Lecture Notes in Computer Science 4778

Commenced Publication in 1973
Founding and Former Series Editors:
Gerhard Goos, Juris Hartmanis, and Jan van Leeuwen

S. Kevin Zhou   Wenyi Zhao   Xiaoou Tang
Shaogang Gong (Eds.)

Analysis and Modeling of Faces and Gestures

Third International Workshop, AMFG 2007
Rio de Janeiro, Brazil, October 20, 2007
Proceedings

 Springer

Volume Editors

S. Kevin Zhou
Siemens Corporate Research
755 College Road East, Princeton, NJ 08540, USA
E-mail: kzhou@scr.siemens.com

Wenyi Zhao
Intuitive Surgical Inc.
950 Kifer Road, Sunnyvale, CA 94086, USA
E-mail: wyzhao@ieee.org

Xiaoou Tang
Microsoft Research Asia
5F, Beijing Sigma Center, 49 Zhichun Road, Haidian District, Beijing 100080, China
E-mail: xitang@microsoft.com

Shaogang Gong
Queen Mary, University of London
Department of Computer Science
London E1 4NS, UK
E-mail: sgg@dcs.qmul.ac.uk

Library of Congress Control Number: 2007936691

CR Subject Classification (1998): I.4, I.5, I.3.5, I.2.10, I.2.6, F.2.2

LNCS Sublibrary: SL 6 – Image Processing, Computer Vision, Pattern Recognition, and Graphics

ISSN   0302-9743
ISBN-10   3-540-75689-2 Springer Berlin Heidelberg New York
ISBN-13   978-3-540-75689-7 Springer Berlin Heidelberg New York

Springer is a part of Springer Science+Business Media

springer.com

© Springer-Verlag Berlin Heidelberg 2007
Printed in Germany

Typesetting: Camera-ready by author, data conversion by Scientific Publishing Services, Chennai, India
Printed on acid-free paper   SPIN: 12174645   06/3180   5 4 3 2 1 0

Preface

The 2007 IEEE International Workshop on Analysis and Modeling of Faces and Gestures (AMFG) is the third workshop of its type organized in conjunction with ICCV, this time in Rio de Janeiro, Brazil. Our primary goal is to bring together researchers and research groups to review the status of recognition, analysis and modeling of face, gesture, activity, and behavior; to discuss the challenges that we are facing; and to explore future directions.

This year we received 55 submissions. Each paper was reviewed by three program committee members. The whole reviewing process was double blind. However, due to size limit, we were only able to accommodate 22 papers, among which 8 are orals and 14 are posters. The topics covered by these accepted papers include feature representation, 3D face, robust recognition under pose and illumination variations, video-based face recognition, learning, facial motion analysis, body pose estimation, and sign recognition.

A special word of thanks goes to Dr. Feng Zhao, our organizing chair, for his dedication and great efforts in maintaining both the online submission system and workshop website and in handling most of the author contacts. We are indebted to the advisory committee members for their valuable suggestions and to the program committee members for their hard work and timely reviews. Finally, we thank Cognitec System GmbH and Siemens Corporate Research for their sponsorship.

October 2007

S. Kevin Zhou
Wen-Yi Zhao
Xiaoou Tang
Shaogang Gong

Organization

AMFG 2007 was held in conjunction with ICCV 2007.

Workshop Chairs

S. Kevin Zhou	Siemens Corporate Research
Wen-Yi Zhao	Intuitive Surgical, Inc.
Xiaoou Tang	Microsoft Research
Shaogang Gong	Queen Mary, University of London

Advisory Committee

Rama Chellappa	University of Maryland
Thomas Huang	University of Illinois at Urbana-Champaign
Anil Jain	Michigan State University

Organizing Chair

Feng Zhao	Chinese University of Hong Kong

Sponsoring Institutions

Cognitec System GmbH
Siemens Corporate Research

Program Committee

Jake Aggarwal	UT Austin, USA
Aaron Bovick	GaTech, USA
Kevin Bowyer	Notre Dame, USA
Rama Chellappa	Maryland, USA
Tsuhan Chen	Carnegie Mellon, USA
Jeff Cohn	Pittsburgh, USA
Robert Collins	Penn State, USA
Tim Cootes	Manchester, UK
James Davis	Ohio State, USA
Larry Davis	Maryland, USA
David Hogg	Leeds, UK

David Jacobs	Maryland, USA
Anil Jain	Michigan State, USA
Mike Jones	MERL, USA
Ron Kimmel	Technion, Israel
Josef Kittler	Surrey, UK
David Kriegman	UCSD, USA
Stan Li	NLPR, China
Chengjun Liu	NJIT, USA
Qingshan Liu	NLPR, China
Jiebo Luo	Kodak, USA
Aleix Martinez	Ohio State, USA
Gerard Medioni	USC, USA
Dimitris Metaxas	Rutgers, USA
Alice O'Toole	UT Dallas, USA
Jonathon Phillips	NIST, USA
Matti Pietikainen	OULU, Finland
Long Quan	UST, HK
Amit Roy-Chowdhury	UCRiverside, USA
Stan Sclaroff	Boston, USA
Matthew Turk	UCSB, USA
Harry Wechsler	George Mason, USA
Shuicheng Yan	UIUC, USA
Ming-Hsuan Yang	Honda Research, USA
Zhengyou Zhang	Microsoft Research, USA
Feng Zhao	CUHK, HK

Table of Contents

Oral - I

Poster - I

Oral - II

Poster - II

Learning Personal Specific Facial Dynamics for Face Recognition from Videos

Abdenour Hadid[1], Matti Pietikäinen[1], and Stan Z. Li[2]

[1] Machine Vision Group, P.O. Box 4500, FI-90014, University of Oulu, Finland
http://www.ee.oulu.fi/mvg
[2] Institute of Automation, Chinese Academy of Sciences, 95 Zhongguancun Donglu
Beijing 100080, China

Abstract. In this paper, we present an effective approach for spatiotemporal face recognition from videos using an Extended set of Volume LBP (Local Binary Pattern features) and a boosting scheme. Among the key properties of our approach are: (1) the use of local Extended Volume LBP based spatiotemporal description instead of the holistic representations commonly used in previous works; (2) the selection of only personal specific facial dynamics while discarding the intra-personal temporal information; and (3) the incorporation of the contribution of each local spatiotemporal information. To the best of our knowledge, this is the first work addressing the issue of learning the personal specific facial dynamics for face recognition.

We experimented with three different publicly available video face databases (MoBo, CRIM and Honda/UCSD) and considered five benchmark methods (PCA, LDA, LBP, HMMs and ARMA) for comparison. Our extensive experimental analysis clearly assessed the excellent performance of the proposed approach, significantly outperforming the comparative methods and thus advancing the state-of-the-art.

Keywords: Facial Dynamics, Local Binary Patterns, Face Recognition, Boosting.

1 Introduction

Psychological and neural studies [1] indicate that both fixed facial features and dynamic personal characteristics are useful for recognizing faces. However, despite the usefulness of facial dynamics, most automatic recognition systems use only the static information as it is unclear how the dynamic cue can be integrated and exploited. Thus, most research has limited the scope of the problem by applying methods developed for still images to some selected frames [2]. Only recently have researchers started to truly address the problem of face recognition from video sequences [3,4,5,6,7,8,9].

In [3], an approach exploiting spatiotemporal information is presented. It is based on modeling face dynamics using identity surfaces. Face recognition is performed by matching the face trajectory that is constructed from the discriminating features and pose information of the face with a set of model trajectories constructed on identity surfaces. Experimental results using 12 training sequences and the testing sequences of three subjects were reported with a recognition rate of 93.9%.

S.K. Zhou et al. (Eds.): AMFG 2007, LNCS 4778, pp. 1–15, 2007.

In [4], Li and Chellappa used the trajectories of tracked features to identify persons in video sequences. The features are extracted using Gabor attributes on a regular 2D grid. Using a small database of 19 individuals, the authors reported performance enhancement over the frame to frame matching scheme. In another work, Zhou and Chellappa proposed a generic framework to track and recognize faces simultaneously by adding an identification variable to the state vector in the sequential important sampling method [5].

An alternative to model the temporal structures is the use of the condensation algorithm. This algorithm has been successfully applied for tracking and recognizing multiple spatiotemporal features. Recently, it was extended to video based face recognition problems [6,5]. More recently, the Auto-Regressive and Moving Average (ARMA) model [10] was adopted to model a moving face as a linear dynamical system and perform recognition [7].

Perhaps, the most popular approach to model temporal and spatial information is based on the Hidden Markov models (HMM) which have also been applied to face recognition from videos [8]. The idea is simple: in the training phase, an HMM is created to learn both the statistics and temporal dynamics of each individual. During the recognition process, the temporal characteristics of the face sequence are analyzed over time by the HMM corresponding to each subject. The likelihood scores provided by the HMMs are compared. The highest score provides the identity of a face in the video sequence.

Unfortunately, most of the methods described above use spatiotemporal representations that suffer from at least one of the following drawbacks: (1) the local information which is shown to be important to facial image analysis [11] is not well exploited with holistic methods such as HMMs; (2) while only personal specific facial dynamics are useful for discriminating between different persons, the intra-personal temporal information which is related to facial expression and emotions is also encoded and used; and (3) equal weights are given to the spatiotemporal features despite the fact that some of the features contribute to recognition more than others. To overcome these limitations, we propose an effective approach for face recognition from videos that uses local spatiotemporal features and selects only the useful facial dynamics needed for recognition. The idea consists of looking at a face sequence as a selected set of volumes (or rectangular prisms) from which we extract local histograms of Extended Volume Local Binary Pattern (EVLBP) code occurrences. Our choice of adopting LBP (Local Binary Patterns) for spatiotemporal representation is motivated by the recent results of LBP approach [12] in facial image analysis [13] and also in dynamic texture recognition [14].

In this paper, noticing the limitations of volume LBP operator in handling the temporal information, we first extend the operator and derive a rich set of volume LBP features denoted EVLBP. Then, instead of ignoring the weight of each feature or simply concatenating the local EVLBP histograms computed at predefined locations, we propose an effective approach for automatically determining the optimal size and locations of the local rectangular prisms (volumes) from which EVLBP features should be computed. More importantly, we select only the most discriminative spatiotemporal EVLBP features for face recognition while discard the features which may hinder the recognition process. For this purpose, we use AdaBoost learning technique [15] which has shown its efficiency in feature selection task. The goal is to classify the EVLBP based spatiotemporal features into intra and extra classes, and then use only the extra-class information for recognition. To the best of our knowledge, this is the first work addressing the issue of learning personal specific facial dynamics for face recognition.

2 Extended Volume LBP Features (EVLBP)

The LBP texture analysis operator, introduced by Ojala *et al.* [16,12], is defined as a gray-scale invariant texture measure, derived from a general definition of texture in a local neighborhood. It is a powerful means of texture description and among its properties in real-world applications are its discriminative power, computational simplicity and tolerance against monotonic gray-scale changes.

The original LBP operator forms labels for the image pixels by thresholding the 3×3 neighborhood of each pixel with the center value and considering the result as a binary number. Fig. 1 shows an example of an LBP calculation. The histogram of these $2^8 = 256$ different labels can then be used as a texture descriptor. Each bin (LBP code) can be regarded as a micro-texton. Local primitives which are codified by these bins include different types of curved edges, spots, flat areas etc.

The calculation of the LBP codes can be easily done in a single scan through the image. The value of the LBP code of a pixel (x_c, y_c) is given by:

$$LBP_{P,R} = \sum_{p=0}^{P-1} s(g_p - g_c)2^P \qquad (1)$$

where g_c corresponds to the gray value of the center pixel (x_c, y_c), g_p refers to gray values of P equally spaced pixels on a cicrle of radius R, and s defines a thresholding function as follows:

$$s(x) = \begin{cases} 1, if \ x \ \geq \ 0; \\ 0, otherwise. \end{cases} \qquad (2)$$

The occurrences of the LBP codes in the image are collected into a histogram. The classification is then performed by computing histogram similarities. For an efficient representation, facial images are first divided into several local regions from which LBP histograms are extracted and concatenated into an enhanced feature histogram. In such a description, the face is represented in three different levels of locality: the LBP labels for the histogram contain information about the patterns on a pixel-level, the labels

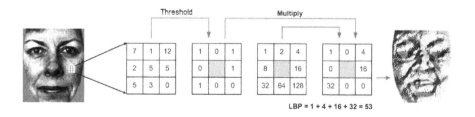

Fig. 1. Example of an LBP calculation

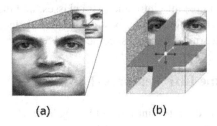

(a)   (b)

Fig. 2. (a): A face sequence is seen as a rectangular prism and (b): An example of 3D neighborhood of a pixel in Volume LBP

are summed over a small region to produce information on a regional level and the regional histograms are concatenated to build a global description of the face. This locality property, in addition to the computational simplicity and tolerance against illumination changes, are behind the success of LBP approach for facial image analysis [13].

The original LBP operator (and also its later extension to use neighborhoods of different sizes [12]) was defined to deal only with the spatial information. For spatiotemporal representation, Volume LBP operator (VLBP) has been recently introduced in [14]. The idea behind VLBP is very simple. It consists of looking at a face sequence as rectangular prism (or volume) and defining the neighborhood of each pixel in three dimensional space. Fig. 2 explains the principle of rectangular prism and shows an example of 3D neighborhood for Volume LBP.

There are several ways of defining the neighboring pixels in VLBP. In [14], P equally spaced pixels on a circle of radius R in the frame t, and $P + 1$ pixels in the previous and posterior neighboring frames with time interval L were used. This yielded in VLBP operator denoted $\text{VLBP}_{L,P,R}$. Fig. 3 (top) illustrates an example of VLBP operator with $P=4$ and $R=1$.

We noticed in our experiments on face recognition from videos that $\text{VLBP}_{L,P,R}$ does not encode well enough the temporal information in the face sequences since the operator considers neighboring points only from three frames and therefore the information in the frames with time variance less than L are missed out. In addition, a fixed number of neighboring points (i.e. P) are taken from each of the three frames, yielding in a less flexible operator with large set of neighboring points. To overcome these limitations, we introduce here an extended set of VLBP patterns by considering P points in $frame_t$, Q points in the $frames_{t\pm L}$ and S points in the $frames_{t\pm 2L}$. This yields in Extended Volume LBP (EVLBP) operator that we denote by $\text{EVLBP}_{L,(P,Q,S),R}$.

By setting

$$\begin{cases} Q = P + 1 \\ S = 0 \end{cases} \tag{3}$$

$\text{EVLBP}_{L,(P,Q,S),R}$ will be equivalent to $\text{VLBP}_{L,P,R}$. Therefore, $\text{VLBP}_{L,P,R}$ can be seen as a special case of $\text{EVLBP}_{L,(P,Q,S),R}$. Fig. 3 (bottom) illustrates an example of Extended Volume LBP operator with $P=4$, $Q=S=1$ and $R=1$ ($\text{EVLBP}_{L,(4,1,1),1}$), while Fig. 3 (top) illustrates an example of $\text{VLBP}_{L,4,1}$ operator which is equivalent to $\text{EVLBP}_{L,(4,5,0),1}$.

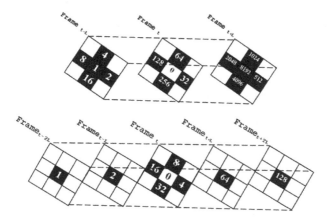

Fig. 3. Top: $VLBP_{L,4,1}$. Bottom: $EVLBP_{L,(4,1,1),1}$

Once the neighborhood function is defined, we divide each face sequence into several overlapping rectangular prisms of different sizes, from which we extract local histograms of EVLBP code occurrences. Then, instead of simply concatenating the local histograms into a single histogram, we use AdaBoost learning algorithm for automatically determining the optimal size and locations of the local rectangular prisms, and more importantly for selecting the most discriminative EVLBP patterns for face recognition while discarding the features which may hinder the recognition process.

3   Learning EVLBP Features for Face Recognition

To tackle the problem of selecting only the spatiotemporal information which is useful for recognition while discarding the information related to facial expressions and emotions, we adopt AdaBoost learning technique [15] which has shown its efficiency in feature selection tasks. The idea is to separate the facial information into intra and extra classes, and then use only the extra-class EVLBP features for recognition.

First, we segment the training face sequences into several overlapping shots of F frames each in order to increase the number of training data. Then, we consider all combinations of face sequence pairs for the intra and extra classes. From each pair ($sequence_i^1$, $sequence_i^2$), we scan both face sequences with rectangular prisms of different sizes. At each stage, we extract the EVLBP histograms from the local rectangular prisms and compute the χ^2 (Chi-square) distances between the two local histograms. χ^2 dissimilarity metric for comparing a target histogram ξ to a model histogram ψ is defined by:

$$\chi^2(\xi, \psi) = \sum_{j=0}^{l-1} \frac{(\xi_j - \psi_j)^2}{\xi_j + \psi_j}, \tag{4}$$

where l is the length of feature vector used to represent the local rectangular prisms.

Thus, for each pair of face sequences, we obtain a feature vector X_i whose elements are χ^2 distances. Let us denote $Y_i \in \{+1, -1\}$ the class label of X_i where $Y_i = +1$

if the pair $(sequence_i^1, sequence_i^2)$ defines an extra-class pair (*i.e.* the two sequences are from different persons) and $Y_i = -1$ otherwise. This results in a set of training samples $\{(X_1, Y_1), (X_2, Y_2), ..., (X_N, Y_N)\}$. Algorithm 1 summarizes our procedure of constructing the training data.

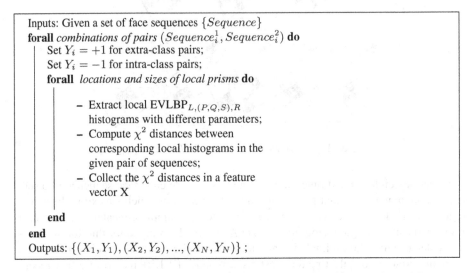

Algorithm 1. The construction of the training samples for feature selection using AdaBoost

Given the constructed training sets, we then apply the basic AdaBoost learning algorithm [15] in order to (i) select a subset of rectangular prisms from which EVLBP features should be computed, and (ii) learn and determine the weights of these selected features.

Once the rectangle prisms are selected and their weights are determined, we perform the recognition of a given probe video sequence by extracting local histograms of EVLBP patterns from the selected prisms and then applying nearest neighbor classification using weighted χ^2 distance:

$$\chi_\alpha^2(\xi, \psi) = \sum_{t=0}^{T-1} \sum_{i=0}^{l_t-1} \alpha_t \frac{(\xi_{i,t} - \psi_{i,t})^2}{\xi_{i,t} + \psi_{i,t}} \qquad (5)$$

where T is the number of selected local prisms; α_t are the weighting coefficients resulted from AdaBoost learning, and l_t the lengths of the feature vectors used to represent local rectangular prisms.

4   Experimental Analysis

4.1   Benchmark Methods

For comparison, we implemented five different algorithms including Hidden Markov models (HMMs) [8] and Auto-Regressive and Moving Average (ARMA) models [7] as benchmark methods for spatiotemporal representations, and PCA, LDA and LBP [13] for still image based ones. In the following, we briefly describe the implementation of these benchmark methods.

a) **HMMs**

The principle of using HMMs to model the facial dynamics and perform video-based face recognition is quite simple [8,17]. Let the face database consist of video sequences of P persons. We construct a continuous hidden Markov model for each subject in the database. A continuous HMM, with N states $\{S_1, S_1, , ..., S_N\}$, is defined by a triplet $\lambda = (A, B, \pi)$, where $A = \{a_{ij}\}$ is the transition matrix, $B = \{b_i(O)\}$ are the state conditional probability density functions (pdf) and $\pi = \{\pi_i\}$ are the initial distributions. The model λ is built using a sequence of feature vectors, called observation sequence $O = \{o_1, o_2, ..., o_l\}$, extracted from the frames of the video sequence (l is the number of frames). Different features can be extracted and used as observation vectors (e.g. pixel values, DCT coefficients etc.). In [8], the PCA projections of the face images were considered. Here in our experiments, we implemented a similar approach using 30 eigenvectors for dimensionality reduction and 16-state fully connected HMM.

During our training, using the Baum-Welch procedure [17], a model λ_p , ($p = 1, 2, ..., P$), is built for all the subjects in the gallery. During the testing, given the gallery models $\{\lambda_1, \lambda_2, ..., \lambda_P\}$ and the sequence of the PCA feature vectors $O = \{o_1, o_2, ..., o_l\}$, the identity of the test face sequence is given by:

$$\underset{p}{argmax}\ P(O|\lambda_p) \qquad (6)$$

In other terms, the likelihood scores $P(O|\lambda_p)$ provided by the HMMs are compared, and the highest score defines the identity of the test video sequence.

b) **ARMA**

In the ARMA framework, a moving face is represented by a linear dynamical system and described by Eqs. 7 & 8:

$$x(t + 1) = Ax(t) + v(t) \qquad v(t) \sim N(0, R) \qquad (7)$$

$$I(t) = Cx(t) + w(t) \qquad w(t) \sim N(0, Q) \qquad (8)$$

where, $I(t)$ is the appearance of the face at the time instant t, $x(t)$ is a state vector that characterizes the face dynamics, A and C are matrices representing the state and output transitions, $v(t)$ and $w(t)$ are IID sequences driven from some unknown distributions.

We build an ARMA model for each face video sequence. To describe each model, we need to estimate the parameters A, C, Q and R. Using the tools from the system identification literature, the estimation of the ARMA model parameters is closed-form and therefore easy to implement [10,7]. While the state transition A and the output transition C are intrinsic characteristics of the model, Q and R are not significant for the purpose of recognition [10]. Therefore, we need only the matrices A and C to describe a face video sequence. Once the models are estimated, recognition can be performed by computing distances between ARMA models corresponding to probe and gallery face sequences. The gallery model which is closest to the probe model is assigned as the identity of the probe (nearest neighbor criteria).

Several distance metrics have been proposed to estimate the distance between two ARMA models [18]. Since it has been shown that the different metrics do not alter the results significantly, we adopted in our experiments the Frobenius distance (d_F^2), defined by :

$$d_F^2 = 2 \sum_{i=1}^{n} sin^2\theta_i(\lambda_j, \lambda_k) \qquad (9)$$

where, θ_i are the subspace angles between the ARMA models λ_j and λ_k, defined in [18].

c) PCA, LDA and LBP

For comparison, we also considered still image based methods such as PCA, LDA and LBP. However, in video-based face recognition schemes both training and test data (galleries and probes) are video sequences. Therefore, performing still-to-still face recognition when the data consists of video sequences is an ill-posed problem (i.e. which frame from the test sequence to compare to which frame in the reference sequence?). Here, we adopt a scheme proposed in [19] to perform static image based face recognition that exploits the abundance of face views in the videos. The approach consists of performing unsupervised learning to extract a set of K most representative samples (or exemplars) from the raw gallery videos (K=3 in our experiments). Once these exemplars are extracted, we build a view-based system and use a probabilistic voting strategy to recognize the individuals in the probe video sequences.

4.2 Experimental Data

For experimental analysis, we considered three different publicly available video face databases (MoBo [20], Honda/UCSD [9] and CRIM [21]) in order to ensure an extensive evaluation of our proposed approach and the benchmark methods against changes caused by different factors including face image resolution, illumination variations, head movements, facial expressions and the size of the database.

The first database, MoBo (Motion of Body), is the most commonly used in video-based face recognition research [5,22,8], although it was originally collected for the purpose of human identification from distance. The considered subset from MoBo database contains 96 face sequences of 24 different subjects walking on a treadmill. Some example images are shown in Fig. 4. Each sequence consists of 300 frames. From each

Fig. 4. Examples of cropped facial images from MoBo video database

Fig. 5. Examples of facial images from CRIM video database

video sequence, we automatically detected and rescaled the faces, obtaining images of 40×40 pixels.

The second database, Honda/UCSD, has been collected and used by Lee *et al.* in their work on video-based face recognition [9]. It was also used in the recent study of Aggarwal et al. [7]. The considered subset from Honda/UCSD database contains 40 video sequences of 20 different individuals (2 videos per person). During the data collection, the individuals were asked to move their face in different combinations (speed, rotation and expression). From the video sequences, we cropped the face images in the same way as we did for the MoBo database. The size of the resulted facial images is 20×20 pixels.

In order to experiment with a large amount of facial dynamics, resulted for example from the movements of the facial features when the individuals are talking, we considered a third video database called CRIM. This is large set of 591 face sequences showing 20 persons reading broadcast news for a total of about 5 hours. The database is originally collected for audio-visual recognition. There are between 23 and 47 video sequences for each individual. Some cropped images are shown in Fig. 5. The size of the extracted face images is 130×150 pixels.

4.3   Experimental Results and Analysis

From each of the three video databases (MoBo, USCD/HONDA and CRIM), we randomly selected half of the face sequences of each subject for training while the other half was used for testing. In addition, given the limited number of training samples in MoBo and Honda/UCSD databases, we also segmented the face sequences into several overlapping shots in order to increase the number of training samples. In all our experiments, we considered the average recognition rates of 100 random permutations.

First, we applied PCA, LDA, LBP, HMMs and ARMA to the test sequences in the three databases. The performances of these methods are shown in Tables 1-3. From the results on MoBo database (Table 1), we notice that all the methods perform quite well and the spatiotemporal based methods (*i.e.* HMMs and ARMA) are slightly better that the static image based methods (PCA, LBP and LDA). The better performance of the spatiotemporal methods is in agreement with the neuropsychological evidence [1] stating that facial dynamics are useful for recognition. From these results we can also see that the benefit of the spatiotemporal approach is not very significant. Perhaps, in MoBo database, this is due to the few amount of facial dynamics which are mainly limited to rigid head movements.

However, the results on Honda/UCSD database (Table 2) show that the low-image resolution (20×20 pixels) affects all these five methods and that image based ones are more affected. This is also in agreement with the neuropsychological findings that

Table 1. Comparative recognition results of 5 benchmark methods on MoBo database

Method	Recognition rate
PCA	87.1%
LDA	90.8%
LBP [13]	91.3%
HMM [8]	92.3%
ARMA [7]	93.4%

Table 2. Comparative recognition results of 5 benchmark methods on Honda/UCSD database

Method	Recognition rate
PCA	69.6%
LDA	74.5%
LBP [13]	79.6%
HMM [8]	84.2%
ARMA [7]	84.9%

Table 3. Comparative recognition results of 5 benchmark methods on CRIM database

Method	Recognition rate
PCA	89.7%
LDA	91.5%
LBP [13]	93.0%
HMM [8]	85.4%
ARMA [7]	80.0%

indicate that facial movement contributes more to the recognition under degraded viewing conditions.

Surprisingly, the results on CRIM database (Table 3) show that HMM and ARMA approaches gave worse results than PCA, LDA, and LBP based methods. While one may not expect worse performances using spatiotemporal representations, the obtained results attest that PCA, LDA and LBP based representations might perform better. This means that combining face structure and its dynamics in an *ad hoc* manner does not systematically enhance the recognition performance.

From the experiments, we also noticed that the basic LBP approach [13] performed quite well and outperformed PCA and LDA in all our tests. This confirms the validity of LBP based descriptions in face analysis. A bibliography of LBP-related research can be found at $http://www.ee.oulu.fi/research/imag/texture/lbp/bibliography/$.

We also experimented with Volume LBP spatiotemporal approach which has been successfully applied to dynamic texture analysis in [14]. We divided each face sequence into several overlapping local rectangular prisms of fixed sizes. Then, we extracted the VLBP based spatiotemporal representation using different VLBP operator parameters. For recognition, we adopted the χ^2 distance. Using such an approach, we obtained best recognition rates of 90.3%, 78.3% and 88.7% with $VLBP_{2,4,1}$, $VLBP_{1,4,1}$

and $VLBP_{1,4,1}$ on MoBo, Honda/UCSD and CRIM databases, respectively. Surprisingly, these results are worse than those obtained using still image LBP based approach which yielded in recognition rates of 91.3% (versus 90.3%), 79.6% (versus 78.3%) and 93.0% (versus 88.7%) on MoBo, Honda/UCSD and CRIM databases, respectively. This supports our earlier conclusion indicating that using spatiotemporal representations do not systematically enhance the recognition performances. The most significant performance degradations of VLBP approach are noticed on CRIM database which contains the largest amount of facial dynamics. This indicates that some of these facial dynamics are not useful for recognition. In other terms, this means that some part of the temporal information is useful for recognition while another part may also hinder the recognition. Obviously, the useful part is that defining the extra-personal characteristics while the non-useful part concerns the intra-class information such as facial expressions and emotions. For recognition, one should then select only the extra-personal characteristics.

To verify this hypothesis, we considered our proposed approach which consists of using AdaBoost for learning and selecting only the most discriminative spatiotemporal features. First, we tested AdaBoost with VLBP features and obtained recognition rates of 96.5%, 89.1% and 94.4% on MoBo, Honda/UCSD and CRIM databases, respectively. As shown in Tables 4-6, performing feature selection yields in significant performance enhancement on all these three databases. This validates our hypothesis that only some part of the temporal information is useful for recognition while another part may hinder the recognition process.

Then, we experimented with the proposed extended set of VLBP features (EVLBP) introduced in Section 2 and used AdaBoost for learning the most discriminative spatiotemporal EVLBP features. As expected, this enhanced further the performances, yielding in excellent recognition rates of 97.9%, 96.0% and 98.5% on MoBo, Honda /UCSD and CRIM databases, respectively. This additional performance enhancement explains the benefit of enriching the VLBP feature set by deriving EVLBP and shows the limitations of $VLBP_{L,P,R}$ operator which does not encode well enough the temporal information in the face sequences since the operator considers neighboring points only from three frames and therefore the information in the frames with time variance less than L are missed out.

Notice that the obtained results significantly outperform those of all benchmarks methods (PCA, LDA, LBP, HMM and ARMA) on the three databases (comparison between Tables 1-3 and Table 4-6). To our knowledge, this is also the best performance on these databases. Perhaps, these excellent results can be explained as follows: (i) the spatiotemporal representation using extended volume LBP features, in contrast to the HMM based approach, is very efficient as it codifies the local and global facial dynamics and structure; and more importantly (ii) the temporal information extracted by the extended volume LBP features consisted of both intra and extra personal information (facial expression and identity). Therefore, there was need for performing feature selection. In addition, the selected EVLBP spatiotemporal features were assigned different weights reflecting their contributions to recognition, while this was not the case in other methods.

Table 4. Recognition results of VLBP, VLBP with AdaBoost and EVLBP with AdaBoost on MoBo database

Method	Recognition rate
VLBP [14]	90.3%
VLBP+AdaBoost	96.5%
EVLBP+AdaBoost	**97.9%**

Table 5. Recognition results of VLBP, VLBP with AdaBoost and EVLBP with AdaBoost on Honda/UCSD database

Method	Recognition rate
VLBP [14]	78.3%
VLBP+AdaBoost	89.1%
EVLBP+AdaBoost	**96.0%**

Table 6. Recognition results of VLBP, VLBP with AdaBoost and EVLBP with AdaBoost on CRIM database

Method	Recognition rate
VLBP [14]	88.7%
VLBP+AdaBoost	94.4%
EVLBP+AdaBoost	**98.5%**

Analyzing the selected local regions (the rectangular prisms) from which the EVLBP features were collected, we noticed that the dynamics of the whole face and the eye area are more important than that of the mouth region for identity recognition. This is a little surprising in the sense that one can expect that the mouth region would play an important role as it is the most non-rigid region of the face when an individual is talking. Perhaps, mouth region does play an important role but for facial expression recognition. Fig. 6 shows examples of the most discriminative spatiotemporal regions returned by AdaBoost for CRIM face sequences and from which EVLBP spatiotemporal features are extracted. Notice that these four first selected features are extracted from global and local regions. This supports the results of other researchers indicating that both global and local features are useful for recognition. From how many selected regions the EVLBP features are computed? Fig. 7 shows the recognition results as a function of the number of regions selected by AdaBoost. The best results are obtained with 9, 16 and 6 regions on MoBo, Honda/UCSD and CRIM databases, respectively. Using additional regions did not enhance the recognition performance.

Table 7 summarizes the obtained results using the different methods (PCA, LDA, LBP, HMM, ARMA, VLBP and EVLBP) on the three databases (MoBo, Honda/UCSD and CRIM).

Fig. 6. Examples of the four first selected rectangular prisms from which EVLBP spatiotemporal features are extracted on CRIM face sequences

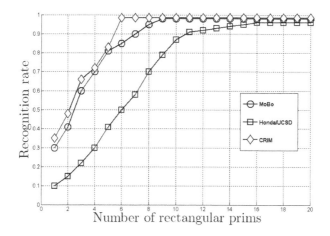

Fig. 7. The recognition rates function of the number of selected regions with AdaBoost from which EVLBP features are extracted

Table 7. Summary of the obtained results using the different methods on the three databases

Method	Results on MoBo	Results on Honda/UCSD	Results on CRIM
PCA	87.1%	69.9%	89.7%
LDA	90.8%	74.5%	91.5%
LBP [13]	91.3%	79.6%	93.0%
HMM [8]	92.3%	84.2%	85.4%
ARMA [7]	93.4%	84.9%	80.0%
VLBP [14]	90.3%	78.3%	88.7%
VLBP+AdaBoost	96.5%	89.1%	94.4%
EVLBP+AdaBoost	**97.9%**	**96.0%**	**98.5%**

5   Conclusion

The few works attempting to use spatiotemporal representations for face recognition from videos ignore the fact that some of the facial information may also hinder the recognition process. Indeed, while one may not expect worse results using spatiotemporal representations instead of still image based ones, our results showed that still image based methods can perform better than spatiotemporal based ones. This suggests that the existing spatiotemporal representations have not yet shown their full potential and need further investigation.

From this observation, we presented a novel approach for spatiotemporal face recognition with excellent results. The efficiency of the proposed approach can be explained by the local nature of the spatiotemporal EVLBP based description, combined with the use of boosting for selecting only the personal specific information related to identity while discarding the information which is related to facial expression and emotions.

Acknowledgment

The partial financial support of the National Agency for Technology and Innovation (Tekes) is gratefully acknowledged.

References

1. O'Toole, A.J., Roark, D.A., Abdi, H.: Recognizing moving faces: A psychological and neural synthesis. Trends in Cognitive Science 6, 261–266 (2002)
2. Zhao, W., Chellappa, R., Phillips, P.J., Rosenfeld, A.: Face recognition: A literature survey. ACM Computing Surveys 34(4), 399–458 (2003)
3. Li, Y.: Dynamic Face Models: Construction and Applications. PhD thesis, Queen Mary, University of London (2001)
4. Li, B., Chellappa, R.: Face verification through tracking facial features. Journal of the Optical Society of America 18, 2969–2981 (2001)
5. Zhou, S., Chellappa, R.: Probabilistic human recognition from video. In: European Conf. on Computer Vision, pp. 681–697 (May 2002)
6. Zhou, S., Krueger, V., Chellappa, R.: Face recognition from video: A condensation approach. In: IEEE Int. Conf. on Automatic Face and Gesture Recognition, pp. 221–228. IEEE Computer Society Press, Los Alamitos (May 2002)
7. Aggarwal, G., Chowdhury, A.R., Chellappa, R.: A system identification approach for video-based face recognition. In: 17th International Conference on Pattern Recognition, vol. 4, pp. 175–178 (August 2004)
8. Liu, X., Chen, T.: Video-based face recognition using adaptive hidden markov models. In: IEEE Int. Conf. on Computer Vision and Pattern Recognition, pp. 340–345. IEEE Computer Society Press, Los Alamitos (June 2003)
9. Lee, K.C., Ho, J., Yang, M.H., Kriegman, D.: Video-based face recognition using probabilistic appearance manifolds. In: IEEE Int. Conf. on Computer Vision and Pattern Recognition, pp. 313–320. IEEE Computer Society Press, Los Alamitos (June 2003)
10. Soatto, S., Doretto, G., Wu, Y.: Dynamic textures. In: International Conference on Computer Vision, Vancouver, BC, Canada, vol. 2, pp. 439–446 (July 2001)
11. Heisele, B., Ho, P., Wu, J., Poggio, T.: Face recognition: Component based versus global approaches. Computer Vision and Image Understanding 91(1-2), 6–21 (2003)
12. Ojala, T., Pietikäinen, M., Mäenpää, T.: Multiresolution gray-scale and rotation invariant texture classification with local binary patterns. IEEE Transactions on Pattern Analysis and Machine Intelligence 24, 971–987 (2002)

13. Ahonen, T., Hadid, A., Pietikäinen, M.: Face description with local binary patterns: Application to face recognition. IEEE Transactions on Pattern Analysis and Machine Intelligence 28(12), 2037–2041 (2006)
14. Zhao, G., Pietikäinen, M.: Dynamic texture recognition using local binary patterns with an application to facial expressions. IEEE Transactions on Pattern Analysis and Machine Intelligence 29(6), 915–928 (2007)
15. Freund, Y., Schapire, R.: A decision-theoretic generalization of on-line learning and an application to boosting. Journal of Computer and System Sciences 55(1), 119–139 (1997)
16. Ojala, T., Pietikäinen, M., Harwood, D.: A comparative study of texture measures with classification based on feature distributions. Pattern Recognition 29, 51–59 (1996)
17. Rabiner, L.R.: A tutorial on hidden markov models and selected applications in speech recognition. In: Proceedings of the IEEE, vol. 77(2), pp. 257–286. IEEE Computer Society Press, Los Alamitos (1989)
18. Cock, K., Moor, B.D.: Subspace angles between ARMA models. Systems and Control Letters 46(4), 265–270 (2002)
19. Hadid, A., Pietikäinen, M.: Selecting models from videos for appearance-based face recognition. In: 17th International Conference on Pattern Recognition, vol. 1, pp. 304–308 (August 2004)
20. Gross, R., Shi, J.: The CMU Motion of Body (MoBo) database. Technical Report CMU-RI-TR-01-18, Robotics Institute, Carnegie Mellon University (June 2001)
21. CRIM: http://www.crim.ca/
22. Krueger, V., Zhou, S.: Exemplar-based face recognition from video. In: European Conf. on Computer Vision, pp. 732–746 (May 2002)

A New Probabilistic Model for Recognizing Signs with Systematic Modulations

Sylvie C.W. Ong and Surendra Ranganath

Department of Electrical and Computer Engineering, National University of Singapore, 4 Engineering Drive 3, Singapore 117576, Singapore

Abstract. This paper addresses an aspect of sign language (SL) recognition that has largely been overlooked in previous work and yet is integral to signed communication. It is the most comprehensive work to-date on recognizing complex variations in sign appearances due to grammatical processes (inflections) which systematically modulate the temporal and spatial dimensions of a root sign word to convey information in addition to lexical meaning. We propose a novel dynamic Bayesian network – the Multichannel Hierarchical Hidden Markov Model (MH-HMM)– as a modelling and recognition framework for continuously signed sentences that include modulated signs. This models the hierarchical, sequential and parallel organization in signing while requiring synchronization between parallel data streams at sign boundaries. Experimental results using particle filtering for decoding demonstrate the feasibility of using the MH-HMM for recognizing inflected signs in continuous sentences.

1 Introduction

In sign language (SL) communication, a large number of complex variations in manual sign (i.e. hand/arm gesture) appearances are possible due to grammatical processes that systematically change the sign appearance to convey information in addition to the lexical meaning. This includes information expressed in English through prefixes, suffixes or additional words like adverbs. Hence, while information is expressed in English by using additional syllables and words as necessary rather than changing a given word's form, in SL, it is often expressed through a change in the form of the root sign word. Thus, just as there is a large variety of prefixes, suffixes, and adverbs that may be used with a particular word in English, there is also a large variety of different systematic appearance changes that can be made to a root word in SL.

Much of SL recognition research has focused on solving problems similar to those that occur in speech recognition, such as scalability to large vocabulary, robustness to noise and person independence. These are worthy problems to consider and solving them is crucial to building a practical SL recognition system. However, the almost exclusive focus on these problems has resulted in systems that can only recognize the lexical meanings conveyed in signs, and bypass the richness and complexity of expression inherent in manual signing. Our work is a step towards addressing this imbalance by focusing on recognizing the different

S.K. Zhou et al. (Eds.): AMFG 2007, LNCS 4778, pp. 16–30, 2007.

sign appearances formed by modulating a root word, and extracting both the lexical meaning and the additional grammatical information that is conveyed by the different appearances.

Specifically, we model and extract information conveyed by two types of grammatical processes that produce systematic changes in manual sign appearance, viz., **directional use of verbs** and **temporal aspect inflections**, described in the next section. The signs and grammar described are with reference to American Sign Language (ASL), which is extensively used by the deaf in North America and is also well-researched by sign linguists and researchers in machine recognition.

For the rest of this paper, the terms **word** and **sign** are defined as follows. If the lexical/word meaning *and* grammatical information conveyed by two SL hand gestures is the same, then we consider it to be the same **sign**. However, gestures that convey the same lexical/word meaning but different grammatical information are defined to be the same **word** but different and distinct signs. So for example, the same word inflected in different ways results in different signs.

1.1   Grammatical Processes in Signs

Sign linguists agree that signs have internal structure that can be broken down into smaller parts [17], and they generally distinguish the basic parts or components as consisting of the handshape, hand orientation, location and movement. Handshape refers to the finger configuration, orientation to the direction in which the palm and fingers are pointing, and location to where the hand is placed relative to the body. Hand movement includes both path movement that traces out a trajectory in space, and movement of the fingers and wrist. Each of these components have a limited number of possible categories, or "primes". In the following sections, we describe two types of grammatical processes and their effect on the different sign components.

Directional Verbs. Signs with directional verb inflections are made with various handshapes and movement path shapes to encode the lexical meaning of the verb. Meanwhile, the movement path direction (the direction in which the hand is moving in 3-dimensional space) serves as a pointing action to identify the subject and the object of the verb [11].

Example 1. Figure 1(a) shows the sign which has lexical meaning TEACH and with subject and object being the signer and the addressee, respectively (English translation: "I teach you"). Figure 1(b) shows the sign with the same lexical meaning of TEACH, this time with subject and object being the addressee and the signer, respectively ("You teach me"). In Figure 1(c), the subject of the verb is indicated as the signer. The object is neither the signer nor the addressee but a third person standing (off-camera) to the left of the signer.

Note that movement direction modulation is accompanied by changes in location and palm orientation. For example, the final location of the hand depends on the locations of entities these verbs are directed towards and the signer's judgement in tracing a path that leads from the starting point of the sign towards the entity that is the verb's object.

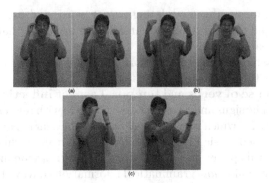

Fig. 1. The sign TEACH pointing towards different subjects and objects : (a) "I teach you", (b) "You teach me", (c) "I teach her/him (someone standing to the left of the signer)"

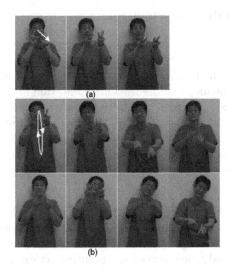

Fig. 2. (a) The sign LOOK-AT (without any additional grammatical information), (b) the sign LOOK − AT$^{[\mathrm{DURATIONAL}]}$, conveying the concept "look at continuously"

Temporal Aspect Inflections. These inflections are represented by systematic changes in the sign's movement path, in terms of the path shape, size, rhythm and speed.

Example 2. In Figure 2(a), the sign is uninflected and conveys the lexical meaning LOOK-AT. It has a linear, straight movement path shape. In Figure 2(b), the sign is modulated with the [DURATIONAL] inflection to give the meaning "look at continuously". The handshape of this inflected sign is the same as in its uninflected form but the movement of the sign is modified to show how the action is performed with reference to time. The sign is performed repetitively in a circular path shape with smooth motion. Examples of other signs that can be inflected in this way are WRITE, SIT, LOOK-AT and 33 other signs listed by Klima and Bellugi in [10].

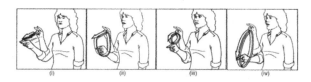

Fig. 3. Signs with the same lexical meaning, ASK, but with different temporal aspect inflections (from [15]) (i) [HABITUAL], meaning "ask regularly", (ii) [ITERATIVE], meaning "ask over and over again", (iii) [DURATIONAL], meaning "ask continuously", (iv) [CONTINUATIVE], meaning "ask for a long time"

Figure 3 shows illustrations of the signs expressing the lexical meaning ASK, with different types of aspectual inflections - [HABITUAL], [ITERATIVE], [DU-RATIONAL], and [CONTINUATIVE]. In terms of rhythm and speed, the [DU-RATIONAL] and [HABITUAL] inflections induce smooth motion at a constant rate while the [CONTINUATIVE] and [ITERATIVE] inflections induce uneven motion.

The meanings conveyed through these modulations in movement are associated with aspects of the verbs that involve frequency, duration, recurrence, permanence, and intensity [10,15]. Besides the examples mentioned above, other meanings that may be conveyed include "incessantly", "from time to time", "starting to", "increasingly", "gradually", "resulting in", "with ease", "readily", "approximately" and "excessively". Klima and Bellugi [10] lists 11 different types of aspectual meanings that can be expressed. Note that the aspectual information is conveyed in addition to and without changing the lexical meaning of the root word.

Multiple Simultaneous Grammatical Information. In ASL, multiple grammatical information may be conveyed through a single sign, by creating complex spatio-temporal sign forms [10]. This is possible because the modulations of sign movement due to different categories of grammatical processes affect different characteristics of movement. For example, a directional verb points to its subject and object through the direction of the movement. Whereas, if the verb is marked for aspectual meaning, this is expressed through the movement path shape, size and speed. So for example, we can express the meaning "you give to me regularly" as distinct from "you give to me continuously" or "I give to you regularly" and so on. The sign vocabulary in the experiments reported in Section 4 includes signs conveying such multiple simultaneous grammatical information.

Previous Work. Generally there have been very few works that address grammatical processes that affect sign appearance in systematic ways. Sagawa and

Takeuchi [16] deciphered the subject-object pairs of Japanese Sign Language (JSL) verbs in sentences by learning the (Gaussian) probability densities of various spatial parameters of the verb's movement from training examples and thereby calculated the probabilities of spatial parameters in test data. Six different sentences constructed from two verbs and three different subject-object pairs, were tested on the same signer that provided the training set, and were recognized with an average word accuracy of 93.4%. Braffort [4] proposed an architecture where hidden Markov models (HMMs) were employed for classifying lexical words using all the features of the sign gesture (glove finger flexure values, tracker location and orientation), while directional verbs were classified by their movement trajectory alone. Sentences comprising seven signs were successfully recognized with 92-96% word accuracy. The main weaknesses of these works is that firstly they recognize a very limited number of different signs. There are six different sign appearances in [16] and seven signs in [4]. Secondly, they tackle signs that exhibit spatial variations only. Thirdly, only one type of variation is expressed in the signs at any one time, and there are no instances of multiple simultaneous grammatical information being expressed through multiple simultaneous systematic variations. Compared to the above, the work presented in this paper recognizes a much more expansive vocabulary of 98 signs, including signs exhibiting temporal as well as spatial variations. Signs with multiple inflections are also recognized. This paper extends our work on isolated gestures previously reported in [14].

2   Proposed Approach

Our approach to recognizing inflected signs is to probabilistically model the effect of lexical and grammatical information on the sign appearance and then use the model to infer the information conveyed, through observing the physical sign appearance.

Besides movement path attributes, directional verb and temporal aspect inflections also affect the location and orientation sign components, as follows:

- Directional verb inflections: the movement direction modulation is accompanied by a change in hand location and palm orientation.
- Temporal aspect inflections: the movement path shape and size modulations also affect the hand location.

We use the fact that the effect of the inflections above appear in both the location and orientation components to reduce the number of sign components that need to be modelled. Thus taking into account that lexical word meaning affects the handshape, location and orientation sign components, we find that only three sign components need to be modelled – handshape, location and orientation. These components are assumed to be independent, with distinct values ("primes") that are classified from separate feature sets. The advantage of this simplifying assumption is that we need never model the interaction between all the components in a sign, thereby greatly reducing the number of model parameters. We consider a sign as consisting of synchronized sequences of distinct values in each of the three components. The synchronization is at the start and end of the sign, since each component expresses the same sign at the same time.

3   Modelling Signs with the Multichannel Hierarchical Hidden Markov Model (MH-HMM)

Hierarchical hidden Markov models (H-HMM) [6,12] have been proposed as a suitable dynamic Bayesian network (DBN) structure for modelling domains with hierarchical processes that evolve at multiple time scales. An example of such a process is speech, where phones combine sequentially to form words, and combinations of words form sentences. Each level (sentence, word, phone) evolves at a different time scale, with state evolutions at higher levels dependent on state sequences finishing at the lower levels. For example, the next word in a sentence can start only when the phone sequence of the current word has ended.

SL manual sign sequences differ from the above domains in that they not only exhibit hierarchical structure, but also consist of multiple data streams, corresponding to each sign component. Our approach represents signs as parallel and simultaneous sequences of values in each of the sign components of handshape, location and orientation. We can consider these component values as the equivalent of phone subunits in speech. So a sign is decomposed as a sequence of phones in each component stream. And we require that for any particular sign in the sentence, the phone sequence for that sign in each component stream should start and end at the same time.

We propose the Multichannel Hierarchical Hidden Markov model (MH-HMM) as a DBN suitable for simultaneously modelling both the hierarchical and the parallel structure in sign sequences. This structure is shown in Figure 4. The MH-HMM models a sentence as made up of a sequence of signs, and each sign as made up of parallel phone sequences, one in each sign component. In our applications, component 1 corresponds to handshape, component 2 is orientaion, and component 3 is location. Most of the previous work in combining multiple data streams either modelled a flat structure for the parallel data streams (e.g multistream HMM [3], product HMM [9], parallel HMM [18], coupled HMM [5] and factorial HMM [7]) or where multiple time-scales and a hierarchical structure was considered, modelled the higher and lower-levels of the hierarchy in a decoupled manner (eg. layered HMM [13]). In contrast, the MH-HMM models multiple data streams with hierarchical structure and different levels of the hierarchy are jointly modelled. In addition, sign-level synchronization between component streams is accomplished through the use of a sync node, S_t^2 in Figure 4, such that none of the components have priority in terms of synchronization. This is unlike the model proposed in [8] where an acoustic feature stream and a video data stream are modelled to perform audio-visual speech recognition, and the word transition times are solely determined by the acoustic data stream. Another advantage of the MH-HMM framework is that it allows training to be performed separately on each component's observation feature stream (described in the next section).

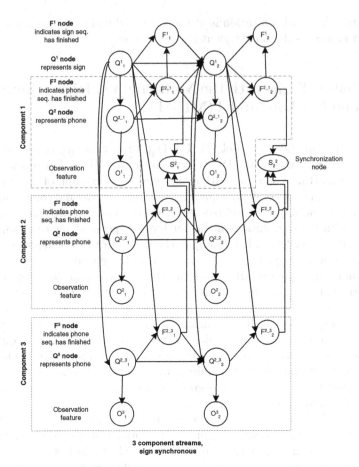

Fig. 4. MH-HMM with two Q-levels and with synchronization between components at sign boundaries (shown for a model with three components streams, and two time slices). Dotted lines enclose component-specific nodes.

We define the conditional probability distributions (CPDs) for $t > 1$ in the MH-HMM of Figure 4 as below.

$$P(Q_t^1 = j | Q_{t-1}^1 = i, F_{t-1}^{2-1} = b, F_{t-1}^1 = f) = \begin{cases} \delta(i,j) & \text{if } b = 0 \\ \tilde{A}^1(i,j) & \text{if } b = 1 \text{ and } f = 0 \\ \pi^1(j) & \text{if } b = 1 \text{ and } f = 1 \end{cases}$$

$$P(F_t^1 = 1 | Q_t^1 = i, F_t^{2-1} = b) = \begin{cases} 0 & \text{if } b = 0 \\ A^1(i, end) & \text{if } b = 1 \end{cases}$$

$$P(Q_t^{2-c} = j | Q_{t-1}^{2-c} = i, F_{t-1}^{2-c} = f, Q_t^1 = k) = \begin{cases} \tilde{A}_k^{2-c}(i,j) & \text{if } f = 0 \\ \pi_k^{2-c}(j) & \text{if } f = 1 \end{cases}$$

$$P(F_t^{2-c} = 1 | Q_t^1 = k, Q_t^{2-c} = i) = A_k^{2-c}(i, end)$$

$$P(O_t^c = \underline{o}_t^c | Q_t^{2-c} = k) = N(\underline{o}_t^c; \underline{\mu}_k^c, \Sigma_k^c)$$

for $c = 1, 2, 3$. Observed component features, O_t^c, are assumed to be continuous-valued with Gaussian densities. $A_k^d(i, j)$ is the state transition probability at level d, indexed by parent value k (if parents exist). $A_k^d(i, end)$ is the probability of ending at state sequence. $\pi_k^d(j)$ is the initial state probability at level d, indexed by parent value k. $\tilde{A}_k^d(i, j)$ and $A_k^d(i, j)$ are related as follows.

$$\tilde{A}_k^d(i, j)(1 - A_k^d(i, end)) = A_k^d(i, j)$$

The CPD of S_t^2 is defined as the EX-NOR function (see Table 1).

The key difference between the MH-HMM and the H-HMM is that in the MH-HMM, there is one set of sign-level nodes, Q_t^1 and F_t^1, but multiple sets of phone-level and observation feature nodes. In Figure 4 there are three component streams and therefore three sets each of $Q_t^{2\text{-}c}$, $F_t^{2\text{-}c}$, and O_t^c nodes, with $c = 1, 2, 3$. (In general, we can expand the model to as many sets, N_c, of the above nodes as required to model multiple component data streams.) The phone-level nodes share the same parent sign node (Q_t^1). So at any instant in time, the phone sequences in each component are associated with a common sign value. However, each component c has a separate set of phone-level nodes $(Q_t^{2\text{-}c}$ and $F_t^{2\text{-}c}$, $c = 1, \ldots, N_c)$, and observation feature nodes $(O_t^c, c = 1, \ldots, N_c)$. So within the time period of a sign, the different component data streams can have different phone state evolution dynamics, where the phone values in one component stream may be changing faster or slower than those in another component stream. At sign boundaries however, the phone sequences for the current sign in all N_c components are required to end, and the phone sequences in all components for the next sign must start. In the MH-HMM, this is achieved by forcing $F_t^{2\text{-}c}$ (which indicates when the phone sequence of the c-th component has ended), for $c = 1, \ldots, N_c$, to all have values of 0 or all have values of 1. The synchronization node S_t^2, is the common child of the $F_t^{2\text{-}c}$ nodes and since the CPD of S_t^2 is defined as the EX-NOR function, $S_t^2 = 1$ only when its parents either all have values of 1 or all have values of 0. When the MH-HMM is used for recognizing continuous signing, for example, when we input the

Table 1. CPD for the sign synchronization node S_t^2 in a MH-HMM modelling three components. The CPD implements the EX-NOR function.

$F_t^{2\text{-}1}$	$F_t^{2\text{-}2}$	$F_t^{2\text{-}3}$	$P(S_t^2\|F_t^{2\text{-}1}, F_t^{2\text{-}2}, F_t^{2\text{-}3})$	
			$S_t^2 = 0$	$S_t^2 = 1$
0	0	0	0	1
0	0	1	1	0
0	1	0	1	0
0	1	1	1	0
1	0	0	1	0
1	0	1	1	0
1	1	0	1	0
1	1	1	0	1

data from a test sentence, we set $S_t^2 = 1$ in all time slices to enforce sign-level synchronization.

3.1   MH-HMM Training and Testing Procedure

In the MH-HMM, the sentence model, i.e. the possible sign sequences, are encoded in the CPD parameters of the sign-level nodes Q_t^1 and F_t^1. For a particular sign, there is not one but N_c sets of component-specific phone-level state initial, transition and ending probabilities encoded in the CPD parameters for nodes $Q_t^{2\text{-}c}$ and $F_t^{2\text{-}c}$. For each phone in the c-th component, the output probability distributions for phone are also specific to the component and are defined by the CPD of the component's observation feature O_t^c.

Our training and modelling strategy is to learn the component-specific phone-level state initial, transition and ending probabilities and output probability distributions by learning each component's parameters independently of each other and with independent observation feature sets. This training is done using the (single channel) H-HMM (refer Figure 5). The parameters of this DBN are estimated with the maximum likelihood (ML) criterion, using the expectation-maximization (EM) training algorithm. All the terms required in the E-step can be obtained from any DBN inferencing algorithm such as the forward interface algorithm [12]. After training, the learned component-specific parameters are combined in the MH-HMM by specifying the CPD parameters for the component-specific phone-level nodes ($Q_t^{2\text{-}c}$ and $F_t^{2\text{-}c}$), and observation feature nodes (O_t^c), for $c = 1, \ldots, N_c$. The sentence model for a particular set of sentences can be straight-forwardly determined from knowledge of the sign sequences that appear in the sentence set. For example, the probability of a particular sign starting a sentence is simply the relative frequency of that sign appearing at the start of the sentences within the set. We thus specify the sentence model, i.e. the CPD parameters of sign-level nodes (Q_t^1 and F_t^1), by taking into account the sign sequences that appear in the training sentence set. The remaining node in the MH-HMM is the sychronization node S_t^2 whose CPD parameters are specified to implement the EX-NOR function.

After the procedure above, the MH-HMM can be used for recognition of continuously signed sentences. To recognize a test sentence, the values of all observed nodes in each time slice are input to the MH-HMM, and the most-likely sign sequence that could have produced the observed values is inferred (here observed nodes refers to nodes with known values). In our testing procedure, the observed nodes at time t include not just the observation features of all the components, O_t^c, for $c = 1, \ldots, N_c$, but also the nodes S_t^2 and F_t^1. As mentioned above, in order to enforce synchronization between component streams at sign boundaries, the value of the S_t^2 node must be set as 1 in all time slices. We also set $F_t^1 = 0$ for $t = 1 \ldots, T - 1$ and $F_T^1 = 1$, indicating that for each test sequence, the sentence ends only at the last time slice and not before [12].

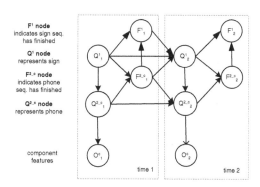

Fig. 5. H-HMM with two Q-levels for training sign component c. Nodes indexed by superscript c pertain to the specific component (e.g. Q_t^{2-c} refers to the phone node at time t for component c). Dotted lines enclose nodes of the same time slice.

Time and space complexity is an issue for decoding because of the large number of hidden variables in our network. Hence, it is necessary to use approximate inferencing methods to reduce time and space requirements to a manageable level. Particle filtering (PF) and other sampling-based algorithms have the advantage of being easy to implement on various kinds of models and giving exact answers in the limit of infinite number of samples [12]. Thus we apply PF for decoding test sentences in the MH-HMM (details omitted here).

4 Experimental Results

4.1 Sign Vocabulary and Sentences

The collected data is obtained from a deaf individual who is a native signer of the local (Singaporean) sign language. The signed sentences, which adhered to ASL grammar, were continuous, with no pauses between signs. There were 73 distinct sentences between 2 to 6 signs long, constructed from a 98-sign vocabulary. Each distinct sentence was signed approximately 5 times, providing a total of 343 sentences and 1927 signs. The 98-sign vocabulary includes signs formed from a combination of a root lexical word and one or more directional verb and temporal aspect inflection values. There are 29 different lexical words present in the vocabulary, three different temporal aspect inflection values ([DURATIONAL], [HABITUAL], [CONTINUATIVE]) and 11 different directional verb inflection values (see Table 2) that may combine with a root lexical word.

Examples of directional verb and temporal aspect inflected signs in the vocabulary are given below:

– The root verb HELP, combined with inflection values indicating different subjects and objects, yields: $\text{HELP}^{I \rightarrow YOU}$, $\text{HELP}^{YOU \rightarrow I}$, $\text{HELP}^{I \rightarrow GIRL}$, $\text{HELP}^{I \rightarrow JOHN}$, $\text{HELP}^{JOHN \rightarrow I}$, $\text{HELP}^{JOHN \rightarrow YOU}$, $\text{HELP}^{YOU \rightarrow HELP}$, $\text{HELP}^{GIRL \rightarrow I}$, $\text{HELP}^{GIRL \rightarrow YOU}$, $\text{HELP}^{YOU \rightarrow GIRL}$, $\text{HELP}^{GIRL \rightarrow JOHN}$.

Table 2. Directional verb inflections used in constructing signs for the experiments

---

$VERB^{I \to YOU}$, $VERB^{YOU \to I}$, $VERB^{I \to GIRL}$, $VERB^{GIRL \to I}$, $VERB^{I \to JOHN}$, $VERB^{JOHN \to I}$, $VERB^{YOU \to GIRL}$, $VERB^{GIRL \to YOU}$, $VERB^{YOU \to JOHN}$, $VERB^{JOHN \to YOU}$, $VERB^{GIRL \to JOHN}$

- The root word EAT, combined with different temporal aspect inflections yields: $EAT^{[DURATIONAL]}$, $EAT^{[HABITUAL]}$, $EAT^{[CONTINUATIVE]}$.

Some of the inflected signs are formed with two inflection values which appear simultaneously, further increasing the complexity of the vocabulary. Examples of these signs are: $(GIVE^{[DURATIONAL]})^{I \to GIRL}$, $(GIVE^{[HABITUAL]})^{I \to GIRL}$, $(GIVE^{[CONTINUATIVE]})^{I \to GIRL}$. A few of the lexical root words are used in combination with various inflection values to form many different signs, for example, the lexical word GIVE appears in 16 different signs.

4.2   Data Measurement and Feature Extraction

Data was obtained using the Polhemus electromagnetic tracker [1] which consists of an electromagnetic field-emitting transmitter and sensors that detect their 3-dimensional position and orientation within the field. Sensors were placed on the back of the signer's right hand and the base of his spine. Conceptually, each sensor has an attached orthogonal coordinate frame. The position and orientation of the right hand's sensor is represented by the 3-dimensional coordinates of its origin, x, y, and z axes ($\underline{o}_H, \underline{x}_H, \underline{y}_H$, and $\underline{z}_H$), relative to the waist sensor's coordinate frame. The waist sensor's coordinate frame was used as a reference to discount variations in the signer's position and the direction he is facing, relative to the transmitter. In addition, we also collected data from a Virtual Technologies Cyberglove [2] worn on the right hand. This records the fingers' joint and abduction angles, and the wrist pitch and yaw, from 18 sensors in the glove. The tracker and glove data are synchronized and were recorded at approximately 31.1ms frame rate.

The features used as observations for the three sign components in our model are given below:

- Handshape component. Data measured by 16 sensors of the Cyberglove, reporting the joint and abduction angles of the right hand's fingers and thumb. The data reported by the two sensors measuring wrist yaw and pitch were not used because this data does not represent the finger configurations. The feature vector for the handshape component is 16-dimensional.
- Location component. The 3-dimensional position of the right hand, $\underline{o}_H$, taken to be the origin of the sensor's coordinate frame. The feature vector for the location component is 3-dimensional.
- Orientation component. The unit vector corresponding to the z-axis, $\underline{z}_H$, of the right hand sensor, with reference to the waist sensor's coordinate frame.

Recall from Section 1.1 that the hand orientation is defined as the direction in which the palm and fingers are pointing. Here however, we only extract features measuring the palm direction because measurements pertaining to the fingers are already extracted in the feature vector of the handshape component. Figure 6 shows a schematic of how the sensor is mounted on the back of the right hand. The x, y and z-axes of the right hand sensor's coordinate frame are shown. The sensor's z-axis direction is roughly coincident with the direction in which the palm is pointing thus its corresponding unit vector indicate the palm orientation. We note that left-right rotation (i.e. hand rotations in the x-y plane) would not register a change in the z-axis direction. So our choice of features is based on a simplifying assumption that the direction in which the palm is pointing is more relevant than the left-right wrist rotation. The feature vector for the orientation component is 3-dimensional.

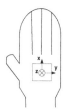

Fig. 6. Schematic representation of how the Polhemus tracker sensor is mounted on the back of the right hand. The z-axis of the sensor's coordinate frame is pointing into the page, i.e. it is approximately coincident with the direction that the palm is facing.

4.3   Training and Testing on a Single Component

The training procedure for learning component-specific CPD parameters is as described in Section 3.1. Starting from initial model parameters for the H-HMM, the iterative steps in the EM algorithm are repeated until it converged. Training uses constrained sentence models reflecting the correct sign sequence in training sentences. In the E-step, inferencing uses the forward interface inferencing algorithm for DBNs [12]. The observations features for all three components are as described in Section 4.2.

The trained H-HMM models for handshape, orientation and location components are tested for sign recognition on the test sentence set. Inferencing during testing obtains the most-probable assignment of values to all the hidden nodes in the model. We use the forward interface algorithm in this decoding step. The sign accuracy results for the three trained models are shown in Table 3.

Note that a sign is recognized as correct if values of all the sign-level nodes are inferred correctly, i.e. the lexical word, directional verb inflection and temporal aspect inflection values must all be correct. With this criterion, sign accuracy is defined as follows. Let N_s denote the total number of signs appearing in the test set, S_s the number of substitutions, D_s the number of deletions, and I_s the number of insertions. The sign accuracy, Acc_s, is thus:

Table 3. Test results on trained models for two Q-level H-HMMs for handshape, orientation and location components

Trained model	Acc_s (%)	$AccSent_s$ (%)	D_s	S_s	I_s	N_s
Handshape component H-HMM	73.1	12.7	11	199	2	788
Orientation component H-HMM	85.0	36.6	16	95	7	788
Location component H-HMM	78.4	18.3	11	150	9	788

$$Acc_s = \frac{N_s - S_s - D_s - I_s}{N_s}$$

Sentence accuracy, $AccSent_s$, is defined by the fraction of sentences without any recognition errors.

4.4 Testing on Combined Model

A MH-HMM modelling the location, handshape and orientation components is constructed by combining the component-specific CPD parameters learned in Section 4.3 (also see Section 3.1). The MH-HMM is shown in Figure 4. We presented the observed values of the component features O_t^c, for components $c = 1, 2, 3$ from the test set sentences. Synchronization between component streams at sign boundaries was enforced by setting $S_t^2 = 1$, for $1 \leq t \leq T$. We also set $F_t^1 = 0$ for $t = 1 \ldots, T - 1$ and as $F_T^1 = 1$. With these observed node values, the most probable sign sequence in each sentence was inferred using PF. The sign accuracy results for this MH-HMM are shown in Table 4 for different number of samples used in the PF algorithm.

Table 4. Test results on MH-HMM combining trained models of location, handshape and orientation components

Num. of samples	Acc_s (%)	$AccSent_s$ (%)	D_s	S_s	I_s	N_s
3000	92.0	58.5	7	56	0	788
5000	92.4	62.0	4	53	3	788
10000	92.6	61.3	6	50	2	788
15000	92.6	62.7	5	50	3	788
20000	93.4	66.2	4	45	3	788
25000	93.9	68.3	5	42	1	788
30000	92.9	64.8	8	45	3	788
40000	93.7	68.3	6	40	4	788

The sign recognition accuracy is greatly improved compared to single component decoding results (compare Table 3). Since more data is available as observed features streams in the combined model, the improved sign recognition results is to be expected. The PF algorithm is expected to give better inferencing results with increased number of samples, theoretically approaching results that would be obtained using exact inferencing at the limit of infinite number of samples. The results in Table 4 show an improvement in sentence accuracy, $AccSent_s$, with increased number of samples. It might be worth increasing the number of samples beyond the maximum 40000 that we experimented with, to investigate if this would produce further improvement in the sentence accuracy, which is currently quite low considering the relatively high sign accuracy.

The correspondence between sample number and accuracy is however not seen in the other accuracy measurements. The maximum sign accuracy (Acc_s) of 93.9% was obtained with 25000 samples and not with the maximum number of 40000 samples that we ran experiments with. The maximum word accuracy (Acc_w) of 98.9% was also obtained with less than 40000 samples. Due to the stochastic nature of the inferencing algorithm, we would have to run a few sets of experiments with the same number of samples before we can conclude if it is indeed the case that we get diminishing returns in sign and word accuracy beyond 20000 to 25000 samples.

5   Conclusions

We have shown decoding results on experimental sign vocabulary including signs with complex and multiple inflection values. Best sign and sentence accuracies of 93.9% and 68.3% respectively indicate the feasibility of our approach using the MH-HMM. We are currently working on modelling movement path attributes explicitly in the MH-HMM, including direction, shape, size and speed. Some features currently being explored include curvature, centroid distance function and Fourier transform based features.

References

1. Polhemus 3Space User's Manual. Polhemus, Colchester, VT (1991)
2. CyberGlove User's Manual. Virtual Technologies Inc. (1995)
3. Bourlard, H., Dupont, S.: A new ASR approach based on independent processing and recombination of partial frequency bands. In: Proc. Int'l. Conf. on Spoken Language Processing, vol. 1, pp. 426–429 (1996)
4. Braffort, A.: Argo: An architecture for sign language recognition and interpretation. In: Proc. Gesture Workshop, pp. 17–30 (1996)
5. Brand, M., Oliver, N., Pentland, A.: Coupled hidden Markov models for complex action recognition. In: Proc. IEEE Int'l. Conf. Comp. Vision and Pattern Recogn., pp. 994–999. IEEE Computer Society Press, Los Alamitos (June 1997)
6. Fine, S., Singer, Y., Tishby, N.: The hierarchical hidden Markov model: Analysis and applications. Machine Learning 32, 41–62 (1998)
7. Ghahramani, Z., Jordan, M.: Factorial hidden Markov models. In: Touretzky, D., Mozer, M., Hasselmo, M. (eds.) Proc. Conf. Advances in Neural Information Processing Systems, vol. 8, pp. 472–478. MIT Press, Cambridge, Mass. (1995)

8. Gowdy, J., Subramanya, A., Bartels, C., Bilmes, J.: DBN based multi-stream models for audio-visual speech recognition. In: IEEE Intl. Conf. Acoustics, Speech and Signal Processing, IEEE Computer Society Press, Los Alamitos (May 2004)
9. Gravier, G., Potamianos, G., Neti, C.: Asynchrony modeling for audio-visual speech recognition. In: Proc. Human Language Technology Conf. (March 2002)
10. Klima, E., Bellugi, U.: The Signs of Language. Harvard Univ. Press, Cambridge, Mass. (1979)
11. Liddell, S.: Grammar, Gesture, and Meaning in American Sign Language. Cambridge Univ. Press, Cambridge (2003)
12. Murphy, K.: Dynamic Bayesian Networks: Representation, Inference and Learning. PhD thesis, UC Berkeley, Computer Science Division (2002)
13. Oliver, N., Horvitz, E., Garg, A.: Layered representations for human activity recognition. In: ICMI 2002. Proc. of the Fourth IEEE Int'l. Conf. on Multimodal Interfaces, IEEE Computer Society Press, Los Alamitos (2002)
14. Ong, S., Ranganath, S., Venkatesh, Y.: Understanding gestures with systematic variations in movement dynamics. Patt. Recog. 39, 1633–1648 (2006)
15. Poizner, H., Klima, E., Bellugi, U., Livingston, R.: Motion analysis of grammatical processes in a visual-gestural language. In: Proc. ACM SIGGRAPH/SIGART Interdisciplinary Workshop, pp. 271–292. ACM Press, New York (1983)
16. Sagawa, H., Takeuchi, M.: A method for analyzing spatial relationships between words in sign language recognition. In: Braffort, A., Gibet, S., Teil, D., Gherbi, R., Richardson, J. (eds.) GW 1999. LNCS (LNAI), vol. 1739, pp. 197–210. Springer, Heidelberg (2000)
17. Valli, C., Lucas, C.: Linguistics of American sign language: a resource text for ASL users. Gallaudet Univ. Press, Washington, D.C. (1992)
18. Vogler, C.: American Sign Language Recognition: Reducing the Complexity of the Task with Phoneme-based Modeling and Parallel Hidden Markov Models. PhD thesis, Univ. of Pennsylvania (2003)

Model-Based Stereo with Occlusions

Fabiano Romeiro and Todd Zickler

School of Engineering and Applied Sciences
Harvard University
romeiro@fas.harvard.edu, zickler@eecs.harvard.edu

Abstract. This paper addresses the recovery of face models from stereo pairs of images in the presence of foreign-body occlusions. In the proposed approach, a 3D morphable model (3DMM) for faces is augmented by an occlusion map defined on the model shape, and occlusion is detected with minimal computational overhead by incorporating robust estimators in the fitting process. Additionally, the method uses an explicit model for texture (or reflectance) in addition to shape, which is in contrast to most existing multi-view methods that use a shape model alone. We argue that both model components are required to handle certain classes of occluders, and we present empirical results to support this claim. In fact, the empirical results in this paper suggest that even in the absence of occlusions, stereo reconstruction using existing shape-only face models can perform poorly by some measures, and that the inclusion of an explicit texture model may be worth its computational expense.

1 Introduction

Being able to automatically recognize faces, track them, and estimate their expression and pose are important for many applications. Performing these tasks reliably requires the ability to represent the appearance of faces over large variations in illumination and viewpoint. It also requires the ability to model the effects of occlusions—both self-occlusions caused by the face itself and occlusions caused by "foreign bodies" (eye glasses, long facial hair, clothing, hands and limbs, etc.) in the environment.

Illumination effects can often be well-represented using purely image-based methods (e.g. [1,2,3,4]), but to effectively handle extreme changes in 3D pose, one typically requires a mechanism for "warping" 2D images. 3D morphable models (3DMMs), which are parametric models of shape and reflectance, are useful for this purpose because they explicitly represent 3D shape and therefore handle self-occlusions in a natural way.

In a 3D model-based approach, one is faced with the problem of finding the parameters of the model that best explain the input data. The estimated model parameters can then be used to perform recognition, track the face, detect expressions, synthesize new images, etc. The fitting problem is complicated in the presence of foreign-body occluders, because unlike self-occlusions, the image effects induced by foreign bodies cannot be explained by the face model.

In this paper we present a 3D model-based method for face reconstruction and recognition that exploits stereo imaging to handle foreign body occlusions. In the proposed approach, occlusion is represented using a single occlusion map defined on the 3D

S.K. Zhou et al. (Eds.): AMFG 2007, LNCS 4778, pp. 31–45, 2007.

shape model, and this occlusion map is recovered efficiently by incorporating robust estimators in the fitting process.

In addition to including an occlusion map, we differentiate between two types of constraints for fitting a model to multiple views. According to the first constraint, each image should agree with a given model's shape and reflectance; and according to the second, the images should agree with each other given the model's shape. We find that the importance of these two constraints (roughly speaking, the "texture match" and the "stereo match") varies depending on the type of foreign body occluders that are present. We also find that even in the absence of occluders, explicitly enforcing the texture match constraint significantly improves fitting accuracy in comparison to an approach that uses the stereo match constraint alone (suggested in [5]).

1.1 Related Work

3D Morphable Models (3DMMs) [6] use high resolution linear 3D shape and texture models to represent faces. Typically, this model is fit to an input image by minimizing an energy function that measures the difference between intensities in the observed image and those predicted by the model. Recognition can be performed based on the model parameters [7] or by using the model to synthesize new views of the face in a canonical pose and lighting configuration [8].

Using a stereo pair for the fitting of a 3DMM imposes additional geometric constraints on the face shape, which can improve the quality of results. Also, by imposing a stereo matching constraint, the fitting of the shape and texture parameters can be decoupled [5]. According to this approach, the shape parameters are recovered by minimizing the per vertex intensity differences between two calibrated views, and the texture is estimated separately using this shape. While the decoupling of shape and texture is appealing from an efficiency standpoint, the results we show here suggest that there are significant benefits to estimating both components jointly.

Explicit handling of foreign-body occlusions has been addressed for the case of monocular fitting of 3DMMs in [9], where a generalized EM algorithm is used to alternate between the estimation of a visibility map given the model and the model parameters given the visibility map. To account for spatial coherence of occluders the visibility map is modeled by a Markov random field (MRF) on the image plane. In contrast, we model occlusions using a visibility map on *the surface*, and approximate the occlusion process using a robust estimator. While it gives up the preference for spatial coherence, the proposed approach can be implemented with little computational overhead. In addition, it can be easily extended to more views, since the occlusion map is on the surface.

Also related to this work are 2D active appearance models (AAMs), which trade precision for speed and are often used for tracking. 2D AAMs [10] typically use low-resolution 2D deformable shapes along with linear texture models. The fitting is done by matching a warped face image (with the warping being given by the linear shape model) against the linear texture model, and solving for the shape and texture parameters that give the best fit. Performance can be improved using an extension to the inverse compositional image alignment algorithm [11], by including 3D constraints [12], or by using multiple views [13, 14]. Fitting AAMs in the presence of occlusions can also be approached using robust estimators [15]. The main advantages of the 3D approach over 2D AAMs are the ability to directly model lighting effects because it has access to surface normals and to more easily handle self-occlusions.

2 Background

2.1 3D Morphable Models for Faces

As a 3D morphable model for faces, we use the shape and texture bases (3DFS-100) made available by the University of Freiburg [6]. These bases were obtained by first concatenating the N vertices (or RGB color values in the case of texture) of each scan i of a large set of high resolution 3D face scans into vectors (FS_i for shape, and FT_i for texture), and putting them into correspondence. That is, the vectors are made such that the same entry in each vector corresponds to the same facial feature [16, 17, 18]. These vectors are denoted:

$$FS_i = [[X_1^i Y_1^i Z_1^i]...[X_N^i Y_N^i Z_N^i]], \quad FT_i = [[R_1^i G_1^i B_1^i]...[R_N^i G_N^i B_N^i]]$$

Principal component analysis (PCA) is performed on this set of vectors, and the most significant eigenvectors are used as bases for shape and texture. Shape and texture are then expressed as linear combinations of these basis elements:

$$S = S_0 + \sum_{i=1}^{m} \alpha_i S_i, \quad T = T_0 + \sum_{i=1}^{m} \beta_i T_i,$$

where S_0 and T_0 are the average face shape and texture and $(S_1,...,S_m)$ and $(T_1, ..., T_m)$ are the eigenvectors of shape and texture respectively. Here, $S_i, T_i \in \mathbb{R}^{3N}$. Thus, in this model, faces are represented by the set of coefficients $\alpha = (\alpha_1, ..., \alpha_m)$ and $\beta = (\beta_1, ..., \beta_m)$ that correspond to their shape and texture.

If one assumes the coefficients are drawn from independent normal distributions, PCA also gives an estimate of their probability distributions;

$$P(\alpha) \propto exp(-\frac{1}{2}\sum_{i=1}^{m} \frac{\alpha_i^2}{\sigma_i^2}), \quad P(\beta) \propto exp(-\frac{1}{2}\sum_{i=1}^{m} \frac{\beta_i^2}{\gamma_i^2}), \tag{1}$$

where σ_i and γ_i are determined by the respective eigenvalues of the covariance matrices of $\{FS_i\}$ and $\{FT_i\}$.

2.2 Image Formation Model

We assume faces to be in or close to the space spanned by the shape and texture bases of Sect. 2.1. Then, given a face's shape parameters α and a suitable rigid body transformation (rotation R and translation t, that align the face model with the actual face), the true color value ($\gamma(k)$) of the face at the position corresponding to the face model's vertex k will equal that predicted by the model:

$$\gamma(k) \approx I_m(k), \tag{2}$$

where $I_m(k)$ is the RGB value of the texture at v_k as given by the texture parameters β, and a suitable set of lighting parameters.

For a lighting model, we assume the surface is Lambertian, and use (R_{amb}, G_{amb}, B_{amb}) for the ambient light color, (R_{dir}, G_{dir}, B_{dir}) for the directional light color, (R_{offset}, G_{offset}, B_{offset}) for the color channels offsets, and l for the directional light direction. Then we have:

$$I_m(k)_R = R_{offset} + t_{kR} \cdot (R_{amb} + R_{dir} \cdot (n_k \cdot l)), \tag{3}$$

with similar definitions for the G,B channels. The symbol t_k represents the kth RGB value in the face model's texture vector representation given the texture coefficients β, and n_k represents the surface normal at v_k.

Assume we are given a stereo pair (I_1, I_2) of face images captured from a pair of calibrated cameras. Letting P_1 and P_2 denote the two camera projection matrices, and assuming we are given the shape parameters α and rigid body transformation parameters (R, t), we have two available measurements of $\gamma(k)$. These can be written $I_1(P_1(R(v_k - c) + c + t))$ and $I_2(P_2(R(v_k - c) + c + t))$, where c is the centroid of the average face shape. Assuming that the cameras are radiometrically calibrated (i.e., have the same exposure, white balance, etc.) with additive Gaussian noise, a reasonable estimator for $\gamma(k)$ is:

$$\hat{\gamma}(k) = \bar{I}(v_k, R, t) \overset{\triangle}{=} \frac{I_1(P_1(R(v_k - c) + c + t)) + I_2(P_2(R(v_k - c) + c + t))}{2}. \tag{4}$$

Thus a simple approximation for the distribution of $I_m(k)$, given I_1, I_2, α, R, t is a normal distribution with mean $\bar{I}$ and standard deviation σ_t (say):

$$I_m(k) \sim N(\bar{I}(v_k, R, t), \sigma_t). \tag{5}$$

In addition, when α, I_2, R, t are given, and again assuming that the cameras are radiometrically calibrated, we can use the following model for the noisy observation in I_1 of a vertex v_k that is visible in both images:

$$I_1(P_1(R(v_k - c) + c + t)) \sim N(I_2(P_2(R(v_k - c) + c + t)), \sigma_s). \tag{6}$$

Note that if the cameras are not radiometrically calibrated, this can be generalized by incorporating camera-dependent gains and offsets into I_1 and I_2.

For simplicity, we make use of the following notation in the next section:

ρ - the 6 parameters of the rigid body transformation (3 for R, 3 for t).

τ - the 11 lighting parameters (3 for i_{amb}, 3 for i_{dir}, 3 for i_{offset}, i={R,G,B}, and 2 for l).

s_k - the position of the kth model vertex given pose parameters (R,t) and shape parameters α; $s_k = R(v_k - c) + c + t$.

3   Robust Stereo Fitting of 3DMMs

3.1   Joint Shape and Texture Stereo Fitting

We use an energy function that incorporates both a shape model and a texture model by combining terms derived from Eqs. 5 and 6, with regularization:

$$
E = \underbrace{\sum_{k|v_k \in V} \frac{||I_1(P_1 s_k) - I_2(P_2 s_k)||^2}{\sigma_s^2}}_{\text{Stereo Match}} + \underbrace{\sum_{i=1}^{m} \frac{\alpha_i^2}{\sigma_i^2}}_{\text{Shape Prior}} + \tag{7}
$$

$$
\underbrace{\sum_{k|v_k \in V} \frac{||I_m(k) - \bar{I}(s_k)||^2}{\sigma_t^2}}_{\text{Texture Model Match}} + \underbrace{\sum_{i=1}^{m} \frac{\beta_i^2}{\gamma_i^2}}_{\text{Texture Prior}} .
$$

Here, the symbol V is used to denote the set of vertices v_k of the face model with parameters (α,ρ) that are visible in both I_1 and I_2.

Model-fitting is performed by finding parameters α,β,ρ,τ that minimize E. This can be interpreted in a MAP framework as a search for parameters (α,β,ρ,τ) for which the posterior $P(\alpha,\beta,\rho,\tau|I_1,I_2)$ is maximal, and such an interpretation highlights the assumptions underlying our approach. First, we expand the posterior as $P(\alpha,\beta,\rho,\tau|I_1,I_2) = P(\alpha,\rho|I_1,I_2) \cdot P(\beta,\tau|I_1,I_2,\alpha,\rho)$. The first term is then rewritten $P(\alpha,\rho|I_1,I_2) \propto P(I_1|\alpha,\rho,I_2) \cdot P(\alpha)$, which by Bayes' rule, assumes that α,ρ,I_2 are mutually independent and that the distribution of face poses (ρ) is uniform. The assumption that shape (α) and pose (ρ) are independent from I_2 may seem non-trivial. But without knowledge of face texture (β), little can be inferred about I_2, because any image I_2 can be explained by a suitably selected texture.

Using Eq. 6 we write:

$$
P(I_1|\alpha,\rho,I_2) \propto \prod_{k|v_k \in V} exp\left(-\frac{1}{2} \frac{||I_1(P_1 s_k) - I_2(P_2 s_k)||^2}{\sigma_s^2} \right). \tag{8}
$$

and using Eq. 5 (assuming the texture (β) and scene lighting (τ) independent, and τ uniformly distributed), we write:

$$
P(\beta,\tau|I_1,I_2,\alpha,\rho) \propto P(\beta) \cdot \prod_{k|v_k \in V} exp\left(-\frac{1}{2} \frac{||I_m(k) - \bar{I}(s_k)||^2}{\sigma_t^2} \right). \tag{9}
$$

Finally, we obtain the energy E by substituting Eqs. 1,8 and 9 into our expression for the posterior, taking the logarithm, negating it and ignoring constant factors.

One can make the following observations about this energy function. First, suppose one were to include only the last three terms in Eq. 7, which would correspond to maximizing $P(I_1|\alpha,\beta,\rho,\tau) \cdot P(I_2|\alpha,\beta,\rho,\tau) \cdot P(\alpha,\beta)$. This approach would not account for the correlation between I_1 and I_2. The two images are not independent given (α,β,ρ,τ) because the true appearance of the face deviates from that given by the face model, and consequently, the two prediction errors are correlated.

Second, suppose we were to ignore the third and the fourth terms in Eq. 7. This is the approach taken in [5], and it corresponds to maximizing $P(\alpha,\rho|I_1,I_2)$ without including a texture model. As we will show experimentally in Sect. 4, this approach can perform poorly because it does not necessarily ensure that important features (eyes, eyebrows, lips) are properly aligned.

Finally, we can compare our approach to an uncalibrated case in which one has no information about the stereo cameras. In this case, separate pose parameters (ρ_1,ρ_2) could be used for each image, and one might seek to maximize $P(\alpha,\beta,\tau,\rho_1,\rho_2|I_1,I_2)$. In this case, by the same argument as in the first observation, I_1 and I_2 are still not independent given $\alpha,\beta,\tau,\rho_1,\rho_2$, therefore maximizing $P(I_1|\alpha,\beta,\tau,\rho_1) \cdot P(I_2|\alpha,\beta,\tau,\rho_2) \cdot P(\alpha,\beta)$ (which would be the trivial extension of the monocular fitting case to two images [6]) does not necessarily maximize $P(\alpha,\beta,\tau,\rho_1,\rho_2|I_1,I_2)$.

3.2 Handling Occlusion

While the approach in the previous section correctly handles cases of self-occlusion (where one part of the face occludes another), it does not account for the possibility of foreign-body occlusions. To handle such situations, we use a modified version of the energy function in Eq. 7, introducing a robust estimator h_a:

$$E' = \sum_{k|v_k \in V} h_a \left(\frac{||I_1(P_1 s_k) - I_2(P_2 s_k)||^2}{\sigma_s^2} + \frac{||I_m(k) - \bar{I}(s_k)||^2}{\sigma_t^2} \right) + \sum_{i=1}^{m} \frac{\alpha_i^2}{\sigma_i^2} + \sum_{i=1}^{m} \frac{\beta_i^2}{\gamma_i^2} \quad (10)$$

This modification requires little change in the optimization procedure, and allows the fitting to be significantly more robust to foreign-body occlusions (see Sect. 4.2). Intuitively, by introducing the robust estimator we are limiting the impact in the energy function of vertices whose stereo matching term or texture matching term are high. More formally, this approach can be justified by introducing a binary occlusion map $O: \{1,..,N\} \rightarrow \{0,1\}^N$, defined on the set of all vertices of the face model. This map dictates whether a vertex of the face model is occluded by a foreign-body in at least one of the images ($O(k) = 1$) or not occluded in either ($O(k) = 0$). Thus, the image formation model is altered so that the visible parts of the face present in the images are generated only by vertices v_k for which $O(k) = 0$.

In this setting, it can be shown that minimizing E' corresponds to searching for α,β,ρ,τ,O for which $P(\alpha,\beta,\rho,\tau,O|I_1,I_2)$ is maximal. Again, we can write $P(\alpha,\beta,\rho,\tau,O|I_1,I_2) = P(\alpha,\rho,O|I_1,I_2) \cdot P(\beta,\tau|I_1,I_2,\alpha,\rho,O)$. We expand the first term by making the same assumptions as those used in the previous section, obtaining $P(\alpha,\rho,O|I_1,I_2) \propto P(I_1|\alpha,\rho,O,I_2) \cdot P(\alpha,O)$. The term $P(I_1|\alpha,\rho,O,I_2)$ is then approximated as in Eq. 8, where the product is now over $\{k|v_k \in V, O(k) = 0\}$. In favor of simplicity and efficiency, we ignore spatial coherence of occlusions, and assume $O(k) \sim$ i.i.d. Bernoulli, obtaining the following prior on O:

$$P(O) \propto \prod_{k|v_k \in V} exp(-\eta_o \cdot O(k)). \tag{11}$$

Using this prior avoids the trivial labeling of all vertices being occluded during the optimization process.

Combining these terms and assuming the shape (α) and occlusion map (O) to be independent, we obtain an expression for $P(\alpha, \rho, O|I_1, I_2)$. Substituting this expression into the posterior along with an expression for the posterior's second term similar to Eq. 9 (but with the product over $\{k|v_k \in V, O(k) = 0\}$, one sees that maximizing the posterior corresponds to minimizing:

$$E'' = \sum_{k|v_k \in V} f(\alpha, \beta, \rho, \tau, O, k) + \sum_{i=1}^{m} \frac{\alpha_i^2}{\sigma_i^2} + \sum_{i=1}^{m} \frac{\beta_i^2}{\gamma_i^2}, \tag{12}$$

where

$$f(\alpha, \beta, \rho, \tau, O, k) = g(\alpha, \beta, \rho, \tau, k) \cdot (1 - O(k)) + 2\eta_o \cdot O(k), \tag{13}$$

and

$$g(\alpha, \beta, \rho, \tau, k) = \frac{||I_1(P_1 s_k) - I_2(P_2 s_k)||^2}{\sigma_s^2} + \frac{||I_m(k) - \bar{I}(s_k)||^2}{\sigma_t^2}. \tag{14}$$

The minimization of E'' can be rearranged as:

$$\min_{\alpha, \beta, \rho, \tau, O} E'' = \min_{\alpha, \beta, \rho, \tau} \{\min_O \{\sum_{k|v_k \in V} f(\alpha, \beta, \rho, \tau, O, k)\} + \sum_{i=1}^{m} \frac{\alpha_i^2}{\sigma_i^2} + \sum_{i=1}^{m} \frac{\beta_i^2}{\gamma_i^2}\} \tag{15}$$

$$= \min_{\alpha, \beta, \rho, \tau} \{\sum_{k|v_k \in V} h(g(\alpha, \beta, \rho, \tau, k), k) + \sum_{i=1}^{m} \frac{\alpha_i^2}{\sigma_i^2} + \sum_{i=1}^{m} \frac{\beta_i^2}{\gamma_i^2}\} \tag{16}$$

where

$$h(g(\alpha, \beta, \rho, \tau, k), k) = \min_{O(k)} \{g(\alpha, \beta, \rho, \tau, k) \cdot (1 - O(k)) + 2\eta_o \cdot O(k)\}. \tag{17}$$

Relaxing the binary process $O(k)$ to an outlier process that varies continuously $0 \leq O_a(k) \leq 1$, we can approximate $h(g, k)$ by a robust function h_a,

$$h_a(g) = -\sigma_o \cdot ln((1 - exp(-\frac{e_o}{\sigma_o})) \cdot exp(-\frac{g}{\sigma_o}) + exp(-\frac{e_o}{\sigma_o})) \tag{18}$$

with suitable parameters e_o and σ_o. These parameters are determined empirically to provide a smooth approximation of the min function (see Fig. 1). This leads to E' as in Eq. 10, where the minimization is over $\alpha, \beta, \rho, \tau$.

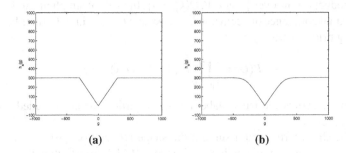

Fig. 1. Robust estimator $h_a(g)$ (Eq. 18) used to handle foreign-body occlusions in the fitting process: (a) $e_o = 300, \sigma_o = 1$ (b) $e_o = 300, \sigma_o = 50$

Following optimization, the occlusion map is recovered from (for $v_k \in V$):

$$O^*(k) = 1, \text{ if } h_a(g(\alpha^*, \beta^*, \rho^*, \tau^*, k)) \geq 2\eta_o - \varepsilon$$
$$O^*(k) = 0, \text{ if } h_a(g(\alpha^*, \beta^*, \rho^*, \tau^*, k)) < 2\eta_o - \varepsilon,$$

where

$$(\alpha^*, \beta^*, \rho^*, \tau^*) = arg \min_{\alpha, \beta, \rho, \tau} E'. \tag{19}$$

3.3   On Foreign Body Occlusions

In a stereo setup, there can be several cases of foreign-body occlusion of a vertex of the face model. We can classify these cases with respect to the positioning of the occluder in (see Fig. 2): half-occlusion (HO), where the vertex is occluded in one of I_1 or I_2; full-occlusion-near (FO_n), where the vertex is occluded in both I_1 and I_2 and the occluding object is close to the face; and full-occlusion-far (FO_f), where the occluder is far from the face relative to the face size. We can also classify occluders with respect to their texture, which can be one of: texture-less (non-skincolor); texture-less (skincolor); and textured.

Depending on the type of occlusion, we expect either the stereo match term or the texture match term to play a more prominent role in the fitting process (see Table 1). For example, in the case of half-occlusion (HO) by a non-skinlike surface, one can expect the stereo match term to provide an important cue as to whether a vertex is occluded. This is because the observed intensities at the projections of a half-occluded vertex correspond to observations of two very different surfaces. When the occlusion is of type full-occlusion-near (FO_n) on the other hand, the stereo match term will not provide much help in determining an occlusion because the two observed intensities will come from nearby locations on the occluder and will be very similar. In this case, provided that the occluder has non-skinlike color, the texture match will be the most helpful in determining its presence. Of course, when the occluder lacks texture and is skinlike, there is little visual information to discriminate between it and the face.

Experimental results are shown in Sect. 4.2.

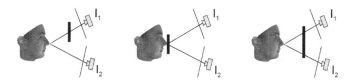

Fig. 2. Categories of foreign-body occlusions. From left to right, occlusions can be one of: half-occlusion (HO), full-occlusion-near (FO_n), full-occlusion-far (FO_f). The stereo and texture terms play different roles in each case (see Table 1).

Table 1. Most relevant terms in the energy function for each of the occlusion cases: S for stereo match term and T for texture match term (see Fig. 2)

Occluder classification	HO	FO_n	FO_f
texture-less (non-skincolor)	S	T	T
texture-less (skincolor)	X	X	X
textured	S	T	S+T

3.4 Optimization Procedure

Initial Fit. Like previous approaches [5,17], we assume that either by user selection, or by means of an automated detection process, image coordinates of a subset of specific feature points of the face (e.g. corners of the eyes, corners of the mouth, tip of the nose, corners of the ears) in both I_1 and I_2 are available. (Some of the feature points may be occluded in one or both images).

Let $j_1, .., j_p$ denote the indices of the vertices in the face model corresponding to these feature points. Starting from the average shape parameters ($\alpha = 0$), we use a quasi-newton gradient descent method to minimize

$$E_f = \sum_{i=1,...,p} \delta_{1i} \|P_1 s_{j_i} - p_{1i}\|^2 + \delta_{2i} \|P_2 s_{j_i} - p_{2i}\|^2, \tag{20}$$

and obtain a rough initial estimate of the shape and rigid body transformation parameters. Here, $\delta_{1i} = 1$ if the ith feature is visible in image I_1 and 0 otherwise (and similarly for δ_{2i} and I_2), p_{1i} is the image coordinate of the ith feature in image I_1, and p_{2i} is the image coordinate of the ith feature in image I_2.

Optimization. For comparison purposes we evaluate the fitting performance of E and E' with and without the texture model terms. In experiments where we utilize only the stereo terms in E (or E'), we start with model parameters α, ρ from the initial fit. In experiments that include texture we also start with the average texture parameters ($\beta = 0$), and lighting parameters τ such that $i_{\text{amb}} = 1$, $i_{\text{dir}} = 1$ (i.e., white ambient and directional lights), and $i_{\text{offset}} = 0$ (zero offset), where $i = R, G, B$. The lighting direction l is initialized to be the bisector of the two cameras viewing directions.

We minimize:

$$E + \lambda \cdot E_f \tag{21}$$

with respect to the suitable parameters, using a stochastic quasi-newton gradient descent method.

To avoid local minima, we use a coarse-to-fine approach, with 3 levels of resolution. At the coarsest resolution, we use versions of I_1 and I_2 that are downsampled by a factor of four, together with a corresponding low resolution version of the 3D face model. As we progress toward the finest level of resolution, we use smaller and smaller values for λ, σ_s and σ_t, which gives smaller weights to the feature term and the shape and texture priors. At regular intervals (more frequently at coarser levels), we recompute the self-occluded vertices (and thus V) as well as the normals (n_k). Instead of computing the energy using all the vertices $v_k \in V$, at each iteration we randomly select a sub-set of these vertices on which to compute the energy (we use 1000, 2000 and 3000, at each level of resolution). In this selection process, we select vertices with probability proportional to the average (over the stereo pair) foreshortened area of the patch around them. When we utilize the complete E or E', we sample at the baricenters of the triangles of the mesh instead of the vertices because that allows for easier computation of the gradient of the energy. In this case, both V and the occlusion map are defined over the set of triangles, and k indexes the triangles that compose the model.

4 Experimental Results

We evaluated the procedure of Sect. 3.4 using the original energy (E) and the robust energy (E'), along with modifications of these energies obtained by excluding the texture terms. Throughout this section, we refer to these as stereo+ texture, stereo, robust stereo+texture, and robust stereo, respectively. To ensure a valid comparison between the different cases, we used equivalent parameters for the feature match weight (λ) and the model priors (σ_s and σ_t) in each experiment. Only the first 40 shape and texture basis vectors were used, since this was found to provide adequate results.

4.1 Accuracy in the Absence of Occlusions

To evaluate the benefits of incorporating a texture model in the absence of occlusions, testing was performed on a subset of sixty individuals from the K.U. Leuven stereo face database [5], which contains stereo pairs of each individual in eight different positions. We obtained fitting results using the stereo and the stereo+texture methods for all eight poses in each of the sixty people, for a total of 480 model fits. Note that the stereo fitting approach is that proposed in [5].

Figures 3 and 4 exemplify the differences between the fits obtained using stereo (first two terms of E) and stereo+texture (E). At first glance, the results in Fig. 3 suggest that the shape estimates using both methods are quite similar. The stereo matching cost ($\sum_{k|v_k \in V} \frac{||I_1(P_1 s_k) - I_2(P_2 s_k)||^2}{|V|}$) was computed to be 280.77 for the stereo method and 340.17 for the stereo+texture method, so the shape obtained using only the stereo term is better in terms of the per-vertex stereo intensity match. However, from Fig. 4 it is clear that the eye, eyebrow and mouth alignment between the model and the images is significantly more accurate when the texture model is included.

These results suggest that either approach may be sufficient if the desired output is a depth map or 3D model for image synthesis. For recognition, however, where one links shape parameters to identity, it is important for features in the fitted model to be

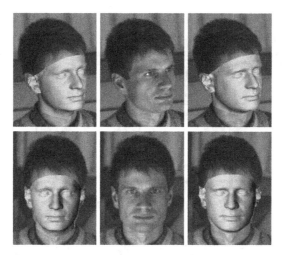

Fig. 3. Comparison of a fit using both stereo and texture to that obtained using stereo alone. Rows indicate left and right images of the stereo pair. First column: shape estimate using stereo, second column: input images, third column: shape estimate using stereo and texture.

Fig. 4. Same comparison as that in Fig. 3, but mapped with estimated textures and rendered semi-transparently over input images. While both the shape obtained using stereo (top) and that obtained using stereo and texture (bottom) provide reasonable depth maps for the input stereo pair (Fig. 3), only the joint use of stereo and texture ensures feature alignment.

aligned with the features in the database models. Our experiments suggest that one way to ensure this alignment is to include a texture model in the fitting procedure.

The same effect can be observed by studying the distribution of the 480 recovered shape models (60 individuals under 8 poses) in the forty-dimensional whitened shape parameter space. Two statistics relate to the quality of the fitting procedure from a recognition standpoint. First, for a single individual, we would like the difference between the fits for different poses to be small. Second, we would like the difference between the

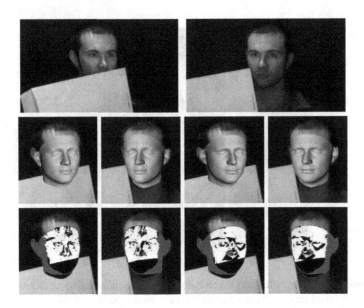

Fig. 5. Models are fit to an input stereo pair (top row) using robust stereo (left columns) and robust stereo and texture (right columns). Here, the face is half-occluded (occluder type HO) by a textureless object. The results from the two methods are very similar, showing that the stereo match term alone suffices for detecting the occluder. The bottom row shows the estimated occlusion map with black indicating foreign-body occlusion ($O(k) = 1$), white indicating visible vertices ($O(k) = 0$ and $v_k \in V$), and red indicating self-occlusion ($v_k \notin V$).

fits for distinct individuals to be large. These can be measured based on the within-class (within-subject) scatter matrix (S_w) and the between-class scatter matrix (S_b). Roughly speaking, the larger the determinant and trace of ($S_w^{-1} S_b$) are, the more accurate a classifier based on these fits will be. Using results from the 480 fits we found the determinants of $S_w^{-1} S_b$ to be $2.9640e^{-5}$ and $1.3418e^{-11}$ and the traces of $S_w^{-1} S_b$ to be 104.0478 and 69.4101 for the stereo+texture method and the stereo method, respectively. These quantitative results support the qualitative observations in Figs. 3 and 4 and suggest that fits obtained with the inclusion of the texture model are significantly more robust to pose changes.

4.2 Accuracy with Occlusions

We also tested the occlusion cases described in Sect. 3.3 by applying the robust fitting process to captured data. For these fitting results, a value of $n_o = 250$ was used for the robust stereo method, and a value of $n_o = 800$ was used for the robust stereo+texture method.

Figure 5 shows results obtained using the robust stereo and robust stereo+texture method in the case of half-occlusion (case HO) by a textureless foreign body. As described in Sect. 3.3, in this case we expect the results for both methods to be similar because the stereo cue is sufficient to detect the occluder. As shown in the figure, this

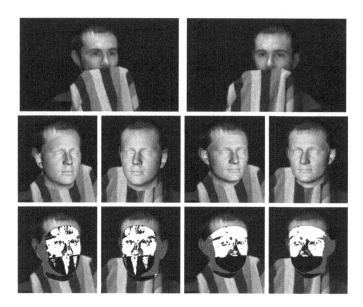

Fig. 6. Same as in Fig. 5, but for the case of a textured foreign-body occluder that is close to the face (occluder of type FO_n). In this case, as evidenced by the occlusion map on the bottom left, the stereo match term alone is not enough to detect the occluder, and the recovered model is inaccurate. Including the texture model (bottom right) significantly improves the result.

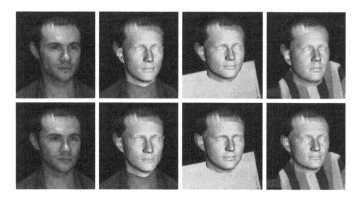

Fig. 7. Comparison of the shapes recovered using robust stereo (first row) and robust stereo and texture (second row) in cases of (from left to right) no occlusion, half-occlusion, and full-occlusion-near. Here, the estimates are overlayed on top of one of their input images. While stereo handles the half occlusion case reasonably well, only combined use of stereo and texture ensures that the recovered model is close to the 'ground truth' shape—at least in its visible regions—in both occlusion cases.

is indeed the case. Notice that the occlusion map captures not only the occluder, but also artifacts that are not predicted by the model, including specular highlights and cast shadows.

Figure 6 shows similar results for the case of a textured occluder that is close to the surface (case FO_n). In this case, the stereo constraint is insufficient for detecting the occluder, and the addition of a texture term provides substantial improvement.

The results from the two occlusion cases are compared to the 'ground truth' shape obtained in the absence of occlusion in Fig. 7. The results obtained by the robust stereo+texture method are relatively consistent over all cases, but the same cannot be said for those obtained using the stereo match alone. Notice that in all cases, the recovered models deviate from the unoccluded model in the unobserved regions of the face. This is to be expected, since there is no shape or texture information available in these regions.

5   Conclusions

We have presented a method for the recovery of face models from stereo pairs of images in the presence of foreign-body occlusions. In this approach, a face model (a 3DMM) is augmented by an occlusion map defined on the model shape, and foreign-body occlusions are detected efficiently using robust estimators. The approach uses an explicit model for texture in addition to shape in an energy-based stereo fitting process.

Experimental results demonstrate robustness to occlusions, and they highlight the relative importance of the stereo match term and the texture match term in the energy. They suggest that both shape and texture components of a 3DMM should be incorporated if one seeks to detect general classes of occluders. The results also suggest that even in the absence of foreign-body occlusions, an explicit texture model can significantly improve stereo fitting results. The texture model provides one way of ensuring proper alignment of features (eyes, eyebrows, lips, etc) in the fitted model.

Another possible approach to achieve alignment, and one we plan to explore in the future, is to use only shape in the stereo fitting process and to incorporate a stereo matching term that is more sophisticated than simple per-vertex intensity differences. This is the approach taken in [19], for example, where window-based matching is employed. One may also look at other feature spaces for fitting (e.g. [20]), as well as better models for the distribution of the error in the modeling of texture (Eq. 5).

Finally, if one is to perform recognition based on models obtained in the presence of occlusions, one would likely want a second model refinement step in which one breaks the initial model into segments [6] in a way that respects the occlusion boundaries. The goal would then be to infer identity using only the unoccluded segments of the model.

Acknowledgements

This work was supported by an NSF CAREER award, IIS-0546408.

References

1. Georghiades, A., Kriegman, D., Belhumeur, P.: Illumination cones for recognition under variable lighting: Faces. CVPR, 52–59 (1998)
2. Belhumeur, P., Hespanha, J., Kriegman, D.: Eigenfaces vs. Fisherfaces: recognition using class specific linear projection. IEEE TPAMI 19(7), 711–720 (1997)
3. Basri, R., Jacobs, D.: Lambertian reflectance and linear subspaces. IEEE TPAMI 25(2), 218–233 (2003)
4. Lee, K.C., Ho, J., Kriegman, D.J.: Nine points of light: acquiring subspaces for face recognition under variable lighting. CVPR 1, 519–526
5. Fransens, R., Strecha, C., Van Gool, L.: Parametric Stereo for Multi-Pose Face Recognition and 3D-Face Modeling. In: Zhao, W., Gong, S., Tang, X. (eds.) AMFG 2005. LNCS, vol. 3723, pp. 109–124. Springer, Heidelberg (2005)
6. Blanz, V., Vetter, T.: A morphable model for the synthesis of 3D faces. In: Proceedings of ACM SIGGRAPH, pp. 187–194. ACM Press, New York (1999)
7. Blanz, V., Vetter, T.: Face recognition based on fitting a 3D morphable model. IEEE TPAMI 25(9), 1063–1074 (2003)
8. Blanz, V., Grother, P., Phillips, P., Vetter, T.: Face recognition based on frontal views generated from non-frontal images. CVPR 2 (2005)
9. De Smet, M., Fransens, R., Van Gool, L., Esat-Psi, K.: A Generalized EM Approach for 3D Model Based Face Recognition under Occlusions. CVPR 2, 1423–1430 (2006)
10. Cootes, T., Edwards, G., Taylor, C.: Active appearance models. IEEE TPAMI 23(6), 681–685 (2001)
11. Baker, S., Matthews, I.: Lucas-Kanade 20 Years On: A Unifying Framework. IJCV 56(3), 221–255 (2004)
12. Xiao, J., Baker, S., Matthews, I., Kanade, T.: Real-time combined 2D+ 3D active appearance models. CVPR 2, 535–542 (2004)
13. Hu, C., Xiao, J., Matthews, I., Baker, S., Cohn, J., Kanade, T.: Fitting a single active appearance model simultaneously to multiple images. In: Proc. British Machine Vision Conference (2004)
14. Koterba, S.C., Baker, S., Matthews, I., Hu, C., Xiao, J., Cohn, J., Kanade, T.: Multi-View AAM Fitting and Camera Calibration. In: ICCV, vol. 1, pp. 511–518 (2005)
15. Gross, R., Matthews, I., Baker, S.: Active Appearance Models with Occlusion. Image and Vision Computing 24(6), 593–604 (2006)
16. Basso, C., Vetter, T., Blanz, V.: Regularized 3D morphable models. In: IEEE Int. Workshop on Higher-Level Knowledge in 3D Modeling and Motion Analysis, pp. 3–10. IEEE Computer Society Press, Los Alamitos (2003)
17. Blanz, V., Basso, C., Poggio, T., Vetter, T.: Reanimating Faces in Images and Video. Computer Graphics Forum 22(3), 641–650 (2003)
18. Basso, C., Paysan, P., Vetter, T.: Registration of Expressions Data using a 3D Morphable Model. FGR, 205–210 (2006)
19. Dimitrijevic, M., Ilic, S., Fua, P.: Accurate face models from uncalibrated and ill-lit video sequences. CVPR 2 (2004)
20. Romdhani, S., Vetter, T.: Estimating 3D Shape and Texture Using Pixel Intensity, Edges, Specular Highlights, Texture Constraints and a Prior. CVPR (2005)

View Invariant Head Recognition by Hybrid PCA Based Reconstruction

Qingquan Wu and Jezekiel Ben-Arie

ECE department, University of Illinois at Chicago,
851 S. Morgan, M/C 154, Chicago, IL 60607, U.S.A.
benarie@ece.uic.edu
http://vision.ece.uic.edu

Abstract. We propose a novel method for 3D head reconstruction and view-invariant recognition from single 2D images. We employ a deterministic Shape From Shading (SFS) method with initial conditions estimated by Hybrid Principal Component Analysis (HPCA) and multi-level global optimization with error-dependent smoothness and integrability constraints. Our HPCA algorithm provides initial estimates of 3D range mapping for the SFS optimization, which is quite accurate and yields much improved 3D head reconstruction. The paper also includes significant contributions in novel approaches to global optimization and in SFS handling of variable and unknown surface albedo, a problem with unsatisfactory solutions by prevalent SFS methods. In the experiments, we reconstruct 3D head range images from 2D single images in different views. The 3D reconstructions are then used to recognize stored model persons. Empirical results show that our HPCA based SFS method provides 3D head reconstructions that notably improve the accuracy compared to other approaches. 3D reconstructions derived from side view (profile) images of 40 persons are tested against 80 3D head models and a recognition rate of over 90% is achieved. Such a capability was not demonstrated by any other method we are aware of.

Keywords: 3D face reconstruction, face recognition, Hybrid PCA, Shape From Shading, Optimization.

1 Introduction

3D face reconstruction from one or multiple 2D face images is an interesting topic that receives a lot of attention. Blanz and Vetter proposed a morphable model for 3D faces reconstruction using an analysis-by-synthesis approach in [4] and later developed a face recognition method in [5], which is based on matching eigenvector coefficients. Jiang et al. [10] used detected face features to determine coefficients for synthesis from shape eigenvectors. Hu et al. [8] utilized a generic 3D face model and detected face features to reconstruct 3D faces with the help of a Shape From Shading (SFS) method and Radial Basis Functions (RBFs). The last two methods reconstruct faces only from frontal face images. In addition, surface albedo was assumed constant in [8], which led to inaccurate height

S.K. Zhou et al. (Eds.): AMFG 2007, LNCS 4778, pp. 46–57, 2007.

on some feature points. Smith and Hancock [13] used an image normalization algorithm to decouple surface normal directions from variable surface albedo. Illumination cones and a Point Distribution Model were employed in a geometric SFS method to refine estimated normals. However, the overall performance of this method is determined by the accuracy of the normalization process. As we can see from above, pose and variable albedo are major concerns in 3D face reconstruction. We propose in this paper a novel method for 3D head reconstruction by SFS which addresses these concerns. Our method reconstructs facial range images from 2D face images in any pose. Furthermore, our approach provides the capability to estimate variable surface albedo. Whereas, such a capability is absent in most of the prevalent SFS methods.

Research on SFS has been conducted for decades. Ikeuchi and Horn [9] proposed to recover shape information by minimizing a cost function. The stereographic plane was employed in their method to express orientations of surface patches. In [7], Horn and Brooks applied the calculus of variations to solve SFS problems. Zheng and Chellappa [17] proposed to estimate illumination direction, albedo, and surface shape by minimizing a cost function with a new smoothness constraint, which was aimed at decreasing the gradient difference between the reconstructed intensity image and the input image. Worthington and Hancock [15] replaced estimated normals with the closest normalized vector on illumination cones to ensure accuracy of recovered surface normals. Samaras and Metaxas [11] incorporated illumination constraints with deformable models in resolving SFS problems. Crouzil et al. [6] developed a multiresolution SFS method, in which cost functions were minimized by fuzing deterministic and stochastic minimization approaches. During the examination of these SFS methods, we find that surface albedo was assumed either constant or given. Assuming constant albedo results in inaccurate reconstruction of surfaces with variable albedo as was demonstrated by the experiments in [16].

Existing SFS methods almost always yield unsatisfactory results when applied to realistic imagery when the initial estimation of the true surface is unavailable or inaccurate. In experiments described in this paper, we demonstrate that providing an accurate initial estimation in SFS methods yields much better results. The Hybrid Principal Component Analysis algorithm provides head surface estimations which are quite accurate. These estimations serve as initial conditions for our multiple-level optimization. The introduction of HPCA and the multiple-level global optimization combined with albedo estimation, are the innovative parts of our approach.

The rest of the paper is arranged as follows: The HPCA algorithm is described in section 2; In section 3, we present results from HPCA; section 4 describes the SFS method; section 5 presents SFS results; section 6 concludes the paper.

2   Hybrid Principle Component Analysis

In this section, we describe the HPCA algorithm. To perform the HPCA algorithm, we need a set of M training images. Each image is a hybrid composed of a 2D $[n \times m]$ gray scale image and a corresponding $[n \times m]$ range image. These training images are lexicographically reordered into M pairs of vectors, denoted by

$$\{\vec{f_i}, \vec{r_i}\} \qquad i = 1, 2, \cdots, M \tag{1}$$

where $\vec{f_i}$ is the vector that represents the ith gray scale image and $\vec{r_i}$ is the vector that represents the corresponding range image. These two vectors are concatenated to generate a $2nm$ dimensional hybrid vector $\vec{h_i}$,

$$\vec{h_i} = \left(\vec{f_i}^T, \vec{r_i}^T \right)^T \tag{2}$$

The training set H for HPCA consists of all the M hybrid vectors $\vec{h_i}$. The mean vector $\vec{\mu_h}$ and covariance matrix C_h for H are calculated as follows

$$\vec{\mu_h} = \frac{1}{M} \sum_{i=1}^{M} \vec{h_i} \tag{3}$$

$$C_h = \frac{1}{M} \sum_{i=1}^{M} (\vec{h_i} - \vec{\mu_h})(\vec{h_i} - \vec{\mu_h})^T \tag{4}$$

Next, the eigenvectors $\{\vec{v_j}; j = 1, 2, \cdots, \omega\}$ for C_h are computed. $\omega \leq 2nm$ is the rank of C_h. The first P eigenvectors, which correspond to the P largest eigenvalues, are taken as the principal eigenvectors. Every eigenvector $\vec{v_j}$ is then split into two sub-vectors with nm dimensions each. We name the two sub-vectors as the top vector $\vec{t_j}$ and the bottom vector $\vec{b_j}$ respectively, i.e.

$$\vec{v_j} = \left(\vec{t_j}^T, \vec{b_j}^T \right)^T \qquad \vec{t_j} \in R^{nm}, \vec{b_j} \in R^{nm} \tag{5}$$

The vector set $\{\vec{t_j}\}$ corresponds to the gray scale images while the set $\{\vec{b_j}\}$ corresponds to the range images. Similarly, the mean vector $\vec{\mu_h}$ is split into two sub-vectors as well.

$$\vec{\mu_h} = \left(\vec{\mu_f}^T, \vec{\mu_r}^T \right)^T \tag{6}$$

We also perform PCA on the set of range images $\{\vec{r_i}; i = 1, 2, \cdots, M\}$ and obtain P principal eigenvectors $\{\vec{e_j}; j = 1, 2, \cdots, P\}$ for the range image space $S_r \in R^{nm}$. Obviously, The set $\{\vec{e_j}\}$ for S_r would be different from the set $\{\vec{b_j}\}$ for the hybrid space. However, we can approximate $\{\vec{e_j}\}$ with $\{\vec{b_j}\}$, i.e., we use $\{\vec{b_j}\}$ as an estimation of the principal eigenvectors for the range image space S_r. As shown in the experiments, this approximation is pretty accurate. Similarly, we use $\{\vec{t_j}\}$ as an estimation of the principal eigenvectors of the gray scale image space $S_g \in R^{nm}$.

The underlying principle of HPCA is that a range image $\vec{r}$ can be approximated by a linear combination of the set $\{\vec{b_j}\}$ using the projection coefficients obtained by projecting the corresponding gray scale image $\vec{f}$ onto the

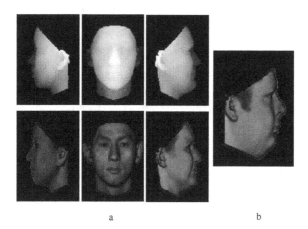

Fig. 1. (a) 3 pairs of training images (Top row - Range images; Bottom row - Corresponding gray scale images); (b) A test image

set $\{\vec{t_j}\} \in S_g$, namely

$$\vec{f} = T\vec{d} + \vec{\mu_f} \tag{7}$$
$$\implies \quad \vec{d} = (T^TT)^{-1}T^T(\vec{f} - \vec{\mu_f}) \tag{8}$$
$$\implies \quad \vec{r} = B\vec{d} + \vec{\mu_r} \tag{9}$$

where $T = (\vec{t_1}\ \vec{t_2} \cdots \vec{t_\omega})$, $B = (\vec{b_1}\ \vec{b_2} \cdots \vec{b_\omega})$ and $\vec{d}$ is the coefficient vector.

3   Experimental Results for HPCA

To achieve reconstruction of heads in different poses, we need a set of gray scale images and range images taken in intervals of few degrees about the vertical axes of the heads. For this purpose, we synthesize the gray scale images from a 3D head model library provided by USF [1]. A few synthetic gray scale images are illustrated in Fig. 1. These synthetic images still look realistic since the variable albedo is taken also into account.

The library from USF includes 100 3D head models and corresponding texture maps. We use 40 head models in the experiment. Every model is rotated about the vertical axis from -90 to +90 degrees in a step size of 5 degrees. A gray scale image and a range image are generated for every pose, which leads to 1480 hybrids for all 40 models. Few pairs of training images are illustrated in Fig. 1.

It is straightforward to obtain model range images while it is more difficult to obtain model gray scale images. Here we need to make two assumptions:

1. Head surfaces exhibit Lambertian reflectance.
2. The light is perpendicular to the image plane.

With these two assumptions, the gray scale value at a point A can be calculated as

$$R_A = \rho\alpha(\overrightarrow{l} \cdot \overrightarrow{n}) = u(\overrightarrow{l} \cdot \overrightarrow{n}) \tag{10}$$

where ρ is the illuminant strength, α is the surface albedo, u is the composite albedo [17] representing the product of ρ and α, $\overrightarrow{l} = (0,0,1)^T$ represents the illuminant direction, and $\overrightarrow{n}$ is the normalized surface normal at point A.

$$\overrightarrow{n} = \frac{1}{\sqrt{1 + p^2 + q^2}} \times (-p, -q, 1)^T \tag{11}$$

p and q are the surface derivatives along x and y axes respectively. Substitute Eq.11 into Eq.10, we get

$$R_A = \frac{\rho\alpha}{\sqrt{1 + p^2 + q^2}} = \frac{u}{\sqrt{1 + p^2 + q^2}} \tag{12}$$

$\rho = 1$ is used in our experiment. As for the surface albedo α, note that there is a texture map for every model in the library from USF. We map the texture to the 3D model and take the normalized gray scale value at every point as its albedo. The gray scale images for testing are obtained in a similar manner from 3D head models which are not included in the training. A test image is shown in Fig.1b. Two views of the corresponding original range image are shown in Fig.2a and 2d. The range image reconstructed by HPCA is illustrated in Fig.2b and 2e. As can be observed, the reconstruction is close to the original range image.

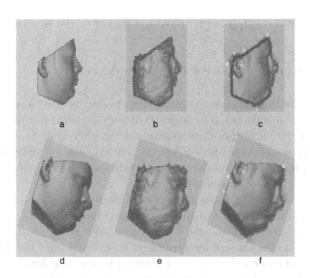

Fig. 2. (a)&(d) The original range image in x-y and 3D view; (b)&(e) The reconstructed range image from HPCA in x-y and 3D view. This reconstruction serves as initial estimation for the optimization algorithm; (c)&(f) Are the x-y and 3D view of the final reconstruction after applying the SFS optimization.

4   Shape from Shading Reconstruction

Starting from the initial reconstruction provided by HPCA, we further improve the reconstruction using a novel SFS method. SFS is usually modeled as an optimization problem [16], in which cost functions are minimized subject to various constraints. Existing methods either try to estimate the surface height directly [14], or to divide the problem into two subproblems[6] [15] . First, to compute the surface's gradient field and then to calculate surface height from the gradient field. Our method belongs to the second category.

Henceforth, we refer to the estimated 3D surface as $z(x, y)$, where z is the surface height and x, y are coordinates. The two components of the gradient field are

$$p(x, y) = \partial z(x, y)/\partial x \quad q(x, y) = \partial z(x, y)/\partial y \tag{13}$$

We present the fundamental equation for SFS, Image Irradiance Equation [7], as

$$I(x, y) = R(\vec{l}, p(x, y), q(x, y)) \tag{14}$$

where R and I are the reflectance map and the input gray scale image respectively, and $\vec{l}$ is the illuminant direction. The cost function shown below is minimized to find the gradient field in image domain Ω.

$$\begin{aligned} C_1(p, q) &= \iint_\Omega [R(\vec{l}, p(x, y), q(x, y)) - I(x, y)]^2 dxdy \\ &= \iint_\Omega [\frac{u(x, y)}{\sqrt{1 + p^2(x, y) + q^2(x, y)}} - I(x, y)]^2 dxdy \end{aligned}$$

$$\tag{15}$$

To get a well-posed solution, an integrability constraint and a smoothness constraint are usually added [7] [6] and the augmented cost function is given below.

$$\begin{aligned} C_2(p, q) &= C_1(p, q) + \lambda_i \iint_\Omega [p_y(x, y) - q_x(x, y)]^2 dxdy \\ &+ \lambda_{s1} \iint_\Omega [p_x^2(x, y) + p_y^2(x, y) + q_x^2(x, y) \\ &+ q_y^2(x, y)]dxdy \end{aligned} \tag{16}$$

where λ_i is the integrability factor and λ_{s1} is the smoothing factor. Both factors are set to positive values. The second and the third terms on the right-hand side represent the integrability constraint and the smoothness constraint respectively.

To handle the variable albedo of faces, we add to $C_2(p, q)$ a smoothness constraint for the composite albedo u and estimate the gradient field and u simultaneously. The new constraint for u is inspired by the observation that abrupt changes of albedo usually only occur on boundaries between special face regions (e.g. lips, eyebrows, eyes or pigmentation). Other than that, the albedo usually varies smoothly, especially on cheeks and foreheads. As a matter of fact, even

albedo inside some special regions, e.g. lips, doesn't vary abruptly. As for illuminant strength, in most cases it remains constant or varies smoothly on faces.
Therefore, u should also vary smoothly on most face regions. Hence, imposing
a smoothness constraint on u is justified almost everywhere. The cost function
with the new constraint is

$$C = C_2(p, q) + \lambda_{s2} \iint_\Omega [u_x^2(x, y) + u_y^2(x, y)] dx dy \tag{17}$$

where λ_{s2} is the smoothing factor for u.

Next we will convert the cost function into discrete form. Hereafter we will
use subscripts to indicate the coordinates of pixels. We apply either forward or
backward finite differences in the conversion. Without loss of generality, we will
discuss the case where forward finite differences are applied. According to the
definition of forward finite differences, we have

$$p_x|_{(i,j)} = p(i, j + 1) - p(i, j) = p_{i,j+1} - p_{i,j} \tag{18}$$
$$p_y|_{(i,j)} = p(i + 1, j) - p(i, j) = p_{i+1,j} - p_{i,j} \tag{19}$$

Hence, Eq.17 changes into

$$C = \sum_{(i,j) \in \Phi} c_{i,j} \tag{20}$$

where Φ is the discrete image domain and $c_{i,j}$ is the cost component for the pixel
at (i, j) given by:

$$
\begin{aligned}
c_{i,j} = [&\frac{u_{i,j}}{\sqrt{1 + p_{i,j}^2 + q_{i,j}^2}} - I_{i,j}]^2 \\
&+ \lambda_i[(p_{i+1,j} - p_{i,j}) - (q_{i,j+1} - q_{i,j})]^2 \\
&+ \lambda_{s1}[(p_{i+1,j} - p_{i,j})^2 + (p_{i,j+1} - p_{i,j})^2 \\
&+ (q_{i+1,j} - q_{i,j})^2 + (q_{i,j+1} - q_{i,j})^2] \\
&+ \lambda_{s2}[(u_{i+1,j} - u_{i,j})^2 + (u_{i,j+1} - u_{i,j})^2]
\end{aligned}
\tag{21}
$$

To minimize the cost function C with respect to $(p_{i,j}, q_{i,j}, u_{i,j})$ at every pixel
is very difficult if the image is large. Therefore, we choose to split a large image
into small patches and run the optimization patch by patch. We use 10×10
patches in our experiment. Starting from the lower right corner of the input
image, a window is moved row-wise from right to left, from bottom to top. The
window is moved by 5 pixels every time so that the patch in the window always
has a half overlapping with any neighboring patch. When the upper left corner
is reached, the window is moved in the other direction from left to right, from
top to bottom. In this way, the window is moved back-and-forth between the two
corners and the cost on every patch is minimized. The iteration is stopped when
the norm of the changes in the gradient field between two iterations is smaller
than a predefined threshold.

We assume that the gradients on the global boundary of an image are zero. when the window is moved from the lower right corner to the upper left corner, the right and bottom boundary conditions of patches can be obtained from either the image boundary conditions or from results of previous patches. That allows us to impose these two boundary conditions during the optimization. As explained in the appendix, we apply forward finite differences in this case to simplify the calculation of the gradient for the cost function. when the window is moved from the upper left corner to the lower right corner, the left and top boundary conditions of patches are available instead. In this case, these two boundary conditions are imposed and then backward finite differences are applied.

Direct minimization of the cost function is performed on those patches using Nonlinear Polak-Ribière Conjugate Gradient method [12]. For every patch, we specify the initial vector set for the optimization as

$$\nu^{(0)} = \{\nu_{i,j}^{(0)}\} = \{(p_{i,j}^{(0)}, q_{i,j}^{(0)}, u_{i,j}^{(0)})_{(i,j)\in\Phi}\} \tag{22}$$

where the gradient field $(p_{i,j}^{(0)}, q_{i,j}^{(0)})_{(i,j)\in\Phi}$ is derived from the initial range image provided by HPCA and $u_{i,j}^{(0)}$ is set to zero, i.e. $(u_{i,j}^{(0)} = 0)_{(i,j)\in\Phi}$. Before running the optimization, we smooth the gradient field using a smoothing filter. By smoothing the gradient field, the cost function surface also becomes smoother. If the smoothing is large enough, all the local minima are eliminated leaving only the global minimum. Beginning with the smoothed $\nu^{(0)}$ and an initial set of constraint factors $(\lambda_i, \lambda_{s1}, \lambda_{s2})$, the Nonlinear Polak-Ribière Conjugate Gradient method is carried out to find a minimum of the cost function and the corresponding vector set $\nu^{(1)}$. Next, the set of constraint factors are reduced by a factor of 2 and a smaller smoothing filter is applied to smooth the gradient field a bit less. When the optimization is repeated, we initiate it with the previous minimum location, which is quite close to the true global minimum. Each iteration, with less smoothing, achieves more accurate minimum location. After each iteration, the constraint factors are reduced by half and the size of the smoothing filter is reduced as well before being applied to the gradient field. The process is stopped when the constraint factors fall below predefined thresholds. After that, the factors are set to zero (no constraints are imposed) and a final iteration of minimization is carried out on each pixel individually. No smoothing filter is applied in this iteration as well. Removing constraints allows the gradient field and the composite albedo to vary more freely to account for abrupt changes on the face.

Evidently, patches on faces have different smoothness. Another advantage of our patch-by-patch method is that different initial constraint factors can be applied to handle different smoothness. The smoothness can be roughly estimated from the range ξ and the standard deviation σ of the gray scale values in a patch, which is taken from the normalized input image. The smaller ξ and σ, the smoother the patch is. Therefore, large factors are used if ξ and σ are small. On the other hand, smaller factors are used if ξ and σ are large.

The Nonlinear Polak-Ribière Conjugate Gradient method is outlined as follows [12]:

1. $g^{(0)} = s^{(0)} = -\nabla C(\nu^{(0)})$ where $\nabla C(\nu^{(0)})$ is the gradient of the cost function at the vector set $\nu^{(0)}$. Details on gradient calculation can be found in the appendix.
2. Perform line search to find a value $\gamma^{(m)}$ that minimizes $C(\nu^{(m)} + \gamma^{(m)} g^{(m)})$ using the Secant method. $\nu^{(m)}$ is the vector set at iteration $m(m = 0, 1, 2, \cdots)$
3. $\nu^{(m+1)} = \nu^{(m)} + \gamma^{(m)} g^{(m)}$
4. $s^{(m+1)} = -\nabla C(\nu^{(m+1)})$
5. $\delta^{(m+1)} = max\{\frac{(s^{(m+1)})^T(s^{(m+1)} - s^{(m)})}{(s^{(m)})^T s^{(m)}}, 0\}$
6. $g^{(m+1)} = s^{(m+1)} + \delta^{(m+1)} g^{(m)}$

The error minimization is stopped when $\|g^{(m+1)}\|$ falls below a predefined threshold.

After the gradient field is estimated, we calculate the final surface using the M-estimators algorithm [2].

5   Experimental Results

Results after SFS optimization are shown in Fig.2c and Fig.2f. Compared to the HPCA results, we can see that details on the face are improved and noise is reduced significantly. In addition, we can also observe that the reconstruction is very close to the original range image. Another example that is reconstructed from a frontal view image is illustrated in Fig.3.

To verify the reconstruction accuracy, we further use the reconstructions in face recognition experiments, in which the reconstructed range images are tested against 3D head models. 40 profile images are synthesized from 40 new 3D head models that are not included in the training. Reconstructions are obtained for those images and tested against the 40 new models plus those used in training. The subject for a reconstructed range image is recognized by a recognition program based on the Iterative Closest Point algorithm [3]. 37 out of 40 test images are recognized correctly. The recognition rate is 92%, which is satisfactory for such a hard task, in which 2D images are tested against 3D models. The good

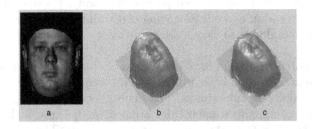

Fig. 3. (a) The test image; (b)The original range image; (c) Reconstruction after SFS optimization

performance on recognition demonstrates the accuracy of our reconstruction method as well.

6   Conclusions

We describe in this paper a novel method for 3D head reconstruction and view-invariant recognition, which is based on Shape From Shading (SFS) combined with Hybrid Principal Component Analysis (HPCA). Our HPCA algorithm provides initial estimates of 3D range mapping for the SFS optimization, which is quite accurate and yields much improved 3D head reconstruction. We also employ in the SFS method a novel multi-level global optimization approach with error-dependent smoothness and integrability constraints. Additional contribution of our paper is the successful handling of variable and unknown surface albedo in SFS. Experimental results show that our HPCA based SFS method provides accurate 3D head reconstructions and high recognition rates. Our work could have many practical applications such as person recognition from side views when only frontal views are available for modeling.

References

1. USF HumanID Face Database. University of South Florida, Tampa, FL, USA.
2. Agrawal, A., Raskar, R., Chellappa, R.: What is the range of surface reconstructions from a gradient field. In: Leonardis, A., Bischof, H., Pinz, A. (eds.) ECCV 2006. LNCS, vol. 3951, pp. 578–591. Springer, Heidelberg (2006)
3. Besl, P., McKay, N.: A method for registration of 3-d shapes. IEEE Trans. Pattern Anal. Mach. Intell. 14(2), 239–256 (1992)
4. Blanz, V., Vetter, T.: A morphable model for the synthesis of 3d faces. In: SIGGRAPH 1999. Proceedings of the 26th annual conference on Computer graphics and interactive techniques, pp. 187–194. ACM Press, New York (1999)
5. Blanz, V., Vetter, T.: Face recognition based on fitting a 3d morphable model. IEEE Trans. Pattern Anal. Mach. Intell. 25(9), 1063–1074 (2003)
6. Crouzil, A., Descombes, X., Durou, J.-D.: A multiresolution approach for shape from shading coupling deterministic and stochastic optimization. IEEE Trans. Pattern Anal. Mach. Intell. 25(11), 1416–1421 (2003)
7. Horn, B.K.P., Brooks, M.J.: The variational approach to shape from shading. Comput. Vision Graph. Image Process. 33(2), 174–208 (1986)
8. Hu, Y., Zheng, Y., Wang, Z.: Reconstruction of 3d face from a single 2d image for face recognition. In: Proceedings 2nd Joint IEEE International Workshop on VS-PETS, pp. 217–222. IEEE Computer Society Press, Los Alamitos (2005)
9. Ikeuchi, K., Horn, B.K.P.: Numerical shape from shading and occluding boundaries. shape from shading, 245–299 (1989)
10. Jiang, D., Hu, Y., Yan, S., Zhang, L., Zhang, H., Gao, W.: Efficient 3d reconstruction for face recognition. Pattern Recognition 38(6), 787–798 (2005)
11. Samaras, D., Metaxas, D.: Incorporating illumination constraints in deformable models for shape from shading and light direction estimation. IEEE Trans. Pattern Anal. Mach. Intell. 25(2), 247–264 (2003)

12. Shewchuk, J.R.: An introduction to the conjugate gradient method without the agonizing pain. Carnegie Mellon University, Pittsburgh, PA (1994)
13. Smith, W.A.P., Hancock, E.R.: Recovering facial shape using a statistical model of surface normal direction. IEEE Trans. Pattern Anal. Mach. Intell. 28(12), 1914–1930 (2006)
14. Szeliski, R.: Fast shape from shading. CVGIP: Image Underst. 53(2), 129–153 (1991)
15. Worthington, P.L., Hancock, E.R.: New constraints on data-closeness and needle map consistency for shape-from-shading. IEEE Trans. Pattern Anal. Mach. Intell. 21(12), 1250–1267 (1999)
16. Zhang, R., Tsai, P.-S., Cryer, J.E., Shah, M.: Shape from shading: A survey. IEEE Transactions on Pattern Analysis and Machine Intelligence 21(8), 690–706 (1999)
17. Zheng, Q., Chellappa, R.: Estimation of illuminant direction, albedo, and shape from shading. IEEE Trans. Pattern Anal. Mach. Intell. 13(7), 680–702 (1991)

Appendix: Gradient Calculation for the Cost Function in Eq.20

Here we demonstrate how to calculate the gradient of the cost function C in Eq.20 with respect to variables $p_{i,j}, q_{i,j}, u_{i,j}$ for $(i,j) \in \Phi$. We limit our discussion here to patches with the right and bottom boundary conditions imposed. Similar derivation can be developed for patches when top and left boundary conditions are imposed. Without loss of generality, we will demonstrate the calculation of the derivative with respect to $p_{i,j}$. Due to the application of forward finite differences, there are 4 different cases for pixels in a $N \times N$ patch.

1. For pixels (i,j) where $i, j \neq 1, N$: from Eq.18 and 19, we know that $p_{i,j}$ is involved in the derivative approximation at and only at these 3 locations: $(i,j), (i-1,j), (i,j-1)$. For example, at $(i-1,j)$,
   $P_y|_{(i-1,j)} = p_{i,j} - p_{i-1,j}$
   Hence, $\frac{\partial C}{\partial p_{i,j}} = \frac{\partial c_{i,j}}{\partial p_{i,j}} + \frac{\partial c_{i-1,j}}{\partial p_{i,j}} + \frac{\partial c_{i,j-1}}{\partial p_{i,j}}$

2. For the pixel $(1,1)$: $\frac{\partial C}{\partial p_{1,1}} = \frac{\partial c_{1,1}}{\partial p_{1,1}}$

3. For pixels (i,j) where $i = 1$ and $j \neq 1, N$:
   $\frac{\partial C}{\partial p_{i,j}} = \frac{\partial c_{i,j}}{\partial p_{i,j}} + \frac{\partial c_{i,j-1}}{\partial p_{i,j}}$

4. For pixels (i,j) where $i \neq 1, N$ and $j = 1$:
   $\frac{\partial C}{\partial p_{i,j}} = \frac{\partial c_{i,j}}{\partial p_{i,j}} + \frac{\partial c_{i-1,j}}{\partial p_{i,j}}$

Here we will explain why we use forward finite differences when the right and bottom boundary conditions are imposed. Let us take a look at a pixel (i,j) on the left boundary of a patch This pixel doesn't have a neighboring pixel $(i,j-1)$ on the left. As a result, derivatives along the horizontal direction can't be calculated if backward finite differences are applied. However, forward finite differences doesn't pose such a problem in this case and therefore are employed.

The calculation of $\frac{\partial c_{i,j}}{\partial p_{i,j}}$, $\frac{\partial c_{i-1,j}}{\partial p_{i,j}}$, and $\frac{\partial c_{i,j-1}}{\partial p_{i,j}}$ is straightforward. Only the calculation of $\frac{\partial c_{i-1,j}}{\partial p_{i,j}}$ is presented for demonstration.

$$
\begin{aligned}
c_{i-1,j} = [& \frac{u_{i-1,j}}{\sqrt{1 + p_{i-1,j}^2 + q_{i-1,j}^2}} - I_{i-1,j}]^2 \\
& + \lambda_i[(p_{i,j} - p_{i-1,j}) - (q_{i-1,j+1} - q_{i-1,j})]^2 \\
& + \lambda_{s1}[(p_{i-1,j+1} - p_{i-1,j})^2 + (p_{i,j} - p_{i-1,j})^2 \\
& + (q_{i-1,j+1} - q_{i-1,j})^2 + (q_{i,j} - q_{i-1,j})^2] \\
& + \lambda_{s2}[(u_{i-1,j+1} - u_{i-1,j})^2 + (u_{i,j} - u_{i-1,j})^2]
\end{aligned}
$$

(23)

$$
\begin{aligned}
\frac{\partial c_{i-1,j}}{\partial p_{i,j}} = & \; 2\lambda_i[(p_{i,j} - p_{i-1,j}) - (q_{i-1,j+1} - q_{i-1,j})] \\
& + 2\lambda_{s1}[p_{i,j} - p_{i-1,j}]
\end{aligned}
$$

(24)

Person-Independent Monocular Tracking of Face and Facial Actions with Multilinear Models

Yusuke Sugano and Yoichi Sato

Institute of Industrial Science, The University of Tokyo
4-6-1 Komaba, Meguro-ku, Tokyo, 153-8505, Japan
{sugano,ysato}@iis.u-tokyo.ac.jp

Abstract. In tracking face and facial actions of unknown people, it is essential to take into account two components of facial shape variations: shape variation between people and variation caused by different facial actions such as facial expressions. This paper presents a monocular method of tracking faces and facial actions using a multilinear face model that treats interpersonal and intrapersonal shape variations separately. We created this method using a multilinear face model by integrating two different frameworks: particle filter-based tracking for time-dependent facial action and pose estimation and incremental bundle adjustment for person-dependent shape estimation. This unique combination together with multilinear face models is the key to tracking faces and facial actions of arbitrary people in real time with no pre-learned individual face models. Experiments using real video sequences demonstrate the effectiveness of our method.

1 Introduction

Real-time face and facial action tracking is a key component of applications in various fields including human-computer interactions, video surveillance, and intelligent transport systems. Techniques suited to such applications must be able to estimate 3D face poses and facial actions correctly using a single camera even when large facial shape deformations due to different facial expressions are present. To be used practically, the techniques must be able to work with arbitrary people without preliminary preparations, e.g., building a face model for each person. The aim of this study is to develop a novel tracking technique that satisfies these two requirements. Therefore, we have developed a person-independent monocular tracking technique for face and facial actions.

Many model-based methods have been proposed for face and facial action tracking [1,2,3,4,5]. Using a linear face model typically obtained by principal component analysis (PCA), these methods estimate the pose and coefficients of deformation bases of a face. However, most previous methods [1,2,4,5] used face models that were created for each person before estimation. Requiring preparation of person-specific face models is often too restrictive for practical applications. In order to use person-specific models without preliminary model preparation, Oka et al. proposed a multi-view method for simultaneously modeling faces and estimating motion [3]. However, their method was still too costly in terms of system installation, using multiple cameras that need to be accurately calibrated beforehand.

S.K. Zhou et al. (Eds.): AMFG 2007, LNCS 4778, pp. 58–70, 2007.

Meanwhile, another approach can be taken using a generic face model that represents facial shape deformation across multiple people with one parameter set [6,7]. Gross et al. presented an interesting empirical study on performance comparison between generic and person-specific models that were not 3D models but 2D active appearance models [6]. It was reported that the use of generic models often resulted in a much worse rate of convergence in model parameter estimation. Especially in the case of 3D models, generic models inescapably contain a deformation factor that normally does not happen for a single person, such as scaling. These factors are hard to distinguish from the head pose, thus decreasing the tracking accuracy. Zhu et al. [7] used an AAM-based generic face model to estimate 3D head pose and facial actions in real time. However, no quantitative evaluation was performed on their head pose estimation result.

To cope with this problem, some methods used 3D face models with two separate sets of parameters (a set of *shape parameters* for interpersonal deformation and a set of *action parameters* for intrapersonal deformation). The use of such models limits the required number of parameters for each set without degrading the expressiveness of the model. In addition, these two sets of parameters with different behavior can be treated separately. Dornaika et al. used a model with separate sets of parameters in real-time face tracking [8]. Their method estimates time-dependent action parameters sequentially. However, shape parameters for person-dependent facial shape variations are set manually, and their method does not adjust shape parameters during the tracking process. Vlasic et al. [9] used a multilinear face model that describes interpersonal and intrapersonal deformations separately. However, the purpose of their method was to capture facial expression from a video segment, so it is not clear how their method can be extended to real-time estimation. DeCarlo et al. [10] used tracking residuals from model-based optical flow to adjust all of the parameters, including shape parameters. However, their method was computationally too costly to be executed in real time.

As stated above, there is no method which is capable of estimating both shape and action parameters in real-time. In contrast, our method executes shape adjustment simultaneously with real-time non-rigid head pose tracking, by using a model-based bundle adjustment with a multilinear face model.

As shown in Fig. 1, our method consists of two steps. The first step, called the *Estimation Step*, estimates action parameters, i.e., intrapersonal deformation, as well as the person's 3D head pose for each input frame by using a particle filter. It also finds correct 2D positions of facial feature points in the image. This step enables a head pose and facial action tracking that is robust to partial occlusion or depth-directional movement.

The second step, called the *Modeling Step*, incrementally refines shape parameters, i.e., interpersonal deformation, by model-based bundle adjustment based on 2D facial feature positions obtained from the *Estimation Step*. This step enables a stable adjustment of shape parameters that includes factors indistinguishable from head pose. Updated shape parameters are then used in the succeeding *Estimation Step*. In this way, our method enables progressive refinement of the estimation accuracy and personal customization of the face model.

This unique combination of particle filter-based tracking and incremental bundle adjustment enables monocular estimation of non-rigid 3D facial motion without

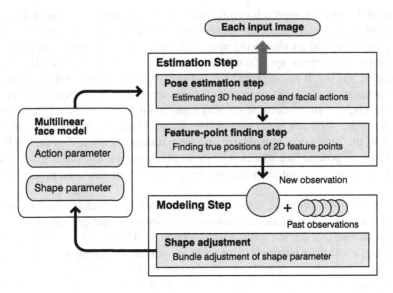

Fig. 1. System overview

preliminary learning of face models tailored for each person. As far as we know, this is the first research to propose a method using this approach.

The rest of this paper is organized as follows. In Section 2, we begin by describing how multi-linear facial models with separate parameter sets are constructed prior to tracking. Then we describe the two steps in our method; the *Modeling Step* in Section 3 and the *Estimation Step* in Section 4. We present our experimental results in Section 5. Finally, we present concluding remarks in Section 6.

2 Preliminary Construction of Multilinear Face Models

In this section, we describe how a multilinear face model with shape and action parameters is prepared by using N-mode singular value decomposition (SVD) [9] prior to tracking.

A person's face is represented in terms of its shape and appearance. More specifically, the face's shape is represented as a $3K$-dimensional shape vector M composed of 3D coordinates of K feature points[1]. These are defined in the local coordinate system fixed to the person's head. The appearance of the face is modeled as appearances of the feature points, which are registered as image templates automatically at the beginning of each tracking.

A multilinear face model that represents facial shapes is built from a data tensor $\mathcal{T}$ that varies with people's identity and facial expressions (Fig. 3). The first mode (noted

---

[1] In this study, K is set to 10. Those feature points are the inner and outer corners of both eyes, both corners of the mouth, both nostrils, and the inner corner of both brows (indicated with plus signs in Fig. 2).

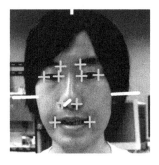

Fig. 2. Example of facial deformation

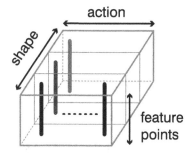

Fig. 3. Data tensor

as feature points in the figure) corresponds to each shape vector M, while the second (shape) and the third (action) modes correspond to identity and facial expression, respectively. The data is arranged so that shape vectors of the same person making different facial expressions are aligned in a slice along the second mode, and shape vectors of different persons making the same expressions are aligned in a slice along the third mode. Based on N-mode SVD, the data tensor $\mathscr{T}$ is expressed as a mode product of an orthonormal matrix U_i of the ith mode and a core tensor $\mathscr{C}$:

$$
\begin{aligned}
\mathscr{T} &= \mathscr{C} \times_{\text{feature}} U_{\text{feature}} \times_{\text{shape}} U_{\text{shape}} \times_{\text{action}} U_{\text{action}} \\
&= \mathscr{M} \times_{\text{shape}} U_{\text{shape}} \times_{\text{action}} U_{\text{action}},
\end{aligned} \tag{1}
$$

where the model tensor $\mathscr{M}$ contains basis vectors of the $3K$-dimensional face vector space. Moreover, an approximated representation of $\mathscr{T}$ is obtained with the truncated basis of action and shape spaces:

$$
\mathscr{T} \approx \mathscr{M} \times_{\text{shape}} \check{U}_{\text{shape}} \times_{\text{action}} \check{U}_{\text{action}}. \tag{2}
$$

Using this approximated model tensor, we can generate an arbitrary face vector M using shape and action parameters defined as coefficient vectors of $\mathscr{M}$.

To construct the data tensor $\mathscr{T}$, we first need to prepare shape vectors for different persons moving their faces in different ways. In this study, we used a multiview-based face and facial action tracking technique [3] to obtain shape vectors. While K facial features were being automatically tracked, S people were asked to move their faces in 2 different ways: horizontally move the corners of their mouth, and vertically move their mouths and eyebrows. Then, 5 intermediate facial shapes were chosen for each facial action (from beginning to completion of the action) for a total of $A = 10$ shape vectors for each person.

This gives us $S \times A$ samples of face shape. After calculating and subtracting mean shape $\bar{M}$, we construct a data tensor $\mathscr{T} \in \mathbb{R}^{3K \times S \times A}$. By calculating the model tensor $\mathscr{M}$ with approximated shape $(S \to S')$ and action $(A \to A')$ spaces as Eq. (2), we can describe an arbitrary face vector M using a shape parameter $s \in \mathbb{R}^{S'}$, an action parameter $a \in \mathbb{R}^{A'}$ and the mean shape $\bar{M}$:

$$
M = \bar{M} + \mathscr{M} \times_{\text{shape}} s^{\text{T}} \times_{\text{action}} a^{\text{T}}. \tag{3}
$$

Here, each row of $\breve{U}_{\text{shape}} = (\breve{s}_1, \ldots, \breve{s}_S)^{\text{T}}$ and $\breve{U}_{\text{action}} = (\breve{a}_1, \ldots, \breve{a}_A)^{\text{T}}$ in Eq. (2) is a parameter vector corresponding to each of the $A \times S$ data. We calculate the mean vector $\bar{s}$ and the vector σ_s composed of standard deviations of elements of $\{\breve{s}_i\}$, and the mean vector $\bar{a}$ and the vector σ_a composed of standard deviations of elements of $\{\breve{a}_i\}$. These four vectors are later used to determine the constraint of a bundle adjustment (Section 3), and the diffusion and weighting process of a particle filter (Section 4).

This model enables us to describe any facial state of any person with a person-dependent shape vector s, a time-dependent action vector a and a head pose vector p defined as a translation and a rotation from the world coordinate system to the model coordinate system. In the following sections, we explain the details of our real-time face and facial action tracking method using this face model.

3   Modeling Step: Estimation of Interpersonal Shape Variations

In this section, we describe the *Modeling Step* of our method of incrementally adjusting shape parameter vector s, which represents interpersonal facial shape variation, using model-based bundle adjustment.

Bundle adjustment is a maximum likelihood estimation method that optimizes parameters in 3D space by minimizing the 2D reprojection error in multiple images. In the context of facial shape estimation, it is used to model rigid faces [11], estimate rigid head motions in real time [12], and adjust the shapes of deformable face models acquired from a non-rigid factorization method [13].

In this research, we used model-based bundle adjustment to incrementally adjust the shape parameter vector s of a multilinear face model. We introduce two modifications to stabilize estimation of shape parameters. One is an incremental construction of an adjustment frame set based on the result from the *Estimation Step* with a particle filter. The other is the use of parameter constraints determined on the basis of the distribution of the shape parameter and estimated pose and action parameters. We first explain how to choose a set of observation frames and then explain model-based bundle adjustment with parameter constraints.

3.1   Incremental Construction of the Bundle Adjustment Frame Set

Using the face model presented in Section 2, the bundle adjustment problem is formulated as follows. First, we calculate the face shape vector M_t from Eq. (3). Then K feature points in shape vector M_t are projected onto the image plane as:

$$m_t = \mathcal{P}(p_t, M_t(a_t, s)), \tag{4}$$

where $\mathcal{P}$ is a projection function given by camera parameters that are obtained prior to tracking, and m_t is a $2K$-dimensional vector that consists of 2D coordinates of K projected feature points.

Let $\hat{m}_t$ be a vector that represents the true 2D coordinates of K feature points. This $2K$-dimensional vector $\hat{m}_t$ is obtained in the *Estimation Step* as explained later in Section 4.2. Finally, we can define an error function for the sum of the reprojection errors over a set of observation frames as:

$$F_t = \sum_{i \in f_t} D(\hat{m}_i, m_i(p_i, a_i, s))^2, \tag{5}$$

where f_t means a set of n observation frames used in the bundle adjustment at time t, as illustrated in Fig. 4.

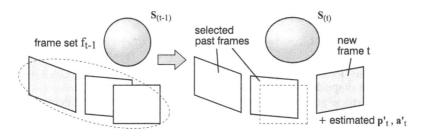

Fig. 4. Flow of incremental bundle adjustment

Our method generates the frames of this frame set f_t one at a time, by replacing one frame of the previous set f_{t-1} with a new frame. For the new frame t, pose p'_t and action a'_t estimated in the *Estimation Step* are assigned as initial values for the minimization of F_t. Meanwhile, selected $n - 1$ frames are initialized from previous minimization results of F_{t-1} and adjusted on an ongoing basis.

Zhang et al. [14] used a similar approach of updating a set of observation frames by replacing the oldest frame with a new incoming frame. However, it is often the case in real-time tracking that object appearances do not change much between consecutive frames, and, as a result, depth ambiguities cannot be resolved reliably with bundle adjustment. This problem is avoided in our method by maximizing the variation of poses in the adjustment frame set. More specifically, we choose the frame set with the widest pose variance at the initial state of the minimization, from among all n frame combinations possible at the time. By repeating this selection scheme, the pose variation in the frame set increases as the tracking proceeds.

3.2 Error Minimization with Parameter Constraints

Next, we describe in detail the minimization procedure of F_t (Eq. (5)) with parameter constraints, which is meant to stabilize the adjustment process. F_t is minimized using a Levenberg-Marquardt method under the parameter constraints [15]:

$$\min_{\{p_i\},\{a_i\},s} F_t , \quad p_i \in C_{p_i}, \ a_i \in C_{a_i}, \ s \in C_s, \tag{6}$$

where C_{p_i}, C_{a_i} and C_s denotes the constraints on each parameter.

As mentioned above, initial pose $\hat{p}_t$ and action parameter $\hat{a}_t$ for the minimization are estimated almost exactly, based on the value obtained in the *Estimation Step*.

Accordingly, tight constraints C_{p_i} and C_{a_i} are imposed such that only small changes are allowed in each iteration:

$$C_{p_i} = \{p_i \mid \hat{p}_i - \lambda_p \leq p_i \leq \hat{p}_i + \lambda_p\}, \tag{7}$$

where λ_p is a constant vector that denotes the adjustment range. The action constraint, C_{a_i}, is set in the same way. Currently, λ_a and λ_p are determined empirically.

In contrast, a relatively weak constraint is imposed on shape parameter s based on the vector of standard deviations σ_s from Section 2:

$$C_s = \{s \mid \bar{s} - 2\sigma_s \leq s \leq \bar{s} + 2\sigma_s\}. \tag{8}$$

This allows shape parameters to be adjusted to the shape of the person's face smoothly while excessive shape deformations are prohibited.

Finally, the shape parameter $s_{(t)}$ for the next *Estimation Step* is calculated as the mean of the estimation results up to the present time:

$$s_{(t)} = \frac{t-1}{t} s_{(t-1)} + \frac{1}{t} s', \tag{9}$$

where s' denotes the result of estimation at time t, calculated from the process mentioned above. Eq. (9) reduces the influence of short-term fluctuation in the adjustment.

4   Estimation Step: Estimation of Head Pose and Facial Actions

In this section we describe the *Estimation Step* (Fig. 1). It is important to note that time-varying action and pose parameters cannot be estimated properly with the model-based bundle adjustment process of the *Modeling Step* for several reasons. First, the estimation result tends to jitter, especially in the depth direction. Second, 2D positions of feature points required for the bundle adjustment cannot be obtained stably with simple 2D tracking or detection. Last, if some of the feature points are not observed, the pose and action parameters cannot be estimated correctly. To solve these problems, we use a particle filter to estimate pose and action parameters based on a 3D model-based motion prediction.

As shown in Fig. 1, the *Estimation Step* consists of two components: the *Pose estimation step*, which estimates pose p_t and action a_t, and the *Feature-point finding step*, which calculates the true 2D positions of feature points $\hat{m}_t$ which are used as the observation vector in Eq. (5) in the *Modeling Step*. In the following sections, we first explain the *Pose estimation step*, and then explain the *Feature-point finding step*.

4.1   Head Pose Estimation Using Particle Filter

To estimate facial action, the multilinear model in Eq. (3) is rewritten as a linear deformation model with the shape parameter $s_{(t-1)}$ calculated in the previous frame:

$$M_t = \bar{M} + \mathcal{M}_t a_t \quad (\mathcal{M}_t = \mathcal{M} \times_{\text{shape}} s_{(t-1)}^T). \tag{10}$$

Using this model, we estimate a $(6 + A')$ dimensional state vector $x_t = (p_t^T, a_t^T)^T$ at frame t. The sample set $\{(u_t^{(i)}; \pi_t^{(i)})\}$ for the particle filter in our method consists of N discrete samples $u_t^{(i)}$ in the $(6 + A')$ dimensional state space and of associated weights $\pi_t^{(i)}$.

To generate N new samples at each time t, we define a uniform linear motion model as follows:

$$u_t^{(i)} = u'_{t-1} + \tau v_{t-1} + \omega, \tag{11}$$

where u'_{t-1} is a chosen sample from the previous sample set, τ is the interval between frames, and v_{t-1} is the velocity of the state vector x calculated at the previous frame $t - 1$. Note that the elements of v_{t-1} corresponding to the action parameter a_t are set to 0, because a_t does not always match the assumption of uniform linear motion.

ω is a system noise that affects the diffusion property, and each element of ω is a Gaussian noise with a zero mean and a uniquely defined variance. The elements corresponding to the head pose are adaptively controlled depending on velocity [3]. Meanwhile, the standard deviation of the Gaussian noise for the other elements corresponding to the action parameter is set to $\kappa \sigma_a$ based on the parameter distribution calculated in Section 2. Here, κ is empirically set to 0.2.

Weight $\pi_t^{(i)}$ of each sample $u_t^{(i)}$ is calculated as:

$$\pi_t^{(i)} \propto \exp\left(-\frac{\left(K - \mathcal{N}(u_t^{(i)})\right)^2}{2\sigma^2}\right) \cdot \exp\left(-\frac{1}{2}\sum_{b=1}^{A'}\left(\frac{a_{t,b}^{(i)} - \bar{a}_b}{\varsigma_b}\right)^2\right), \tag{12}$$

where $\mathcal{N}(u_t^{(i)})$ is a sum of the normalized correlation score for all K feature points based on template image T, which has a value between $-K$ and K. The first term of Eq. (12) is a Gaussian function evaluating $\mathcal{N}(u_t^{(i)})$, and the standard deviation σ is set to 1.0. The second term is an evaluation function for the action parameter $a_t^{(i)}$, which prevents excessive face deformation. Here, $a_{t,b}^{(i)}$, $\bar{a}_b$ and ς_b is the b-th element of $a_t^{(i)}$, $\bar{a}$ and σ_a, respectively.

After the calculation, each weight $\pi_t^{(i)}$ is normalized so that the sum is equal to 1. Eventually, the current state vector x_t is computed as a weighted average of all samples.

Note that the initial state vector x_0 is calculated from the bundle adjustment. After a person's face and K feature points are automatically detected over n frames (using OKAO Vision library developed by OMRON Corporation), all parameters are initialized by minimizing Eq. (6). In this case, we use predefined values as the start point of the iteration: a head pose facing the center of the camera and mean parameters $\bar{a}$ and $\bar{s}$.

4.2   Finding True Feature Positions in Images

Next, we describe the *Feature-point finding step* in detail. The 2D positions m'_t of the estimated feature points can be calculated from the estimated state vector x_t and the projection function $\mathcal{P}$ (Eq. 4). However, if the adjustment of the shape parameter is not done properly, the estimated positions do not always correspond with the true positions

estimated position **m'**   true position **m̂**

Fig. 5. Finding true feature points

(as shown in Fig. 5). In this step, we find the true 2D positions $\hat{m}_t$ around the estimated positions m'_t.

We define the following energy function E_t similar to the one used in Gokturk et al. [1], and calculate the difference $d\hat{m} = \hat{m}_t - \hat{m}_{t-1}$ by successively minimizing it.

$$E_t = \sum_{\text{ROI}} \left\{ \rho ||\hat{I}_t - \hat{I}_{t-1}||^2 + ||\hat{I}_t - \hat{I}_1||^2 \right\} + \epsilon ||\hat{m}_t - m'_t||^2. \tag{13}$$

The first term of Eq. (13) denotes the difference between the appearances of regions of interest (ROIs) around the feature points. $\hat{I}_t \in \mathbb{R}^K$ is an intensity vector corresponding to $\hat{m}_t$, whose kth element is the intensity of the input image at the kth 2D position of $\hat{m}_t$. We use both the difference from the previous image and the difference from the first image, which [1] also uses. This avoids the problem of drift of the calculated feature points. ρ is empirically set to 4, and the size of ROI is 16×16. In contrast, the second term denotes the geometric difference between m'_t and $\hat{m}_t$. Using this term, we find the true positions $\hat{m}_t$ in the neighboring region of estimated positions m'_t. ϵ is empirically set to 4000.

5   Experimental Results

We have conducted a number of experiments to evaluate the performance of our method. First, we compared our method with the multiview-based tracking method [3]. In addition, to evaluate the effect of the use of the multilinear model and the bundle adjustment, we made another comparison with the particle filter-based estimation result using a generic PCA model with one parameter set.

The face model was built from $S = 26$ persons $\times$ $A = 10$ actions, and the resulting model had $S' = 15$ shape parameters and $A' = 5$ action parameters. The generic model was also built from the same data set using PCA, and had 20 deformation parameters. Note that the target person in the experiment was not included among the 26 persons.

Table 1. Comparison of estimation errors

[mm]	x	y	z	[deg.]	roll	pitch	yaw
Particle filter-based estimation using the generic PCA model							
Mean	6.14	4.71	51.32	Mean	0.34	6.54	3.34
Std. Dev.	4.88	4.09	38.29	Std. Dev.	0.29	4.71	2.73
Our method using the multilinear model							
Mean	3.26	4.37	20.18	Mean	0.41	3.12	2.33
Std. Dev.	2.62	2.83	11.18	Std. Dev.	0.27	2.49	1.98

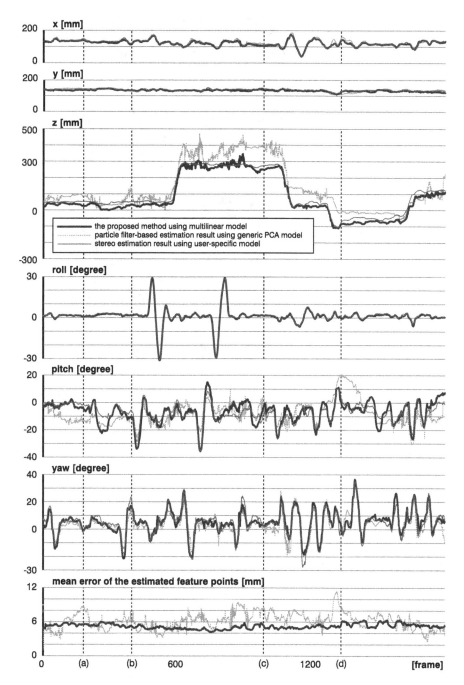

Fig. 6. Estimation results: x, y, and z are the horizontal, vertical, and depth-directional translation, and $roll$, $pitch$, and yaw are the rotation around the z, y, and x axes, respectively. The bottom graph shows the facial shape estimation error in the model coordinate system.

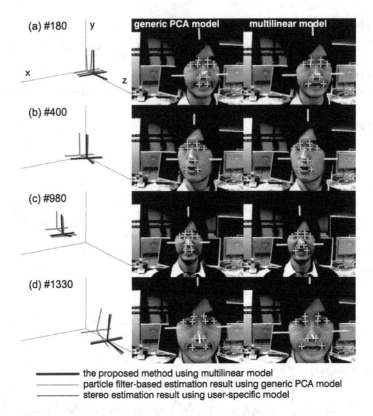

(a) #180

(b) #400

(c) #980

(d) #1330

generic PCA model   multilinear model

———— the proposed method using multilinear model
———— particle filter-based estimation result using generic PCA model
———— stereo estimation result using user-specific model

Fig. 7. Result images: the right column shows actual estimation results of our method using the multilinear model, and the center column shows results of the generic model-based method. The left column shows these results rendered from a different viewpoint.

Our tracking system consisted of a Windows-based PC with Intel Core 2 Duo E6700. We captured 60-second long (1800 frames) video sequences from two calibrated BW cameras via IEEE-1394. The image resolution was 640×480, the size of image templates T was set to 16×16. A set of 1000 samples was used for particle filtering. $n = 7$ frames were used for the bundle adjustment. The initialization step, with 10 iterations of LM minimization, took approximately 90 [ms], and the overall tracking process, with 5 iterations per frame, took approximately 32 [ms/frame].

Table 1 shows the estimation error of our method and the generic model-based method. x, y, and z are the horizontal, vertical, and depth-directional translation, and $roll$, $pitch$, and yaw are the rotation around the z, y, and x axes, respectively. Additionally, Fig. 6 shows the detailed estimation results and the facial shape estimation error in the model coordinate system. The difference between two monocular estimation methods is evident here. In Fig. 7, the right and center columns show actual images of the estimation results, and the left column shows these results rendered from a different viewpoint. The whole sequences can be seen on our website.[2] These results demon-

---

[2] http://www.hci.iis.u-tokyo.ac.jp/~sugano/research/3d-face-tracking/

strate that our method is more accurate than the method using the generic PCA model, and favorably compares with stereo estimation.

6   Conclusion

In this work, we presented a person-independent monocular method for real-time 3D face and facial action tracking. The key idea of our method is a unique combination of i) particle filter-based tracking for time-dependent pose and facial action estimation and ii) incremental model-based bundle adjustment for person-dependent shape estimation, together with multilinear face models. To our knowledge, this is the first work to achieve fully automatic 3D tracking of face and facial actions without preliminary training of person-specific face models. Our experimental results demonstrate that our method performs significantly better than monocular tracking with a generic face model, confirming the effectiveness of our real-time tracking method based on a multilinear face models. In our future work, we are planning to use our tracking method for real-time facial expression analysis.

Acknowledgement

We thank OMRON Corporation for providing the OKAO Vision library used in this work.

References

1. Gokturk, S.B., Bouguet, J.Y., Grzeszczuk, R.: A data-driven model for monocular face tracking. In: Proc. IEEE Int. Conf. Computer Vision, vol. 2, pp. 701–708. IEEE Computer Society Press, Los Alamitos (2001)
2. Munoz, E., Buenaposada, J.M., Baumela, L.: Efficient model-based 3d tracking of deformable objects. In: Proc. IEEE Int. Conf. Computer Vision, pp. 877–882. IEEE Computer Society Press, Los Alamitos (2005)
3. Oka, K., Sato, Y.: Real-time modeling of face deformation for 3-d head pose estimation. In: Zhao, W., Gong, S., Tang, X. (eds.) AMFG 2005. LNCS, vol. 3723, pp. 308–320. Springer, Heidelberg (2005)
4. Xiao, J., Baker, S., Matthews, I., Kanade, T.: Real-time combined 2d+3d active appearance models. In: Proc. IEEE Int. Conf. Computer Vision and Pattern Recognition, vol. 2, pp. 535–542. IEEE Computer Society Press, Los Alamitos (2004)
5. Zhu, Z., Ji, Q.: Robust real-time face pose and facial expression recovery. In: Proc. IEEE Int. Conf. Computer Vision and Pattern Recognition, pp. 681–688. IEEE Computer Society Press, Los Alamitos (2006)
6. Gross, R., Matthews, I., Baker, S.: Generic vs. person specific active appearance models. Image and Vision Computing 23(11), 1080–1093 (2005)
7. Zhu, J., Hoi, S.C.H., Lyu, M.R.: Real-time non-rigid shape recovery via active appearance models for augmented reality. In: Leonardis, A., Bischof, H., Pinz, A. (eds.) ECCV 2006. LNCS, vol. 3951, pp. 186–197. Springer, Heidelberg (2006)
8. Dornaika, F., Davoine, F.: On appearance based face and facial action tracking. IEEE transactions on circuits and systems for video technology 16(9), 1107–1124 (2006)

9. Vlasic, D., Brand, M., Pfister, H., Popovic, J.: Face transfer with multilinear models. In: ACM Transactions on Graphics (Proc. ACM SIGGRAPH 2005), vol. 24(3), pp. 426–433. ACM Press, New York (2005)

10. DeCarlo, D., Metaxas, D.: Adjusting shape parameters using model-based optical flow residuals. IEEE Trans. Pattern Analysis and Machine Intelligence 24(6), 814–823 (2002)

11. Xin, L., Wang, Q., Tao, J., Tang, X., Tan, T., Shum, H.: Automatic 3d face modeling from video. In: Proc. IEEE Int. Conf. Computer Vision, vol. 2, pp. 1193–1199. IEEE Computer Society Press, Los Alamitos (2005)

12. Vacchetti, L., Lepetit, V., Fua, P.: Stable real-time 3d tracking using online and offline information. IEEE Trans. Pattern Analysis and Machine Intelligence 26(10), 1380–1384 (2004)

13. Del Bue, A., Smeraldi, F., Agapito, L., Mary, Q.: Non-rigid structure from motion using non-parametric tracking and non-linear optimization. In: Proc. IEEE Workshop on Articulated and Non-Rigid Motion, vol. 1, IEEE Computer Society Press, Los Alamitos (2004)

14. Zhang, Z., Shan, Y.: Incremental motion estimation through modified bundle adjustment. In: Proc. IEEE Int. Conf. Image Processing, vol. 2, pp. 343–346. IEEE Computer Society Press, Los Alamitos (2003)

15. Lourakis, M.I.A.: levmar: Levenberg-marquardt nonlinear least squares algorithms in C/C++ (2004), http://www.ics.forth.gr/~lourakis/levmar/

Automatic Facial Expression Recognition Using Boosted Discriminatory Classifiers

Stephen Moore and Richard Bowden

Centre for Vision Speech and Signal Processing
University of Surrey, Guildford, GU2 7JW, UK
{stephen.moore,r.bowden}@surrey.ac.uk

Abstract. Over the last two decades automatic facial expression recognition has become an active research area. Facial expressions are an important channel of non-verbal communication, and can provide cues to emotions and intentions. This paper introduces a novel method for facial expression recognition, by assembling contour fragments as discriminatory classifiers and boosting them to form a strong accurate classifier. Detection is fast as features are evaluated using an efficient lookup to a chamfer image, which weights the response of the feature. An Ensemble classification technique is presented using a voting scheme based on classifiers responses. The results of this research are a 6-class classifier (6 basic expressions of anger, joy, sadness, surprise, disgust and fear) which demonstrate competitive results achieving rates as high as 96% for some expressions. As classifiers are extremely fast to compute the approach operates at well above frame rate. We also demonstrate how a dedicated classifier can be consrtucted to give optimal automatic parameter selection of the detector, allowing real time operation on unconstrained video.

1 Introduction

Our objective is to detect facial expressions in static images. This is a difficult task due to the natural variation in appearance between individuals such as ethnicity, age, facial hair and occlusion (glasses and makeup) and the effects of pose, lighting and other environmental factors. Our approach relies upon a boosted discriminatory classifier based upon contour information. Contours are largely invariant to lighting and, as will be shown, provide an efficient discriminatory classifier using chamfer matching.

Given a cartoon or line drawing of a face, it is taken for granted that the human brain can recognize the expression or emotional state of the character. Sufficient information must therefore be present in this simplified representation for a computer to recognize key features associated with expressions. Using only contour information provides important advantages as it offers some invariance to lighting and reduces the complexity of the problem. Our approach relies upon finding edges/contours on the face that are consistent across individuals for specific expressions. From a large set of facial images, candidate edges are extracted

S.K. Zhou et al. (Eds.): AMFG 2007, LNCS 4778, pp. 71–83, 2007.

and a subset of consistent features selected using boosting. The final classifier is then a set of weighted edge features which are matched to an image quickly using chamfer-matching resulting in a binary classifier that detects specific emotions.

This paper is split into a number of sections, firstly a brief background of research into automatic facial expression recognition is presented. Section 3 explains the methodology of this research. Section 4 evaluates different expression classifiers and results. Real time implementation of this work is described in section 5 where the work is adapted for robust, continuous use. Parameterisation is addressed through the use of a dedicated classifier for automatic selection. Finally conclusions and future work are described in section 6.

2   Background

Automatic facial expression research has gained inertia over the last 20 years. Furthermore, recent advances in the area of face recognition and tracking, coupled with relatively inexpensive computational power has fueled recent endeavors.

Early work on Automatic Facial expression recognition by Ekman [8], introduced the Facial Action Coding System (FACS). FACS provided a prototype of the basic human expressions and allowed researchers to study facial expression based on an anatomical analysis of facial movement. A movement of one or more muscles in the face is called an action unit (AU) and all expressions can then be described by a combination of one or more of 46 AU's.

Feature extraction methods applied to facial expression recognition can be categorized into two groups, deformation methods or motion extraction methods. Deformation methods applied to facial expression recognition include Gabor wavelets [3] [6] [21], neural networks (intensity profiles) [1] and Active Appearance Models [15]. Gabor wavelets have achieved very accurate results as they are largely invariant to lighting changes and have been widely adopted in both facial detection and recognition, but are computationally expensive to convolve with an image. Motion extraction methods using optical flow [20] or difference images [5] have also been applied to facial expression recognition. Essa and Pentland [9] combined these approaches and demonstrated accurate recognition using optic flow with deformable models. This work also introduced FACS+, an extension of FACS into the temporal domain.

Expression recognition is closely related to face detection, and many approaches from detection (such as the Gabor methods previously mentioned) have been applied to expression recognition. Since the popularization of boosting in the vision community by Viola and Jones [17], this type of machine learning has received considerable attention. In Adaboost, a strong classifier is built as a simple linear combination of seemingly very weak classifiers. Viola and Jones built a fast and reliable face detector using Adaboost from simple, weak classifiers based upon 'haar wavelet like' block differences [17]. It is arguably the current state-of-the-art in face detection and has resulted in boosting being applied to many computer vision problems with many variants to the learning algorithm [13], [19]. Wang et al [18] extended this technique to facial expression recognition by building separate classifiers of 'haar like' features for each expression. Shan and Gong [4] also applied boosting to facial expression recognition, but boosted local binary patterns (LBP) using conditional mutual information based boosting (CMIB). CMIB learns a sequence of weak classifiers that maximize their mutual information.

Shotton and Blake [16] presented a categorical object detection scheme based upon boosted local contour fragments. They demonstrate that the boundary contour could be used efficiently for object detection. This paper shows how internal contour features can be used for extremely fast discriminatory classification.

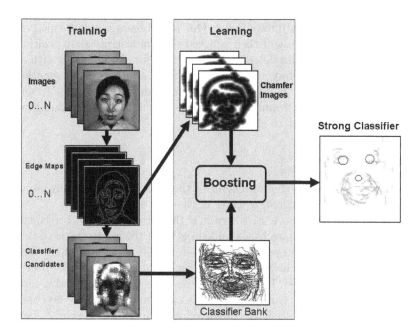

Fig. 1. System Overview

3   Methodology

3.1   Overview

In this section we introduce how the proposed approach works, illustrated in figure 1. A training set of images is extracted from a FACS encoded database. Images are annotated (eyes and tip of the nose) so that features can be transformed to a reference co-ordinate system. Each image then undergoes edge detection. From each edge image, small coherent edge fragments are extracted from the area in and around the face. A classifier bank (figure 2) is then assembled from candidate edge fragments from all the training examples. A weak classifier is formed by assembling an edge fragment combined with a chamfer score.

Boosting is then used to choose an optimal subset of features from the classifier bank to form a strong discriminatory classifier. The final boosted classifier provides a binary decision for object recognition. To build an n-class discriminatory classifier we use probability distributions built from classifier responses to allow likelihoods ratios to be used to compare across different classifiers. Also an investigation of fusion methodologies, a one against-many classifier and an ensemble classifier [7] are presented.

3.2   Image Alignment

To overcome the problem of image registration, each facial image must be transformed into the same co-ordinate frame. Our initial tests are performed using a 3 point basis. However we will then proceed to demonstrate that position and scale of a face (obtained via detection) is sufficient for classification with a minimal loss of accuracy. Before training, the images are manually annotated to identify the two eyes and the tip of the nose, to form a 3-point basis (points are non-collinear). Only near frontal faces are considered in this work and therefore a 3-point basis is sufficient to align examples.

3.3   Weak Classifiers

Expressions are based on the movement of the muscles, but visually we distinguish expressions by how these features of the face deform.

The contour fragments $e \in E$, where E is the set of all edges, are considered from the area around the face based on heuristics of the golden ratio of the face. The distance between the eyes is approximately half the width of the face and one third of the height. This identifies the region of interest (ROI) from which contours will be considered. Following an edge detection, connected component analysis is performed and from each resulting contour fragment, the contour is sampled randomly to form short connected edge features. Figure 2 shows an example of a classifier bank built from a training set of faces.

Fig. 2. Classifier Bank

3.4   Chamfer Image

To measure support for any single edge feature over a training set we need some way of measuring the edge strength along that feature in the image. This can be computed efficiently using Chamfer matching. Chamfer matching was first introduced by Barrow et al [2]. It is a registration technique whereby a drawing consisting of a binary set of features (contour segments) is matched to an image. Chamfer matching allows features to be considered as point sets and matching is efficient as the image is transformed into a chamfer image (distance) only once and the distance of any feature can then be calculated to the nearest edge as a simple lookup to that chamfer image. The similarity between two shapes can be measured using their chamfer distance.

All images in the training set undergo edge detection with the canny edge detector to produce an edge map. Then a chamfer image is produced using a distance transform DT. Each pixel value q, is proportional to the distance to its nearest edge point in E:

$$DT_E(q) = min_{e \in E} \|q - e\|_2 \qquad (1)$$

To perform chamfer matching, two sets of edges are compared. The contour fragment (T) and image edge strength E, producing an average Chamfer score:

$$d_{cham}^{(T,E)}(x) = \frac{1}{N} \sum_{t \in T} min_{e \in E} \|(t + x) - e\|_2 \qquad (2)$$

where N is the number of edge points in T. This gives the Chamfer score as a mean distance between feature T and the edge map E. Chamfer images are expensive to compute, however this needs only be computed once per image. The function $d_{cham}^{(T,E)}(x)$ is an efficient lookup to the chamfer image for all classifiers. An example of a chamfer image is shown in figure 1.

3.5   Learning

Boosting is a machine learning algorithm for supervised learning. Boosting produces a very accurate (strong) classifier, by combining weak classifiers in linear combination. Adaboost (adaptive boosting) was introduced by Freund and Schapire [10] and has been successfully used in many problems such as face detection [17] and object detection [16]. Adaboost can be described as a greedy feature selection process where a distribution of weights are maintained and associated with training examples. At each iteration, a weak classifier which minimizes the weighted error rate is selected, and the distribution is updated to increase the weights of the misclassified samples and reduce the weights of correctly classified examples. The Adaboost algorithm tries to separate training examples by selecting the best weak feature $h_j(x)$ that distinguish between the positive and negative training examples.

$$h_j(x) = \begin{cases} 1 \ if \ d_{cham}^{(T,E)}(x) < \theta_j \\ 0 \ otherwise \end{cases} \qquad (3)$$

θ is the weak classifier threshold. Since setting a fixed threshold requires a priori knowledge of the feature space, an optimal θj is found through an exhaustive search for each weak classifier. An image can have up to 1,000 features, thus over the training set, many thousands of features are evaluated during the learning algorithm. This allows the learning algorithm to select a set of weak classifiers with low thresholds that are extremely precise allowing little deviation, and weak classifiers with high thresholds which allows consistent deformation of the facial features. This increases the performance but as will be seen, does not result in over fitting the data.

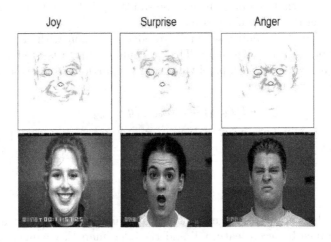

Fig. 3. Strong Classifier Visualization

Positive training examples are taken from the target expression and negative examples from other sets of expressions. Following boosting the final strong classifier consists of edge features which can be visualized. Figure 3 shows the classifiers for joy, surprise and anger trained against neutral expressions, the circles depict the position of the 3 point basis. Note that these visualizations reflect what we assume about expressions, eg surprise involves the raising of the eyebrows and anger 'the deformation' around the nose. However perhaps surprisingly, the mouth does not play an important role in the joy classifier, which is both counter intuitive and contradictory to AU approaches. This is partly due to higher variability away from the center of the 3 point basis, but more importantly the variability across subjects. People smile with their mouth open or closed, so boosting decides that the lines on the cheeks are more consistent features than those of the mouth. What boosting is doing is deciding its own optimal set of AU's based upon the data.

Training expressions against only neutral images results in a classifier that learns all the deformation for that expression. While this is beneficial for visualisation or single class detection it presents problems to multi class detection as many positive expressions will be confused by the classifiers. Training against all

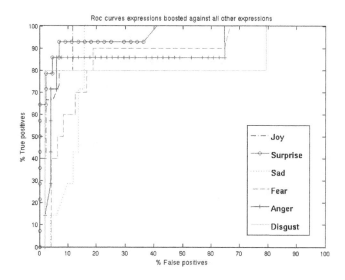

Fig. 4. Roc curves for each expression trained one against many

other expressions forms classifiers that only learn the deformation that is unique to that expression, which reduces the number of false positives. Figure 4 shows receiver operating characteristic (ROC) curves for each of the expression classifiers. Expressions were boosted using all other expressions as negative examples and over 1000 rounds of boosting.

3.6   N-Class Discriminatory Classifier

The following section is an investigation into different classifier approaches. In this paper we investigated using the threshold response from the strong classifier, likelihoods and ensemble methods for classification.

As our n-class classifier is to be built from binary classifiers some way of combining classifiers responses is required in order to disambiguate between expressions. The unthresholded classifier response cannot be used, as each classifier has a different number of weak classifiers, different thresholds and therefor different responses and ranges.

A more principled way to compare responses is to use likelihoods. Positive and negative probability distribution functions (pdf's) were constructed for each classifier, using a validation set. Noise in terms of x,y translation was added to the validation set in order to artificially increase the set. Positive and negative responses from the validation set were then used to build histograms (figure 5 and figure 6). Parzen windowing was used to populate these histograms. To calculate the likelihoods a comparison is made between the response of the positive pdf's for each classifier.

The likelihood ratio was evaluated for each classifier by dividing the response of the positive pdf by the response of the negative pdf for each classifier (equation

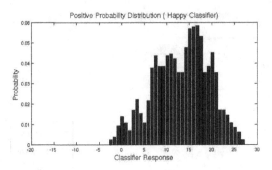

Fig. 5. Positive Probability Distribution

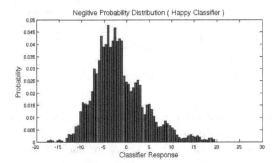

Fig. 6. Negative Probability Distribution

[4]). Where LR is the likelihood ratio, L is the likelihood and the positive and negative pdf's are Pp and Pn respectively.

$$LR(x) = MAX_{\forall n} \left\{ \frac{L(x, Pp)}{L(x, Pn)} \right\} \qquad (4)$$

Dietterich [7] argues that ensembles methods can often perform better than a single classifier. [7] proposes three reasons why classifier ensembles can be beneficial (statistical, computational and representational). Statistical reasons are based on the learning algorithm choosing a non-optimal hypothesis, given insufficient training data. By constructing an ensemble from accurate classifiers, the algorithm can average the vote and reduce the risk of misclassification. For a n-class classifier system, this can be broken into $\frac{n(n-1)}{2}$ binary classifiers respectively, allowing each expression to be exclusively boosted against every other expression. Using a binary threshold each classifier has a vote. Each n expression ensemble classifier can receive (n-1) votes, and classification is done using a winner takes all strategy.

4   Expression Classification

The Cohn Kanade facial expression database [12] was used in the following experiments. Subjects consisted of 100 university students ranging in age from 18 - 30. 65% were female, 15% were African American, and three percent were Asian or Latino. The camera was located directly in front of the subject. The expressions are captured as 640 x 480 eps images. In total 365 images were chosen from the database. The only criteria was that the image represented one of the prototypical expressions. This database is FACS encoded and provides ground truth for experiments. Each image has a FACS code and from this code images are grouped into different expression categories. This dataset and the selection of data was used to provide a comparision between other similiar expression classifiers [4] and [3].

Initial experiments were carried out by training each expression against 1) neutral expressions only, 2) against all other expressions, selecting candidate features from positives training examples only and 3) against all other expressions, selecting negative and positive features from all images in the training set. Training expressions against only neutral images results in a classifier with the poorest performance as there is little variance in the negative examples and many other expressions are misclassified by the detector. Training against all other expressions improves performance as the classifier learns what deformation is unique to that expression. The better classifier is one that selects negative features to reduce false detections. This classifier outperforms the other two methods as each expression has unique distinguishing features which act as negative features. To give a crude baseline we normalize the classifier responses into the range 0-1 and the highest response wins. As expected likelihoods is a better solution with marginal performance gains. However the Likelihood ratio gives a significant boost . Using 5-fold cross validation on the 6-basis expressions and 7-class (neutral class included) a recognition rate of 67.69% and 57.46% is achieved.

Table 1. Recognition results 6 class

Method	Joy	Surprise	Sad	Fear	Anger	Disgust	Overall
Classifier Response	78.67	81.43	55.72	38	77.14	40	61.83
Likelihood	78.67	82.86	57.14	56	60	40	62.45
Likelihood Ratio	90.67	91.43	51.43	36	88.57	48	67.69
Ensemble Classifier Response	96	95.72	82.86	72	91.43	72	85

The recognition results were poor when compared to the roc curves (figure 4) for the classifiers. This is because when confusion between classifiers occurs, examples are misclassified. To overcome this confusion several more principled approaches were evaluated. Table 1 and table 2 show results using likelihoods and likelihood ratio's. All results presented in table 1 and table 2 are obtained using 5-fold cross validation with training and test sets divided 80-20. As expected, likelihood ratios outperform likelihoods yielding a 5% increase in performance. From the results it was apparent that the more subtle expressions (disgust, fear and sad) are outperformed by expressions with a large amount of deformation (Joy, surprise,anger). Subtle changes in appearance are difficult to distinguish when using one reference co-ordinate frame due to the variability across subjects.

Table 2. Recognition results 7 class

Method	Joy	Surprise	Sad	Fear	Anger	Disgust	Neutral	Overall
Classifier Response	78.67	68.57	48.57	50	65.71	12	46	52.78
Likelihood	70.69	71.43	25.71	44	71.43	20	64	52.47
Likelihood Ratio	73.35	68.57	31.43	50	82.85	32	64	57.46
Ensemble Classifier Res	95.99	92.86	65.71	58	92.28	84	76	80.69

In this research we have a 6-class and 7-class classifier system, this can be broken down into 15 and 21 binary classes respectively, allowing each expression to be exclusively boosted against every other expression. Using a binary threshold (chosen from the equal error rate on the ROC curve) each classifier has a vote. Each n expression ensemble classifier can receive (n-1) votes. When confusion occurs, a table of likelihood responses is kept, the product of these is compared for each class of confusion and the highest likelihood wins. Using the binary voting scheme with the ensemble classifier gives an increase of up to 27% in recognition performance.

Table 3 compares this work with other facial expression classifiers. For a direct comparison we compare our results to other methods that use Adaboost and the Cohn Kanade database. Bartlett et al [3] performed similar experiments on the same dataset using Adaboost to learn Gabor wavelet features and achieved 85% accuracy. Further more Shan and Gong [4] learnt LBP through Adaboost and achieved 84.6% accuracy. Table 3 summarises that using contour fragments as a discriminatory classifier is comparably to Gabor wavlet and LBP features. It is important to note that while performance equals the state of the art, the application of our classifier is extremely efficient. A worst case classifier of 1000 weak classifiers takes only 3ms to assess within a half pal image based upon our implementation on a 3GHz P4 machine.

Table 3. Comparisons between other boosting based expression classifiers using Cohn Kanade database

Methods	Results
Local Binary Patterns with Adaboost [4]	84.6%
Gabor wavelets with AdaBoost [3]	85%
Edge/chamfer features with Adaboost	85%

5   Real Time Implementation

For real time detection in video sequences this work has been implemented with the Viola-Jones [17] face detector from the openCV libraries [11]. The initial experiments above required annotating the 3 point basis. For this implementation we use a 2 point basis from the bounding box returning by the face detector. Figure 7 shows the comparison of the three point basis (two eyes and nose) and the two point basis (points returning by face detector). Interestingly only a small performance drop is seen going from a 3 point basis to 2.

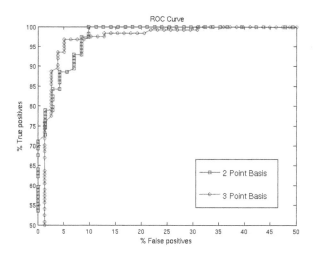

Fig. 7. Comparison between 2 and 3 point basis

Detection is reliant upon a good edge detection and therefore Chamfer map, however, edge information varies with lighting conditions, scale and subject. For reliable recognition, a suitable edge threshold is required for the given subject. An optimal threshold (OT) classifier was therefore constructed in a similar way to the previous classifiers, this is then used to alter the edge threshold at run time. This allows continuous parameter selection and thus our system is more robust to subject change and lighting conditions. The OT classifier is build using positives examples from different expressions with an optimal threshold selected manually. The negative examples are the same expressions with extremely low (high noise ratio) edge thresholds. This allows boosting to select features which are consistent across all expressions at an optimal edge threshold and more importantly negative features consistent across expressions at low edge thresholds. Since the features of the face provide strong edge information across a range of edge thresholds the OT classifier was predominantly constructed from negative features which are consistent only at low edge thresholds. At runtime the response of the OT classifier will peak at a suitable threshold which can then be used with the other classifiers.

6   Conclusions and Future Work

In this paper a novel automatic facial expression classifier is presented. Unlike other popular methods using Gabor wavelets, we have developed a real time system. For a 6 class (Joy, Surprise, Sadness, Fear, Anger and Disgust) system a recognition rate of 85% is achieved. Recognition is done on a frame by frame basis. As suggested in the literture [7], ensemble methods can often outperform single classifiers. In our experiments, the ensemble classifier approach provided an increase of up to 27% in recognition rates.

Bassili [14] demonstrated how temporal information can improve recognition rates in humans. Some faces are often falsely read as expressing a particular emotion, even if their expression is neutral, because their proportions are naturally similar to those that another face would temporarily assume when emoting. Temporal information can overcome this problem by modeling the motion of the facial features. Future work will incorporate temporal information into the current approach.

Acknowledgement

This work is partly funded by EPSRC through grant LILiR (EP/E027946) to the University of Surrey.

References

1. Alessandro, L.F.: A neural network facial expression recognition system using unsupervised local processing. In: ISPA 2001. 2nd international symposium on image and signal processing and analysis, Pula, CROATIE, pp. 628–632 (2001)
2. Barrow, H.G., Tenenbaum, J.M., Bolles, R.C., Wolf, H.C.: Parametric correspondence and chamfer matching: Two new techniques for image matching. In: DARPA 1977, pp. 21–27 (1977)
3. Bartlett, M., Littlewort, G., Fasel, I., Movellan, J.: Real time face detection and facial expression recognition: Development and application to human-computer interaction (2003)
4. Gong, S., McOwan, P., Shan, C.: Conditional mutual information based boosting for facial expression recognition. In: British Machine Vision Conference (2005)
5. Choudhury, T., Pentland, A.: Motion field histograms for robust modeling of facial expressions. In: ICPR 2000. Proceedings of the International Conference on Pattern Recognition (2000)
6. Dailey, M.N., Cottrell, G.W.: Pca = gabor for expression recognition. Technical report, La Jolla, CA, USA (1999)
7. Dietterich, T.G.: Ensemble methods in machine learning. In: Kittler, J., Roli, F. (eds.) MCS 2000. LNCS, vol. 1857, pp. 1–15. Springer, Heidelberg (2000)
8. Ekman, P., Friesen, W.V., Hager, J.C.: Facial action coding system. Palo Alto, CA, USA (1978)
9. Essa, I.A., Pentland, A.: Facial expression recognition using a dynamic model and motion energy. In: ICCV, pp. 360–367 (1995)

10. Freund, Y., Schapire, R.E.: Experiments with a new boosting algorithm. In: International Conference on Machine Learning, pp. 148–156 (1996)
11. OpenCV User Group. OpenCV Library Wiki (2006),
    http://opencvlibrary.sourceforge.net
12. Kanade, T., Tian, Y., Cohn, J.F.: Comprehensive database for facial expression analysis. In: FG 2000. Proceedings of the Fourth IEEE International Conference on Automatic Face and Gesture Recognition 2000, p. 46. IEEE Computer Society Press, Washington, DC, USA (2000)
13. Mahamud, S., Hebert, M., Shi, J.: Object recognition using boosted discriminants. In: CVPR 2001. IEEE Conference on Computer Vision and Pattern Recognition, Hawaii, IEEE Computer Society Press, Los Alamitos (December 2001)
14. Bassili, J.N.: Facial motion in the perception of faces and of emotional expression.
15. Saatci, Y., Town, C.: Cascaded classification of gender and facial expression using active appearance models. In: FGR 2006. Proceedings of the 7th International Conference on Automatic Face and Gesture Recognition, pp. 393–400. IEEE Computer Society Press, Washington, DC, USA (2006)
16. Shotton, J., Blake, A., Cipolla, R.: Contour-based learning for object detection. In: ICCV 2005. Proceedings of the Tenth IEEE International Conference on Computer Vision, vol. 1, pp. 503–510. IEEE Computer Society Press, Washington, DC, USA (2005)
17. Viola, P., Jones, M.J.: Robust real-time face detection. Int. J. Comput. Vision 57(2), 137–154 (2004)
18. Wang, Y., Ai, H., Wu, B., Huang, C.: Real time facial expression recognition with adaboost. In: ICPR, vol. 03, pp. 926–929 (2004)
19. Whitehill, J., Omlin, C.W.: Haar features for facs au recognition. In: FGR 2006. Proceedings of the 7th International Conference on Automatic Face and Gesture Recognition, pp. 97–101. IEEE Computer Society Press, Washington, DC, USA (2006)
20. Yacoob, Y., Davis, L.S.: Recognizing human facial expressions from long image sequences using optical flow. IEEE Trans. Pattern Anal. Mach. Intell. 18(6), 636–642 (1996)
21. Zhang, Z., Lyons, M., Schuster, M., Akamatsu, S.: Comparison between geometry-based and gabor-wavelets-based facial expression recognition using multi-layer perceptron. In: FG 1998. Proceedings of the 3rd. International Conference on Face & Gesture Recognition, p. 454. IEEE Computer Society Press, Washington, DC, USA (1998)

Generating Body Surface Deformation Using Level Set Method

Satoru Morita

Faculty of Engineering, Yamaguchi University,
2-16-1 Tokiwadai Ube 755-8611, Japan
smorita@yamaguchi-u.ac.jp

Abstract. Recently skeletal motion data is obtained from the motion capture and is used for movie and sports. The movie production does not need the skeletal motion data but the body surface data. It is difficult to generate body surface data from only skeletal motion data because muscle deforms according to the skeletal motion. Muscle deformation occurs with arm and leg joint rotation. In this paper, we visualize body surface deformation based on the deformation mechanism that is applicable to human motion according to anatomy based modeling. We propose the method generating body surface by covering the skeletal muscles using a thin film based on the level set method. We demonstrate the effectiveness of the system through the generation of the movement of a body builder by using the proposed system.

1 Introduction

It is studied to measure and calculate the human motion in the several fields. Recently, body surfaces[1][2] and skeletal motions[3] have been measured using cameras and range sensors. It is possible to scan not only the body surface but also the inside of the body using MRI and CT in the medical field[4]. A part from this, a bipedal walking robot has been studied [5]. The composite method of the human motion based on the physical model was studied[6].

The importance of anatomy based modeling has been discussed[7][8]. We can find the muscles and they deform according to the finite element methods[9][10]. However we cannot appear the model of muscle fibers in the paper. Face deformation based on the countenance muscle was studied to generate angry and cheerful countenance[11]. The deformation mechanism of face muscle is basically different from that of skeletal muscle[12]. Although the visualization of the human body based on motion has been studied[1][2][13], the muscle deformation was not simulated based on the muscle deformation mechanism according to skeletal motion. We do not generate only muscles but also muscle fibers. In this paper, we visualize the skeletal muscle based on its deformation according to skeletal motion.

If the skeletal muscle contracts and decreases in length, it becomes thick. However the skeletal muscle stretches and its length increases, it becomes thin. These situation occurs because muscle fibers move with the contractions and streching

S.K. Zhou et al. (Eds.): AMFG 2007, LNCS 4778, pp. 84–95, 2007.

of the skeletal muscle. We visualize skeletal muscle deformation according to the human motion based on the mechanism.

While the body surface is generated using the cylinder model[14] in the case of representing the human body related to the anatomy, it is difficult to generate the human body using only cylinders. Though we follow the anatomy based modeling, we do not generate the body surface by using the cylinder model but covering the skeletal muscles using a thin film. We generate the three dimensional image by mapping the points on the body surface in the three dimensional space that an animal exists. Thus we propose the method generating the human body by using the level set method[15] from the obtained three dimensional image. In this paper, we extend the region partition method based on level set method[16] applying for the two dimensional image to the method applying for the three dimensional image. It is enable to to visualize the body surface deformation using only skeletal motion data obtained from the motion capture.

The importance generating the several body types such as overweight and underweight human by deforming a body surface obtained using range sensors is discussed[17]. We show that the trained muscle and the normal muscle can be visualized by changing the skeletal muscle parameters according to the concept.

We discuss the skeleton and the skeletal muscle in section 2, and the muscle fiber model in section 3, and the generation of the body surface in section 4. We demonstrate the effectiveness of the method by visualizing muscle deformation based on skeletal motion in section 5.

2   Skeleton and Muscle

2.1   Skeleton

The skeletons of a human were generated their based on images in medical book[18][19]. Bones are connected together through joints. The number of joints in the human skeleton for the human model used in the experiment is 56, including the 38 in the hands. Each joint has three degrees of freedom. The number of human bones for the human model used in the experiment is 59 including 33 bones in the hands.

The neighbor skeletons share a parent child relationship and we define the joint angle between them. The human motion is calculated from the joint angle by using forward kinematics[20]. As the body motion can be calculated using motion capture data, we can use the motion capture data to determine the body motion.

2.2   Skeletal Muscle

The human body is composed of several tissues in skin, muscle, skeleton, viscera, and neuron. These tissues are classified into epithelial, connective, muscle and nervous tissue. Among these tussues, only the muscle tissue can contract and stretch. The muscle tissue is classified into skeletal muscle, cardiac muscle, and smooth muscle tissue. The skeletal muscle is used to cover and move the

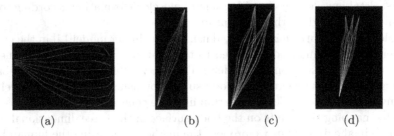

Fig. 1. The muscle fibers: (a) deltloid muscle, (b) spindle muscle, (c) bicepts muscle, and (d) triceps muscle

bones. The strength and velocity of muscle contraction and stretching can be consciously controlled. The smooth muscle tissue is called viscera as it is used as the wall of the viscera and it contracts and stretches unconsciously. The cardiac muscle is in the heart and it contracts and stretchs unconsciously. As muscle fibers are soft and fragile, they have strength by collecting many fibers. If skeletal muscle contracts and stretchs, the body moves. The number of the skeletal muscle is about 400, and it occupies about 40% in the human body weight.

A skeletal muscle is the symmetrical shape for the rotation. A skeletal muscle is composed of eight muscle fibers covering a skeletal muscle. Figures 1(a), (b), (c), and (d) show deltoid, mitotic spindle, biceps and triceps muscles respectively. The one side of the biceps muscle connects to bone and another side connects to the two bones. The one side of the triceps muscle connects to bone and another side connects to the three bones. In this paper, a muscle type is generated by using some skeletal muscles of the spindle shape. The number of the human skeletal muscle types is 34. The number of the human skeletal muscles is 178. Their skeletal muscles are generated based on medical books[18][19]. Figures 2(a) and (b) show the skeletal muscle of the human body for the initial model as viewed from the fromt and the rear, respectively. Figure 2(c) shows the skeletal muscle of the human hand for the initial model. We use them as the initial model of the human body.

3   Muscle Fiber Model

A skeletal muscle is located between two neighbor skeletons that connect at a joint. The angle joint can be varied by contracting the skeletal muscle. If the skeletal muscle decrease in length, the muscle fibers moves sideways, and the skeletal muscle swells. If the skeletal muscle increases in length, the muscle fibers move lengthwise and the skeletal muscle thins. Figure 3 shows the muscle deformation. The biceps of the brachii muscle contracts and expands, as the joint between an upper and a lower arm bends.

A joint between a bone and a skeletal muscle moves with the rotation of a joint between neighboring bones rotates. As bones move, the connection between a skeletal muscle and a bone also moves and there is a change in the thickness

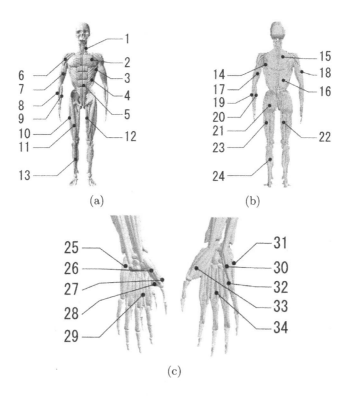

(a)

(b)

(c)

Fig. 2. (a) The skeletal muscle of the human body for the initial model as viewed from the front. (b) The skeletal muscle of the human body for the initial model as viewed from the rear. (c)The skeletal muscle of the human hand for the initial model.

of the skeletal muscle. If the muscle length is $|a|$ and the distance between the muscle fiber and the center line of the skeletal muscle is r, then the cylinder volume is $V = r^2 \cdot \pi \cdot |a|$. On the other hand, if the muscle length $|a|$ changes to $|b|$, the volume changes to $V' = r'^2 \cdot \pi \cdot |b|$. The volume does not change as the radius r changes to $r' = k \cdot r \cdot \sqrt{\frac{|a|}{|b|}}$. That is, the radius of the muscle is $r' = k \cdot r \cdot \sqrt{\frac{|a|}{|b|}}$ after the joint between two bones rotates. If the radius is k times the radius of the initial model, the volume changes to $k \cdot k$ times the initial volume. We refer to parameter k as the thickness parameter of the skeletal muscle. If $k = 0.9$, the volume decreases to 0.81 times as big as the initial volume.

The movement of the muscle fiber is estimated on the basis of this model. At first, we put the initial model of skeletal muscles and skeletons in the three dimensional world coordinate space represented as (x, y, z). If the center axis of the skeletal muscle in the initial model is (x_{a1}, y_{a1}, z_{a1}), (x_{a2}, y_{a2}, z_{a2}), then the center axis of the skeletal muscle after the joint between two bones rotates is defined as (x_{b1}, y_{b1}, z_{b1}), (x_{b2}, y_{b2}, z_{b2}) and the center of the rotation

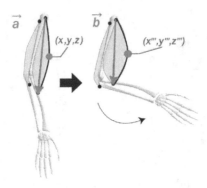

Fig. 3. The position of the muscle fiber is calculated from the initial model. The left figure shows the initial model. The right figure shows the muscle at the current time.

is (x_{a1}, y_{a1}, z_{a1}), (x_{a2}, y_{a2}, z_{a2}). The start point (x_{b1}, y_{b1}, z_{b1}) and the end point (x_{b2}, y_{b2}, z_{b2}) after the joint between the bones rotates can be calculated, because the start and end point have the information of the connecting bones.

The muscle fiber position (x''', y''', z''') can be calculated using the muscle fiber position (x, y, z) in the initial model, the center axis of the skeletal muscle (x_{b1}, y_{b1}, z_{b1}), (x_{b2}, y_{b2}, z_{b2}) after the rotation of the joint and the center axis of the skeletal muscle (x_{a1}, y_{a1}, z_{a1}), (x_{a2}, y_{a2}, z_{a2}) in the initial model. If $a = (x_{a2}, y_{a2}, z_{a2}) - (x_{a1}, y_{a1}, z_{a1})$, $b = (x_{b2}, y_{b2}, z_{b2}) - (x_{b1}, y_{b1}, z_{b1})$,

$$
\begin{bmatrix} \frac{x_{a2}-x_{a1}}{|a|} \\ \frac{y_{a2}-y_{a1}}{|a|} \\ \frac{z_{a2}-z_{a1}}{|a|} \end{bmatrix} = \mathbf{R_x}(\alpha)\mathbf{R_y}(\beta) \begin{bmatrix} 0 \\ 0 \\ 1 \end{bmatrix}. \tag{1}
$$

As the variables except the rotation angles α and β are known, the rotation angles α and β can be gotten by solving the equation. The matrix $R_x(\alpha)$ shows the rotation matrix that rotates α degree around x axis, and the matrix $R_y(\alpha)$ shows the rotation matrix that rotates β degree around y axis.

$$
\begin{bmatrix} \frac{x_{b2}-x_{b1}}{|b|} \\ \frac{y_{b2}-y_{b1}}{|b|} \\ \frac{z_{b2}-z_{b1}}{|b|} \end{bmatrix} = \mathbf{R_x}(\alpha')\mathbf{R_y}(\beta') \begin{bmatrix} 0 \\ 0 \\ 1 \end{bmatrix} \tag{2}
$$

As the variables except the rotation angles α' and β' are known, the rotation angles α' and β' can be gotten by solving the equation.

The muscle fiber position (x, y, z) of the initial model moves to the position (x', y', z') on the z axis.

$$
\begin{bmatrix} x' \\ y' \\ z' \end{bmatrix} = \mathbf{R_y}(-\beta)\mathbf{R_x}(-\alpha) \begin{bmatrix} x - x_{a1} \\ y - y_{a1} \\ z - z_{a1} \end{bmatrix} \tag{3}
$$

If $\theta = tan^{-1}\frac{y'}{x'}$, $r = \sqrt{x'^2 + y'^2}$, the muscle fiber position (x', y', z') that the center of the skeletal muscle is on the z axis moves to the position (x'', y'', z'') by constructing the muscle fiber.

$$
\begin{bmatrix} x'' \\ y'' \\ z'' \end{bmatrix} = \begin{bmatrix} k \cdot r \cdot \sqrt{\frac{|a|}{|b|}} cos\theta \\ k \cdot r \cdot \sqrt{\frac{|a|}{|b|}} sin\theta \\ \sqrt{\frac{|b|}{|a|}} \cdot z' \end{bmatrix}
\tag{4}
$$

The muscle fiber position (x'', y'', z'') that the center of the skeletal muscle is on the z axis moves to the position (x''', y''', z''') by the translational motion in the following equation.

$$
\begin{bmatrix} x''' \\ y''' \\ z''' \end{bmatrix} = \mathbf{R_x}(\alpha')\mathbf{R_y}(\beta') \begin{bmatrix} x'' \\ y'' \\ z'' \end{bmatrix} + \begin{bmatrix} x_{b1} \\ y_{b1} \\ z_{b1} \end{bmatrix}
\tag{5}
$$

The muscle fiber position (x''', y''', z''') at this point of time is calculated using the muscle fiber position (x, y, z) of the initial model. Thus we can calculated the muscle deformation from the initial model of the skeletal muscles, the initial model of the skeletons and the body motion data.

4 Generating Body Surface That Covers the Skeletal Muscle

We generate a body surface that covers the skeletal muscle. We mapped the three dimensional image from the space where the animal exists. In this study, the body surface is composed of many triangles. We can increase the surface points on the surface in the three dimensional image by dividing a triangle into a number of smaller triangles. The body surface is thus generated from the three dimensional image.

Recently, an image processing method based on a moving curved surface was proposed using a partial differential equation[16]. As the level of the function $\phi = 0$, based on a geometric measure is defined using the partial differential equation, this method is referred to as the level set method. An active contour model was proposed to detect from the image with noise. In this study, we employ the active contour model based on the method of the defining the level of the function $\phi = 0$, which in turn is based on a geometric measure. The original image is u_0, and the phase ϕ is the function required to detect the region. This enables us to define an arbitarily initial value. The contour is $\phi = 0$ in the phase ϕ. The function u is the result of the region partition. The variable ν is the surface smoothing parameter.

$$
\frac{\partial \phi}{\partial t} = \delta(\phi)(\nu\nabla \cdot (\frac{\nabla\phi}{|\nabla\phi|}) -
$$
$$
((u_0 - c_1)^2 - (u_0 - c_0)^2))
\tag{6}
$$

$$c_1 = \frac{\int u_o H(\phi)dxdy}{\int H(\phi)dxdy}$$

$$c_0 = \frac{\int u_o(1 - H(\phi))dxdy}{\int(1 - H(\phi))dxdy}$$

$$u = c_0(1 - H(\phi_1)) + c_1(H(\phi_0)) \tag{7}$$

We extend this method to detect the three dimensional regions in this paper. The function H is the Heaviside function and the function $\delta(x)$ which satisfies $\delta(x) = \frac{\partial H(x)}{\partial x}$. In the present method, the point that a number of phases are used to detect certain regions is different from active contour model based on partial differential equation If n is the number of ϕ, the image is classified into 2^n regions. As shown the partial differential equation divides a three dimensional image into four regions. Hence, if three phases are used, the image will be classified into eight regions. We define the initial phases arbitrarily. We define the positive values in the interior of the objects and the negative values for all locations except the interior of the objects. The initial phase ϕ at an image point is defined as the distance between the $\phi = 0$ contour and the image point. We extend the method for the two dimensional image to the method for the three dimensional image.

$$\frac{\partial \phi_1}{\partial t} = \delta(\phi_1)(\nu\nabla \cdot (\frac{\nabla\phi_1}{|\nabla\phi_1|})$$
$$-(((u_0 - c_{11})^2 - (u_0 - c_{01})^2)H(\phi_2)$$

$$+ ((u_0 - c_{10})^2 - (u_0 - c_{00})^2)(1 - H(\phi_2)) \tag{8}$$

$$\frac{\partial \phi_2}{\partial t} = \delta(\phi_2)(\nu\nabla \cdot (\frac{\nabla\phi_2}{|\nabla\phi_2|})$$
$$-(((u_0 - c_{11})^2 - (u_0 - c_{10})^2)H(\phi_1)$$
$$+ ((u_0 - c_{01})^2 - (u_0 - c_{00})^2)(1 - H(\phi_1)) \tag{9}$$

$$c_{11} = \frac{\int u_0 H(\phi_1)H(\phi_2)dxdydz}{\int H(\phi_1)H(\phi_2)dxdydz}$$

$$c_{10} = \frac{\int u_0 H(\phi_1)(1 - H(\phi_2))dxdydz}{\int H(\phi_1)(1 - H(\phi_2))dxdydz}$$

$$c_{01} = \frac{\int u_0(1 - H(\phi_1))H(\phi_2)dxdydz}{\int(1 - H(\phi_1))H(\phi_2))dxdydz}$$

$$c_{00} = \frac{\int u_0(1 - H(\phi_1))(1 - H(\phi_2))dxdydz}{\int(1 - H(\phi_1))(1 - H(\phi_2))dxdydz} \tag{10}$$

$$u = c_{11}H(\phi_1)H(\phi_2) + c_{10}H(\phi_1)(1 - H(\phi_2))$$
$$+ c_{01}(1 - H(\phi_1))H(\phi_2) + c_{00}(1 - H(\phi_1))(1 - H(\phi_2)) \tag{11}$$

Some regions can be detected from an three dimensional image.

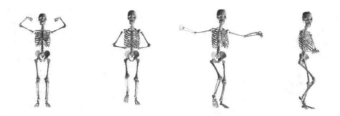

Fig. 4. The skeletal motion of the posing body builder. These figures show 20th, 60th, 90th, and 110th frame from the left side.

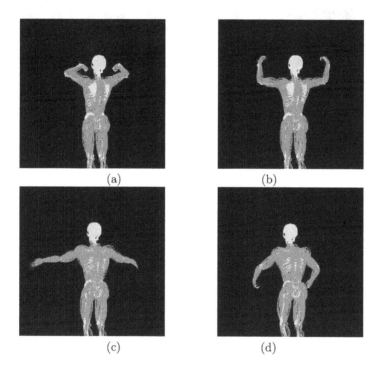

Fig. 5. The muscle deformation of the posing body builder visualized using the thickness parameter $k = 1.5$. (a) The 40th frame. (b) The 45th frame. (c) The 50th frame. (d) The 55th frame.

5   Visualizing Muscle Deformation Based on Skeletal Motion

We explain the process for visualizing muscle deformation.

- The articulated body motion for the skeleton is calculated as shown in section 2.

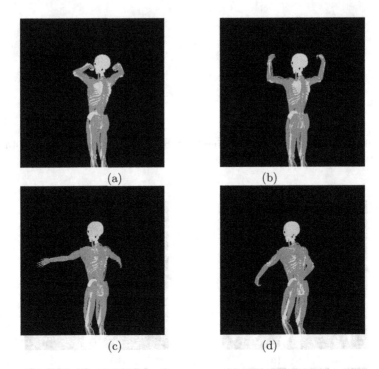

Fig. 6. The muscle deformation of the posing human visualized using the thickness parameter $k = 1.0$. (a) The 40th frame. (b) The 45th frame. (c)The 50th frame. (d) The 55th frame.

- Skeletal muscle deformation is calculated as shown in section 3.
- The body surface that covers the skeletal muscle with thin film is generated as shown in section 4.

Figure 4 shows the human motion generated by the posing of a body builder. The animation for this motion is composed of 120 frames. The muscle deformation is calculated using the human muscle. In general, if the thickness of the skeletal muscle changes, the contraction power also changes. The thickness of the skeletal muscle in Figure 5 is different from the thickness in Figure 6. The muscle deformation of the human model shown in Figures 5 and 6 is generated based on the mechanism of the human motion shown in Figure 4. The thickness parameter of the skeletal muscle is $k = 1.5$ and $k = 1.0$ in Figure 5 and 6, respectively. Figures 5 as well as Figures 6(a), (b), (c) and (d) show the images of the 40th, 45th, 50th, and 55th frames, respectively. The skeletal muscle of Figure 5 is thicker in comparison with that of Figure 6. You can have more muscular impression for human shown in Figure 5 than the human shown in Figure 6.

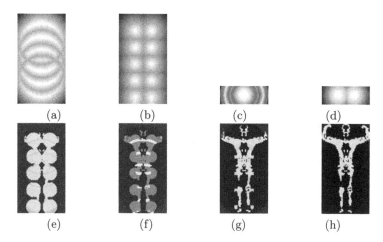

(a)   (b)   (c)   (d)

(e)   (f)   (g)   (h)

Fig. 7. Figures (a) and (b) show the x-y cross section of the phases ϕ_0 and ϕ_1 at the iteration number $t = 0$. Figures (c) and (d) show the x-z cross section of the phases ϕ_0 and ϕ_1 at the iteration number $t = 0$. Figures (e), (f),(g), and (h) show the x-y cross section of the u image at the iteration numbers $t = 8$, $t = 64$, $t = 512$ and $t = 4096$ respectively.

As the thickness of the skeletal muscle changes according to the mechanism of the muscle deformation.

We calculate the body surface from the skeletal motion shown in Figure 4. A triangle existing on the muscle surfaces is subdivided into a number of smaller triangles. We generate the three dimensional image u_0 by mapping the points on the body surface in the three dimensional space that an animal exists. The image size is $74 \times 135 \times 26$ pixels. The parameter ν and time constant $d\tau$ required for the calculation is defined as 0.03 and 0.0001 respectively. Two phases are used. Figures 7(a), (b), (c), and (d) show the phase images for the iteration number $t = 0$. The x-y cross sections of the phases ϕ_0 and ϕ_1 for $z = 13$ are shown in Figures 7(a) and (b), respectively and the x-z cross sections of the phases ϕ_0 and ϕ_1 for $y = 67$ are shown in Figures 7(c) and (d), respectively. Figures 7(e), (f), (g), and (h) show the x-y cross section of the u image for $z = 13$ at the iteration numbers $t = 8$, $t = 64$, $t = 512$, and $t = 4096$, respectively. It is found that the human body appears gradually as the iteration number increases. Figure 8 shows the thin film covering of the skeletal muscle. The human body surfaces covering the muscle of the posing body builder is visualized using the thickness parameter $k = 1.5$. Figures 8(a) and (b) are generated from the 43th frame, and Figures 8(c) and (d) are generated from 58th frame. Figure 8(a) and (c) are the body surface viewed from the front and figure 8(b) and (d) is the body surface viewed from the rare. It is found that the muscles deform with the motion of the human skeletons.

(a)

(b)

(c)

(d)

Fig. 8. The human body surfaces covering the muscle of the posing body builder is visualized using the thickness parameter $k = 1.5$ for the 43th frame in figures (a)(b) and 58th frame in figures (c)(d) . The body surfaces seen from the forward and backward directions are shown in figures (a)(c) and figures (b)(d).

6   Conclusions

We visualized muscle deformation and the body surface covering of the skeletal muscle from the human motion. We demonstrated that this method can be applied for certain subjects such as humans as well as for certain motions such as posing and running. It is shown that several types of muscles such as trained muscle and normal muscle can be also visualized.

References

1. Sand, P., McMilan, L., Popovic, J.: Continuous capture of skin deformation. In: Proc. of SIGGRAPH 2003, pp. 578–586 (2003)
2. Allen, B., Curless, B., Popovic, Z.: The spaces of human body shapes reconstruction and parameterization from range scans. In: Proc. of SIGGRAPH 2003, pp. 587–594 (2003)
3. Allen, B., Curless, B., Popovic, Z.: Articulated body deformations from range scan data. In: Proc. of SIGGRAPH 2002, pp. 20–30 (2002)
4. Suto, Y.: Three-dimensional surgical simulation system using x-ray ct and mri images. Medical Review 35, 32–43 (1991)
5. Kaneko, K., et al.: Humanoid robot hrp-2. In: Proc. of ICRA 2004, pp. 1083–1090 (2004)
6. Fang, A.C., Pollard, N.S.: Efficient synthesis of physically valid human motion. In: Proc. of SIGGRAPH 2003, pp. 417–426 (2003)
7. Scheepers, F., Parent, R.E., Carlson, W.E., May, S.F.: Anatomy-based modeling of the human musculature. In: Proc. of SIGGRAPH 1997, pp. 163–172 (1997)
8. Wilhelms, J., Gelder, A.V.: Anatomically based modeling. In: Proc. of SIGGRAPH 1997, pp. 173–180 (1997)
9. Teran, J., Blemker, S.: Finite volume methods for the simulation of skeletal muscle. In: Proc. of Eurographics Simposium on Computer Animation, pp. 68–74 (2003)
10. Albrecht, L., Haber, J., Seidel, H.P.: Construction and animation of anatomically based human hand models. In: Proc. of Eurographics Symposium on Computer Animation, pp. 98–109 (2003)
11. Kahler, K., Haber, J., Seidel, H.: Reanimating the dead: Reconstruction of expressive faces from skull data. In: Proc. of SIGGRAPH 2003, pp. 554–561 (2003)
12. Tortora, G.J., Grabowski, S.R.: Principles of anatomy and physiology. 35, 32–43 (1991)
13. Mohr, A., Gleicher, M.: Building efficient accurate character skins from examples. In: Proc. of SIGGRAPH 2003, pp. 562–568 (2003)
14. Chadwck, J., Haumann, D.R., Parent, R.E.: Layered construction for deformable animated characters. In: Proc. of SIGGRAPH 1989, pp. 243–252 (1989)
15. Sethian, J.A.: Level set methods and fast marching methods (1999)
16. Vese, L.A., Chan, T.F.: A multiphase level set framework for image segmentation using the mumford and stah model. International Journal of Computer Vision 50(3), 271–293 (2002)
17. Allen, B., Curless, B., Popovic, Z.: The space of human body shapes: reconstruction and parameterization from range scans. In: Proc. of SIGGRAPH 2003, pp. 587–594 (2003)
18. Rohen, J.W., Yoichi, C., Lutjen-Drecoll, E.: Color atlas of anatomy: A photographic study of the human body (2002)
19. Done, S.H.: Color atlas of veterinary anatomy: The dog & cat (1996)
20. Zatsiorsky, V.M.: Kinematics of human motion (1999)

Patch-Based Pose Inference with a Mixture of Density Estimators

David Demirdjian and Raquel Urtasun

Computer Science and Artificial Intelligence Laboratory
32 Vassar Street, Cambridge, MA 02139, USA

Abstract. This paper presents a patch-based approach for pose estimation from single images using a kernelized density voting scheme. We introduce a boosting-like algorithm that models the density using a mixture of weighted 'weak' estimators. The 'weak' density estimators and corresponding weights are learned iteratively from a training set, providing an efficient method for feature selection. Given a query image, voting is performed by reference patches similar in appearance to query image patches. Locality in the voting scheme allows us to handle occlusions and reduces the size of the training set required to cover the space of possible poses and appearance. Finally, the pose is estimated as the dominant mode in the density. Multimodality can be handled by looking at multiple dominant modes. Experiments carried out on face and articulated body pose databases show that our patch-based pose estimation algorithm generalizes well to unseen examples, is robust to occlusions and provides accurate pose estimation.

1 Introduction

We consider the problem of pose estimation from monocular images. To date, many successful pose estimation algorithms have been proposed, but most of them rely on retinotopic representations. Such a representation requires preprocessing, *i.e.* the object or person must be normalized in location and scale to fit a canonical view. This simplifies the representation, but puts the burden on detecting the location and scale of the object in the image, which is not a trivial task. In addition, global representations are relatively sensitive to occlusions and normalization errors.

Using local and sparse descriptors has proven to be useful for tasks such as object categorization [12,10,11]. Local feature-based approaches provide a robust representation because object classes are modeled by a set of local descriptors, which are usually more discriminative than global descriptors. These approaches can handle missing data (e.g. occlusions and partial views), and generalize better than global methods since they have compositional properties, e.g. descriptors from different poses can be combined to produce a pose that is not in the training set.

In this paper we advocate the use of patches as local descriptors, but it raises two challenges. First, there is the *bag-of-features* dilemma. If patch descriptors are too local, or if their relative position is not taken into account, the geometric relationships between patches might be lost making impossible to estimate the pose. Then, the patches are ambiguous: as they will, in general, correspond to multiple poses, it is important

S.K. Zhou et al. (Eds.): AMFG 2007, LNCS 4778, pp. 96–108, 2007.

to define a good pose distribution model that can represent the wide range of poses associated with a patch.

In this paper, we propose a learning-based approach for pose estimation from a density-based voting scheme. We first construct a database containing a set of pose-patch associations. Our approach avoids the use of complex part-based models being able to learn the geometric structure from images. Given a query image, the pose density is approximated by kernels associated with patches from the training set similar to patches in the image. Modes of the density correspond then to most likely poses.

When the number of training examples is large and the pose space is high dimensional, the computational cost of the density estimation becomes prohibitive. To mitigate the problem we propose a boosting-based feature selection algorithm that builds a density estimator by iteratively adding a (weak) density estimator using a subset of the training patches, selected to minimize the overall training error. Our algorithm retains the most discriminative patches for pose estimation and provides accurate density estimates. Moreover, it is directly amenable to integration with prior models for probabilistic tracking.

2   Previous Work

Discriminative approaches to pose estimation learn a mapping from image to pose. Shakhnarovich et al. [15] propose to locally regress k-nearest neighbors. This approach relies on a large database generated using a rendering software (POSER [2]). Although fast and accurate for small dimensional spaces, it requires extremely large training sets that grow exponentially with the pose dimensionality. Agarwal et al. [3] use RVM to learn a continuous mapping between image measurements (i.e., shape context from silhouettes) and 3D pose. To reduce the sensitivity to the presence of clutter, recent work [4] uses sparse (grid-based) image features for pose estimation and non-negative matrix factorization to learn clutter. Manifold learning techniques [20,9,21] have also been investigated to learn low dimensional representations of the pose distribution, but in general have been limited to a restricted set of activities.

All previously mentioned approaches are limited in their use of retinotopic representations, i.e., pose is computed on normalized images where the person has a somewhat known fixed size and location. Such approaches are usually not robust to occlusions, clutter and normalization errors. In this paper, we propose a local representation to address these issues.

Model-based approaches [6,16,18] usually minimize the reprojection of a parametric model to the image. These techniques, however, rely on good initialization, require complex and precise models and are computationally expensive. In [7,14,17,19], specialized appearance models or detectors are trained on individual body parts and combined with geometric constraints. This requires expensive manual labeling of the body parts and modeling appearance under different view-points might be difficult.

In a similar manner, methods using part-based representations have been developed for object categorization [12,13,10,11]. The approach described in [10,11] employs an Implicit Shape Model (ISM) that consists of both the local appearance and the spatial probability distribution of each codebook entry. Pose estimation is possible with this approach but it is limited to the estimation of the scale and 2D center location of an object in the image.

In this paper, we advocate a part-based approach and generalize the technique developed by [10,11] to generic 2D and 3D pose estimation (*e.g.* fiducial, head pose, articulated body pose). Here, the spatial probability of codebook entries is modeled relative not just to the object center and scale, but to the object *pose*. As in [10,11], we estimate the pose distribution associated with each image patch by comparing the query patch to reference patches for which the pose is known. All image patches contribute to the density by soft voting. Analysis of the density allows probabilistic inference of the global pose associated with the image.

3   Density from Image Patches

Given a training set of pairs $\{(I_i, x_i)\}$ where I_i is an image and $x_i \in \mathbb{R}_n$ a pose we wish to learn a function $\Phi(x, I)$ that models the conditional density distribution $p(x|I)$ for all the images in the training set. Given a query image I', the pose $x' = f(I')$ can be estimated at the modes of $\Phi(x, I')$.

For a face pose could refer, for example, to the 2D location of fiducial points $m_i = (u_i, v_i)$. In this case, $x = (m_1, \ldots, m_N)^\top$. In case pose represents the orientation of the face, x is a 2-dimensional vector containing horizontal and vertical components. For an articulated body, pose can represent the 3D joint locations $M_i = (X_i, Y_i, Z_i)$. In this case, $x = (M_1, \ldots, M_N)^\top$.

3.1   Building a Patch Database

For each image I, interest points u_i are extracted (e.g. Harris) and descriptors d_j are evaluated at multiple scales in order to capture both local and semi-local information. Our approach does not rely on a specific image descriptor. As pose is sensitive to the orientation and translation components of patches, we choose descriptors which are not invariant to affine or Euclidean transformations. Descriptors can be normalized intensity vectors or silhouette patches, edge orientation histograms or SIFT descriptors.

We build hashing functions by extracting descriptors and associated poses for all training image/pose pairs in the database. Each patch has an associated triplet $\{(d_j, \sigma_j, x_j)\}$, where σ_j is the scale. If the pose is given with respect to a referential, *e.g.* the pose is defined relative to the location of the keypoint u_j and geometric constraints can be captured by the voting process.

3.2   Implicit Geometric Constraints

We define $\bar{x}$ a patch-relative pose that is independent from the keypoint location by defining a mapping $g_u(x)$.

If x corresponds to a set of 2D image points $x = (m_1, \ldots, m_N)^\top$, with $m_i = (u_i, v_i)$, we choose g_u as:

$$\bar{x} = g_u(x) = \sigma(x - (u, \ldots, u)^\top) \tag{1}$$

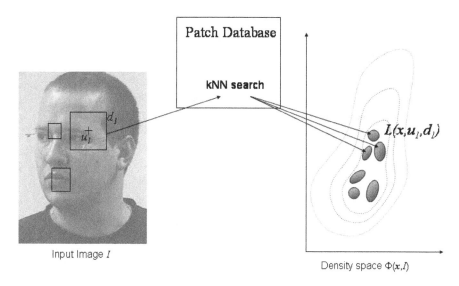

Fig. 1. Density estimation from image parts. Each patch from image I is matched to the database. k-nearest neighbors are retrieved and populate the density space with a set of kernels representing the pose distribution associated with the query patch. In this example, k=3.

If x corresponds to a set of 3D image points $x = (M_1, \ldots, M_N)^\top$, with $M_i = (X_i, Y_i, Z_i)$ the 3D coordinates. We can choose g_u to be

$$g_u(x) = (M_1 - U, \ldots, M_N - U)^\top$$

with $U = k_f(u - p_0)$ where k_f is the size (in metric units) of a pixel and p_0 is the principal point of the camera.

4   Pose Density Estimate

Let $S = \{(d_j, \sigma_j, \bar{x}_j)\}$ be a database of reference pose-patches. Let I be a query image from which we wish to retrieve the pose density $p(x|I)$.

For each descriptor, the k closest reference patches (in terms of descriptor distance) from S are extracted. For each retrieved reference patch, an 'absolute' pose x_j is computed from the relative pose $\bar{x}_j$ as $x_j = g_u^{-1}(\bar{x}_j)$.

Let $n(j)$ be the index of the jth nearest neighbor of the descriptor d. Vectors $x_j = g_u^{-1}(\bar{x}_{n(j)})$ are the absolute poses corresponding to a feature point located at location ui in the image.

Let N be the number of patches in the image. A kernel-based density estimator $\Phi_S(x, I)$ can be defined at an arbitrary pose x as:

$$\Phi_S(x, I) = \frac{1}{Z} \sum_{i=1}^{N} L(x, u_i, d_i) \tag{2}$$

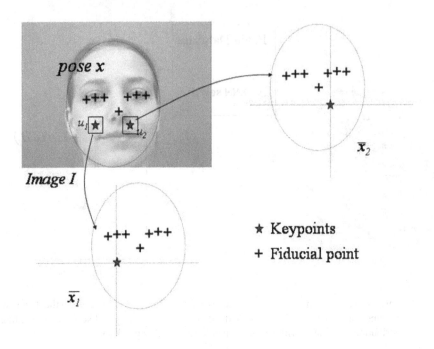

Fig. 2. Pose x corresponds here to the 2D locations of fiducial points. For each keypoint u_1 and u_2, the 'relative' pose is computed locally as $\bar{x}_1$ and $\bar{x}_2$. In case pose is in 3D, the same mechanism can be applied: the pose of the 3D points $\bar{x}$ are given in a referential centered at the point location u, considered as a 3D point on the image plane.

where Z is a normalization constant

$$L(x, u, d) = \sum_{i=1}^{k} K(x, x_j) \tag{3}$$

with x_j the absolute poses of the k-most similar patches to d in S. $K(x_i, x_j)$ is a Gaussian kernel defined as:

$$K(x_i, x_j) = \lambda e^{(x_i, x_j)^\top \Sigma (x_i, x_j)} \tag{4}$$

where Σ is the covariance of kernel. $L(x, u, d)$ can be seen as a *factored* representation of x for patch d. For a given x, the function $\Phi_S(x, I)$ provides an estimation of $p(x|I)$. This is illustrated by Figure 3. Computing Σ from training data can become relatively intractable for large databases. In general, we choose Σ that minimizes the training errors. However, when pose $x = (m_1, \ldots, m_n)$ corresponds to a set of 2D points, we define Σ as a block diagonal matrix

$$\Sigma = diag(\Lambda_1, \ldots, \Lambda_n) \tag{5}$$

where Λ_i is a 2x2 matrix defined as $\Lambda_i = \mu^2 \|m_i - u\|^2 I_2$ where μ is a user-defined constant. This gives lower confidence to the location of points away from u.

The modes of $\Phi_S(\boldsymbol{x}, I)$ can be obtained with the mean-shift clustering algorithm [5]. Our approach can be seen as a soft voting scheme where larger values of $\Phi_S(\boldsymbol{x}, I)$ are obtained for regions corresponding to an accumulation of kernels.

Clutter is handled naturally as it will usually be matched to arbitrary reference patches, creating thus some noise in the density.

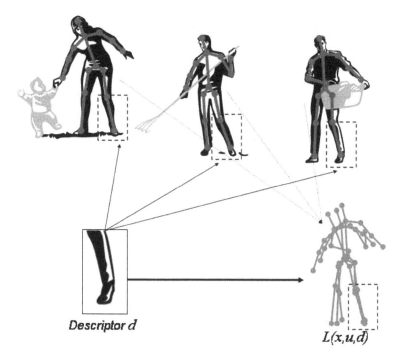

Fig. 3. Inference: each image patch is compared to the database. In this example, 3 nearest neighbors are extracted from the database providing 3 kernels. The green skeleton represents the 'factored' distribution L.

5   Feature Selection

When the number training patches is large, the computational cost of evaluating eq. (2) might be prohibitive. Here, we propose to approximate the posterior probability by a mixture of experts, where each expert takes into account a much smaller set of patches.

$$p(\boldsymbol{x}|I) \approx \Phi(\boldsymbol{x}, I) = \sum_{i=1}^{C} \alpha_i p(\boldsymbol{x}|i, I) = \hat{\alpha}\Psi \,, \tag{6}$$

where $\alpha_i = p(i|\boldsymbol{x})$ is the probability of each experts (i.e. gaiting function), $\hat{\alpha} = [\alpha_1, \cdots \alpha_N]$ is the matrix of gaiting functions and $\Psi = [p(\boldsymbol{x}|1, I), \cdots, p(\boldsymbol{x}|N, I)]$ is the matrix composed of the estimation of all the experts.

When the experts have a parametric form they are usually trained with Expectation-Maximization (EM). Since our experts are non parametric (i.e. we use a kernel-based voting scheme), such training procedure does not apply. Instead, learning is done by maximizing the KL divergence between the probability estimated from all the training data, $p(\boldsymbol{x}|I)$, and the approximation made by the mixture of experts, Φ.

$$\epsilon = \sum_i D_{KL}(p(\boldsymbol{x}|I_i)||\Phi(\boldsymbol{x}, I_i)) \tag{7}$$

$$= \int p(\boldsymbol{x}|I_i) \log(\frac{p(\boldsymbol{x}|I_i)}{\Phi(\boldsymbol{x}, I_i)}) d\boldsymbol{x} \tag{8}$$

If the true distribution $p(\boldsymbol{x}|I_i)$ is a dirac centered at x_i, a first order approximation of eq. (8) gives:

$$\epsilon = -\sum_i \log(\Phi(\boldsymbol{x}, I_i)) \approx C - \sum_i \Phi(\boldsymbol{x}, I_i). \tag{9}$$

Learning the experts might still be very expensive is the number of experts required to accurate learn the density is large. We further propose a more efficient algorithm that is based on Adaboost.

5.1 Adaboost-Like Learning

At each iteration a new expert is learned and added to the existing mixture, and the relative weights (i.e. gaiting units) of the experts are re-estimated by minimizing (8). We restrict here the choice of the experts to be of the same form as the non parametric density estimators of section 4, but where instead of being estimated from the entire set of patches, they are estimated from a subset of them.

For large databases, finding the optimal set of patches at each iteration is computationally very expensive, instead, we propose to use a RANSAC scheme. Different subsets of patches are randomly sampled. For each subset, the corresponding density estimator is built and the optimal gating units are computed[1]. The selected density estimator at each iteration is the one with the smallest error (8).

6   Experimental Evaluation

In order to evaluate the performance of our density-based pose estimation algorithm, we performed experiments on 3 different datasets.

For each dataset, a patch-pose database was built as described in Section 3.1: for each image of the training set, interest points were extracted and descriptors were computed at their location at multiple spatial scales and stored in the database along with the corresponding pose.

---

[1] Given a set of experts Ψ_i, the gating units that optimize (8) can be computed in closed form as $\hat{\alpha} = \frac{1}{\Sigma_i A_i} A$, where $A_i = \Sigma_j \Psi_i(\boldsymbol{x}_j)$.

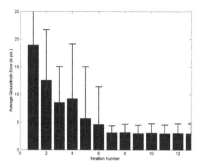 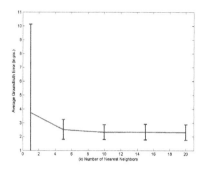

Fig. 4. Experiments on the BioID database. (left) Variation of the ground truth error of the density-based pose estimation algorithm *vs.* Adaboost-like iterations. After the 7-th iteration, the error is already relatively small and very close to the error obtained with the density estimator using the entire dataset. (right) Variation of the ground truth error of the density-based pose estimation algorithm *vs.* Number of nearest neighbors.

6.1 BioID Database

We carried out a set of experiments on the BioID database [1]. This database contains 1521 face images of 23 different persons labeled with pose corresponding to the 2D locations of 20 fiducial points (e.g. nose, pupils, eyes and mouth corners). Most images are frontal views and contain clutter, large variations of expression, appearance (in particular, some people wearing glasses), illumination and location in the image.

We built a patch database from a training set consisting of 1000 images and used another 100 images for testing. Patches have a nominal size of 19x19. The database contains around 90000 pose-patches.

For each weak density estimator, we chose a set of 300 randomly selected patches. As shown in Figure 4 shows, the convergence of the feature selection algorithm is relatively fast (7 iterations). In practice, we stop the algorithm when 10% or more of the database had been selected. In this implementation, gu is defined as in eq. (1) and the covariances Σ are defined as in eq. (5). We used the mean-shift algorithm to find the main mode of the density.

In order to evaluate the efficiency of our feature selection algorithm, we implemented a pose density estimator Φ using the entire database.

To evaluate the efficiency of our feature selection algorithm we compared to two baselines: the full database and to random selection of a subset of patches that comprised 10% of the database: we randomly selected a large number (1000) of subsets corresponding to 10% of the database and retained the subset with lowest training error. Table 1 reports the ground truth error for the three methods. Note that the errors are relatively small (less than 3 pixels) for both the full database and our feature selection algorithm. Note also that the variance is much smaller than randomly selecting the patches.

We also tested the robustness of our method to occlusions. See Figure 6. Black rectangles were generated at a random location in the face. For small rectangles (30x30 pix.^{2}) representing an eighth of the face surface, errors were sensibly similar to non

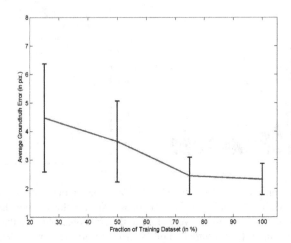

Fig. 5. Experiments on the BioID database. Variation of the ground truth error of the densitybased pose estimation algorithm *vs.* percentage of the initial training dataset used for training.

Table 1. Evaluation of the feature selection algorithm. The accuracy of our feature selection approach is relatively similar to the performance using the full database.

	Error (in pix.)
Feature select. (10%)	2.79 (0.78)
Full database	2.32 (0.52)
Random (10%)	4.98 (9.38)

occluded faces (mean error 2.52 pix. and variance 0.61). For larger rectangles (60x60 pix.^{2}), the estimation degraded (mean error 4.46 pix. and variance 8.41).

6.2 Pointing'04 Database

We performed experiments on the Pointing04 database [8]. This database contains images of 15 subjects (2 sets, each with 93 views per subject). A pose corresponds to head orientation and is defined by 2 angles (horizontal and vertical inclinations), which vary in the database from -90 to +90 degrees. Note that this database is challenging as it contains many occluded views (*e.g.* part of the face not contained in the image). We defined the function g_u as the identity (no geometric constraints) and chose $\Sigma = 5.0\mathbf{I}_2$.

Table 2. Mean and variance (in brackets) error for our pose estimation algorithm as a function of the number of scales used in the database

scales	Error (in deg.)
1	5.24 (10.98)
3	2.45 (7.37)
5	1.52 (6.29)

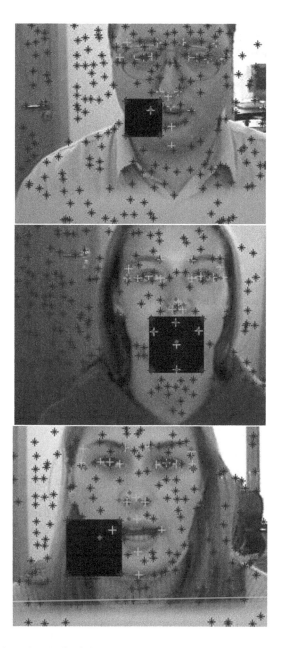

Fig. 6. Example of results obtained for the 'occlusion' experiment. The errors are respectively (from top to bottom) 2.02 pixels, 2.31 pixels and 5.6 pixels. Blue stars (*) are detected keypoints, cyan crosses (+) are the ground truth fiducial points and red dots (.) are estimated by our algorithm.

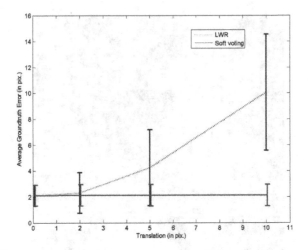

Fig. 7. Experiments on the POSER database. The error (in pixels) of LWR (dotted) and our approach (solid) with respect to misalignment between the training and the testing images. As expected, our approach is perfectly insensitive to translations. In contrast, LWR error grows rapidly with the amount of translation.

We trained our system on all users from one set and tested on a subject from the second set. Table 2 reports the error as a function of the number of scales used by our density-based pose estimation algorithm. Errors are relatively small, the large variances reflect the presence of outliers (*i.e.* errors between 20 to 40 degrees). As expected, increasing the number of scales decrease the error.

6.3   Articulated Pose

We performed experiments on synthetic sequences generated with a rendering software package (POSER) from motion-capture data. These are similar to the sequences used in [15, 4] and include for instance activities such as walking, dancing. The pose corresponds to the 3D location of 20 joints.

We trained our algorithm on individual sequences (averaging 500 frames). We used 90% of the sequence for training and 10% for testing.

We compared our algorithm to Locally Weighted Regression (LWR) as used in [15] for instance. We generated sequences without background and centered in the character. To test the sensibility to translation, we generated a database where the character is exactly at the center of the image for training and we translated the testing images in a random direction. Results are reported Figure 7. As expected, our approach is insensitive to translations. With no translation, our approach and LWR perform similarly. However, LWR error grows on with the amount of translation.

Our approach can also deal with multiple people. Figure 8 depicts an example of 2 people in a very cluttered background. The two people are obtained by detecting the 2 modes of the density by mean-shift clustering. The left image of Figure 8 depicts in red circles the keypoints for which the pose density is high.

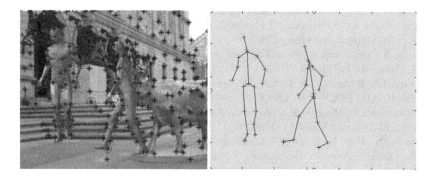

Fig. 8. Experiments on the POSER database. (left) image containing some background and 2 subjects. The blues crosses represent the keypoints. The red circles represent keypoints for which the density is high. (right) pose corresponding to the two principal modes of the density.

7   Conclusion

We presented a density-voting technique for pose estimation from patches. It relies on the use of a local representation of pose that allows to efficiently combine evidence from multiple patch while avoiding the bag-of-feature dilemna. To scale our approach to large training sets, we presented a boosting-like feature selection approach, which efficiently selects the most discriminative subsets of patches for pose estimation.

Our approach is relatively simple and does not require explicitly or implicitly modeling people as parts. Instead, geometric constraints are learned directly from images. The main advantage of our technique is that detection and pose estimation are done simultaneously.

The local voting scheme allows us to use the contribution of individual patches simultaneously, making it robust to occlusions, partial views and the presence of clutter in the scene. Our framework handles multiple people naturally by finding multiple modes in the density. Applications for tracking are obvious as our pose density estimation would integrate nicely with dynamic priors.

Finally, our technique is fast as it takes only a few seconds per image. In fact, most of the running time is spent in the mean-shift algorithm because of the high dimensionality of the pose space. We believe that dimensionality reduction techniques would allow our approach to run in real-time and increase the robustness. As future work, we plan to integrate this approach in a tracking framework by smoothing densities in the pose space based on temporal priors.

References

1. The bioid face database. http://www.bioid.com/downloads/facedb/
2. Curious labs, inc., santa cruz, ca. poser 5 - reference manual (2002)
3. Agarwal, A., Triggs, B.: Learning to Track 3D Human Motion from Silhouettes. In: Proceedings of the 21st International Conference on Machine Learning, Banff, Canada (July 2004)

4. Agarwal, A., Triggs, B.: A local basis representation for estimating human pose from cluttered images. In: Narayanan, P.J., Nayar, S.K., Shum, H.-Y. (eds.) ACCV 2006. LNCS, vol. 3851, Springer, Heidelberg (2006)
5. Cheng, Y.: Mean shift, mode seeking, and clustering. IEEE Trans. Pattern Anal. Mach. Intell. 17(8), 790–799 (1995)
6. Cootes, T.F., Edwards, G.J., Taylor, C.J.: Active appearance models. In: Burkhardt, H., Neumann, B. (eds.) ECCV 1998. LNCS, vol. 1407, p. 484. Springer, Heidelberg (1998)
7. Felzenszwalb, P., Huttenlocher, D.: Pictorial structures for object recognition. International Journal of Computer Vision 61 (June 2005)
8. Gourier, N., Hall, D., Crowley, J.L.: Estimating face orientation from robust detection of salient facial features. In: Proceedings of Pointing 2004, ICPR, International Workshop on Visual Observation of Deictic Gestures, Cambridge, UK (2004)
9. He, X., Yan, S., Hu, Y., Niyogi, P.: Face recognition using laplacianfaces. IEEE Trans. Pattern Anal. Mach. Intell. 27(3), 328–340 (2005)
10. Leibe, B., Leonardis, A., Schiele, B.: Combined object categorization and segmentation with an implicit shape model. In: Pajdla, T., Matas, J(G.) (eds.) ECCV 2004. LNCS, vol. 3021, pp. 17–32. Springer, Heidelberg (2004)
11. Leibe, B., Schiele, B.: Scale invariant object categorization using a scale-adaptive mean-shift search. In: Rasmussen, C.E., Bülthoff, H.H., Schölkopf, B., Giese, M.A. (eds.) DAGM 2004. LNCS, vol. 3175, pp. 145–153. Springer, Heidelberg (2004)
12. Lowe, D.G.: Object recognition from local scale-invariant features. In: International Conference on Computer Vision, Corfu, Greece, pp. 1150–1157 (September 1999)
13. Murphy, K., Torralba, A., Freeman, W.: Using the forest to see the tree: a graphical model relating features, objects and the scenes (2003)
14. Ronfard, R., Schmid, C., Triggs, B.: Learning to parse pictures of people. In: Heyden, A., Sparr, G., Nielsen, M., Johansen, P. (eds.) ECCV 2002. LNCS, vol. 2350, pp. 700–714. Springer, Heidelberg (2002)
15. Shakhnarovich, G., Viola, P., Darrell, T.: Fast Pose Estimation with Parameter-Sensitive Hashing. In: Proceedings of the IEEE International Conference on Computer Vision, Nice, France, IEEE Computer Society Press, Los Alamitos (October 2003)
16. Sidenbladh, H., Black, M., Fleet, D.: Stochastic Tracking of 3D Human Figures Using 2D Image Motion. In: Vernon, D. (ed.) ECCV 2000. LNCS, vol. 1842, pp. 702–718. Springer, Heidelberg (2000)
17. Sigal, L., Isard, M., Sigelman, B., Black, M.: Attractive People: Assembling Loose-Limbed Models using Non-Parametric Belief Propagation. In: Advances in Neural Information Processing Systems, Vancouver, Canada (December 2003)
18. Sminchiesescu, C., Triggs, B.: Kinematic jump processes for monocular 3d human tracking. In: Proc. IEEE Conf. on Computer Vision and Pattern Recognition, IEEE Computer Society Press, Los Alamitos (2003)
19. Sudderth, E.B., Ihler, A.T., Freeman, W.T., Willsky, A.S.: Nonparametric belief propagation. In: IEEE Conference on Computer Vision and Pattern Recognition, IEEE Computer Society Press, Los Alamitos (June 2003)
20. Turk, M.A., Pentland, A.P.: Face recognition using eigenfaces. In: Computer Vision and Pattern Recognition, 1991. Proceedings CVPR 1991, IEEE Computer Society Conference on, pp. 586–591. IEEE Computer Society Press, Los Alamitos (1991)
21. Urtasun, R., Fleet, D.J., Hertzmann, A., Fua, P.: Priors for people tracking from small training sets. In: ICCV 2005. Proceedings of the Tenth IEEE International Conference on Computer Vision, Washington, DC, USA, vol. 1, pp. 403–410 (2005)

Integrating Multiple Visual Cues for Robust Real-Time 3D Face Tracking

Wei-Kai Liao, Douglas Fidaleo, and Gérard Medioni

Computer Science Department,
Institute for Robotics and Intelligent Systems,
University of Southern California,
Los Angeles, CA 90089-0273, USA

Abstract. 3D face tracking is an important component for many computer vision applications. Most state-of-the-art tracking algorithms can be characterized as being either intensity- or feature-based. The intensity-based tracker relies on the brightness constraint while the feature-based tracker utilizes 2D local feature correspondences. In this paper, we propose a hybrid tracker for robust 3D face tracking. Instead of relying on single source of information, the hybrid tracker integrates feature correspondence and brightness constraints within a nonlinear optimization framework. The proposed method can track the 3D face pose reliably in real-time. We have conducted a series of evaluations to compare the performance of the proposed tracker with other state-of-the-art trackers. The experiments consist of synthetic sequences with simulation of different environmental factors, real sequences with estimated ground truth, and sequences from a real-world HCI application. The proposed tracker is shown to be superior in both accuracy and robustness.

1 Introduction

3D face tracking is a fundamental component for solving many computer vision problems. In this paper, we focus on tracking the 3D rigid motion of the head. The estimated 3D pose is useful for various face-related applications. For example, in human-computer interaction, the 3D pose can be used to determine a user's attention and mental status. For expression analysis and face recognition, the 3D head pose can be used to stabilize the face as a preprocess. The pose estimate can also assist in 3D face reconstruction from a monocular video.

The performance of a face tracker is affected by many factors. While higher level choices such as whether or not to use keyframes, how many to use, and whether to update them online can alter the accuracy (and speed) of the tracker, a more fundamental issue is the optimization algorithm and the related objective functional. Most state-of-the-art face tracking algorithms are affected by these three factors:

- Prior knowledge of the approximate 3D structure of the subject's face. In [1], Fidaleo et al. have shown that the accuracy of the underlying 3D model can dramatically affect the tracking accuracy of a feature driven tracker. Much of the performance difference between tracking methods can be attributed to the choice of model: planar [2], ellipse [3], cylinder [4][5], and generic face or precise geometry [6].

S.K. Zhou et al. (Eds.): AMFG 2007, LNCS 4778, pp. 109–123, 2007.

– Observed data in the 2D image. The tracker relies on this information to estimate the head pose. This includes feature locations [6][7], intensity values in a region [4][5][8], or estimated motion flow fields [3][9].
– The computational framework, which can be roughly divided into deterministic optimization and stochastic estimation [10]. For deterministic optimization methods, an error function is defined using the observed 2D data and the corresponding estimated 2D data. Pose parameters are adjusted to minimize this error function. On the other hand, stochastic estimation methods such as particle filtering define the observation and transition density functions for tracking. Deterministic methods are typically more computationally efficient, while stochastic methods are more resistent to local minima.

For real-world applications, there are several constraints besides tracking accuracy, including computational efficiency and robustness of the tracker. For real-time or interactive applications, the tracker must be computationally efficient. Robustness can be defined in several ways including robustness to noise, stability on textureless video, insensitivity to illumination changes, and resistance to the expression changes or other local non-rigid deformation. The tracker should be able to run continuously for long sequences, requiring a mechanism to prevent drift and error accumulation.

In this paper, we propose a hybrid tracker for 3D face tracking. Instead of relying on any single channel of information, the hybrid tracker integrates different visual cues for face tracking. This idea is inspired by detailed comparisons between existing state-of-the-art head trackers [5][6]. Feature-based methods such as [6][7] depend on the ability to detect and match the same features in subsequent frames and keyframes. The quantity, accuracy, and face coverage of the matches fully determines the recovered pose quality. In contrast, intensity-based methods such as [5] do not explicitly require feature matching, but expect brightness consistency between the same image patches in different images to compute the implicit flow of pixels. These two methods are extensively examined in our experiments. Empirical observation suggests that neither's definitely better among the existing face tracking algorithms; each tracker has its own strengths but also comes with its weaknesses. Thus, by design, the hybrid tracker is expected to overcome the flaws of the single channel trackers while retaining their strength. This is clearly demonstrated in our experiments.

The rest of this paper is organized as follows: We start with the discussion and comparison of established ideas for intensity- and feature-based face tracking, in section 2. Based on empirical observation, a hybrid tracking algorithm is proposed. The details of this algorithm are illustrated in section 3. The proposed hybrid tracker, along with the intensity- and feature-based trackers, have been examined thoroughly in various experiments. These results are presented in section 4. Finally, the summary and conclusion are given in section 5.

2   Intensity- Versus Feature-Based Tracker

This section compares intensity- and feature-based trackers. To prepare the readers, we first review the individual algorithms. The selected representative algorithms for each class are [5] and [6] for the intensity- and feature-based methods, respectively. The fundamental concepts of these trackers are summarized, and the reader is referred to the original papers for the specific details.

2.1 Intensity-Based Tracker

The intensity-based tracker performs optimization based on the brightness constraint. To be more specific, let $\mu = \{t_x, t_y, t_z, w_x, w_y, w_z\}^T$ be the motion vector specifying the 3D head pose. Given the pose in frame $t - 1$, μ_{t-1}, we define an error function $E_t(\triangle\mu)$ for $\triangle\mu$, the incremental pose change between frame $t - 1$ and t, as

$$E_t(\triangle\mu; \mu_{t-1}) = \sum_{p \in \Omega} \|I^{t-1}(F(p, 0; \mu_{t-1})) - I^t(F(p, \triangle\mu; \mu_{t-1}))\|_2^2 \quad (1)$$

here Ω is the face region and p is the 3D position of a point on the face. $F = P \circ M$, where $M(p, \triangle\mu)$ will transform the 3D position of p as $\triangle\mu$ specified and P is a weak perspective projection. $I^t(.)$ and $I^{t-1}(.)$ are the frame t and $t - 1$ respectively.

This error function measures the *intensity difference* between the previous frame and the transformed current frame. If the intensity consistency is maintained and the noise of intensity is Gaussian distributed, the minimum of this 2-norm error function is guaranteed to be the optimal solution. Thus, by minimizing this error function with respect to the 3D pose, we can estimate the change of 3D pose and recover the current pose.

Off-line information can also be integrated into the optimization similar to Vacchetti et al. [6]. The error function $E_k(\triangle\mu)$:

$$E_k(\triangle\mu; \mu_{t-1}) = \sum_{i=1}^{N_k} \alpha_i \left[\sum_{p \in \Omega} \|I^i(F(p, 0; \mu_i)) - I^t(F(p, \triangle\mu; \mu_{t-1}))\|_2^2 \right] \quad (2)$$

is defined between the current frame and the keyframes. N_k is the number of keyframes. $I^i(.)$ and μ_i are the frame and pose of the ith keyframe. This error function can use both off-line or on-line generated keyframes for estimating the head pose.

A regularization term

$$E_r(\triangle\mu; \mu_{t-1}) = \sum_{p \in \Omega} \|F(p, 0; \mu_{t-1}) - F(p, \triangle\mu; \mu_{t-1})\|_2^2 \quad (3)$$

can also be included to impose a smoothness constraint over the estimated motion vector.

The final error function for optimization is combination of (1), (2), and (3):

$$E_{\text{int}} = E_t + \lambda_k E_k + \lambda_r E_r \quad (4)$$

where λ_k and λ_r are the weighting constants. This is a nonlinear optimization problem and the iteratively reweighted least square is applied.

2.2 Feature-Based Tracker

The feature-based tracker minimizes the reprojection error of a set of 2D and 3D points matched between frames. A keyframe in [6] consists of a set of 2D feature locations detected on the face with a Harris corner detector and their 3D positions estimated by back-projecting onto a registered 3D tracking model. The keyframe accuracy is dependent on both the model alignment in the keyframe image, as well as the geometric structure of the tracking mesh. These points are matched to patches in the previous frame and combined with keyframe points for pose estimation.

The reprojection error for the keyframe feature points is defined as:

$$E_{k,t} = \sum_{p \in \kappa} \| m_t^p - F(p, \mu_t) \|_2^2 \tag{5}$$

where κ is the set of keyframe feature points, m_t^p is the measured 2D feature point corresponding to the keyframe feature point p at frame t, and $F(p, \mu_t)$ is the projection of p's 3D position using pose parameters μ_t.

To reduce jitter associated with single keyframe optimization, additional correspondences between the current and previous frame are added to the error term:

$$E_t = \sum_{p \in \kappa} \left(\| n_t^p - F(p, \mu_t) \|_2^2 + \| n_{t-1}^p - F(p, \mu_{t-1}) \|_2^2 \right) \tag{6}$$

where the 3D for the new points is estimated by back projection to the 3D model at the current pose estimate.

The two terms are combined into the final error functional:

$$E_{\text{fpt}} = E_{k,t} + E_{k,t-1} + E_t \tag{7}$$

which is minimized using nonlinear optimization.

2.3 Comparison

Both tracking methods are model based, using an estimate of the 3D shape of the face and its projection onto the 2D image plane to define a reprojection error functional that is minimized using a nonlinear optimization scheme. The forms of the error functionals are nearly identical, differing only in the input feature space on which the distance function operates. Figure 1 illustrates the difference between these 2 trackers.

For the feature-based tracker, the reprojection error is measured as the *feature distance* between a set of key 2D features and their matched points in the new image. The tracker relies on robust correspondence between 2D features in successive frames and keyframes, and thus the effectiveness of the feature detector and the matching algorithm is critical for the success of the tracker. In [6], Vacchetti et al. used the standard eigenvalue-based Harris corner detector. Using a more efficient and robust detector should improve the feature-based tracker.

In contrast, the intensity-based tracker utilizes the brightness constraint between similar patches in successive images and defines the error functional in terms of *intensity differences* at sample points.

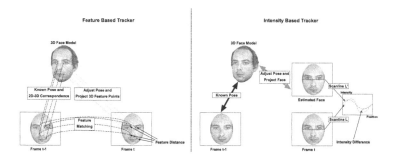

Fig. 1. Difference in optimization source data for the feature-based tracker, T_F, and the intensity-based tracker, T_I. Given a set of key feature points defined on a 3D model, and their projection, T_F minimizes the total distance to matched feature points in pixel space. T_I computes the pose that minimizes the total intensity difference of pixels under the feature points.

To determine the role of this input space on tracking accuracy we perform a set of controlled experiments on synthesized motion sequences (see section 4 for details). Feature-based methods are generally chosen for their stability under changing lighting and other conditions, with the assumption that feature locations remain constant despite these changes. For cases where there is insufficient texture on the face (low resolution, poor focus, etc) the accuracy of feature methods quickly degrades. Intensity-based methods are more widely applicable and can perform well in low or high-texture cases, however they are clearly sensitive to environmental changes. This is demonstrated empirically by testing on the near-infrared sequence.

3   The Hybrid Tracker

The empirical and theoretical comparison of intensity- and feature-based tracker inspires the hybrid tracking algorithm. In this section, we reformulate the 3D face tracking problem as a multi-objective optimization problem, and present an efficient method to solve it. The robustness of the tracker is also discussed.

3.1   Integrating Multiple Visual Cues

Integrating multiple visual cues for face tracking can be interpreted as adjusting the 3D pose to fit multiple constraints. The hybrid tracker has two objective functions with different constraints to satisfy simultaneously: equations 4 and 7. This becomes a multi-objective optimization problem. Scalarization is a common technique for solving multi-objective optimization problems. The final error function is a weighted combination of the individual error functions 4 and 7:

$$E = a_i E_{\text{int}} + a_f E_{\text{fpt}} \tag{8}$$

where a_i and a_f are the weighting constants.

The hybrid tracker searches for the solution to minimize equation 8. The process can be interpreted as a nonlinear optimization based on brightness constraints, but regularized with feature correspondence constraints. Ideally, these two constraints compensate for each other's deficiencies. The feature point correspondences restrict the space of feasible solutions for the intensity-based optimization and helps the optimizer to escape from local minima. The brightness constraint refines and stabilizes the feature-based optimization. When there are not sufficient high quality feature matches, the intensity constraint still provides adequate reliable measurement for optimization.

The convergence of feature-based optimization is much faster than intensity-based methods due to the high dimensionality of the image data and the nature of the associated imaging function. However, when E_{fpt} is close to its optimum, E_{int} still provides information to refine the registration. Therefore, an adaptive scheme is applied to choose the weights a_i and a_f. At the beginning of the optimization, E_{fpt} has higher weight and decreases when it approaches its optimum. At the same time, the weight of E_{int} increases when the optimization proceed. The overall distribution of the weights is also affected by the number of matched features. In the case of few feature correspondences, the tracker reduces the weight of E_{fpt}.

3.2   Efficient Solution

The computational cost of the feature-based tracker is low due to the relatively small number of the matched features and the fast convergence of the optimization. On the other hand, the intensity-based tracker is notorious for its high computational cost. The standard algorithm for solving this iterative least-square problem is slow, due to the evaluation of a large Jacobian matrix $F_\mu = \partial F / \partial \mu$ and Hessian matrix $(I_u F_\mu)^T (I_u F_\mu)$, where I_u is the gradient of the frame I. This can be accelerated using the (forward) compositional algorithm, but the evaluation of Hessian is still required at each iteration.

Speed of the algorithm can be further improved using the inverse compositional algorithm. In [11], Baker and Matthews proposed the inverse compositional algorithm to solve the image alignment problem efficiently. The same modifications to the solver can be made for this problem. In the inverse compositional algorithm, the Jacobian and Hessian matrix are evaluated in a preprocessing step; only the error term is computed during the optimization. To do this, the image is warped at each iteration, and the computed transform is inverted to compose with previous transform. Here, warping the image is equivalent to model projection. Since we know the 2D-3D correspondence in I_{t-1}, warping I_t for intensity difference evaluation is achieved by projecting the 3D model and sampling to get the intensity in I_t.

The inverse compositional version of the algorithm is:

- Preprocess
  For E_{int}: Compute the gradient image, the Jacobian, and the Hessian matrix.
  For E_{fpt}: Perform feature detection on I_t, and feature matching between I_t, I_{t-1}, and keyframes.
- Optimization
  At each iteration:
  1.1. Warp the face region of I_t to get the intensity.

   1.2. Compute the intensity difference and the weight.

   2.1. Project the feature points to get the 2D position.

   2.2. Compute the reprojection error and weights.

   3. Solve the linear system.

   4. Update the pose.

– Postprocess

   Back-project the face region and feature points of I_t into the 3D face model.

In our experiments, for fast convergence and small face region cases, the speed of forward and the inverse compositional algorithm is similar. This is true because the preprocess of the inverse compositional algorithm takes more time. However, as the face region or the iteration number increases, the benefit of the inverse compositional algorithm becomes clear, since each iteration takes less time. Besides, this direct extension of inverse compositional algorithm to 3D-2D alignment is not mathematically equivalent to the forward compositional algorithm, as discussed in [12]. However, in our experiments, it still shows good performance for estimating 3D head pose.

3.3   Improving the Robustness

Robustness is an important issue for 3D face tracking. We employ the m-estimator [13] technique for optimization, which improve the robustness against outlier and noise.

Combining the feature correspondence constraint with the brightness constraint for face tracking intrinsically improves the robustness. With the proper weighting, we overcome the instability of the feature-based optimization due to insufficient or poor feature matching. The sensitivity of the intensity-based optimization is also reduced, as many plausible solutions are ruled out by the feature correspondence constraints. This is especially useful for lighting variation. Lighting changes affect the intensity on the face, and violate the underlying brightness consistency assumption of the intensity-based tracker. However, several existing feature detectors have been shown to be robust (or less sensitive) to the illumination change, for example the SIFT detector [14]. In our implementation, we choose the SIFT detector as the underlying feature detector for its superior performance reported in the literature. Hence, the extracted feature correspondence and the resulting hybrid tracker is more resistent to the illumination change.

Robustness to non-rigid deformation is another issue. Since we only focus on the rigid motion of the head, the local non-rigid motion should be regarded as the noise for this framework. It has been shown that better results are achieved by utilizing feature-based methods. However, it turns out that this performance gain is not strictly due to the use of features over intensity.

A fundamental part of the feature-based tracker is the feature matching stage. During feature matching, candidates with low region-correlation are rejected as outliers and therefore not included in the optimization stage. The effect of this is that the majority of feature points used in the optimization belong to rigid areas of the face. On the other hand, the weighting scheme of the intensity-based method only considers the pixel-wise intensity difference. This difference will be near zero under deformation, as deformation does not alter the intensity of the single pixel. Instead, the deformation alters the composition of local patch. Thus, it suggests the use of region-wise intensity differences instead of pixel-wise intensity differences.

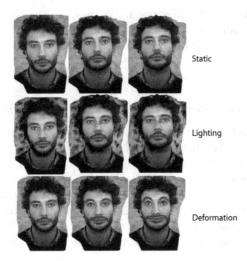

Fig. 2. Example synthetic sequences used for experiments. (top) Static sequence, (middle) Single directional light source. (bottom) Deformation with face muscle system.

The intensity of each pixel is modified as the weighted average of the intensity of its neighbors. The idea is that if this point is located in a highly deformable area, the composition of the region changes significantly, thus the weighted average is changed. Combining with the m-estimator technique, the proposed region-based intensity difference improves the robustness by implicit decreasing the weight of pixels in the highly deformable area.

4 Experiments

A series of tracker evaluations are performed. The first set of experiments uses synthetic sequences. Using synthetic sequences guarantees exact ground truth is available. We have full control over sequence generation, and thus can isolate each factor and test the tracker's response. The next experiment tests the performance of the tracker in real video sequences. The collected video sequences and one public benchmark database are used for evaluation. In a third experiment we test the performance on textureless videos. We have a real-world application that demands the use of a near-infrared camera. The face tracker is used to extract head pose for human-computer interaction. We present tracking results of the proposed hybrid tracker in this challenging setting.

The proposed tracker, and the existing state-of-the-art tracking algorithms are evaluated and compared. The feature-based tracker is an implementation of [6]. The intensity-based and hybrid tracker are C++ implementations of the methods presented in section 2 and 3. The feature detector in the hybrid tracker is the SIFT detector [14]. For computational efficiency, a simplified SIFT detector is implemented; only a single octave is used for feature detection.

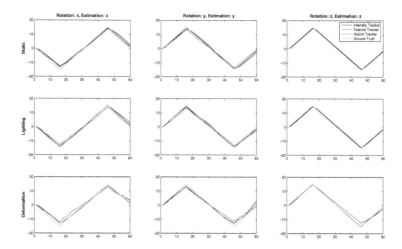

Fig. 3. The estimated pose of synthetic sequences. For the rows, **Top**: the static sequences. **Middle**: the lighting sequences. **Bottom**: the deformation sequences. For the columns, **Left**: the estimated rotation along x-axis for pure x-axis rotation. **Center**: the estimated rotation along y-axis for pure y-axis rotation. **Right**: the estimated rotation along z-axis for pure z-axis rotation. The angle is averaged over all subjects, and the unit is degree.

4.1 Evaluation with Synthetic Sequences

The evaluation sequences are generated by textured 3D face models of four subjects. These models are acquired by the FaceVision modeling system[15]. For each model, three independent sequences of images are rendered. The first consists of pure rotation about the X- (horizontal) axis, the second is rotation about the Y- (vertical) axis, and the third is rotation about the Z-axis. In each case, the sequences begin with the subject facing the camera and proceed to -15 degrees, then to 15 degrees, and return to neutral in increments of 1 degree. A total of 60 frames are acquired for each sequence. Image size is 640×480.

Synthetic perturbations are applied to the sequences to mimic variations occurring due to lighting and facial deformation changes. The following test configurations will be used to evaluate the tracking performance:

Static. In this case the sequences are rendered with constant ambient lighting. This removes all factors influencing the tracking accuracy.

Lighting. We explore the robustness of the trackers in the presence of subtle lighting changes. The models are rendered with a single directional light source.

Deformation. We explore the robustness of the tracker in response to facial deformation. A synthetic muscle system is used to deform the face mesh over the course of the sequence. The muscles are contracted at a constant rate over the duration of the sequence, inducing deformation in the mouth and eyebrow region (two high texture areas on the face).

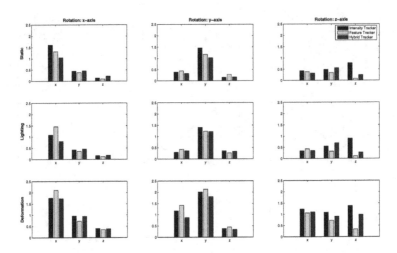

Fig. 4. The averaged error of synthetic sequences. For the rows, **Top**: the static sequences. **Middle**: the lighting sequences. **Bottom**: the deformation sequences. For the columns, **Left**: rotation around x-axis sequences. **Center**: rotation around y-axis sequences. **Right**: rotation around z-axis sequences. Each figure plots the averaged error per frame for x-, y-, and z-axis angle.

Figure 2 shows some examples from the synthetic sequences. The faces in the rendered sequences have a large amount of surface texture and are therefore amenable to feature based tracking.

The proposed hybrid tracker, the intensity- and feature-based tracker are evaluated. All trackers use the precise 3D face model to rule out the effect of model misalignment. Figure 3 shows the averaged estimated pose compared to the ground truth, and figure 4 shows the averaged error per frame. This error measures the absolute difference between the estimated angle and the true angle. In this evaluation, the averaged speed of the proposed tracker is 30 frame-per-second (FPS) on a normal desktop with one Intel XEON 2.4GHz processor.

From this evaluation, we can see that these three trackers are all comparable. In most cases, the hybrid tracker is consistently better than the other two, especially on the rotation axis. In some cases, the hybrid tracker is worse than the other two, but the difference is marginal and not statistically significant.

Static. All trackers perform very well, despite the different optimization functionals.

Lighting. The result is somewhat unintuitive, as we would expect the intensity-based tracker's performance to degrade. However, the performance difference is very marginal, since the points are weighted high in high gradient regions.

Deformation. All trackers perform worse than the optimal cases, but the accuracy is still acceptable. From figure 3, as deformation increases with time the accuracy of all methods declines. The intensity-based method is only slightly worse than the feature-based method, since the usage of the region-based difference compensates for the outliers and improves the robustness.

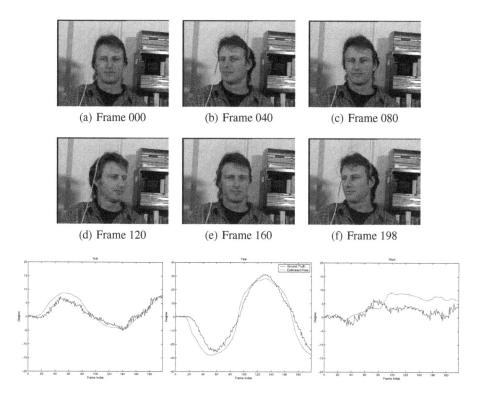

(a) Frame 000   (b) Frame 040   (c) Frame 080

(d) Frame 120   (e) Frame 160   (f) Frame 198

Fig. 5. Evaluation on the BU database. The top rows show some examples from the tracker and the last row show the estimated roll, yaw, and pitch compared with the ground truth from magnetic tracker. The result is for the "jam5.avi" sequence in the uniform lighting class of the BU database.

4.2   Evaluation with Real Sequences

The proposed tracker is also evaluated with many real sequences. One problem of evaluating with real sequences is the lack of ground truth. Only "estimated ground truth" is available. In the literature, several methods are used to estimate the ground truth, such as with a magnetic tracker or off-line bundle adjustment. We perform the evaluation with two different sets of sequences. One is collected by in our lab, and the other is from the Boston University database [4].

The BU database contains 2 sets of sequences: uniform lighting and varying lighting. The uniform lighting class includes 5 subjects, totalling 45 sequences. Figure 5 shows the tracking result of the "jam5.avi" sequence in the uniform lighting class. Overall, the estimated pose is close to ground truth, despite the fact that there is some jitter from the magnetic tracker.

Our sequence is captured in an indoor environment. The ground truth is estimated by commercial bundle adjustment software[16]. These sequences contain large rotations with the maximum angle near 40 degree. The hybrid tracker tracks the 3D pose reliably. Figure 6 shows the tracking result of one sequence.

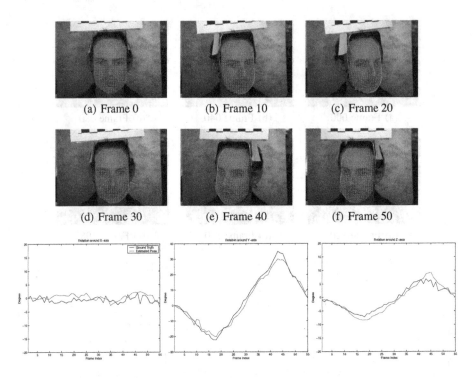

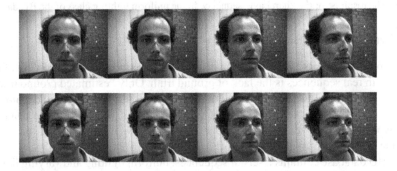

Fig. 6. The estimated rotation around x-, y-, and z-axis of our sequences. The top rows show some result of tracked sequences. The bottom row is the estimated rotation.

Fig. 7. Comparison of intensity-based tracker to hybrid tracker. The top row is the intensity tracker and the bottom is the hybrid tracker for the same sequence. The intensity-based tracker is more sensitive to the strong reflection.

Figure 7 shows the comparison of the hybrid tracker to the intensity-based tracker in a strong reflection case. As shown in the figure, the drift of intensity-based tracker is larger than the hybrid tracker.

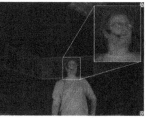

Fig. 8. left Theater environment for head tracking application. Subject is in nearly complete darkness except for the illumination from the screen. Image courtesy of USC's Institute for Creative Technologies. **right** Images from high resolution IR camera placed below the screen.

4.3   Infrared Sequences and Application

Infrared (IR) images are commonly used in vision applications in environments where visible light is either non-existent, highly variable, or difficult to control. Our test sequences are recorded in a dark, theater-like interactive virtual simulation training environment. In this environment, the only visible light comes from the reflection of a projector image off a cylindrical screen. This illumination is generally insufficient for a visible light camera and/or is highly variable. The tracker estimates the head pose, indicating user's attention and is used in a multi-modal HCI application. The theater environment and sample IR video frames are shown in figure 8. Ground truth is not available for this data, therefore only qualitative evaluation is made.

IR light is scattered more readily under the surface of the skin than visible light. Micro-texture on the face is therefore lost (especially at lower resolution), making identification of stable features more difficult and error prone. Due to varying absorption properties in different locations of the face, however, low frequency color variations will persist which satisfy the brightness constraint.

Figure 9 shows the tracking results in this environment. It shows multiple frames across a several minute sequence. The video is recorded at 15 FPS and its frame size is 1024×768. In most cases, the face size is around 110×110. The subject's head moves in both translation and rotation. There are also some mild expression changes (mouth open and close), and strong reflection at some frames. In this experiment, the user is assumed to begin in a frontal view. The tracker uses only one keyframe, the first frame. No off-line training is involved. The proposed hybrid tracker reliably tracks the pose in real-time with large head motion, while the feature-based tracker loses track completely after only 3 frames. Probing deeper we see that when feature-based tracker is lost, only a few features (1-4) are reliably matched on each frame. This exemplifies the problem with feature-based methods on low texture images.

Another interesting observation is related to error accumulation. In figure 9, the center column shows a frame with strong reflection coming from the subject's glasses. At that frame, the tracking accuracy degrades, due to the insufficient number of the features matched in this environment. However, after the reflection disappears,

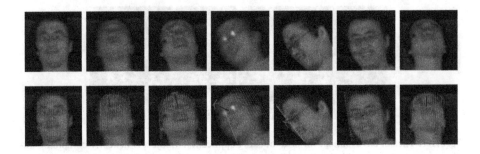

Fig. 9. The top row shows some example frames and the bottom row shows the estimation of the proposed tracker. The arrow indicates the direction that the user is facing. The feature-based tracker fails completely in only 3 frames.

the tracker recovers. This demonstrates how the use of keyframes prevents error accumulation.

5   Conclusions

We have proposed a hybrid tracking algorithm for robust real-time 3D face tracking. Built on a nonlinear optimization framework, the tracker seamlessly integrates intensity information and feature correspondence for 3D tracking. To improve the robustness, we have adopted an m-estimator type scheme for optimization. Patch-based differencing has been used to define the objective function. The inverse compositional algorithm is presented to solve this problem efficiently. The proposed tracker tracks the 3D head pose reliably in various environments. An extensively empirical validation and comparison with state-of-the-art trackers conclusively demonstrates this.

In the future, we plan to use this tracker in several applications. One such application is for HCI, such as in the theater environment presented in section 4.3. The challenge here is stability on very long sequences. We have applied the on-line keyframe generation technique to improve the stability, but the remaining issue is the reliability of the generated keyframe. The generated keyframe should be updated as the tracker gathers more information about the subject's face. Another problem is re-initialization. Expression analysis on the moving head is another future direction. The current tracker has been shown to be robust under moderate facial deformation, thus has the potential for facial gesture analysis. Combining with a deformable model may improve the tracking accuracy and extend the ability to track non-rigid facial features. Other applications include pose estimation for 3D face reconstruction.

Acknowledgements

This research was supported by a grant from the Institute for Creative Technologies.

References

1. Fidaleo, D., Medioni, G., Fua, P., Lepetit, V.: An investigation of model bias in 3d face tracking. In: IEEE International Workshop on Analysis and Modeling of Faces and Gestures, IEEE Computer Society Press, Los Alamitos (2005)
2. Black, M.J., Yacoob, Y.: Recognizing facial expressions in image sequences using local parameterized models of image motion. IJCV 25(1), 23–48 (1997)
3. Basu, S., Essa, I., Pentland, A.: Motion regularization for model-based head tracking. In: ICPR 1996, vol. 3, pp. 611–616 (1996)
4. Cascia, M.L., Sclaroff, S., Athitsos, V.: Fast, reliable head tracking under varying illumination: An approach based on registration of texture-mapped 3d models. PAMI 22(4), 322–336 (2000)
5. Xiao, J., Moriyama, T., Kanade, T., Cohn, J.: Robust full-motion recovery of head by dynamic templates and re-registration techniques. Internal Journal of Imaging Systems and Technology 13, 85–94 (2003)
6. Vacchetti, L., Lepetit, V., Fua, P.: Stable real-time 3d tracking using online and offline information. PAMI 26(10), 1385–1391 (2004)
7. Shan, Y., Liu, Z., Zhang, Z.: Model-based bundle adjustment with application to face modeling. In: ICCV 2001, vol. 2, pp. 644–651 (2001)
8. Schodl, A., Haro, A., Essa, I.: Head tracking using a textured polygonal model. In: Proceedings of Perceptual User Interfaces Workshop (held in Conjunction with ACM UIST 1998), ACM Press, New York (1998)
9. DeCarlo, D., Metaxas, D.: The integration of optical flow and deformable models with applications to human face shape and motion estimation. In: CVPR 1996, pp. 231–238 (1996)
10. Lu, L., Dai, X., Hager, G.: Efficient particle filtering using ransac with application to 3d face tracking. IVC 24(6), 581–592 (2006)
11. Baker, S., Matthews, I.: Lucas-kanade 20 years on: A unifying framework. IJCV 56(3), 221–255 (2004)
12. Baker, S., Patil, R., Cheung, K.M., Matthews, I.: Lucas-kanade 20 years on: Part 5. Technical Report CMU-RI-TR-04-64, Robotics Institute, Carnegie Mellon University, Pittsburgh, PA (November 2004)
13. Huber, P.J.: Robust Statistics. Wiley, New York (1981)
14. Lowe, D.G.: Distinctive image features from scale-invariant keypoints. IJCV 60(2), 91–110 (2004)
15. FaceVision200: Geometrix, http://www.geometrix.com
16. Photomodeler: http://www.photomodeler.com

Model-Assisted 3D Face Reconstruction from Video

Douglas Fidaleo and Gérard Medioni

Institute for Robotics and Intelligent Systems
University of Southern California
dfidaleo@gmail.com, medioni@usc.edu

Abstract. This paper describes a model-assisted system for reconstruction of 3D faces from a single consumer quality camera using a structure from motion approach. Typical multi-view stereo approaches use the motion of a sparse set of features to compute camera pose followed by a dense matching step to compute the final object structure. Accurate pose estimation depends upon precise identification and matching of feature points between images, but due to lack of texture on large areas of the face, matching is prone to errors.

To deal with outliers in both the sparse and dense matching stages, previous work either relies on a strong prior model for face geometry or imposes restrictions on the camera motion. Strong prior models result in a serious compromise in final reconstruction quality and typically bear a signature resemblance to a generic or mean face. Model-based techniques, while giving the appearance of face detail, in fact carry this detail over from the model prior. Face features such as beards, moles, and other characteristic geometry are lost. Motion restrictions such as allowing only pure rotation are nearly impossible to satisfy by the end user, especially with a handheld camera.

We significantly improve the robustness and flexibility of existing monocular face reconstruction techniques by introducing a deformable generic face model only at the pose estimation, face segmentation, and preprocessing stages. To preserve data fidelity in the final reconstruction, this generic model is discarded completely and dense matching outliers are removed using tensor voting: a purely data-driven technique. Results are shown from a complete end to end system.

1 Introduction

3D face models are important for a wide array of applications including surveillance, computer gaming, military simulation, virtual teleconferencing/chat, and surgical simulation. Most existing techniques for face reconstruction require special hardware or multiple cameras to create faces which prevents wide-spread adoption. This is unfortunate, as the rapidly increasing quality of consumer digital cameras has reduced the need for such specialized equipment for high quality reconstruction of faces.

S.K. Zhou et al. (Eds.): AMFG 2007, LNCS 4778, pp. 124–138, 2007.

The goal of this work is to reconstruct high accuracy 3D geometry of human faces from 2D video sequences acquired from a single, consumer quality, monocular, video camera. Performing reconstruction from a single camera enables leveraging of existing ubiquitous surveillance and web camera infrastructure for security and entertainment purposes.

Structure from motion has been used in single camera architectural and terrain modeling with great success [1]. These domains tend to have many distinguishable features that simplify the pose estimation and dense reconstruction phases. Reconstruction of faces from images is challenging as the face has very little texture outside of the eye, eyebrow, and mouth region. The image may be corrupted by noise, shadows, or other environmental aberrations which, combined with the lack of texture, makes it difficult to identify precise feature points required for accurate pose estimation. Inaccuracies in pose estimation translate into geometric distortions and noise.

Existing *model-based* work on single camera face reconstruction utilizes very strong prior knowledge of the structure and appearance of faces to constrain the reconstruction [2][3][4][5][6]. However, by imposing these constraints, these methods do not capture the subtle details present in the original face that are critical for recognition. *Data-driven* approaches can capture more subtle details from faces by disregarding strong face model constraints and relying strictly on the observed data [7][1]. However, rejecting a regularizing model can be dangerous due to more prevalent outliers on faces with limited texture.

It turns out that the use of a generic model for face reconstruction is not always bad, as long as it is used at the appropriate points in the reconstruction process.

We make two significant contributions to face reconstruction literature. First, it was observed in [8][9] that introduction of prior knowledge of the face can significantly improve the stability and accuracy of face pose estimation. We use this knowledge by incorporating the results of a model-based face tracker into the pose estimation stage. To prevent bias in the final face geometry, and to allow for reconstruction of face features such as beards that are not in the model prior, this model is discarded after pose estimation. Second, to deal with outliers in the dense reconstruction phase, we use tensor voting to perform model-free outlier rejection. Both of these contributions result in significant improvement of face reconstruction generality and robustness over existing methods.

This paper describes the entire end-to-end reconstruction system. It should be noted that, while this paper focuses on faces, the technique could be easily extended to reconstruction of other textured surfaces for which a rough initial estimate of the object's structure is available.

2   Previous Work

Several active and passive techniques exist for creating 3D faces. The majority of past work has required the use of specialized hardware, e.g. laser range finders, stereo camera rigs, or structured light projectors. These methods can achieve outstanding accuracy but the hardware requirement prevents use with existing imaging infrastructure such as consumer digital cameras and surveillance cameras. In this work we are only interested in reconstruction methods from a single camera.

Two categories of single camera reconstruction methods exist: data-driven and model-based. Data driven methods are largely based on textbook structure from motion techniques [10]. An example of such an approach is the body of work by Pollefeys et. al. for reconstruction of architectural scenes from a single moving camera. In [1] camera pose is estimated using self calibration on a sparse set of points matched between local image pairs. Following camera estimation and image rectification, dense feature matching is performed to compute a dense disparity map which may be triangulated and textured using image intensity information. Very nice results are achieved with architectural objects having large amounts of surface texture. The direct application of this approach to faces is challenging as faces have large areas of relatively uniform texture and are prone to highlights. This can result in large amounts of noise due to uncertainty in the matching process.

Pesenti et. al. use a similar framework for reconstruction applied to faces [7]. Epipolar geometry estimation and self calibration in Pollefeys' work is replaced with bundle adjustment. The initial bundle configuration is derived from a simplified motion model; assuming the head undergoes pure rotation in a given triplet of frames.

A common approach to deal with geometry and pose uncertainty is to introduce very strong prior models of the face. Fua uses bundle adjustment and a strong prior to model heads [5]. The prior model is tightly integrated with both pose estimation and modeling and hence the final reconstruction, while visually appealing, cannot deviate far from the original model. Morphable models [3] assume the face is a linear combination of a set of basis face shapes and appearance. The reconstruction process involves a minimization of the image reconstruction error over basis vector weights as well as camera and lighting parameters. Similarly, work by Shan et.al. parameterizes the face by a generic model and a set of face "metrics" or deformation parameters [4]. DeCarlo et.al. use optical flow and a component-wise deformable decomposition of the face to regularize feature motion and model the face [2].

By design, these approaches are limited by the constructed parameter space. Though modeling can be performed from single images real faces have variations not within the space defined by the basis shapes, resulting in reconstructions that bear a signature resemblance to a generic (or mean) face. Optimization is performed using an image based error functional and can be very slow to converge. To constrain the search space fewer basis shapes are used, consequently the resulting reconstructions do not capture the subtle details present in the original face. Recently in work by Ilic et. al., the silhouettes from multiple views have been integrated with implicit surfaces to bias a Morphable Model solution towards a more faithful reconstruction [11].

The approach most similar to ours uses a multi-view stereo approach for monocular reconstruction of faces [7]. A set of individual face scans is derived from each pair of images in a video sequence of a user rotating his head. These scans are merged into a single point cloud which is processed for outliers and triangulated to form a final dense mesh. The quality of the final mesh depends on the proper alignment of the individual scans, and hence, the proper estimation of the camera poses in the images.

Pose estimation is dependent on precise feature matching between images. Errors in feature matching propagate to tracking and ultimately to pose and reconstruction errors. Pesenti et.al. determine feature candidates on each face image with an interest operator [12] and match points with maximum correlation. However, most faces have very little texture in the cheek and forehead regions. Hence, unconstrained correlation produces egregious outliers which results in extremely poor pose estimation and reconstruction. To remove outliers and initialize the bundle adjuster, Pesenti uses RANSAC and a pure rigid rotation motion model. While this removes gross outliers, foreshortening effects and lack of texture will still produce erroneous matches that are consistent with the motion model, resulting in poor pose estimation and reconstruction. Furthermore, head motion is almost never purely rotational. Neglecting translation in the motion model imposes serious constraints on the kinds of input sequences that can be reliably reconstructed.

Undoubtedly, there are cases where these errors are small and the resulting reconstruction is reasonable (as shown in the paper), however it is suspected due to the fact that there was no continuation of that work in either journal or conference publication, that these are isolated cases and in general the method fails.

Our work relaxes the constraints imposed in [7] by borrowing principals from the model-based literature. A strong face model is used to dramatically enhance pose accuracy without biasing the geometry solution. Our approach also enables the use of still images with wider baselines for reconstruction. Outliers in dense matching are handled with tensor voting, a model free surface extraction technique, which only becomes possible after accurate pose estimation.

Fig. 1. The problem of reconstructing a single rigid object (static or mobile) with a single camera (static or mobile) can be equivalently modeled as reconstruction from multiple static cameras with the same relative external coordinate system

3   Reconstruction Overview

Given a sequence of images of the face $I = \{I_0, I_1 ... I_k\}$ in different poses our goal is to transform this sequence into an accurate textured 3D model M. Though not required, for simplicity we will assume that the subject's face is frontal in frame I_0, and that indices k are ordered in time.

It is assumed that the subject remains expressionless through the duration of the sequence, providing a rigid surface for reconstruction. Given these parameters and constraints, the "moving head - static camera" problem can be modeled equivalently as an array of multiple static cameras placed around a static object, each acquiring a different view of the face as shown in figure 1.

Figure 2 shows a diagram of the reconstruction process described in detail in this document. Novel contributions are highlighted. We begin with an input video sequence of a subject. It is presumed that multiple views of the subject's head are present in the sequence: as much coverage as desired for the final reconstruction. We utilize a 3D face tracking algorithm to derive an initial head pose estimate and mask for the face. Optimal views are selected from the set of images and passed to a sparse feature tracking module. Sparse feature tracking produces a set of feature correspondences for each successive image pair. Global optimization is performed over the entire sequence of feature points and cameras to refine the tracking camera estimate and compute the 3D structure at the sparse feature locations.

The optimized camera positions are used to rectify pairs of images, constraining the search space for corresponding feature points to a horizontal scanline in the paired image. Dense feature matching is performed across pairs and correspondences are reconstructed by triangulation using the optimized camera poses resulting in a dense 3D point cloud. Point clouds corresponding to individual pairs are merged into a single cloud and outliers are removed.

A connected surface is fit to the final cleaned point cloud and the face texture is acquired from a frontal image. The final result is a clean 3D mesh that is ready to be used for animation, recognition, or rendering.

4   Model-Based Pose Estimation

In the interest of remaining purely data-driven, Pesenti et.al. assume the head in the video sequence undergoes pure rotation and apply a simple motion constraint at the sparse feature matching stage. These constraints are necessary to achieve a decent pose estimate to initialize the bundle adjustment algorithm. Unfortunately, these restrictions are much too prohibitive for a robust system.

We make the observation that we can reap the benefits of a geometric model at the pose estimation stage without biasing the shape at the final reconstruction stage. Therefore, in our system, the initial pose estimate is obtained from the 3D head tracker developed by Vacchetti et.al. [9]. This tracker relies heavily on an approximate generic model of the subject's face.

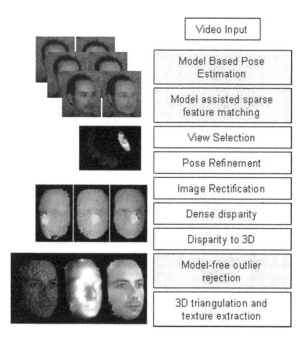

Fig. 2. Overview of the reconstruction system presented in this paper. Highlighted modules are novel contributions.

4.1 Tracking

This section presents a brief overview of the tracking approach, but the reader is referred to the original paper [9] for details.

In the initial frame I_0 a 3D face model is manually aligned to the face. This establishes a reference keyframe consisting of a set of 2d feature locations detected on the face with a Harris corner detector and their 3D positions estimated by back-projecting onto the model. The keyframe accuracy is dependent on both the model alignment in the keyframe image, as well as the geometric structure of the tracking mesh.

As the subject rotates her head, there may be several newly detected feature points not present in any keyframe that are useful to determine inter-frame motion. These points are matched to patches in the previous frame and combined with keyframe points for pose estimation.

The current head pose estimate for I_t serves as the starting point for a local bundle adjustment. Classical bundle adjustment is typically a time consuming process, even when a reasonable estimate of camera and 3D parameters is provided. However, by constraining the 3D points to lie on the surface of the tracking model, the method is modified to run in real-time without substantial sacrifice in accuracy. When an accurate 3D model of the tracked object is used, reported accuracy approaches that of commercial batch processing bundle adjustment packages requiring several minutes per frame.

4.2   Model-Assisted Sparse Feature Matching

We use the result of the model-based tracker to improve the number and accuracy of sparse feature points used in the bundle adjustment stage. Indeed, the accuracy of sparse feature matching is critical as errors in feature matching will propagate into the bundle solution. In general, this problem is difficult, as local image patches may resemble more than one patch in another image, especially in large textureless areas. Our approach utilizes salient feature points and model constraints to converge on a set of accurate feature matches.

Extraction of the feature matches is divided into 2 parts: *feature matching* and *feature chaining*.

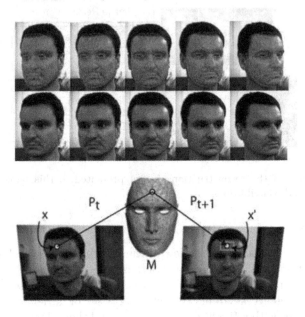

Fig. 3. (top) Model-based face tracking. (bottom) Model assisted feature matching.

Feature matching is performed on consecutive pairs of images I_t and I_{t+1}. Feature points are first detected in each image using a Harris corner detector. A sample window is extracted at the feature location x. The predicted match location of x in the corresponding frame is computed using the transfer function

$$x' = T(x, P_t, P_{t+1}, X) \tag{1}$$

This function is illustrated in Figure 3. T uses P_t to back-project x to the the 3D generic model M. The corresponding 3D point X is then projected to the I_{t+1} using P_{t+1}. This new 2D location x' is the predicted feature location. Note that if we were to use this location as the feature match, the resulting pose estimate would be identical to the tracking estimate, when we know to be imprecise.

Instead, a search area is defined around the predicted location x'. In this area, we find the best correspondence candidate c via normalized cross correlation.

If the match score is below a threshold τ, the match is rejected. In practice we set $\tau = .9$ and the search area to be $21x21$ to ensure only high quality correspondences. Features are chained across image pairs.

4.3   View Selection

The bundle adjustment process is sensitive to the angular baseline between images as well as the number of matched feature points in each frame. The baseline between virtual camera locations is directly related to the uncertainty of the reconstruction estimate [10]. A narrow baseline increases measurement uncertainty but ensures visibility of points in multiple images. A wide baseline decreases measurement uncertainty but increases the chances that a point is occluded.

In practice, we select an angular baseline between 8 and 15 degrees and select frames with at least 6 points matched across a minimum of 3 frames (determined experimentally).

4.4   Bundle Adjustment and Bundle Surface Extraction

The tracker provides a rough estimate of the head pose. However, to accommodate the real-time constraint, only current, previous, and key frames are used in the optimization. This narrow view range causes misalignment between pairs of images at wider baselines and hence distortion in the reconstruction. We therefore introduce an offline pose estimation stage that considers the full set of views.

Given the 2D feature chains identified in section 4.2 we perform a global bundle adjustment to refine the camera poses using the tracking estimate as a starting point for the optimization [13].

The 3D point cloud resulting from bundle adjustment is a coarse estimate of the structure of the subject's face. We create an interpolated version of this surface to filter the dense face reconstruction using scattered data interpolation via radial basis functions [14]. We refer to the resulting interpolated model as the *bundle surface*.

The refined camera poses are used to rectify the images to assist in the dense feature matching stage. We perform rectification using standard computer vision techniques [10].

5   Model-Assisted Face Segmentation

Using the model based face tracker, we do not require the face to be in the foreground as in [7]. The region under the tracking model provides a good approximation of the face area and is used to define a binary reconstruction mask where white pixels are to be reconstructed and black omitted. The initial mask is defined by the entire area under the tracking model as shown.

5.1   Skin Mask

Due to alignment problems, the reconstruction mask derived from the tracking model may not cover the entire face region. Too little coverage may be sufficient for recognition applications, however for animation a complete head model is generally required. If the mask is too large, non-face pixels may interfere with the reconstruction process.

We refine the initial segmentation by segmenting the skin region belonging to the face; learning the skin color distribution and classifying skin pixels.

We make the basic assumption that skin color is largely constant over the face with most variations occuring due to lighting. The skin color sample is defined by the area under the tracking mask. Separation of color from illumination is difficult in the standard RGB space. We therefore convert the image window to HSV space, and discard all but the hue component. The majority of the image under the face rectangle is skin and therefore the strongest mode of a histogram plot of the hue data will belong to the skin color.

A Gaussian model is fit to the data. Each pixel in the image is then classified as skin/non-skin with respect to this model using a fixed threshold. The binary face mask is augmented with new skin pixels.

This process generally performs quite well, but may fail if the image contains multiple overlapping faces or areas with color distributions resembling skin. In this case, the initial reconstruction mask may be used.

5.2   Highlight Removal

Specular highlights on the face cause problems in the reconstruction. The center of the highlights saturate and hence obscure any texture in the area. As the face rotates, the highlights shift, and cause errors in matching along the highlight border. Saturated areas can be detected by analyzing the variance of a window of pixels. If the variance is below a threshold, this window is removed from the reconstruction mask M. To deal with highlight boundaries which may not saturate, the highlight mask is dilated.

5.3   View Angle Filtering

Due to foreshortening effects on face texture, surfaces nearly orthogonal to the camera view ray will have greater matching uncertainty. We use the normal map derived from the tracking model to compute this angle and reject points whose approximated normal is greater than 50 degrees from the view ray. Each mask is combined to produce the final reconstruction mask as shown in Figure 4.

6   Model-Free Dense Reconstruction

6.1   Dense Feature Matching

Dense feature matching determines a dense set of corresponding points in each pair of rectified images. The matching is restricted to the area covered by the

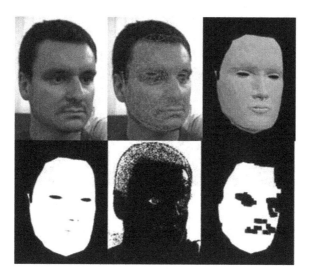

Fig. 4. (top) Input image, aligned tracking mask, normal map. (bottom) Initial reconstruction mask, highlight mask, and final combined reconstruction mask.

reconstruction mask from Section 5. For each pixel in one image, a template is extracted using a fixed window size. This template is matched along the corresponding epipolar line in the paired image. A minimum correlation threshold and restricted disparity range suitable for faces is used to reduce the number of spurious matches. Multiple candidate matches can be retained, but locations with flat correlation plots (no obvious peak) are rejected, as this is an indicator of a textureless, or possibly occluded region.

The result of the matching process is a disparity volume where each (x,y,d) value maps a pixel (x,y) in one rectified image to a pixel (x+d,y) in the paired image.

6.2 3D from Disparity

The known camera poses allow us to convert each disparity value to a true 3D point by triangulation. Each disparity pixel is transformed to the original image space using the inverse of the rectifying transform. The 3D location of each match is given by the intersection of the rays passing through the camera optical centers and the corresponding feature matches in the image planes. In practice, due to imperfect feature matching and camera estimates, these lines will not intersect exactly. We therefore compute the 3D point that minimizes the orthogonal distance to the two rays [10].

6.3 Outlier Rejection

Tensor Voting. Errors in feature matching result in considerable reconstruction noise. If the noise is uncorrelated within and between views, it will appear

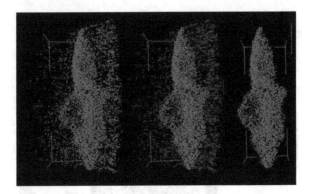

Fig. 5. Tensor Voting Outlier rejection. (left) original points. (middle) Outliers shown in red. (right) 3D points after tensor voting outlier rejection.

as sparse, high frequency variations in the 3D structure. Correct matches will, however, be correlated between views due to the smoothness and continuity of face structure. We use tensor voting to uncover this correlation structure and reject outliers.

Tensor voting is a technique used to uncover the intrinsic dimensionality of data in arbitrary dimensional spaces. Data points share information with their neighbors encoding their saliency in a given dimension. In 3D tensor voting each 3D point can be encoded as a ball tensor (no orientation preference) or stick tensor (if normal information at the point is available). In the voting process, orientation and structural saliency information (dimensionality) are shared with neighboring points. Neighbors with similar structure reinforce each other with the amount of structural reinforcement defined by the initial structural saliency.

When the individual point clouds are integrated, points on face surface are correlated and will reinforce each other during tensor voting. Incorrect matches due to sensor noise, lack of texture, or other artifacts will result in uncorrelated noise in the 3d structure. These points will have very low surface saliency and are removed by simple thresholding. This approach is similar to that of Mordohai et. al. for denoising of disparity maps [15].

In practice, a good initial estimate of point normals is preferred to blindly encoding points as ball tensors. We therefore use the bundle surface to approximate the point normals. Fixing the normal as the first eigenvector in a 3x3 eigensystem, the remaining basis vectors are computed using singular value decomposition (SVD). Initial surface saliency (defined by the difference in magnitude of the first two eigenvectors) is set uniformly for all points initially.

As the 3D from the bundle adjustment is a very accurate sparse estimate of the face structure, these points are added to the tensor voting point set with boosted surface saliency.

After two passes of tensor voting, points with low surface saliency are removed, leaving a dense cloud of points distributed across the surface of the face as shown in Figure 5.

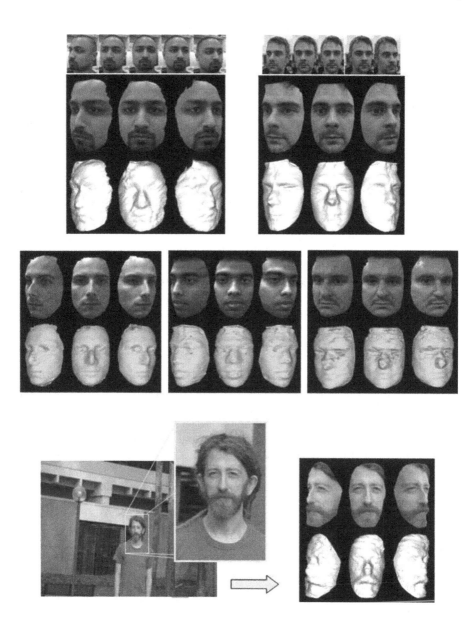

Fig. 6. Reconstruction results. (top) Reconstruction from 5 digital still images shown above models. (middle) Reconstruction from video sequence. (bottom) Reconstruction outdoors at a distance of 15 feet.

Tensor voting is computationally intensive in software. The computation time grows nearly linearly with point set size, assuming a local voting field. This implies that each reconstruction pair adds a constant amount of computational effort. With an average cost of 30 sec. per pair (reconstructing 50k points) this cost can become prohibitive for more interactive applications.

If constant computation time is desired, the final point cloud may be quantized first by voxelizing the set then reducing each voxel to a single point. Tensor voting may then be performed on the quantized set. The speed and accuracy tradeoff may be adjusted by altering the quantization resolution. In practice we break the face volume into 10^6 voxels and take the mean value for each voxel. This results in a set of < 20k 3D points which can be processed by the tensor voting module in less than 15 seconds.

Voxel filtering. Tensor voting removes uncorrelated outliers, however there are many cases where correlated artifacts can arise such as on the boundary of the face or shifting highlights. The bundle surface provides a strong constraint on the allowable 3D computed in the dense reconstruction; the computed structure should not deviate far from the bundle derived structure. This structure is used to filter the data by voxelizing the interpolated bundle structure and rejecting data at a predefined distance from the bundle voxels. It should be noted that this is not the same as using a generic model constraint, as the bundle structure can be considered optimal based on the observed data.

7   Meshing

It is difficult to visualize the reconstruction results from the point clouds alone, therefore the 3D point cloud is converted to a textured 3D mesh using a standard graphics technique. The point cloud is projected to the surface of a cylinder whose axis is aligned with the axis passing through the center of the head with the cylinder axis defined by the tracking model.. The points are triangulated in the 2D cylindrical space. Texture is acquired by projecting the resulting triangles to the image using the optimized camera pose. High frequency noise in the mesh is eliminated using a volume preserving diffusion technique by Desbrun et.al. [16].

8   Results

Figure 6 shows results from the reconstruction system. We demonstrate the robustness and flexibility of the system in different environments using different camera hardware. All images used for reconstruction are 640x480 pixels. Models in the center row were taken in a standard office environment at a distance of roughly 3 feet using a PointGrey Dragonfly video camera. Our system is not limited to video sequences. The model at the top left was created using a set of 6 still images from a Canon Powershot S300 digital camera in a similar environment. We are also not limited to indoor sequences with short focal lengths. The model at the bottom was created outdoors at a distance of 15 feet. Note the ability to capture the prominent facial hair on the subject. Model based methods completely fail in such cases as these personalized variations are difficult to embed in the model space.

9   Conclusion

We have demonstrated a robust system for reconstruction of faces from a single camera. We make a fundamental observation that introduction of prior face knowledge at the pose estimation stage can significantly improve reconstruction results without biasing the geometry solution towards this prior. Performing outlier rejection using tensor voting, a purely data driven method, preserves the subtle details present in the subject's face. The use of the model based face tracker relaxes the constraints on the subject's motion and enables the use of both video sequences with small angular baseline between images, as well as a set of still images with significantly larger baselines.

References

1. Pollefeys, M., Gool, L.V., Vergauwen, M., Verbiest, F., Cornelis, K., Tops, J., Koch, R.: Visual modeling with a hand-held camera. International Journal of Computer Vision 59, 207–232 (2004)
2. DeCarlo, D., Metaxas, D.: The integration of optical flow and deformable models with applications to human face shape and motion estimation (1996)
3. Blanz, V., Vetter, T.: A morphable model for the synthesis of 3D faces. In: Rockwood, A. (ed.) Siggraph 1999, Computer Graphics Proceedings, pp. 187–194. Addison Wesley Longman, Los Angeles (1999)
4. Shan, Y., Liu, Z., Zhang, Z.: Model-based bundle adjustment with application to face modeling. In: International Conference on Computer Vision, Vancouver, Canada (2001)
5. Fua, P.: Using model-driven bundle-adjustment to model heads from raw video sequences. In: Proceedings of the 7th International Conference on Computer Vision, Corfu, Greece, p. 4653 (1999)
6. Romdhani, S., Vetter, T.: Efficient, robust and accurate fitting of a 3d morphable model. In: ICCV 2003. Proceedings of the Ninth IEEE International Conference on Computer Vision, p. 59. IEEE Computer Society Press, Washington, DC, USA (2003)
7. Pesenti, B., Medioni, G.: Generation of a 3d face model from one camera. In: Proceedings of the 16th International Conference on Pattern Recognition, Quebec City, Quebec, Canada, pp. 667–671 (2002)
8. Fidaleo, D., Medioni, G., Fua, P., Lepetit, V.: An investigation of model bias in 3d face tracking. In: IEEE Analysis and Modeling of Faces and Gestures, pp. 125–139. IEEE Computer Society Press, Los Alamitos (2005)
9. Vacchetti, L., Lepetit, V., Fua, P.: Stable real-time 3d tracking using online and offline information. IEEE Trans. Pattern Anal. Mach. Intell. 26, 1385–1391 (2004)
10. Hartley, R., Zisserman, A.: Multiple View Geometry in Computer Vision. Cambridge University Press, Cambridge, UK (2000)
11. Ilic, S., Fua, P.: Implicit meshes for surface reconstruction. IEEE Transactions on Pattern Analysis and Machine Intelligence 28, 328–333 (2006)

12. Shapiro, L., Haralick, R.: Image matching - an interest operator. In: Computer and Robot Vision Volume II, pp. 341–343. Prentice-Hall, Englewood Cliffs (1992)
13. Lourakis, M., Argyros, A.: The design and implementation of a generic sparse bundle adjustment software package based on the levenberg-marquardt algorithm. Technical Report 340, Institute of Computer Science - FORTH, Heraklion, Crete, Greece (2004)
14. Powell, M.J.D.: Radial basis functions for multivariable interpolation: a review, 143–167 (1987)
15. Mordohai, P., Medioni, G.: Stereo using monocular cues within the tensor voting framework. IEEE Transactions on Pattern Analysis and Machine Intelligence 28, 968–982 (2006)
16. Desbrun, M., Meyer, M., Schröder, P., Barr, A.H.: Implicit fairing of irregular meshes using diffusion and curvature flow. In: ACM SIGGRAPH Proceedings, vol. 33, pp. 317–324. ACM Press, New York (1999)

Human Perambulation as a Self Calibrating Biometric

Michela Goffredo, Nicholas Spencer, Daniel Pearce, John N. Carter,
and Mark S. Nixon

ISIS, School of Electronics and Computer Science,
University of Southampton, SO17 1BJ, UK
mg2@ecs.soton.ac.uk

Abstract. This paper introduces a novel method of single camera gait recons-truction which is independent of the walking direction and of the camera parameters. Recognizing people by gait has unique advantages with respect to other biometric techniques: the identification of the walking subject is completely unobtrusive and the identification can be achieved at distance. Recently much research has been conducted into the recognition of fronto-parallel gait. The proposed method relies on the very nature of walking to achieve the independence from walking direction. Three major assumptions have been done: human gait is cyclic; the distances between the bone joints are invariant during the execution of the movement; and the articulated leg motion is approximately planar, since almost all of the perceived motion is contained within a single limb swing plane. The method has been tested on several subjects walking freely along six different directions in a small enclosed area. The results show that recognition can be achieved without calibration and without dependence on view direction. The obtained results are particularly encouraging for future system development and for its application in real surveillance scenarios.

Keywords: Human motion analysis, 3D modeling, Gait, Biometrics.

1 Introduction

Many biometrics require either a subject's cooperation or contact for data acquisition; vision-based systems usually require a chosen viewpoint. These methods cannot reliably recognize non cooperating individuals at a distance in the real world under changing environmental conditions. Gait, which concerns recognizing individuals by the way they walk, is a relatively new biometric without these disadvantages [1], [2]. There is a rich literature, including medical and psychological studies, indicating the potential for gait in personal identification [3], [4]. Moreover, early medical studies suggest that if all gait movements are considered then gait is unique [5].

There is a rich literature of various gait recognition techniques that can be broadly divided as model-based and model-free approaches. Model based approaches [6], [7] aim to derive the movement of the torso and/or the legs, recovering explicit features describing gait dynamics of joint angles. On the other hand, model-free approaches are mainly silhouette-based. The silhouette approaches [8], [9] characterize body movement by the statistics of the patterns produced by walking. These patterns

S.K. Zhou et al. (Eds.): AMFG 2007, LNCS 4778, pp. 139–153, 2007.
© Springer-Verlag Berlin Heidelberg 2007

capture both the static and dynamic properties of body shape. A rich variety of data has been collected for evaluation. The widely used and compared databases on gait recognition include: the University of Maryland's surveillance data [10]; the University of South Florida's outdoor data [11]; Carnegie Mellon University's multi-view indoor data [12]; and the University of Southampton's data [13]. The majority of methods and databases found in the literature thus concern a person walking in fronto-parallel [6], [7], [9] or the use of several digital cameras acquiring the movement [7], [8] and thus the knowledge of the calibration parameters.

It appears obvious that for biometric aims the recognition system must be invariant to subject's pose or be able to reconstruct the canonical fronto-parallel view of the gait motion. Recently, in fact, novel approaches on biometrics based on gait are oriented towards synthesizing fronto-parallel views by use of structure from motion, but require some information about camera calibration [14], [15]. Moreover, considering the recent applications of gait recognition in criminal investigation, like the case of the murderer of Swedish Foreign Minister Anna Lindh [16], usually there is no access to the camera and generally only the recorded video sequences are available [17], [18]. Therefore, view-point independent reconstruction of gait would have a major impact on the viability of gait-based biometrics and a system for achieving this purpose is particularly attractive.

This paper presents a new method to reconstruct gait motion from monocular image sequences by taking advantage of the constraints of articulated limb motions. No prior knowledge of the camera calibration is necessary and the limbs landmark points are extracted over all frames in the sequence by tracking reflective markers on subject's legs. This work is part of a wider project (Fig. 1) where the single view human identification based on gait will be completely markerless. Therefore, the aim of this paper is to propose a novel method for reconstructing the gait parameters independently from the view-point and the subject pose.

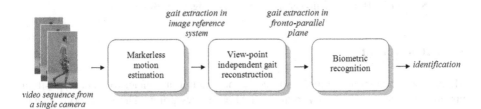

Fig. 1. Flow diagram of the overall project

2   Theory

Walking has been widely studied in medical research and biomechanics [19] and the characteristics of the gait cycle for subjects without any pathology are well-known. Each leg has two distinct periods: a stance phase, when the foot is in contact with the floor; and a swing phase, when the foot is off the floor moving forward to the next step. The time interval between successive instances of initial foot-to-floor contact 'heel strike' for the same foot is the gait cycle.

The proposed method for a pose invariant gait analysis is based on three main assumptions: the nature of human gait is cyclic; the distances between the bone joints are invariant during the execution of the movement; and the articulated leg motion is approximately planar, since almost all of the perceived motion is contained within a single limb swing plane.

Considering a subject walking along a straight line, the multiple periods of linear gait motion appear analogous to a single period viewed from many cameras related by linear translation. Following this rationale, the positions of the points of interest, i.e. the leg joints, lie in an auto-epipolar configuration consistent with the imaged motion direction. The epipole is thus estimated by computing the intersection of the set of lines formed by linking the correspondent points of interest in each phase of the gait cycle. In order to find these correspondences, the gait periodicity is calculated by applying the stereopsis transformation that maps the epipole e to the ideal point $[1,0,0]^T$ and then by computing the cost based on dot product between matching limb segment vectors.

After estimating the periodicity of gait, assuming linear velocity between consecutive frames, the set of points of interest are recomputed in order to lie on straight lines starting from the epipole. At first the set of points is mapped to the unit square $x_0 = K_n x$ with the matrix K_n. Similarly the epipole $e_0 = K_n e$ is re-normalized to the unit norm $\|e_0\| = 1$. Subsequently, the optimal points are found by estimating the positions $\bar{x}_i$ that lie on the epipolar line and that satisfies the condition

$$\bar{x}_i^T [e_0] \times \bar{x}_i = 0 \tag{1}$$

Therefore the back projected rays, formed from a set of optimal points, intersect in a single worldspace point: the epipole.

The back projection of all sets of points generates the cluster of 3D points for an assumed single period of reconstructed gait motion. The Direct Linear Transform, DLT [20], is thus used in order to triangulate each worldspace point X

$$([\bar{x}_k] \times P_k) \cdot X = 0 \tag{2}$$

with the set of camera projection matrices

$$P_k = [R_e^T | -k \cdot e_0] \tag{3}$$

where $\bar{x}_k$ is the image of the worldspace point X in the kth period image, R_e is the 3 by 3 rotation matrix that aligns the epipolar vector with the X (horizontal) axis, and k is an integer describing the periodicity of the subject's translation.

Considering the assumption that the articulated leg motion is approximately planar the 3D limb points can be reasonably fitted to two planes. Since the epipolar vector is aligned with the X axis, the ideal point $[1,0,0]^T$ do lie on each of the worldspace planes. Therefore, the pencil of planes that intersect this ideal point have the form $p = (0, v_2, v_3, v_4)^T$. Consequently the problem is reduced to finding two lines within the YZ plane cross section data.

After computing the mean $[y,z]^T$ of the point distribution, the translation $\mathbf{H_t}$ that maps this point to the origin is applied. The two cross section plane lines $l_1 = [v_2, v_3, v_4]^T$ and $l_2 = [v_2', v_3', v_4']^T$ are then achieved by orthogonal regression and then aligned parallel with the Y (vertical) axis by applying a rotation $\mathbf{H_r}$. The intersection point of the two lines is then called $\mathbf{u}$ and is given by the cross product between the two lines.

Consequently, the pair of transformed lines are mapped to $l_1' = \mathbf{H_r} l_1$ and the rotation matrix $\mathbf{H_r}$ and the perspective transformation $\mathbf{H_\alpha}$

$$\mathbf{H_\alpha} = \begin{pmatrix} 1 & 0 & 0 \\ 0 & 1 & 0 \\ \alpha & 0 & 1 \end{pmatrix} \tag{4}$$

are applied to the point $\mathbf{u'}$ in order to transform it to the ideal point $[1,0,0]^T$.

Since $\mathbf{u'}$ lies on the Y axis and has the form $[y,0,w]^T$, the transformation $\mathbf{H_\alpha u'}$ gives $\alpha = -w/y$ and the corresponding line mapping $\mathbf{H_\alpha l_i'}$ effectively zeros the first component of the two normal lines. Since the lines are parallels, they are normalized

$$l_1'' = (0,1,-c_1)^T \qquad l_2'' = (0,1,-c_2)^T \tag{5}$$

so that is it possible to find the point (c_1, c_2) of intersection with Z (depth) axis. A further similarity transform $\mathbf{H_s}$ that translates the midpoint $(c_2 + c_1)/2$ to the origin and scales in the Z direction to rectify the lines to the form $l = [0,1,\pm 1]^T$ is then applied.

The translation by ± 1 mapping the selected set of points onto the z=0 plane is then computed with the matrix $\mathbf{H_\beta}$. The combined set of transformations thus forms the limb plane transformation $\mathbf{H_v} = \mathbf{H_\beta} \mathbf{H_s} \mathbf{H_\alpha} \mathbf{H_r} \mathbf{H_t}$. In order to change the matrix order, a similar set of transformation is constructed:

$$\begin{aligned} \mathbf{H_v} &= \mathbf{H_\beta} \mathbf{H_\alpha} (\mathbf{H_\alpha^{-1}} \mathbf{H_s} \mathbf{H_\alpha}) \mathbf{H_r} \mathbf{H_t} \\ \mathbf{H_v} &= \mathbf{H_\beta} \mathbf{H_\alpha} \mathbf{H_s'} \mathbf{H_r} \mathbf{H_t} \end{aligned} \tag{6}$$

Therefore, the projection transform mapping the back projected points into the image can be decomposed as:

$$\bar{\mathbf{x}}(k) = \begin{bmatrix} \mathbf{R_e^T} \mathbf{I} - k \cdot \mathbf{e'} \end{bmatrix} \begin{pmatrix} 1 & 0 \\ 0 & \mathbf{H_v^{-1}} \end{pmatrix} \begin{pmatrix} 1 & 0 \\ 0 & \mathbf{H_v} \end{pmatrix} \mathbf{X} \tag{7}$$

where

$$\mathbf{H_v} = \begin{bmatrix} 1 & m_2 & m_3 & m_4 \\ 0 & 0 & 0 & 1 \end{bmatrix} \begin{pmatrix} 1 & 0 & 0 & 0 \\ 0 & 1 & 0 & 0 \\ 0 & 0 & 1 & -\beta \\ 0 & -\alpha & 0 & 1 \end{pmatrix} \tag{8}$$

The corresponding transformation of worldspace points $(u,v,0,w)^T$ into the image is given by

$$\overline{\mathbf{x}}' = \mathbf{H_p} \cdot (u,v,w)^T \tag{9}$$

where

$$\mathbf{H_p} = \begin{bmatrix} \mathbf{e}' & m_2' - \alpha \cdot (m_4' - k \cdot \mathbf{e}') & (m_4' - k \cdot \mathbf{e}') - \beta \cdot m_3' \end{bmatrix} \tag{10}$$

with

$$m_i' = \mathbf{R_e^T} m_i \qquad \mathbf{e}' = \mathbf{R_e^T}[1,0,0]^T \tag{11}$$

Finally the sets of optimal z=0 plane points is found by solution of the

$$\left(\mathbf{x}'_{k,\beta}\right) \times \mathbf{H_p}(k,\beta)\overline{\mathbf{w}} = 0 \tag{12}$$

for each point $\mathbf{w}$ in order to minimize the reprojection error.

Structure on the z=0 plane has been recovered up to an affine ambiguity $\mathbf{H_\mu}$ that maps the imaged circular points $(1,\mu \pm i\ \lambda,0)^T$ back to their canonical positions $(1,\pm i,0)^T$:

$$\mathbf{H_\mu} = \begin{pmatrix} 1 & 0 & 0 \\ -\dfrac{\mu}{\lambda} & \dfrac{1}{\lambda} & 0 \\ 0 & 0 & 1 \end{pmatrix} \tag{13}$$

For estimating the metric structure, the lengths of the articulated limbs is assumed to be known and constant over all the frames. Thus the squared distance between two points $\mathbf{x_0}$ and $\mathbf{x_1}$ can be written

$$d^2 = \Delta\mathbf{x}^T \Delta\mathbf{x} \tag{14}$$

where

$$\Delta\mathbf{x} = [u_1 - u_0, v_1 - v_0]^T \tag{15}$$

If $\Delta\mathbf{x_1}$ and $\Delta\mathbf{x_2}$ are the pose difference vectors for a limb segment at two consecutive frames, then the equal limb length constraint can be written

$$\Delta\mathbf{x_1^T}\mathbf{H^T}\mathbf{H}\Delta\mathbf{x_1} = \Delta\mathbf{x_2^T}\mathbf{H^T}\mathbf{H}\Delta\mathbf{x_2} \tag{16}$$

Therefore, writing $\Delta\mathbf{x_i} = [\delta x_i, \delta y_i]$ and the element of the matrix $\mathbf{M} = \mathbf{H^T}\mathbf{H}$ as $\mathbf{m} = [M_{11}, M_{12}, M_{22}]^T$, the equation is

$$\left| \delta x_1^2 - \delta x_2^2 \quad 2 \cdot \left(\delta x_1^2 \delta y_1^2 - \delta x_2^2 \delta y_2^2 \right) \quad \delta y_1^2 - \delta y_2^2 \right| m = 0 \tag{17}$$

Since m is defined up to scale then a minimum of two corresponding pose constraints are required. All constrains formed from all sets of combinations of same limb frame poses are stacked on each swing plane.

The rectification matrix $\mathbf{H}_\mu$ is formed from the extracted parameters of $\mathbf{H}^T\mathbf{H}$, where $\mu = -m_2/m_3$ and

$$\lambda = \sqrt{\frac{m_1}{m_3} - \mu^2} \tag{18}$$

The ideal epipole $[1,0,0]^T$ is then mapped by $\mathbf{H}_\mu$ to $[1,-\mu/\lambda,0]^T$ so a rotation $\mathbf{H}_r$ is necessary in order to align the epipole back along the X axis such that $\mathbf{H}_a = \mathbf{H}_r \mathbf{H}_\mu$ is the affine transform that recovers metric angles and length ratios on both planes.

Points on the metric plane w are then mapped into the image as:

$$\bar{x} = \mathbf{H}_p \mathbf{H}_a^{-1} \left(\mathbf{H}_a \bar{u} \right) = \bar{H} \bar{w} \tag{19}$$

Scaling is then applied to both planes in order to transform each first limb segment to unit length. The mean set of limb lengths for both planes is estimated as $\mathbf{d}, \mathbf{d'}$. These lengths are related by the inter-plane scaling: $\mathbf{d}_i = \tau \mathbf{d}_i'$. A minimal solution to this trivial set of linear equations requires at least one valid length correspondence within the set of limb segments. With $\mathbf{H}_\tau$ now known the optimal first limb segment length $\mathbf{D}_1$ on the first plane can be evaluated. The scaling transform $\mathbf{H}_s$ that maps $\mathbf{D}_1$ to the unit length and update both sets of points and projection homographies is then calculated.

$$\mathbf{H}_1 = \bar{\mathbf{H}}_p \bar{\mathbf{H}}_s^{-1} = \begin{bmatrix} \dfrac{p_1}{s} & \dfrac{p_2}{s} & p_3 \end{bmatrix}$$

$$\bar{\mathbf{H}}_2 \mathbf{H}_\tau^{-1} \mathbf{H}_s^{-1} = \begin{bmatrix} \dfrac{p_1}{s} \cdot \tau & \dfrac{p_2}{s} \cdot \tau & p_3' \end{bmatrix} \tag{20}$$

$$\mathbf{H}_2 = \begin{bmatrix} \dfrac{p_1}{s} & \dfrac{p_2}{s} & \tau \cdot p_3' \end{bmatrix}$$

where

$$p_2 = m_2' - \alpha \cdot m_4'$$
$$p_3 = m_4' - m_3' \tag{21}$$
$$p_3' = m_4' + m_3'$$

defined in equation 10.

The true metric structure $\mathbf{w}_i$ is then recomputed from the real normalized image points $\mathbf{x}_i'$ by applying the inverse mappings

$$\mathbf{w}_i = \mathbf{H}_1^{-1}\mathbf{x}_i' \qquad \mathbf{w}_i' = \mathbf{H}_2^{-1}\mathbf{x}_i' \tag{21}$$

Therefore, the four-fold X,Y reflection ambiguity of the metric plane is resolved by consideration of the gross spatiotemporal motion structure. Two smoothed data vectors $\tilde{u}_0$, $\tilde{u}_0'$ generated from the mean X coordinate positions of limb points over a centred 3 frame window, are computed and fitted to a linear velocity model with a pair of simultaneous equations:

$$\tilde{u}_i = v_x \cdot i + u_0 \qquad \tilde{u}_i' = v_x \cdot i + u_0' \tag{22}$$

The gait sequences is then normalized in order to emulate a left to right walk, so ensureing that v_x is positive by applying a reflection about the Y axis and updating both points $\mathbf{w}_i$, $\mathbf{w}_i'$ and the homographies. The reflection about the X axis, to ensure that the sky is upward, is determined from the Y coordinate ordering of the means of each limb point over all frames. The only remaining ambiguity is then the translation between both sets of plane points.

Since normal gait is bilaterally symmetric with a half phase shift, for each limb segment both plane limb angle sets and their corresponding time sample vectors are computed. Therefore, the angle vectors can be concatenated as $\mathbf{A}=[\mathbf{a}|\mathbf{a}']$ and the time sample vector as $\mathbf{S}=[\mathbf{t}|\mathbf{t}'+\mathbf{T}/2]$.

With the knowledge of the normalized limb lengths $\mathbf{D}$ both sets of origin limb points $\mathbf{o}$, $\mathbf{o}'$ can be found by back substitution. We then compute two vectors of smoothed X origin limb data generated from the mean positions over a centred 3 frame window, and fit the linear velocity model to the pair of simultaneous equations in $\mathbf{t}$. This gives a reasonable estimate of the linear velocity component and initial X offset points $[\mathbf{u}_0, \mathbf{u}_0']$ of gait on the metric plane. We now compute a partitioned bilateral Fourier series representation of the origin point displacement function with sample data $\mathbf{o}$, $\mathbf{o}'$ and fixed fundamental frequency f_0

$$u(t) = v_x \cdot t + \sum_{k=1}^{n} A_k \cos\left(2\pi k f_0 t + \phi_k\right) + u_0$$
$$u'(t) = v_x \cdot t + \sum_{k=1}^{n} A_k \cos\left(2\pi k f_0 \left(t + \frac{T}{2}\right) + \phi_k\right) + u_0' \tag{23}$$

The initial first harmonic is firstly computed by partitioning the parameter vector $\mathbf{P}_1 = [v_x, A_1, \phi_1 \mid u_0, u_0']^{\mathrm{T}}$.

The estimation of $\mathbf{P}_1$ is then used to bootstrap the full partitioned parameterization:

$$\mathbf{P} = \left[v_x, A_1, \phi_1, ..., A_n, \phi_n \mid u_0, u_0' \right] \tag{24}$$

The Y component origin limb point displacement function is similar, though v_y is held fixed (zero). Both are computed using a partitioned Levenberg-Marquardt algorithm [21] with fixed fundamental frequency f_0. The translations $\mathbf{H}_o$, $\mathbf{H}_o'$ then map the starting origin limb point displacements $[u_0, v_0]^{\mathrm{T}}$, $[u_0', v_0']^{\mathrm{T}}$ to the origin.

We finally apply the inverse normalization transform to the updated homography mappings $\mathbf{K_n}^{-1}\mathbf{H_i}'$ in order to map the metric plane points to image points:

$$\mathbf{x}_1(t) = \begin{bmatrix} h_1 & h_2 & h_3 \end{bmatrix} g\left(t : f_0, \mathbf{D}, V_x, V_y, F\right)$$
$$\mathbf{x}_2(t) = \begin{bmatrix} h_1 & h_2 & h_3' \end{bmatrix} g\left(t + T/2 : f_0, \mathbf{D}, V_x, V_y, F\right)$$

(25)

where $g(t)$ is the bilateral Fourier series function, V_x and V_y are the velocity and Fourier coefficients of the metric plane origin limb displacement functions and F are the Fourier coefficients of the set of limb pose angle functions. As a final optimization step we perform a bundle adjustment procedure that minimizes reprojection error with respect to all parameters $\mathbf{P}$ of the gait projection function.

3 Experimental Tests

The method has been tested on 5 subjects walking freely along 6 different directions in a 7x7m^2 area. The video sequences were acquired with a digital camera FLEA IEEE-1394 Digital Camera (Point Grey Research) with a spatial resolution of 1024x768 pixels and 30 fps. Two 575 Watt lights illuminated the scene and 6 reflective markers (Vicon® 14mm) have been applied on the lower limbs (3 on the shank and 3 on the thigh). Fig. 3 shows the experimental setup.

3.1 Markers and Limb Pose Extraction

The aim of this paper is to test the proposed view-point independent gait reconstruction method on reliable and known limb trajectories. For this reason a set of markers has been applied on the subjects' legs and thus the first block of Fig. 1 has been replaced with the marker extraction (Fig. 2). Moreover, this is only the first step of a wider project where the extraction of leg pose will be completely automatic by developing a specialized image processing technique.

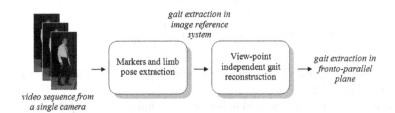

Fig. 2. Flow diagram for testing the proposed method

For the extraction of limb poses frame by frame an algorithm based on color segmentation and blob analysis has been designed.

Because of the special reflective structure of the markers with respect to the background and to the subject clothes, the marker extraction can be easily and robustly achieved by applying an RGB threshold. Robustness to noise and lighting changes has been achieved by comparing the roundness of the objects obtained from the color segmentation. The centroid of the remaining objects is then estimated and a vertical separation of these points is used to classify them into two subsets representing the thigh and the shank (lower leg) points. The individual thigh and shank points are then matched between consecutive frames on the assumption that the same point in the next frame has not moved more than the still closest point, in 2D Euclidian norm, to the point in the present frame. This is of course dependent on the frame rate of the camera system. The frame rate of 30 fps that is used here is enough to make this classification stable for the type of movement captured.

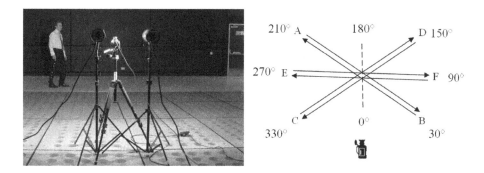

Fig. 3. Experimental setup

Because of the special reflective structure of the markers with respect to the background and to the subject clothes, the marker extraction can be easily and robustly achieved by applying an RGB threshold. Robustness to noise and lighting changes has been achieved by comparing the roundness of the objects obtained from the color segmentation. The centroid of the remaining objects is then estimated and a vertical separation of these points is used to classify them into two subsets representing the thigh and the shank (lower leg) points. The individual thigh and shank points are then matched between consecutive frames on the assumption that the same point in the next frame has not moved more than the still closest point, in 2D Euclidian norm, to the point in the present frame. This is of course dependent on the frame rate of the camera system. The frame rate of 30 fps that is used here is enough to make this classification stable for the type of movement captured.

After applying the method for extracting the markers trajectories to the video sequences, the limbs pose has been estimated frame by frame. Moreover, the hip and knee angles, θ and ϕ respectively, have been evaluated for each walking direction. Fig. 4 shows an example of markers extraction and the corresponding stick body model.

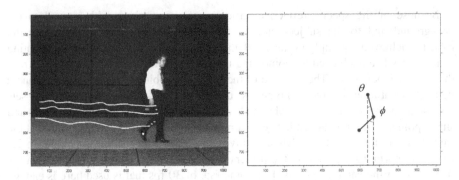

Fig. 4. Marker extraction and stick model

3.2 Gait Reconstruction

From the upper traces in Fig. 5 it is obvious that the mere extraction of limbs position from the 2D images produces angle trends that cannot be used directly for biometric identification. For this reason, the proposed method allows correction of these gait patterns so that they have trends similar to the one that can be achieved by extracting them on the anterior-posterior plane as showed in the lower part of Fig. 5. By inspection the correction achieved by our new approach has aligned the sequences such that they can now be used for identification purposes: the rectification process has led to series which are now closely aligned for the same subject. There is some slight variation between the resulting traces (in the lower part of Fig. 5) consistent with intra-subject variation between the recordings.

Data obtained by analysing the 30 video sequences has been collected and in order to quantify the angle trends matching after the proposed correction, the Mean Correlation Coefficient (MCC) along the i ($i=1,..N$) different directions has been achieved. Let S be the number of subjects, the MCC for the angle θ is defined in the following way:

$$MCC_\theta(i) = \frac{\sum_{k=1}^{S} CC_k^\theta(i)}{S} \tag{26}$$

where $CC_k^\theta(i)$ is the mean correlation coefficient of subject k along the walking direction i:

$$CC_k^\theta(i) = \frac{\sum_{j=1}^{N} R_{i,j}^\theta}{N} \tag{27}$$

and $R_{i,j}^\theta$ is the off-diagonal elements of the correlation coefficients matrix between the directions i and j and similarly for ϕ.

Fig. 6 shows how the MCCs vary with respect to the walking direction i (where $i=0,...,360$ as reported in Fig. 1). The results, with a mean value of 0.996, are particularly encouraging and the peaks corresponding at the two fronto-parallel paths (at 90 and 270 degrees) confirm that the reconstructed angles along different directions are correlated with the canonical view. The front and rear views (at 0 and 180 degrees) show the lowest performance, but this is only where the MCC is still very close to the mean anyway. The errors in the estimates for the shank (lower leg) inclination are slightly greater and the MCC is slightly lower, but still at minimum 0.992. The larger error in the lower leg is due to the greater freedom in movement, and since the shank moves much faster than the thigh reducing effective resolution.

Furthermore, the information regarding the limbs' pose along different directions has allowed estimation of the root mean square (RMS) distance between the detected marker points and the projected ones.

The mean RMS error for the 5 subjects is 0.2% of the image resolution. This result is particularly encouraging especially compared with the 0.1% RMS obtained using Zhang calibration algorithm [22].

Moreover, the video sequences and the marker trajectories have been modified in order to test the method under different circumstances.

Firstly, the sensitivity of the method with respect to the camera characteristics has been evaluated by changing the image resolution and the frame rate.

Table 1 shows the mean MCC and RMS values obtained with the image spatial resolution varying from 320x240 to 640×480 to 1024×768 pixels. The frames have been resized using nearest-neighbor interpolation.

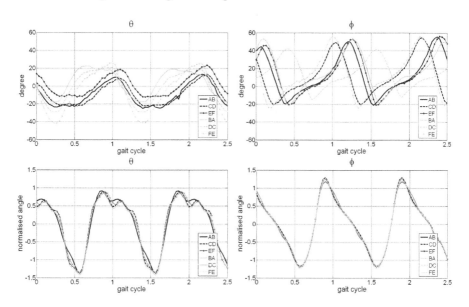

Fig. 5. Hip and knee angles in different walking directions, unprocessed (above) and corrected (below)

It is notable how the image resolution remarkably influences the RMS and how, on the other hand, the mean MCC remains higher than 0.9. The sensitivity of the proposed method to the camera frame rate is reported in Fig. 7, where the video

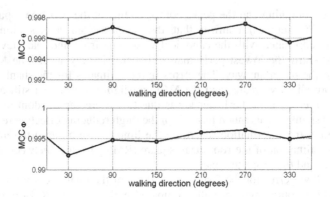

Fig. 6. Mean Correlation Coefficient (MCC) along the different walking directions

sequences have been subsampled from 20 to 30 fps. The mean MCC and RMS show that with a frame rate higher than 25 fps the performance has a linear trend.

In addition, to simulate the limb tracking imprecision, zero-mean Gaussian noise has been added to the markers' trajectories. The standard deviation of the added noise varies from 0 (original data) to 10 pixels. For each noise level, 6 different trials have been conducted and added to each marker trajectory. Obviously the error increases with the level of noise added to the trajectories but the decrease of MCC is particularly interesting because it is higher than 0.9 even at high noise levels.

Table 1. Sensitivity of MCC and RMS with respect to image resolution

	320x240	640x480	1024x768
Mean MCC	0.989	0.992	0.996
RMS (%)	0.990	0.549	0.278

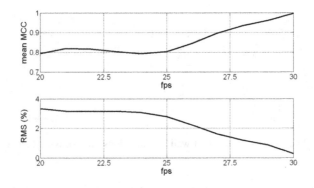

Fig. 7. Sensitivity of MCC and RMS with respect to camera frame rate

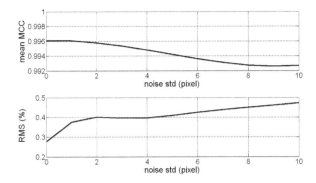

Fig. 8. Sensitivity of MCC and RMS with respect to Gaussian noise in the markers points

Moreover, the noise study allows to understand how the proposed method depends on an accurate limb position extraction and thus to extend the approach in a markerless context.

4   Conclusion

It is widely recognized that gait identification has unique advantages, such as the unobtrusiveness, respect to other biometric techniques. Recently a lot of research has been conducted into the recognition of fronto-parallel gait or using more views after the calibration process. However, considering biometrics aims and the criminal investigation context these approaches appear limited, especially because usually there is no access to the cameras and the subjects do not walk along the canonical direction. For these reasons a system is required which does not rely on the subject's pose or on the calibration of the camera.

In this context this paper has introduced a novel method for a pose invariant gait analysis based on the assumptions that the nature of human gait is cyclic, the distances between the bone joints are invariant and the articulated leg motion is approximately planar.

Experimental tests have been conducted on 5 subjects walking freely along 6 different directions in a $7x7m^2$ area. Different conditions concerning image resolution, frame rate and noisy limb trajectories, have been compared. Moreover the influence of the walking direction on the angle's estimation has been analysed. This quantity of data and the amount is sufficient to demonstrate that the proposed new approach can achieve view-point independent gait reconstruction as described.

The obtained results are particularly encouraging for future system development concerning the markerless extraction of limbs' pose, and for its appliance in real surveillance scenarios.

Acknowledgments. The study was supported by DTC through General Dynamics.

References

1. Sarkar, S., Phillips, P.J., Liu, Z., Vega, I.R., Grother, P., Bowyer, K.W.: The HumanID Gait Challenge Problem: Data Sets, Performance, and Analysis. IEEE Transactions on Pattern Analysis and Machine Intelligence 27(2), 162–177 (2005)
2. Nixon, M.S., Carter, J.N.: Automatic Recognition by Gait. Proceeding of the IEEE 94(11), 2013–2023 (2006)
3. Nixon, M.S., Carter, J.N., Cunado, D., Huang, P.S., Stevenage, S.V.: In: Jain, A., Bolle, R., Pankanti, S. (eds.) Biometrics: Personal Identification in a Networked Society, pp. 231–250. Kluwer Academic Publishing, Dordrecht (1999)
4. Cutting, J., Kozlowski, L.: Recognizing friends by their walk: gait perception without familiarity cues. Bull. Psychonom. Soc. 9, 353–356 (1977)
5. Murray, M.P., Drought, A.B., Kory, R.C.: Walking patterns of normal men. J. Bone and Joint Surgery 46-A(2), 335–360 (1964)
6. BenAbdelkader, C., Cutler, R., Davis, L. et al.: Motion-Based Recognition of People in Eigengait Space. In: Proc. Automatic Face and Gesture Recognition (2002)
7. Wagg, D.K., Nixon, M.S.: On automated model-based extraction and analysis of gait. In: Proc. Automatic Face and Gesture Recognition, pp. 11–16 (2004)
8. Collins, R., Gross, R., Shi, J.: Silhouette-Based Human Identification from Body Shape and Gait. In: Proc. Int. Conf. Automatic Face and Gesture Recognition (2002)
9. Veres, G.V., et al.: What image information is important in silhouette-based gait recognition. In: Proc. IEEE Conf. on Computer Vision and Pattern Recognition (2004)
10. Kale, A., Rajagopalan, A.N., Sundaresan, A., Cuntoor, N., RoyChowdhury, A., Kruger, V., Chellappa, R.: Identification of Humans Using Gait, Image Processing. IEEE Transactions on Publication 13(9), 1163–1173 (2004)
11. Phillips, P.J., Sarkar, S., Robledo, I., Grother, P., Bowyer, K.: The Gait Identification Challenge Problem: Data Sets and Baseline Algorithm. In: 16th ICPR, pp. 385–389 (2002)
12. Gross, R., Shi, J.: The CMU Motion of Body (MoBo) Database, tech. report CMU-RI-TR-01-18, Robotics Institute, Carnegie Mellon University (2001)
13. Shutler, J.D., Grant, M.G., Nixon, M.S., Carter, J.N.: On a Large Sequence-Based Human Gait Database. In: Proc. 4th Int. Conf. RASC, Nottingham (UK) (2002)
14. Spencer, N., And Carter, J.: Towards Pose Invariant Gait Reconstruction. In: IEEE International Conference On Image Processing, vol. 3, pp. 261–264 (2005)
15. Kale, A., Chowdhury, R., Chellappa, R.: Towards a view invariant gait recognition algorithm. In AVSS 2003, pp. 143–150 (2003)
16. Lynnerup, N.: Person Identification by Gait Analysis & Photogrammetry. In: Proc. 2nd Annual Conference Crime Solutions (2006)
17. Yamada, Y.: Advanced method for improvement of obscure video image Security Technology. In: Proceedings. IEEE 33rd Annual 1999 International Carnahan Conference on, pp. 440–445 (1999)
18. Dick, A.R., Brooks, M.J.: Issues in automated visual surveillance. In: Proc. VIIth Digital Image Comp. Tech. and App. pp.195–204, Sydney, (December 2003)
19. Kirtley, C.: Clinical Gait Analysis: Theory and Practice (June 2005) ISBN-10: 0443100098
20. Abdel-Aziz, Y.I., Arara, H.M.: Direct Linear Transformation from comparator coordinates into object space coordinates in close range photogrammetry. In: Proceedings of the Symposium on Close-Range Photogrammetry pp. 1–18 (1971)

21. Hartley, R.I., Zisserman, A.: Multiple View Geometry in Computer Vision. Cambridge University Press, Cambridge (2004)
22. Zhang, Z.: A flexible new technique for camera calibration, Pattern Analysis and Machine Intelligence. IEEE Transactions 22(11), 1330–1334 (2000)

Detecting, Localizing and Classifying Visual Traits from Arbitrary Viewpoints Using Probabilistic Local Feature Modeling

Matthew Toews and Tal Arbel

Centre for Intelligent Machines
McGill University
Montreal, Canada
{mtoews,arbel}@cim.mcgill.ca

Abstract. We present the first framework for detecting, localizing and classifying visual traits of object classes, e.g.gender or age of human faces, from arbitrary viewpoints. We embed all three tasks in a viewpoint-invariant model derived from local scale-invariant features (e.g. SIFT), where features are probabilistically quantified in terms of their occurrence, appearance, geometry and relationship to visual traits of interest. An appearance model is first learned for the object class, after which a Bayesian classifier is trained to identify the model features indicative of visual traits. The advantage of our framework is that it can be applied and evaluated in realistic scenarios, unlike other trait classification techniques that assume data that is single-viewpoint, pre-aligned and cropped from background distraction. Experimentation on the standard color FERET database shows our approach can automatically identify the visual cues in face images linked to the trait of gender. Combined detection, localization and gender classification error rates are a) 15% over a 180-degree range of face viewpoint and b) 13% in frontal faces, lower than other reported results.

1 Introduction

Practical visual processing applications must be able to robustly detect instances of object classes of interest in arbitrary, cluttered images, and make inferences regarding their visual traits. For example, consider an intelligent vision system that must identify all males in a crowded scene, as illustrated in Figure 1. Image features arising from human face instances must first be detected and localized in the midst of unrelated clutter and viewpoint change, after which they can be used to determine traits such as gender for each person detected. Although the tasks of detection, localization and classification are all inextricably linked in such realistic visual processing scenarios, they are typically treated in isolation in the current vision literature. For example, approaches to classifying facial traits such as gender typically assume frontal face data which has been precisely pre-aligned and cropped from distracting background clutter prior to classification [2,25,14,17,9]. As a result, it remains questionable whether such approaches can be applied in conjunction with automatic detection strategies in arbitrary, cluttered scenes where automatic face localization is non-trivial. Likewise, it is unclear whether

S.K. Zhou et al. (Eds.): AMFG 2007, LNCS 4778, pp. 154–167, 2007.

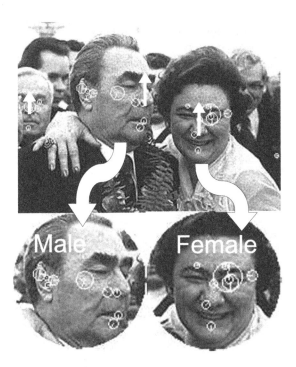

Fig. 1. Illustrating the output of our general framework for detection, localization and trait classi-fication from arbitrary viewpoints. All three tasks are embedded in a viewpoint-invariant model derived from scale-invariant image features. Here, face instances (white arrows above) are first detected and localized from scale-invariant features (white circles) extracted in a cluttered scene. Features associated with each face instance are then used in a Bayesian classifier to determine face gender (lower insets). The image shown is from the CMU face database [5], and the proba-bilistic framework used is learned from 500 FERET [1] face images taken at arbitrary viewpoints.

recent general object class detection strategies [8,7,19,6,4,21] can be extended in order to learn and classify abstract visual traits such as gender from arbitrary viewpoints.

Our contribution in this paper is a general, integrated framework for detecting, lo-calizing and classifying visual traits of object classes from arbitrary viewpoints. Our approach is the first to propose learning visual traits from arbitrary viewpoints, and the first to embed all three tasks in a general appearance model based on local scale-invariant features (e.g. SIFT), where features are probabilistically quantified in terms of their occurrence, appearance and geometry within a common reference frame. Our approach involves first learning a set of model features related to the object class of interest, after which the same features are used to train a Bayesian classifier for visual traits. Classifier training involves estimating the likelihood ratio of feature occurrence given trait presence vs. absence, the underlying premise being that informative features are more likely than not to co-occur with the trait of interest. The resulting framework can be used to detect and localize and classify the traits of object class instances in the presence of viewpoint change, geometrical deformations such as translation, orientation and scale changes, linear illumination changes, partial occlusion and multi-model intra-class variation (e.g. faces with/without sunglasses).

The remainder of this paper is organized as follows: in Section 2 we review related work in general object class detection and visual trait classification. In Section 3 we describe our approach to trait learning and classification based on probabilistic modeling of scale-invariant image features. Although our approach generalizes to a variety of object classes and visual traits, we experiment on the class of faces and the trait of gender in Section 4 using the standard color FERET database. We provide a quantitative performance evaluation for combined detection, localization and gender classification of faces images in both arbitrary and frontal viewpoint contexts, and show how our approach can identify visual cues of gender in face images over a range of viewpoint. A discussion follows in Section 5.

2   Related Work

2.1   Object Class Detection

The general detection task requires identifying and localizing instances of an object class, e.g. cars or faces, in images. General object class detection requires effectively dealing with a wide range of appearance variation due to viewpoint change, geometrical deformations such as translation, orientation and scale changes, illumination changes, partial pattern occlusion and multi-modal intra-class variation (i.e. faces with/without sunglasses). Such variation can only be realistically overcome by learning a model from a set of natural training images. Early approaches advocated learning models of global features, i.e. eigenfaces [22], but proved to be inefficient for detection over geometrical deformations and poorly suited for coping with local appearance variation and occlusion. To overcome these difficulties, researchers have increasingly turned to local image feature representations. Scale-invariant features [15,3,16,13] for instance can be robustly and efficiently extracted from scale-space pyramids in the presence of translation, orientation and scale geometrical deformations and illumination changes. As features are local, they can be used to determine correspondence between different images in the presence of partial occlusion. Geometrical information from the extraction process including feature location, orientation and scale can be used to generate independent hypotheses as to the geometrical transform relating different images, without requiring an expensive explicit search over transform parameters.

While scale-invariant feature correspondences cannot generally be established directly between different instances of the same object class due to intra-class variability, research has shown that learned probabilistic models of features can be used to reliably detect object class instances in arbitrary, cluttered images [8,7,19,6,4,21]. Such models describe the appearance of an object class in terms of a set of local features, including their appearances, occurrences and their geometries (i.e. image location, orientation and scale). Models generally vary in terms of the assumptions made regarding inter-feature geometrical dependencies, e.g. geometry independent models [7,19], naive Bayes dependencies [21,8], Markov dependencies [4], fully-dependent [24], and intermediate approaches [6]. Although geometrical dependence assumptions vary, most models make the assumption of conditional independence of individual feature appearances/occurrences given feature geometry and object class.

Most approaches to invariant feature modeling are based on stable 2D feature configurations in the image plane, and are thus single-viewpoint in nature [8]. Multi-view [20] and viewpoint-invariant [21] representations have emerged to address object class detection and localization from arbitrary viewpoints. Modeling 3D object class appearance over viewpoint change is considerably more challenging than from single viewpoints, as correspondences must be established between different views in addition to different object class instances, and learning techniques typically employ a degree of external supervision. The multi-view modeling approach [20] requires a viewsphere sampled at regular angular intervals, for each of set of different object class instances. Such an approach is not well suited to learning from natural images taken from arbitrary viewpoints around arbitrary 3D object class instances, however. The viewpoint-invariant approach [21] relates features in different images via an object class invariant (OCI), a geometrical reference frame that is uniquely defined for each object class instance and invariant to projective image transform arising from viewpoint change. As the variable of viewpoint is effectively marginalized from the formulation, a viewpoint-invariant model can be learned from natural imagery taken from arbitrary viewpoints from labeled images.

2.2 Visual Trait Classification: Gender from Faces

Visual traits are abstract qualities of an object class identifiable from images, such as the make or model of cars, the age or gender of faces, etc. They represent a mechanism by which members of the same object class can be described or subdivided. Due to the ubiquitous nature of face image analysis, one of the most common visual trait classification tasks is that of determining gender from face images, and the wide range of published approaches highlights the state-of-the-art in general trait classification. Trait learning has been tackled from spatially global feature representations such as templates[14,9], principle components [17] or independent components [10]. Other more recent approaches used pixels as features [2] or Haar wavelets [25,18]. Machine learning techniques such as neural networks [9], support vector machines (SVMs) [17] and boosted classifiers [2] have been brought to bear. In the interest of comparison, most approaches train and test on the standard FERET face database [1] containing accurate labels for visual traits such as gender, age and ethnicity.

To date, all published approaches to trait classification are based exclusively on single viewpoints, i.e. frontal faces [2,25,10,17,9]. With the exception of [18], most approaches assume that, prior to classification, faces are precisely localized and background distraction such as hair and clothing is cropped away. For example, localization is performed by manually specifying eye locations [2] or using special-purpose frontal face alignment software [25,17], and pre-defined facial masks are subsequently applied to remove background clutter. As a result, classification error rates of 4% to 10% represent artificially low, ideal-case results, and offer little insight as to classification performance in a general vision system where object class localization is non-trivial. Indeed, a recent work evaluating the effect of artificial localization perturbations on classification accuracy showed that accuracy drops off rapidly with even small independent perturbations in scale and orientation (i.e. 5 degrees) [2]. An additional fact worth noting is that several published works reporting low error rates use different images of the same person in both classifier training and testing [25,17]. As facial features arising from different frontal images of the same person are highly correlated, one cannot know whether the low classification error reported reflects the ability of the classifier to generalize to new, unseen faces or simply classification-by-recognition.

2.3   Combined Detection, Localization and Trait Classification

To date only a single approach has proposed combined detection, localization and classification within an integrated framework suitable for general object classes [18], using boosted classifiers of Haar wavelet features [23] for all tasks. The approach is single-viewpoint (frontal faces) and not invariant to orientation, and the reported error rate of 21% reflects the increased difficulty of the combined task. This result is based a proprietary database, however, where faces with ambiguous gender are manually removed, as are faces whose in-plane orientation is greater than 30 degrees, and as such a direct comparison cannot be made. The general scale-invariant feature-based approach to modeling object classes offers an attractive alternative for combined detection, localization and classification, as it can provide invariance to viewpoint change, in addition to in addition to translation, orientation and scale changes. To date, the general scale-invariant feature-based modeling approach has not been investigated for visual trait classification, and classifying visual traits such as gender from faces from arbitrary viewpoints has not been addressed.

3   Classifying Visual Traits from Local Features

In realistic scenarios, visual trait classification is inseparable from detection and localization: features must first be detected and localized before they can be classified. We propose embedding all three tasks within a general appearance model derived from local scale-invariant features, which can be used to detect, localize and classify traits of object classes in natural imagery captured from arbitrary viewpoints. A model describing object class appearance is first learned, after which a Bayesian trait classifier is then trained from features in the model.

3.1   Viewpoint-Invariant Appearance Modeling

To effectively capture the subtleties of visual traits, we require a model that can be 1) effectively learned from arbitrary viewpoints 2) used to detect and localize individual object class instances in arbitrary viewpoints and 3) provide a rich, multi-modal description of object class appearance on which trait classification can be based. We thus avoid geometry-free models which are generally less suitable for localizing object class instances [7,19] and models consisting of relatively few features (e.g.10) [8] which may not provide a sufficiently rich image description for visual traits. While our trait classification approach is generally applicable to single-viewpoint models consisting of many features (e.g.100+) [4], effectively learning and classifying visual traits requires

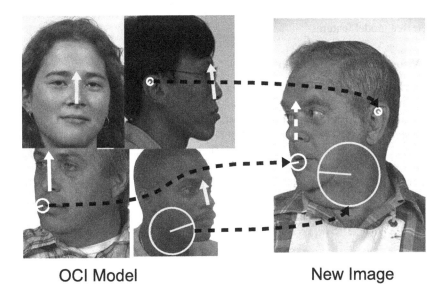

OCI Model   **New Image**

Fig. 2. Illustrating the viewpoint-invariant OCI model relating scale-invariant features (white circles) to an OCI (solid white arrows). The OCI, defined here a line segment from the base of the nose to the forehead, represents a viewpoint-invariant mechanism for grouping scale-invariant image features in images taken from arbitrary viewpoints. A probabilistic model (left) is learned from manually labeled OCIs in training images taken at arbitrary viewpoints. Model instances can then be robustly detected and localized in a new image (right) taken at an arbitrary viewpoint, based on detected model features (dashed black lines) that agree on an OCI (dashed white arrow). Note that OCI shown here 1) exploits the symmetry of faces allowing mirror feature correspondence and 2) is not designed for overhead/underhead views.

addressing the issue of viewpoint change. To do this, we adopt the viewpoint-invariant OCI model [21]. The model relates scale-invariant features to an OCI, an abstract 3D geometrical structure that is uniquely defined with respect to each 3D object class instance and invariant to projective transform arising from viewpoint change, as illustrated in Figure 2. The probabilistic model formulation adopts the assumption of conditional independence of feature geometries and appearances/occurrences, and the naive Bayes assumption of conditional independence of individual features i, given the OCI o. Under these assumptions, the posterior probability of o given feature geometry $G : \{g_i\}$, appearance $A : \{a_i\}$ and occurrence $F : \{f_i\}$ data can be expressed as:

$$p(o|G, A, F) \propto p(o)p(G|o)p(A, F|o),$$
$$\propto p(o) \prod_i p(g_i|o)p(a_i|f_i)p(f_i|o), \qquad (1)$$

where distributions $p(g_i|o)$, $p(a_i|f_i)$ and $p(f_i|o)$ over individual feature geometries, appearances and occurrences are learned from a set of training data containing features and labeled OCIs. Novel object class instances can be detected and localized in new images by maximizing the posterior probability in equation (1) with respect to o based on detected model features.

3.2 Visual Trait Classification

Once a viewpoint invariant model has been learned for a given object class, we seek to identify model features indicative of visual traits using the co-occurrence statistics of individual features with the trait of interest. To do this, we consider the random event $f_i = 1$ signifying the occurrence of model feature i, and we expand the random event of object class occurrence $o = 1$ into a discrete random variable $c : \{c_1, \ldots, c_K\}$ over K trait values of interest, e.g.$gender : \{female, male\}$. A Bayesian classifier $\gamma(c)$ can then be used to express the most probable trait classification given a set of model feature occurrences $\{f_i\}$:

$$\gamma(c_j) = \frac{p(c_j|\{f_i\})}{p(\bar{c}_j|\{f_i\})} = \frac{p(c_j)}{p(\bar{c}_j)} \prod_i \frac{p(f_i|c_j)}{p(f_i|\bar{c}_j)}. \tag{2}$$

where $\frac{p(c_j)}{p(\bar{c}_j)}$ is the prior ratio of trait value presence c_j vs. absence $\bar{c}_j$ (e.g. male vs. not male or female), and $\frac{p(f_i|c_j)}{p(f_i|\bar{c}_j)}$ expresses the likelihood ratio of trait value presence c_j vs. absence $\bar{c}_j$ coinciding with feature observation f_i. Features that are important to classification or highly informative with regard to trait value c_j will have high likelihood ratios. The focus of our approach is to use these likelihood ratios to quantify the association of model features with visual traits, as illustrated in Figure 3.

In order to estimate the likelihood parameters, we use a supervised learning process, based on observed model feature occurrences f_i and trait labels c_j for each training image. Discrete class-conditional likelihoods $p(f_i|c_j)$ can be represented as binomial distributions, parameterized by event counts [12]. During training, $p(f_i|c_j)$ is estimated from $p(c_j)$ and $p(f_i, c_j)$, the probability of observed joint events (f_i, c_j), using the definition of conditional probability:

$$p(f_i|c_j) = \frac{p(f_i, c_j)}{p(c_j)}. \tag{3}$$

The most straightforward manner of estimating $p(f_i, c_j)$ is via ML (maximum likelihood) estimation, by counting the joint events (f_i, c_j) and normalizing with respect to their sum. ML estimation is known to be unstable in the presence of sparse data, leading to noisy or undefined parameter estimates. This is particularly true in models consisting of many local features, where feature occurrences are typically rare events. Bayesian MAP (maximum a posteriori) estimation can be used to cope with data sparsity, and involves regularizing estimates using a Dirichlet hyperparameter distribution [12]. In practice, Dirichlet regularization involves pre-populating event count parameters with samples following a prior distribution embodying assumptions regarding the expected sample distribution. Where no relevant prior knowledge exists, a uniform or maximum entropy prior can be used [11]. Although both ML and MAP estimates converge as the number of data samples increases, MAP estimation using a uniform prior will tend towards conservative parameter estimates while the number of data samples is low. The final estimator we use becomes:

$$p(f_i|c_j) \propto \frac{k_{i,j}}{p(c_j)} + d_{i,j}, \tag{4}$$

where $k_{i,j}$ is the frequency of the joint occurrence event (f_i, c_j), $p(c_j)$ is the frequency of trait value c_j in the training data and $d_{i,j}$ is the Dirichlet regularization parameter used to populate event counts. In the case of a uniform prior, $d_{i,j}$ is constant for all i, j. The proportionality constant for the likelihood in equation (4) can be obtained by normalizing over values of f_i, but is not required for likelihood ratios.

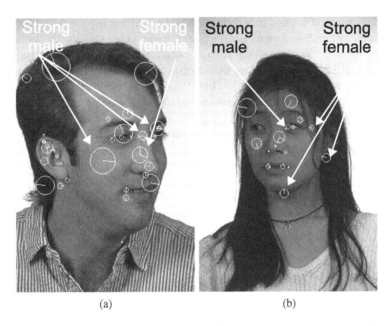

(a)   (b)

Fig. 3. Illustrating classification of the visual trait of gender from local features (white circles). A given face instance consists of a set of local features, a subset of which are reflective of either gender, and it is their ensemble which determines the final decision. To illustrate, we describe a feature as strongly male or female if its likelihood ratio of co-occurring with the indicated gender in training images is greater than 2:1. Of the 63 model features detected in image (a), 15 are strongly male and 1 is strongly female, suggesting a male face. Of the 31 features detected in image (b), 7 are strongly female and 1 is strongly male, suggesting a female face. Many features, although very common in the class of face images, are uninformative regarding gender.

4 Experimentation

For the purpose of experimentation, we consider the combined task of detection, localization and gender classification of faces from arbitrary viewpoints. To compare with the results in the literature, we also provide results for a model trained from frontal faces only. Experimentation is based on the standard, publicly available color FERET face image database [1] for both training and testing. The FERET database consists of images of 994 unique subjects of various ethnicity, age, gender, taken from various viewpoints, illumination conditions, with/without glasses, etc. We process images at a resolution of 256x384 pixels and no subjects are duplicated in either testing or training data, in order to evaluate the generality of our approach.

Learning proceeds as follows: an initial local feature-based model is trained on randomly-selected subsets of face images using the supervised OCI technique, and the remaining images are used for testing. Model learning requires approximate labeling of an OCI in the form of a line segment from the base of the nose to the forehead as in Section 3.1, and automatically extracting scale-invariant features in each training images. Although a variety of different scale-invariant features can be used, we use the SIFT (scale-invariant feature transform) technique [15] for feature detection and appearance description based on robust implementation made public by the author. Once the model has been learned, model feature occurrences identified in the training set along with FERET gender labels are used to estimate likelihood ratios of the Bayesian trait classifier as described in Section 3. In estimating likelihood ratios via equation (4), we used a Dirichlet regularization parameter of $d_{i,j} = 2$ which maximizes training set classification performance.

Once the framework has been learned, combined detection, localization and classification proceed on the remainder of FERET faces not used in training. Scale-invariant features are first extracted in all testing images, after which detection and localization are performed by determining the most probable OCI instance in each of the testing images based on extracted image features. Model features contributing the OCI instance are then used to determine gender using the Bayesian classifier in equation (2), using a prior trait ratio of $\frac{p(c_j)}{p(\bar{c}_j)} = 1$. Note that the FERET database does not necessarily represent the most challenging test for model detection, as most faces are clearly visible, but it does allow evaluating whether or not facial features can be automatically localized with sufficient accuracy for subsequent trait classification. Qualitative experimentation was performed on cluttered imagery from the CMU profile database [5], as illustrated in Figure 1), demonstrating the viability of the system in difficult detection/localization contexts. Performance is generally better for higher resolution faces, where the number of SIFT features extracted is sufficient for reliable detection and classification. Classification appears correct in most cases, although ground truth gender labels are unavailable and difficult to determine in many cases.

4.1 Locating, Detecting and Classifying from Arbitrary Viewpoints

In order to investigate the trait of gender from arbitrary viewpoints, a database of all 994 unique FERET subjects was selected, where each subject image is chosen at random from a 180 degree viewpoint range (i.e. from left to right profile images). Figure 4 illustrates the viewpoint distribution in the dataset. We trained on two randomly selected subsets of 331 and 497 images (1/3 and 1/2 of the data), and performed combined detection, localization and gender classification on the remaining images.

Table 1 summarizes the results obtained, where our approach achieves an error rate of 15% based on 497 training images. Misclassification rates were 12% and 17% for males and females, respectively, examples can be seen in Figure 5. The detection and localization error rate prior to classification was 3.6%, where the discrepancy between

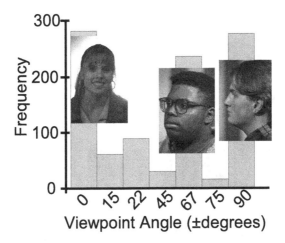

Fig. 4. A histogram illustrating the viewpoint distribution for the 994 unique FERET subject images used in experimentation

Table 1. Error rates for localization, and combined detection, localization and classification over viewpoint. Our Bayesian classifier obtains an error rate of 15% when trained on 497 of 994 images. Localization error rates are based on discrepancy threshold between localized and manual labeled OCIs in testing images.

Database	Loc. Error	Combined Error
FERET (497 training)	3.6%	15%
FERET (331 training)	4.5%	19%

the localized and labeled OCIs was greater than a threshold in scale, orientation and location of $log(1.5)$, 20 degrees and OCI scale/2 pixels, respectively. It is possible that increasing the training data size by several hundred more images would further reduce the error rate by several percentage points.

4.2 Identifying Visual Cues of Gender

As humans, we are all capable of determining visual traits such as face gender of a face image with reasonable certainty. What is more difficult is to identify the visual cues that are operative in making the determination - most faces contain a variety of cues that could be construed as either male or female, and it is their ensemble which determines the final decision. The local feature-based approach provides insight in terms of what local image cues are most important in determining visual traits, insight which is not possible from other representations, e.g. global features or templates. By sorting features according to their likelihood ratios, the image regions most telling regarding the trait of gender can be visualized as in Figure 6. In a viewpoint invariant model, ear features are more indicative of males, as they are less visible due to generally longer female hair. Several features around the mouth are indicative of males, indicative of

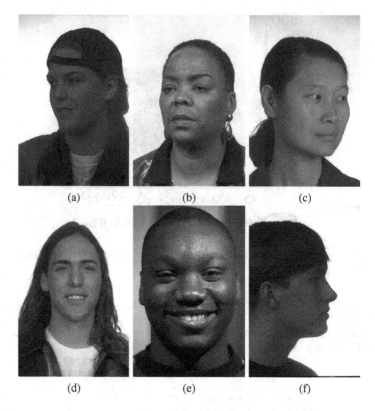

(a)   (b)   (c)

(d)   (e)   (f)

Fig. 5. Illustrating several misclassification examples. Images (a)-(c) are misclassified as male, while (d)-(f) are misclassified as female. Misclassification can occur due to faces containing a disproportionately high number of features indicative of the opposite sex, e.g. (a)-(e), or a lack of gender-informative features e.g. (f).

beards or facial stubble. Females are distinguished by features arising from hairlines, eyes (possible from makeup) and lips. In contrast, certain model features arising from nostrils or cheeks, although very common in the class of face images, were generally less informative regarding gender. Note that although the male:female ratio in training data was close to 1:1, approximately twice as many gender-related features were identified for males as for females, suggesting a greater number of visual cues characteristic of the male gender.

4.3 Locating, Detecting and Classifying from Frontal Views

In order to compare our general approach results in the literature, we also trained and tested on a restricted set of frontal faces. We used the 925 standard FERET frontal images labeled "*_fa.*", models were trained from randomly selected subsets of 100 and 200 images. Table 2 for the combined task of detection, localization and classification, error rates for classification only (i.e. faces pre-aligned and cropped prior to classifica-

Table 2. Published error rates for combined detection, localization and classification for frontal faces. Our Bayesian classifier trained on 200 FERET faces in (a) achieves the lowest error rate of 13%, in comparison with (b) the boosted Haar wavelet classifier [18] of 21%. Results for (b) are based on a proprietary database, however, so a precise comparison cannot be made. Results for classification only (c), i.e. with faces pre-aligned and cropped, represent an ideal-case baseline and are included for completeness.

Task	Method	Features	Database	Error Rate
Combined detection, localization and classification	(a) Bayesian classifier	Scale-invariants	FERET (200 training)	13%
			FERET (100 training)	16%
	(b) Adaboost [18]	Haar wavelets	Proprietary ($\approx$3000 training)	21%
Classification only	(c) Various [2,25,10,17,9]	Various	FERET	4%-10%

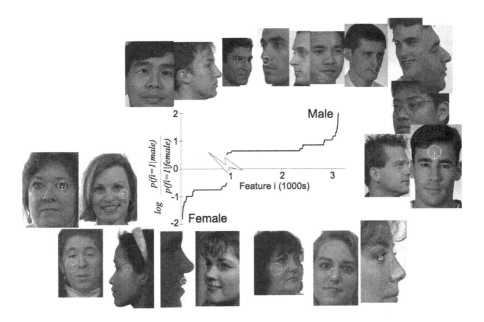

Fig. 6. Illustrating visual cues indicative of face gender, in the form of scale-invariant features. Features are sorted in increasing order of their log likelihood ratio $log(\frac{p(f_i=1|male)}{p(f_i=1|female)})$. Of approx. 15,000 features in a viewpoint invariant face model learned from 497 randomly selected FERET images, approx. 3000 features bear information regarding gender (i.e. $|log(\frac{p(f_i=1|male)}{p(f_i=1|female)})| > 0.5$). Features lying to the left of the graph occur more frequently in female subjects and those to the right more frequently in male subjects. Face images shown illustrate instances of gender-informative features (white circles) with absolute log likelihood ratios ranging from 1.3 to 2.0. Although the male:female ratio in the training data was 28:22, approximately twice as many gender-reflective features are associated with males.

tion) represent an ideal-case baseline and are included for completeness. For the more difficult combined task, our Bayesian gender classifier achieves an error rate of 13% for training based on 200 randomly selected FERET subjects. The misclassification rates are 9.7% and 15% for males and females, respectively. Note that training on only 100 subjects results a marginally higher error rate of 16%, suggesting that the majority of the information regarding face gender is captured from on the order of several hundred subjects. Note that significantly fewer training images are required to obtain similar error rates to modeling viewpoint.

5   Discussion

In this paper, we present the first approach addressing learning and classification of visual traits of object classes from arbitrary viewpoints. As a realistic scenario requires first detecting and localizing object class instances prior to trait classification, we embed all three tasks within a single viewpoint-invariant model of general object class appearance that can be used for combined detection, localization and classification from arbitrary viewpoints. Our approach involves first learning a model of object class appearance, then training a Bayesian classifier for visual traits from model features. Classifier training involves estimating the likelihood ratio of positive feature occurrence given trait presence vs. absence, where features associated with significantly non-zero likelihood ratios indicate visual cues reflective of the trait of interest. We provide the first experimental results on a standard, publicly available database (FERET) for the combined tasks of detection, localization and gender classification of faces. We obtain an error rate of 15% for the combined task over a 180 degree range of face viewpoint, and an error rate of 13% for frontal faces.

Various future avenues exist for learning visual traits from general appearance models based on local scale-invariant features. Computational complexity of detection, localization and classification is low and the combined system should be implementable in real or near-real time. Visual traits of faces can be used as a soft biometric in interactive image-based applications, surveillance or recognition, and the framework could possibly extend to classifying traits such as age or emotion. We experimented with learning the trait of age, by dividing faces into less than/greater than 25 years of age, splitting the data set approximately evenly. A somewhat high classification error rate of 23% was obtained framework trained from the framework trained on 200 frontal faces, indicating that age classification is a more difficult problem than gender, particularly when faces are split at the 25-year old mark. Useful traits can potentially be learned from of different object classes, for example the make or model of cars and motorbikes. Whether different traits such as age and gender are best modeled independently or jointly is an open research question, the Bayesian classifier we present could be used for either although joint modeling becomes computationally complex for large numbers of different traits. Continuous-valued traits such as age could potentially be modeled using continuous-valued likelihoods. A variety of different scale-invariant feature types other than SIFT could be incorporated to potentially improve classification performance by highlighting different image characteristics.

References

1. Feret face database. http://www.itl.nist.gov/iad/humanid/colorferet
2. Baluja, S., Rowley, H.A.: Boosting sex identification performance. IJCV 71(1), 111–119 (2007)
3. Carneiro, G., Jepson, A.: Multi-scale phase-based local features. In: CVPR, vol. 1, pp. 736–743 (2003)
4. Carneiro, G., Lowe, D.G.: Sparse flexible models of local features. In: Leonardis, A., Bischof, H., Pinz, A. (eds.) ECCV 2006. LNCS, vol. 3953, pp. 29–43. Springer, Heidelberg (2006)
5. CMU Face Group. Frontal and profile face databases, http://vasc.ri.cmu.edu/idb/html/face/
6. Crandal, D., Felzenswalb, P., Huttenlocher, D.: Spatial priors for part-based recognition using statistical models. In: CVPR, vol. 1, pp. 10–17 (2005)
7. Dorko, G., Schmid, C.: Selection of scale-invariant parts for object class recognition. In: ICCV, pp. 634–640 (2003)
8. Fergus, R., Perona, P., Zisserman, A.: Weakly supervised scale-invariant learning of models for visual recognition. IJCV 71(3), 273–303 (2006)
9. Gutta, S., Wechsler, H., Phillips, P.: Gender and ethnic classification of human faces using hybrid classifiers. In: FGR, pp. 194–199 (1998)
10. Jain, A., Huang, J., Fang, S.: Gender identification using frontal facial images. In: ICME (2005)
11. Jaynes, E.: Prior probabilities. IEEE Transactions of systems, science, and cybernetics 4(3), 227–241 (1968)
12. Jordan, M.I.: An Introduction to Probabilistic Graphical Models (2003) (in preparation)
13. Kadir, T., Brady, M.: Saliency, scale and image description. IJCV 45(2), 83–105 (2001)
14. Kim, H.-C., Kim, D., Ghahramani, Z., Bang, S.Y.: Appearance-based gender classification with gaussian processes. PRL 27, 618–626 (2006)
15. Lowe, D.G.: Distinctive image features from scale-invariant keypoints. IJCV 60(2), 91–110 (2004)
16. Mikolajczyk, K., Schmid, C.: Indexing based on scale invariant interest points. In: ICCV, pp. I: 525–531 (2001)
17. Moghaddam, B., Yang, M.: Learning gender with support faces. PAMI 24(5), 707–711 (2002)
18. Shakhnarovich, G., Viola, P.A., Moghaddam, B.: A unified learning framework for real time face detection and classification. In: FGR (2002)
19. Sivic, J., Russell, B.C., Efros, A.A., Zisserman, A., Freeman, W.T.: Discovering objects and their localization in images. In: ICCV, pp. 370–377 (2005)
20. Thomas, A., Ferrari, V., Leibe, B., Tuytelaars, T., Schiele, B., Van Gool, L.: Towards multi-view object class detection. In: CVPR (2006)
21. Toews, M., Arbel, T.: Detection over viewpoint via the object class invariant. In: ICPR, pp. 765–768 (2006)
22. Turk, M., Pentland, A.P.: Eigenfaces for recognition. CogNeuro 3(1), 71–96 (1991)
23. Viola, P., Jones, M.: Rapid object detection using a boosted cascade of simple features. In: CVPR, vol. 1, pp. 511–518 (2001)
24. Weber, M., Welling, M., Perona, P.: Unsupervised learning of models for recognition. In: Vernon, D. (ed.) ECCV 2000. LNCS, vol. 1842, pp. 18–32. Springer, Heidelberg (2000)
25. Yang, Z., Li, M., Ai, H.: An experimental study on automatic face gender classification. In: ICPR, pp. 1099–1102 (2006)

Enhanced Local Texture Feature Sets for Face Recognition Under Difficult Lighting Conditions

Xiaoyang Tan and Bill Triggs

INRIA & Laboratoire Jean Kuntzmann, 655 avenue de l'Europe, Montbonnot 38330, France
{xiaoyang.tan,bill.triggs}@imag.fr

Abstract. Recognition in uncontrolled situations is one of the most important bottlenecks for practical face recognition systems. We address this by combining the strengths of robust illumination normalization, local texture based face representations and distance transform based matching metrics. Specifically, we make three main contributions: (*i*) we present a simple and efficient preprocessing chain that eliminates most of the effects of changing illumination while still preserving the essential appearance details that are needed for recognition; (*ii*) we introduce Local Ternary Patterns (LTP), a generalization of the Local Binary Pattern (LBP) local texture descriptor that is more discriminant and less sensitive to noise in uniform regions; and (*iii*) we show that replacing local histogramming with a local distance transform based similarity metric further improves the performance of LBP/LTP based face recognition. The resulting method gives state-of-the-art performance on three popular datasets chosen to test recognition under difficult illumination conditions: Face Recognition Grand Challenge version 1 experiment 4, Extended Yale-B, and CMU PIE.

1 Introduction

One of the key challenges of face recognition is finding efficient and discriminative facial appearance descriptors that can counteract large variations in illumination, pose, facial expression, ageing, partial occlusions and other changes [27]. There are two main approaches: geometric feature-based descriptors and appearance-based descriptors. Geometric descriptors can be hard to extract reliably under variations in facial appearance, while appearance-based ones such as eigenfaces tend to blur out small details owing to residual spatial registration errors. Recently, representations based on local pooling of local appearance descriptors have drawn increasing attention because they can capture small appearance details in the descriptors while remaining resistant to registration errors owing to local pooling. Another motivation is the observation that human visual perception is well-adapted to extracting and pooling local structural information ('micro-patterns') from images [2]. Methods in this category include Gabor wavelets [16], local autocorrelation filters [11], and Local Binary Patterns [1].

In this paper we focus on Local Binary Patterns (LBP) and their generalizations. LBP's are a computationally efficient nonparametric local image texture descriptor. They have been used with considerable success in a number of visual recognition tasks including face recognition [1,2,20]. LBP features are invariant to monotonic gray-level

S.K. Zhou et al. (Eds.): AMFG 2007, LNCS 4778, pp. 168–182, 2007.

changes by design and thus are usually considered to require no image preprocessing before use[1]. In fact, LBP itself is sometimes used as a lighting normalization stage for other methods [12]. However, in practice the reliability of LBP decreases significantly under large illumination variations (*c.f.* table 3). Lighting effects involve complex local interactions and the resulting images often violate LBP's basic assumption that gray-level changes monotonically. We have addressed this problem by developing a simple and efficient image preprocessing chain that greatly reduces the influence of illumination variations, local shadowing and highlights while preserving the elements of visual appearance that are needed for recognition.

Another limitation of LBP is its sensitivity to random and quantization noise in uniform and near-uniform image regions such as the forehead and cheeks. To counter this we extend LBP to Local Ternary Patterns (LTP), a 3-valued coding that includes a threshold around zero for improved resistance to noise. LTP inherits most of the other key advantages of LBP such as computational efficiency.

Current LBP based face recognition methods partition the face image into a grid of fixed-size cells for the local pooling of texture descriptors (LBP histograms). This coarse (and typically abrupt) spatial quantization is somewhat arbitrary and not necessarily well adapted to local facial morphology. It inevitably causes some loss of discriminative power. To counter this we use distance transform techniques to create local texture comparison metrics that have more controlled spatial gradings.

To illustrate the effectiveness of our approach we present experimental results on three state-of-the-art face recognition datasets containing large lighting variations similar to those encountered in natural images taken under uncontrolled conditions: Face Recognition Grand Challenge version 1 experiment 1.0.4 ('FRGC-104') [19]; Extended Yale illumination face database B ('Extended Yale-B') [9,15]; and CMU PIE [22].

2   Related Work

As emphasized by the recent FRVT and FRGC trials [19], illumination variations are one of the most important bottlenecks for practical face recognition systems. Generally, one can cope with this in two ways. The first uses training examples to learn a global model of the possible illumination variations, for example a linear subspace or manifold model, which then generalizes to the variations seen in new images [5,3]. The disadvantage is that many training images are required.

The second approach seeks conventional image processing transformations that reduce the image to a more "canonical" form in which the variations are suppressed. This has the merit of easy application to real images and the lack of a need for comprehensive training data. Given that complete illumination invariants do not exist [7], one must content oneself with finding representations that are resistant to the most common classes of natural illumination variations. Most methods exploit the fact that these are typically characterized by relatively low spatial frequencies. For example, the Multiscale Retinex (MSR) method of Jobson *et al.* [13] normalizes the illumination by dividing the image by a smoothed version of itself. A similar idea (with a different local filter) is used by

---

[1] One exception is Local Gabor Binary Pattern Histogram Sequences [26] whose Gabor magnitude mapping can be regarded as a special kind of preprocessing for LBP.

Wang *et al.* [23] in the Self Quotient Image model (SQI). More recently, Chen *et al.* [8] improved SQI by using Logarithmic Total Variation (LTV) smoothing, and Gross & Brajovic (GB) [10] developed an anisotropic smoothing method that relies on the iterative estimation of a blurred version of the original image. Some comparative results for these and related works can be found in [21].

In this paper we adopt the "canonical form" philosophy, basing our method on a chain of efficient processing steps that normalize for various effects of the changing illumination environment. The main advantages of our method are simplicity, computational efficiency and robustness to lighting changes and other image quality degradations such as blurring.

We describe our LBP/LTP face descriptors and their distance transform based similarity metric in the next two sections, detailing our preprocessing method in §5 and concluding with experiments and discussion.

3   Local Ternary Patterns

3.1   Local Binary Patterns (LBP)

Ojala *et al.* [17] introduced the Local Binary Pattern operator in 1996 as a means of summarizing local gray-level structure. The operator takes a local neighborhood around each pixel, thresholds the pixels of the neighborhood at the value of the central pixel and uses the resulting binary-valued image patch as a local image descriptor. It was originally defined for 3×3 neighborhoods, giving 8 bit codes based on the 8 pixels around the central one. Formally, the LBP operator takes the form

$$LBP(x_c, y_c) = \sum_{n=0}^{7} 2^n \, s(i_n - i_c) \tag{1}$$

where in this case n runs over the 8 neighbors of the central pixel c, i_c and i_n are the gray-level values at c and n, and $s(u)$ is 1 if $u \geq 0$ and 0 otherwise. The LBP encoding process is illustrated in fig. 1.

Two extensions of the original operator were made in [18]. The first defined LBP's for neighborhoods of different sizes, thus making it feasible to deal with textures at different scales. The second defined the so-called *uniform patterns*: an LBP is 'uniform' if it contains at most one 0-1 and one 1-0 transition when viewed as a circular bit string. For example, the LBP code in fig. 1 is uniform. Uniformity is an important concept in the LBP methodology, representing primitive structural information such as edges and corners. Ojala *et al.* observed that although only 58 of the 256 8-bit patterns are uniform,

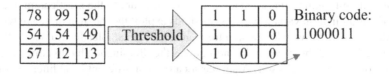

Fig. 1. Illustration of the basic LBP operator

nearly 90 percent of all observed image neighbourhoods are uniform. In methods that histogram LBP's, the number of bins can be thus significantly reduced by assigning all non-uniform patterns to a single bin, often without losing too much information.

3.2   Local Ternary Patterns (LTP)

LBP's are resistant to lighting effects in the sense that they are invariant to monotonic gray-level transformations, and they have been shown to have high discriminative power for texture classification [17]. However because they threshold at exactly the value of the central pixel i_c they tend to be sensitive to noise, especially in near-uniform image regions. Given that many facial regions are relatively uniform, it is potentially useful to improve the robustness of the underlying descriptors in these areas.

This section extends LBP to 3-valued codes, *Local Ternary Patterns*, in which gray-levels in a zone of width $\pm t$ around i_c are quantized to zero, ones above this are quantized to $+1$ and ones below it to -1, *i.e.* the indicator $s(u)$ is replaced by a 3-valued function:

$$s'(u, i_c, t) = \begin{cases} 1, & u \geq i_c + t \\ 0, & |u - i_c| < t \\ -1, & u \leq i_c - t \end{cases} \qquad (2)$$

and the binary LBP code is replaced by a ternary LTP code. Here t is a user-specified threshold (so LTP codes more resistant to noise, but no longer strictly invariant to gray-level transformations). The LTP encoding procedure is illustrated in fig. 2. Here the threshold t was set to 5, so the tolerance interval is $[49, 59]$.

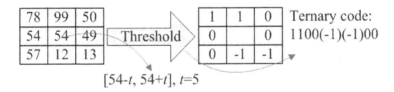

Fig. 2. Illustration of the basic LTP operator

When using LTP for visual matching we could use 3^n valued codes, but the uniform pattern argument also applies in the ternary case. For simplicity the experiments below use a coding scheme that splits each ternary pattern into its positive and negative parts as illustrated in fig. 3, subsequently treating these as two separate channels of LBP descriptors for which separate histograms and similarity metrics are computed, combining these only at the end of the computation.

LTP's bear some similarity to the texture spectrum (TS) technique from the early 1990's [24]. However TS did not include preprocessing, thresholding, local histograms or uniform pattern based dimensionality reduction and it was not tested on faces.

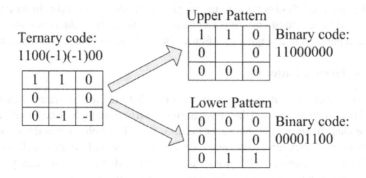

Fig. 3. An example of the splitting of an LTP code into positive and negative LBP codes

4   Distance Transform Based Similarity Metric

T. Ahonen *et al.* introduced an LBP based method for face recognition [1] that divides the face into a regular grid of cells and histograms the uniform LBP's within each cell, finally using nearest neighbor classification in the χ^2 histogram distance for recognition:

$$\chi^2(p, q) = \sum_i \frac{(p_i - q_i)^2}{p_i + q_i} \tag{3}$$

Here p, q are two image descriptors (histogram vectors). Excellent results were obtained on the FERET dataset.

Possible criticisms of this method are that subdividing the face into a regular grid is somewhat arbitrary (cells are not necessarily well aligned with facial features), and that partitioning appearance descriptors into grid cells is likely to cause both aliasing (due to abrupt spatial quantization) and loss of spatial resolution (as position within a grid cell is not coded). Given that the aim of coding is to provide illumination- and outlier-robust appearance-based correspondence with some leeway for small spatial deviations due to misalignment, it seems more appropriate to use a Hausdorff distance like similarity metric that takes each LBP or LTP pixel code in image X and tests whether a similar code appears at a nearby position in image Y, with a weighting that decreases smoothly with image distance. Such a scheme should be able to achieve discriminant appearance-based image matching with a well-controllable degree of spatial looseness.

We can achieve this using Distance Transforms [6]. Given a 2-D reference image X, we find its image of LBP or LTP codes and transform this into a set of sparse binary images b^k, one for each possible LBP or LTP code value k (*i.e.* 59 images for uniform codes). Each b^k specifies the pixel positions at which its particular LBP or LTP code value appears. We then calculate the distance transform image d^k of each b^k. Each pixel of d^k gives the distance to the nearest image X pixel with code k (2D Euclidean distance is used in the experiments below). The distance or similarity metric from image X to image Y is then:

$$D(X, Y) = \sum_{\text{pixels } (i, j) \text{ of } Y} w(d_X^{k_Y (i,j)}(i, j)) \tag{4}$$

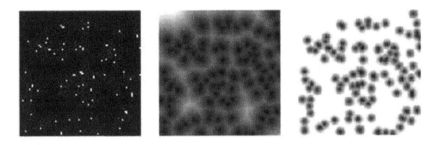

Fig. 4. From left to right: a binary layer, its distance transform, and the truncated linear version of this

Here, $k_Y(i,j)$ is the code value of pixel (i,j) of image Y and $w()$ is a user-defined function[2] giving the penalty to include for a pixel at the given spatial distance from the nearest matching code in X. In our experiments we tested both Gaussian similarity metrics $w(d) = \exp\{-(d/\sigma)^2/2\}$ and truncated linear distances $w(d) = \min(d, \tau)$. Their performance is similar, with truncated distances giving slightly better results overall. The default parameter values (for 120×120 face images in which an iris or nostril has a radius of about 6 pixels) are $\sigma = 3$ pixels and $\tau = 6$ pixels.

Fig. 4 shows an example of a binary layer and its distance transforms. For a given target the transform can be computed and mapped through $w()$ in a preprocessing step, after which matching to any subsequent image takes $\mathcal{O}(\text{number of pixels})$ irrespective of the number of code values.

5   Illumination Normalization

5.1   The Processing Sequence

This section describes our image preprocessing method. It incorporates a series of steps chosen to counter the effects of illumination variations, local shadowing and highlights, while still preserving the essential elements of visual appearance for use in recognition. Although not done by design, the final chain is reminiscent of certain preprocessing stages found in the mammalian visual cortex. In detail, the steps are as follows.

Gamma Correction. This is a nonlinear gray-level transformation that replaces gray-level I with I^γ (for $\gamma > 0$) or $\log(I)$ (for $\gamma = 0$), where $\gamma \in [0,1]$ is a user-defined parameter. It has the effect of enhancing the local dynamic range of the image in dark or shadowed regions, while compressing it in bright regions and at highlights. The basic principle is that the intensity of the light reflected from an object is the product of the incoming illumination L (which is piecewise smooth for the most part) and the local

---

[2] w is monotonically increasing for a distance metric and monotonically decreasing for a similarity one. In D, note that each pixel in Y is matched to the nearest pixel with the same code in X. This is not symmetric between X and Y even if the underlying distance d is, but it can be symmetrized if desired.

surface reflectance R (which carries detailed object-level appearance information). We want to recover object-level information independent of illumination, and taking logs makes the task easier by converting the product into a sum: for constant local illumination, a given reflectance step produces a given step in $\log(I)$ irrespective of the actual intensity of the illumination. In practice a full log transformation is often too strong, tending to over-amplify the noise in dark regions of the image, but a power law with exponent γ in the range $[0, 0.5]$ is a good compromise. Here we use $\gamma = 0.2$ as the default setting.

Difference of Gaussian (DoG) Filtering. Gamma correction does not remove the influence of overall intensity gradients such as shading effects. Shading induced by surface structure is potentially a useful visual cue but it is predominantly low frequency spatial information that is hard to separate from effects caused by illumination gradients. High pass filtering removes both the useful and the incidental information, thus simplifying the recognition problem and in many cases increasing the overall system performance. Similarly, suppressing the highest spatial frequencies reduces aliasing and noise, and in practice it often manages to do so without destroying too much of the underlying signal on which recognition needs to be based. DoG filtering is a convenient way to obtain the resulting bandpass behaviour. Fine spatial detail is critically important for recognition so the inner (smaller) Gaussian is typically quite narrow ($\sigma_0 \leq 1$ pixel), while the outer one might have σ_1 of 2–4 pixels or more, depending on the spatial frequency at which low frequency information becomes misleading rather than informative. Given the strong lighting variations in our datasets we find that $\sigma_1 \approx 2$ typically gives the best results, but values up to about 4 are not too damaging and may be preferable for datasets with less extreme lighting variations. LBP and LTP seem to benefit from a little smoothing ($\sigma_0 \approx 1$), perhaps because pixel based voting is sensitive to aliasing artifacts. Below we use $\sigma_0 = 1.0$ and $\sigma_1 = 2.0$ by default[3].

We implement the filters using explicit convolution. If the face is part of a larger image the gamma correction and prefilter should be run on an appropriate region of this before cutting out the face image. Otherwise extend-as-constant boundary conditions should be used: using extend-as-zero or wrap-around (FFT) boundary conditions significantly reduces the overall performance, in part because it introduces strong gradients at the image borders that disturb the subsequent contrast equalization stage. If DoG is run without prior gamma normalization, the resulting images clearly show the extent to which local contrast (and hence visual detail) is reduced in shadowed regions.

Masking. If a mask is needed to suppress facial regions that are felt to be irrelevant or too variable, it should be applied at this point. Otherwise, either strong artificial gray-level edges are introduced into the convolution, or invisible regions are taken into account during contrast equalization.

---

[3] Curiously, for some datasets it also helps to offset the center of the larger filter by 1–2 pixels relative to the center of the smaller one, so that the final prefilter is effectively the sum of a centered DoG and a low pass spatial derivative. The best direction for the displacement is somewhat variable but typically diagonal. The effect is not consistent enough to be recommended practice, but it might repay further investigation.

Contrast Equalization. The final step of our preprocessing chain globally rescales the image intensities to standardize a robust measure of overall contrast or intensity variation. It is important to use a robust estimator because the signal typically still contains a small admixture of extreme values produced by highlights, garbage at the image borders and small dark regions such as nostrils. One could, *e.g.*, use the median of the absolute value of the signal for this, but here we have preferred a simple and rapid approximation based on a two stage process:

$$I(x,y) \leftarrow \frac{I(x,y)}{(\mathrm{mean}(|I(x',y')|^a))^{1/a}} \tag{5}$$

$$I(x,y) \leftarrow \frac{I(x,y)}{(\mathrm{mean}(\min(\tau,|I(x',y')|)^a))^{1/a}} \tag{6}$$

Here, a is a strongly compressive exponent that reduces the influence of large values, τ is a threshold used to truncate large values after the first phase of normalization, and the mean is over the whole (unmasked part of the) image. By default we use $\alpha = 0.1$ and $\tau = 10$.

The resulting image is now well scaled but it can still contain extreme values. To reduce their influence on subsequent stages of processing, we finally apply a nonlinear function to compress over-large values. Here we use the hyperbolic tangent $I(x,y) \leftarrow \tau \tanh(I(x,y)/\tau)$, thus limiting I to the range $(-\tau, \tau)$.

5.2 Robustness and Computation Time

To illustrate the behavior of the proposed preprocessing method, we examine its effect on the LBP histogram feature set. Fig. 5 shows a matching pair of target and query images chosen randomly from the FRGC dataset (see below). LBP features are extracted from corresponding local regions of the two images (the white squares in fig. 5), both before and after illumination normalization. The resulting histograms are shown in fig. 6. It can be seen that without illumination normalization the descriptors of the

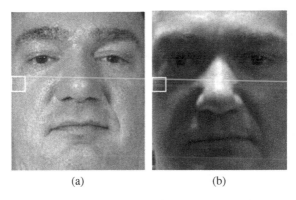

(a)   (b)

Fig. 5. Two face images from the same subject. The LBP histograms from the marked region are shown in fig. 6.

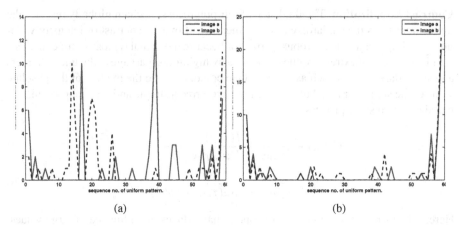

Fig. 6. LBP histograms for the marked region in fig. 5, before (a) and after (b) illumination normalization

two images are very different, but that this is significantly reduced by normalization. In fact, the χ^2 distance between the two spatial histograms reduces from 93.4 before normalization to 25.0 after it.

Since run time is a critical factor in many practical applications, it is also interesting to consider the computational load of our normalization chain. Our method uses only simple closed-form image processing operations so it is much more efficient than ones that require expensive iterative optimizations such as Logarithmic Total Variation [8] and anisotropic diffusion [10]. Our (unoptimized Matlab) implementation takes only about 50 ms to process a 120×120 pixel face image on a 2.8 GHz P4, allowing face preprocessing to be performed in real time. In comparison, the current implementation of LTV is about 300 times slower.

6   Experiments

We now present experiments that illustrate the effectiveness of our method using three publicly available face datasets with large illumination variations: Face Recognition Grand Challenge version 1 experiment 1.0.4 ('FRGC-104') [19]; Extended Yale Face Database B ('Extended Yale-B') [15]; and CMU PIE [22].

6.1   Experimental Settings

We use only frontal face views but lighting, expression and identity may all vary. All of the images undergo the same geometric normalization prior to analysis: conversion to 8 bit gray-scale images; rigid scaling and image rotation to place the centers of the two eyes at fixed positions, using the eye coordinates supplied with the original datasets; and image cropping to 120×120 pixels.

The default settings of the various parameters of our methods are summarized in table 1. Unless otherwise noted, these apply to all experiments. General guidelines on

Table 1. Default parameter settings for our methods

Procedure	Parameter	Value
Gamma Correction	γ	0.2
DoG Filtering	σ_0	1
	σ_1	2
Contrast Equalization	α	0.1
	τ	10
LTP	t	0.1-0.2
LBP/LTP χ^2 cell size		8×8

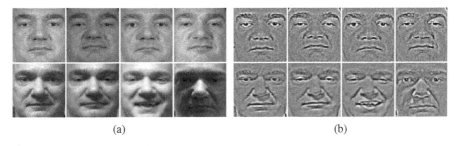

(a)   (b)

Fig. 7. Examples of images from FRGC-104: (a) target images (upper row) and query images (lower row) without illumination preprocessing; (b) the corresponding illumination normalized images from the proposed preprocessing chain

how to set these parameters can be found in section 5. We find that the proposed pre-processing method gives similar results over a broad range of parameter settings, which greatly facilitates the selection of parameters.

For comparison, we also tested the LTP/DT features with our preprocessing chain replaced with several alternative illumination normalization methods including standard histogram equalization (HE), Self-Quotient Image (SQI [23]), Multiscale Retinex (MSR [13]), Logarithmic Total Variation (LTV [8]) and Gross & Brajovic's anisotropic smoothing (GB [10]). The implementations of these algorithms were based in part on the publicly available *Torch3Vision* toolbox (http://torch3vision.idiap.ch) with its default or recommended parameter settings. We would also like to thank Terrence Chen for making his implementation of LTV [8] available to us.

Although we do not show the results here owing to lack of space, our preprocessing method also gives substantial performance gains for the other image descriptors and recognition algorithms tested including eigen- and Fisher-faces under a range of descriptor normalizations and distance metrics, kernelized versions of these, and Gabor features.

6.2   Results on FRGC-104

We now show results on the dataset of the FRGC 1.0.4 experiment [19]. This dataset is challenging because, although the gallery images were obtained under carefully con-

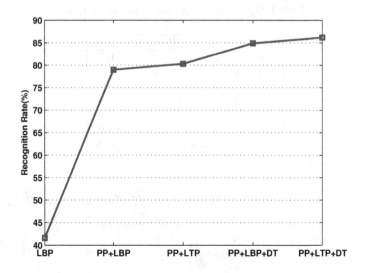

Fig. 8. Overall results for the proposed methods on FRGC-104

trolled conditions, the probe images were captured in uncontrolled indoor and outdoor settings. Fig. 7 shows some example images. There are large changes in illumination, appearance and expression. For the experiments reported here we use nearest-neighbour matching of each of the 943 probe images against each of the 943 gallery images. The training images are not used at all.

Fig. 8 shows the extent to which standard LBP can be improved by combining the three enhancements proposed in this paper: using preprocessing (PP); replacing LBP with LTP; replacing local histogramming and the χ^2 histogram distance with the Distance Transform based similarity metric (DT). Overall the absolute recognition rate is increased by about 45% relative to standard unpreprocessed LBP/χ^2. Preprocessing alone boosts the performance by 37% (from 41.6% to 79.0%). Replacing LBP with LTP improves the recognition rate to 80.4% and adding DT further improves it to 86.3%. LTP consistently outperforms LBP by a small margin, and the DT based similarity metric significantly improves on χ^2 histogram distance independent of the local region size. By way of comparison, the best previous performance that we are aware of on this dataset (unfortunately for a different and hence not strictly comparable experimental setup) is 78.0% [16].

To evaluate the performance of our preprocessing chain, we replaced it with several competing illumination normalization methods. The results are shown in fig. 9. Our method significantly outperforms the other ones tested. In particular, the performance of the sophisticated methods GB and LTV is disappointing on this dataset (*c.f.* their results on Yale-B below). It seems that on average they remove too much information during normalization. The reasons for this deserve further investigation. Note that besides large lighting variations, the dataset contains various other commonly encountered variations including ageing effects and image blurring.

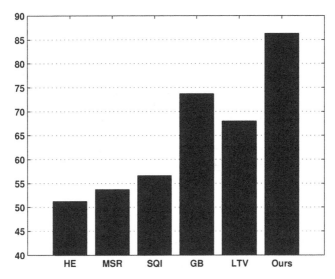

Fig. 9. Comparison of recognition rates of different preprocessing methods on the FRGC-104 database with LTP/DT features (%)

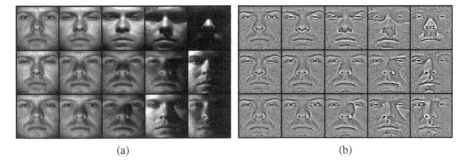

(a)   (b)

Fig. 10. Examples of images of one person from the Extended Yale-B frontal database. The columns respectively give images from subsets 1 to 5. (a) input images. (b) the corresponding illumination normalized images from our preprocessing chain.

6.3   Results on Extended Yale-B

The Yale Face Dataset B [4] containing 10 people under 64 different illumination conditions has been the de facto standard for studies of variable lighting over the past decade. It was recently updated to the Extended Yale Face Database B [15], containing 38 subjects under 9 poses and 64 illumination conditions. In both cases the images are divided into five subsets according to the angle between the light source direction and the central camera axis ($12°, 25°, 50°, 77°, 90°$). Example images are shown in fig. 10. For our experiments, the images with the most neutral light sources ('A+000E+00') were used as the gallery, and all frontal images of each of the standard subsets 1–5 were used as probes (2414 images of 38 subjects for the Extended dataset, 640 of 10 for the standard one).

Table 2. Overall recognition rates (%) on Extended Yale-B

Methods	Subset No.(number of probes)				
	1	2	3	4	5
	(363)	(456)	(455)	(526)	(714)
LBP/χ^2	100.0	100.0	97.6	65.2	44.4
PP+LBP/χ^2	100.0	100.0	99.8	97.3	87.5
PP+LTP/χ^2	100.0	100.0	100.0	98.1	97.1
PP+LBP/DT	100.0	100.0	100.0	**99.4**	95.2
PP+LTP/DT	100.0	100.0	100.0	99.2	**97.2**

Table 3. Recognition rates (%) with different preprocessing methods on Extended Yale-B database

Methods	Subset No.(number of probes)				
	1	2	3	4	5
	(263)	(456)	(455)	(526)	(714)
w/o	100.0	100.0	97.1	66.8	60.6
HE	100.0	100.0	97.4	76.8	66.8
MSR	100.0	99.8	96.7	93.6	82.1
SQI	100.0	99.8	97.8	94.1	82.4
GB	100.0	100.0	99.8	96.9	90.6
LTV	100.0	100.0	98.4	98.9	**97.6**
Ours	**100.0**	**100.0**	**100.0**	99.2	97.2

Table 4. Recognition Rates with different preprocessing methods on the CMU-PIE database (%)

Methods	HE	MSR	SQI	GB	LTV	Ours
Accuracy	98.3	98.3	98.5	99.7	100.0	**100.0**

Our LTP/DT method gives perfect results on all 5 subsets of standard Yale-B[4]. On Extended Yale-B, the overall performance of our methods is shown in table 2 and the effect of using different illumination normalization methods with LTP/DT is shown in table 3. In table 2, note that for the most difficult subset (5), including either LTP or the distance transform increases performance over PP+LBP/χ^2 by respectively about 10.0% and 8.0%. As the first row of table 3 indicates, even without image preprocessing the system performs quite well under the mild lighting changes of subsets 1–3 (*c.f.* fig. 10). However its performance drops significantly under the more extreme lighting conditions of subsets 4–5. In these cases, illumination normalizers such as LTV [8] and GB [10] significantly improve the accuracy. Our three-stage preprocessing chain achieves the top performance on subsets 3–4 and is beaten only marginally by LTV on set 5. As mentioned above, LTV is also about 300 times slower than our preprocessing method.

6.4   Results on the CMU PIE Database

CMU PIE [22] is another dataset that is often used for studies of illumination variations. We tested a subset containing frontal images of 68 individuals illuminated from 21 directions. Images of one individual are shown in fig. 11. As before, the images with the most neutral lighting are used for the gallery and all of the remaining images are used as probes. When preprocessing is included, all of our LBP and LTP based schemes achieve 100.0% on this dataset. Comparative results for LTP/DT with different preprocessing methods are shown in table 4. As before, our preprocessing chain and LTV are the top performers.

---

[4] For comparison, on Yale-B subsets 2,3,4: Harmonic image Exemplars give 100, 99.7, 96.9% [25]; nine point of light gives 100, 100, 97.2% [14]; and Gradient Angle gives 100, 100, 98.6% [7]. These authors do not test on the most difficult set, 5.

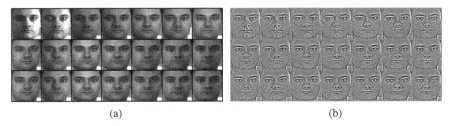

(a)   (b)

Fig. 11. Example images of one person from the CMU PIE database: (a) original images; (b) the corresponding normalized images obtained with the proposed preprocessing chain

7 Conclusions

We have presented new methods for face recognition under uncontrolled lighting based on robust preprocessing and an extension of the Local Binary Pattern (LBP) local texture descriptor. There are three main contributions: (*i*) a simple, efficient image preprocessing chain whose practical recognition performance is comparable to or better than current (often much more complex) illumination normalization methods; (*ii*) a rich descriptor for local texture called Local Ternary Patterns (LTP) that generalizes LBP while fragmenting less under noise in uniform regions; and (*iii*) a distance transform based similarity metric that captures the local structure and geometric variations of LBP/LTP face images better than the simple grids of histograms that are currently used. The combination of these enhancements provides very promising performance on three well-known face datasets that contain widely varying lighting conditions.

Work in progress includes experiments on the much larger FRGC 2.0.4 dataset and tests against subspace based recognition methods.

References

[1] Ahonen, T., Hadid, A., Pietikainen, M.: Face recognition with local binary patterns. In: Pajdla, T., Matas, J(G.) (eds.) ECCV 2004. LNCS, vol. 3021, pp. 469–481. Springer, Heidelberg (2004)

[2] Ahonen, T., Hadid, A., Pietikainen, M.: Face description with local binary patterns: Application to face recognition. IEEE TPAMI 28(12) (2006)

[3] Basri, R., Jacobs, D.: Lambertian reflectance and linear subspaces. IEEE TPAMI 25(2), 218–233 (2003)

[4] Belhumeur, P., Hespanha, J., Kriegman, D.: Eigenfaces vs. Fisherfaces: Recognition using class specific linear projection. IEEE TPAMI 19(7), 711–720 (1997)

[5] Belhumeur, P., Kriegman, D.: What is the set of images of an object under all possible illumination conditions. IJCV 28(3), 245–260 (1998)

[6] Borgefors, G.: Distance transformations in digital images. Comput. Vision Graph. Image Process. 34(3), 344–371 (1986)

[7] Chen, H., Belhumeur, P., Jacobs, D.: In search of illumination invariants. In: Proc. CVPR 2000, pp. I: 254–261 (2000)

[8] Chen, T., Yin, W., Zhou, X., Comaniciu, D., Huang, T.: Total variation models for variable lighting face recognition. IEEE TPAMI 28(9), 1519–1524 (2006)

[9] Georghiades, A.S., Belhumeur, P.N., Kriegman, D.J.: From few to many: illumination cone models for face recognition under variable lighting and pose. IEEE TPAMI 23(6), 643–660 (2001)

[10] Gross, R., Brajovic, V.: An image preprocessing algorithm for illumination invariant face recognition. In: Kittler, J., Nixon, M.S. (eds.) AVBPA 2003. LNCS, vol. 2688, pp. 10–18. Springer, Heidelberg (2003)

[11] Guodail, F., Lange, E., Iwamoto, T.: Face recognition system using local autocorrelations and multiscale integration. IEEE TPAMI 18(10), 1024–1028 (1996)

[12] Heusch, G., Rodriguez, Y., Marcel, S.: Local binary patterns as an image preprocessing for face authentication. In: Proc. FGR 2006, USA, pp. 9–14 (2006)

[13] Jobson, D., Rahman, Z., Woodell, G.: A multiscale retinex for bridging the gap between color images and the human observation of scenes. IEEE TIP 6(7), 965–976 (1997)

[14] Lee, K., Ho, J., Kriegman, D.: Nine points of light: Acquiring subspaces for face recognition under variable lighting. In: Proc. CVPR 2001, pp. I: 519–526 (2001)

[15] Lee, K., Ho, J., Kriegman, D.: Acquiring linear subspaces for face recognition under variable lighting. IEEE TPAMI 27(5), 684–698 (2005)

[16] Liu, C.: Capitalize on dimensionality increasing techniques for improving face recognition grand challenge performance. IEEE TPAMI 28(5), 725–737 (2006)

[17] Ojala, T., Pietikainen, M., Harwood, D.: A comparative study of texture measures with classification based on feature distributions. Pattern Recognition 29 (1996)

[18] Ojala, T., Pietikainen, M., Maenpaa, T.: Multiresolution gray-scale and rotation invarianat texture classification with local binary patterns. IEEE TPAMI 24(7), 971–987 (2002)

[19] Phillips, P.J., Flynn, P.J., Scruggs, W.T., Bowyer, K.W., Chang, J., Hoffman, K., Marques, J., Min, J., Worek, W.J.: Overview of the face recognition grand challenge. In: Proc. CVPR 2005, San Diego, CA, pp. 947–954 (2005)

[20] Rodriguez, Y., Marcel, S.: Face authentication using adapted local binary pattern histograms. In: Leonardis, A., Bischof, H., Pinz, A. (eds.) ECCV 2006. LNCS, vol. 3954, pp. 321–332. Springer, Heidelberg (2006)

[21] Short, J., Kittler, J., Messer, K.: A comparison of photometric normalization algorithms for face verification. In: Proc. AFGR 2004, pp. 254–259 (2004)

[22] Sim, T., Baker, S., Bsat, M.: The cmu pose, illumination, and expression (pie) database of human faces. Technical Report CMU-RI-TR-01-02, Robotics Institute, Carnegie Mellon University (January 2001)

[23] Wang, H., Li, S., Wang, Y.: Face recognition under varying lighting conditions using self quotient image. In: Proc. AFGR 2004 (2004)

[24] Wang, L., He, D.: Texture classification using texture spectrum. Pattern Recognition 23, 905–910 (1990)

[25] Zhang, L., Samaras, D.: Face recognition under variable lighting using harmonic image exemplars. In: Proc. CVPR 2003, pp. I: 19–25 (2003)

[26] Zhang, W., Shan, S., Gao, W., Zhang, H.: Local Gabor Binary Pattern Histogram Sequence (LGBPHS): A novel non-statistical model for face representation and recognition. In: Proc. ICCV 2005, Beijing, China, pp. 786–791 (2005)

[27] Zhao, W., Chellappa, R., Phillips, P.J., Rosenfeld, A.: Face recognition: A literature survey. ACM Computing Survey 34(4), 399–485 (2003)

Structured Ordinal Features for Appearance-Based Object Representation

Shengcai Liao, Zhen Lei, Stan Z. Li, Xiaotong Yuan,
and Ran He

Center for Biometrics and Security Research & National Laboratory of Pattern Recognition,
Institute of Automation, Chinese Academy of Sciences,
95 Zhongguancun Donglu, Beijing 100080, China
{scliao,zlei,szli,xtyuan,rhe}@nlpr.ia.ac.cn
http://www.cbsr.ia.ac.cn

Abstract. In this paper, we propose a novel appearance-based representation, called Structured Ordinal Feature (SOF). SOF is a binary string encoded by combining eight ordinal blocks in a circle symmetrically. SOF is invariant to linear transformations on images and is flexible enough to represent different local structures of different complexity. We further extend SOF to Multi-scale Structured Ordinal Feature (MSOF) by concatenating binary strings of multi-scale SOFs at a fix position. In this way, MSOF encodes not only microstructure but also macrostructure of image patterns, thus provides a more powerful image representation. We also present an efficient algorithm for computing MSOF using integral images. Based on MSOF, statistical analysis and learning are performed to select most effective features and construct classifiers. The proposed method is evaluated with face recognition experiments, in which we achieve a high rank-1 recognition rate of 98.24% on FERET database.

1 Introduction

Object recognition from images is a challenging problem in computer vision. The main difficulties arise due to many uncertainties such as viewpoint and illumination changes. To overcome such problems, appearance-based object representation has been a hot issue in the past two decades. Among these, PCA [17] and LDA [2] are two classical linear methods that have significantly advanced object recognition techniques. But linear, holistic appearance-based methods can not capture subtleties of various objects, and holistic features are unstable under various illumination changes. It is believed that localized appearance-based features, which reflect the intrinsic properties of an object, can be more powerful for object recognition. Thus local features have been investigated a lot by researchers in recent years, such as Local feature analysis (LFA) [10], Gabor wavelet-based features [5,19,7], Local Binary Patterns (LBP) [1], and ordinal measures [15].

Local Binary Pattern (LBP) is a powerful local descriptor for microfeatures of images [9]. The LBP operator labels the pixels of an image by thresholding the 3×3-neighborhood of each pixel with the center value and considering the result as a binary number. Ahonen *et al.* proposed a novel approach for face recognition, which takes advantage of the Local Binary Pattern (LBP) histogram [1]. However, the original LBP

S.K. Zhou et al. (Eds.): AMFG 2007, LNCS 4778, pp. 183–192, 2007.

has its small spatial support area, hence the bit-wise comparison therein made between two single pixel values is much affected by noise. Moreover, features calculated in the local 3×3 neighborhood cannot capture larger scale structure (macrostructure) that may be dominant features of objects.

Recently, ordinal measure is discussed frequently as a method for representing local image structures. Ordinal features are defined based on the qualitative relationship between two image regions and are robust against various intra-class variations [11,15,16]. For example, they are invariant to linear transformations on images and is flexible enough to represent different local structures of different complexity. Sinha [15] shows that several ordinal measures on facial images, such as those between eye and forehead and between mouth and cheek, are invariant with different persons and imaging conditions, and thereby develops a ratio-template for face detection. Schneiderman [13] also uses an ordinal representation for face detection. While in the task of face recognition, which is a more complex problem than face detection, Thoresz [16] believes that ordinal features are not suited because they are too weak. Yet Liao *et al.* propose an ordinal feature based face recognition method for the first try, and obtained a promising results [6].

In this work, we propose a novel representation, called Structured Ordinal Feature (SOF). It is believed that the human vision system uses a series of levels of representation, with increasing complexity. Since one single ordinal feature is too simple to represent complex structures, we propose to combine several ordinal measures together to form a more powerful encoding of local image structures. SOF is a binary string encoded by combining eight ordinal blocks in a circle symmetrically. Using integral images, the comparison of average intensities between two blocks can be calculated very efficiently. Furthermore, Multi-scale Structured Ordinal Feature (MSOF) can be derived via concatenating binary strings of multi-scale SOFs at a fix position. This way, MSOF encodes not only microstructure but also macrostructure of image patterns, thus provides a more complete image representation. Based on MSOF, we define several dissimilarity measures, and perform statistical learning to select the most effective features and construct classifiers. Finally, we apply it to face recognition to illustrate the power and effectiveness of our proposed method.

The rest of this paper is organized as follows: In Section 2, the SOF and MSOF representations are introduced, and several dissimilarity measures based on MSOF are defined for discrimination tasks. In Section 3, statistical learning is applied for MSOF-based feature selection and classifier construction. Later, experiments with face recognition are shown in Section 4, and finally we conclude this paper in Section 5.

2   Structured Ordinal Feature

2.1   Ordinal Feature

Ordinal features come from a simple and straightforward concept that we often use. For example, we could easily rank or order the heights or weights of two persons, but it is hard to answer their precise differences. For computer vision, the absolute intensity information associated with an object can vary because it can change under various illumination settings. However, ordinal relationships among neighborhood image pixels or regions present some stability with such changes and reflect the intrinsic natures of the object.

An ordinal feature encodes an ordinal relationship between two concept. Fig.1 gives an example in which the average intensities between regions A and B are compared to give the ordinal code of 1 or 0. The information entropy of the ordinal measure is maximized because the ordinal code has nearly equal probability of being 1 or 0 for arbitrary patterns.

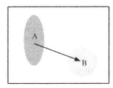 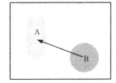

Fig. 1. Ordinal measure of relationship between two regions. An arrow points from the darker region to the brighter one. Left: Region A is darker than B, *i.e.* $A \prec B$. Right: Region A is brighter than B, *i.e.* $A \succ B$.

2.2 Structured Ordinal Feature

It is believed that the human vision system uses a series of levels of representations, with increasing complexity. Since one single ordinal feature is too simple to represent complex structures, we propose to combine several ordinal measures together to form a more powerful encoding of local image structures. We call this combination of ordinal encoding Structured Ordinal Feature (SOF). SOF is a binary string encoded by combining eight square ordinal blocks in a circle symmetrically, which is inspired by the encoding of local binary patterns [9]. Fig.2 illustrates an example of how SOF encoded.

There are two parameters in SOF: one is the size s of the square blocks, the other is the radius r of the circle. The parameter pair (s, r) denotes the scale of SOF. An SOF feature of scale (s, r) at pixel location (x, y) can be denoted as $SOF_{s,r}(x, y)$.

Structured Ordinal Feature extends the original ordinal feature, and can be used to represent various image structures, which may be some intrinsic properties of image object. The original ordinal feature can only show the contrast information between two regions, while using SOF, more local image structures can be represented. Fig. 3 shows some image structures that can only be represented by SOF. These structures are basic properties within many image objects. Therefore, SOF provides a more efficient and flexible way for appearance-based object representation.

Note that the scalar values of averages over blocks can be computed very efficiently [14] from the summed-area table [3] or integral image [18]. For this reason, the computation of SOF is very fast. Also note that the comparison result between averages of two blocks is invariant when the image is linearly transformed, thus the encoding of SOF is invariant to linear transformations on images.

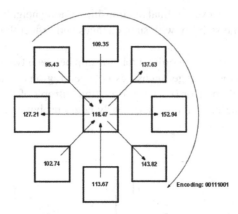

Fig. 2. An example of SOF encoding. Eight square ordinal blocks are combined in a circle symmetrically to form a structured filter. The number in each block is the average intensity within the corresponding image region. The arrows represent the ordinal relationships. According to these relationships, the result is encoded as a binary string.

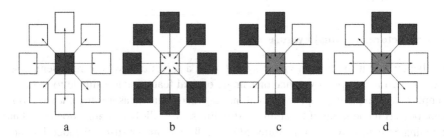

Fig. 3. Some image structures represented by SOF. a. Centered darker region; b. Centered brighter region; c. Brighter strip; d. Cross strips.

2.3 Multi-scale Structured Ordinal Feature

To construct a more complete image representation, we develop the operator of multi-scale SOF (MSOF). MSOF can be derived via concatenating binary strings of multi-scale SOFs at a fix position. See Fig.4 for an example. Suppose there are n scales of SOF, then an MSOF at location (x, y) is encoded as

$$MSOF(x, y) = SOF_{s_0, r_0}(x, y) \oplus SOF_{s_1, r_1}(x, y) \oplus \cdots \oplus SOF_{s_{n-1}, r_{n-1}}(x, y),$$

where $\oplus$ denotes binary concatenation operator. In this way, MSOF encodes not only microstructure but also macrostructure of image patterns, thus provides a more complete image representation.

The scale parameters of MSOF should be carefully designed so that the operator will cover the neighborhood as well as possible while minimizing the amount of redundant information. Consequently, the square blocks are set to fill the eight directions well within the same circle, while touching each other as well as possible between circles.

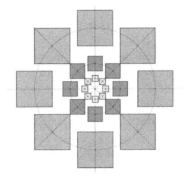

Fig. 4. An example of MSOF operator. Three scales of SOFs are combined at the center. The encodings are concatenated to form a binary string of 24 bits.

2.4 Dissimilarity Measure

For discrimination tasks, the Hamming distance can be used between two MSOFs at the same position. Since the encoding of MSOF is a concatenated binary string at a fix position, Hamming distance between two MSOFs at the same position can be used to measure the difference of two images at that position. Let $Hamm(\cdot, \cdot)$ denote the Hamming distance between two binary strings, then distance between two MSOFs at location (x, y) of image I' and I'' can be measured as

$$d_{hamm}(x, y) = Hamm(MSOF'(x, y), MSOF''(x, y)) \tag{1}$$

This kind of difference measures the percentage of bitwise difference between two MSOFs, ranging from 0 to 1.

Consequently, Hamming distances at all positions provides a discriminative feature set for object recognition, and classifiers can be further developed based on these features. One simple classifier is Nearest Neighbor (NN) classifier, using MSOF distance summed over the whole image as a dissimilarity measure. Suppose all images are H pixels high and W pixels wide, then such dissimilarity measure between two images I' and I'' can be defined as

$$d_{hamm} = \frac{1}{H \times W} \sum_{x,y} d_{hamm}(x, y) \tag{2}$$

The NN classifier can be used to provide a baseline performance. The latter section will demonstrate promising results given by MSOF-based NN classifier.

Another discriminative feature set can be constructed considering spacial information. Let $B = \{B_0, B_1, \cdots, B_{m-1}\}$ be a set of m-1 blocks of various sizes and positions over the whole image, then a set of features containing local region information can be defined as

$$d_{hamm}(B_i) = \frac{1}{H_i \times W_i} \sum_{(x,y) \in B_i} d_{hamm}(x, y), \quad i = 0, 1, \cdots, m - 1, \tag{3}$$

where H_i and W_i are height and width of block B_i respectively. Accordingly m discriminative features are defined for object recognition. We call them block-based MSOF Hamming dissimilarity measures.

Hamming distance based MSOF dissimilarity measure is effective when images are well aligned. However, based on pixel-wise comparison, Hamming distances are influenced by image misalignment. For more robust and efficient discrimination, we construct a feature set based on spatially distributed histograms, which are also used in [1]. Using the above notations, the MSOF histogram is defined as

$$Hist(B_i, j) = \frac{1}{H_i \times W_i \times n} \sum_{(x,y) \in B_i} \sum_{k=0}^{n} I\{SOF_{s_k, r_k}(x, y) = j\},$$

$$i = 0, 1, \cdots, m - 1, \; j = 0, 1, \cdots, L - 1, \tag{4}$$

where j is an SOF code, and $L = 2^8$, thus the histogram has 256 bins. Based on these spatially distributed histograms, discriminative features can be defined as difference between two corresponding histogram bins:

$$d_{hist}(B_i, j) = |Hist'(B_i, j) - Hist''(B_i, j)|,$$

$$i = 0, 1, \cdots, m - 1, j = 0, 1, \cdots, L - 1. \tag{5}$$

We call the above dissimilarity measure histogram-based MSOF dissimilarity measure. These features provide local histogram information and hence will be more efficient for discrimination tasks. However, considering blocks of all sizes and locations, the feature dimensions will be very large ($m \times 256$). Therefore, a proper technique should be used to reduce the dimension and construct classifiers.

3   Statistical Learning for Object Recognition

The above MSOF-based dissimilarity measures provide an over-complete discriminative feature set. The only question remained is how to use them to construct a powerful classifier. Because those excessive measures contain much redundant information, a further processing is needed to remove the redundancy and build effective classifiers. In this paper we use Gentle AdaBoost algorithm [4] to select the most effective MSOF-based dissimilarity measures.

Boosting can be viewed as a stage-wise approximation to an additive logistic regression model using Bernoulli log-likelihood as a criterion [4]. Developed by Friedman et al, Gentle AdaBoost modifies the popular version of the Real AdaBoost procedure [12], using Newton stepping rather than exact optimization at each step. Empirical evidence suggests that Gentle AdaBoost is a more conservative algorithm that has similar performance to both the Real AdaBoost and LogitBoost algorithms, and often outperforms them both, especially when stability is an issue.

While an AdaBoost procedure essentially learns a two-class classifier, we convert the multi-class problem into a two-class one using the idea of intra- and extra-class difference [8]. However, here the difference data are derived from the MSOF-based dissimilarity measures rather than from the images. An MSOF-based dissimilarity measure is taken between two MSOF representations, which is intra-class if the two images are of the same class, or extra-class if not. The MSOF-based dissimilarity measures are used to construct weak classifiers for the above AdaBoost learning. The best current weak classifier is the one for which the weighted intra-class MSOF-based dissimilarity measure (over the training set) is minimized while that of the extra-class is maximized. After AdaBoost learning, the feature dimensions of the MSOF-based dissimilarity measures are dramatically reduced, meanwhile a powerful classifier is constructed.

With the two-class scheme and the learned classifier, the object recognition procedure will work in the following way: It takes a probe image and a gallery image as the input, and computes a feature vector from the two images using the selected MSOF-based dissimilarity measures, then it calculates a similarity score for the feature vector using the learned AdaBoost classifier. Finally a decision is made based on the score, to classify the feature vector into the intra-class (the same objects) or the extra-class (different objects).

4   Experiments

To evaluate the proposed MSOF-based representation, we apply it to face recognition, which is a typical object discrimination task and also a hard problem. Experiment is evaluated on FERET fa/fb face database. Face images are cropped into 150 pixels high and 130 pixels wide, according to their eye coordinates. The non-face area is excluded using an elliptical mask, and the gray histogram within the elliptical mask is equalized. The FERET training CD contains 1002 frontal face images from 429 subjects. The test set contains 1196 galleries and 1195 probes from 1196 subjects.

First, we want to show some basic effects of MSOF filtering. Fig. 5 shows three examples of face images, and Fig. 6 demonstrates the corresponding filtered images, each of which is filtered by a 5-scale MSOF operator. The scale parameters we use in this paper are: (1,1), (3,3), (5,7), (9,14), (17,27), which are determined according to the principle we mentioned in Section 2.3. From Fig. 6 we could see that large scale of SOF encodes macrostructure of image objects, while small scale reveals fine details of local structures. Hence combining all these scales, MSOF provides a complete object representation.

Dissimilarity measures of a pair of intra-personal images and a pair of extra-personal ones are shown in Fig. 5. The difference image is generated using Equ. (1), where the brighter pixels indicate larger differences. From Fig. 5 we could see clearly that images of extra-personal pair have larger differences than that of intra-personal pair. Using Equation of (2), we could exactly measure the dissimilarity between two images. In this example, the intra-personal dissimilarity is 0.1603, while the extra-personal one is 0.2974. It follows that the MSOF-based dissimilarity measure is able to provide promising power for discriminating intra-/extra-class differences.

The next experiment is designed to evaluate the baseline performance of NN classifier using dissimilarity measure of Equ. (2). We follow the standard FERET test protocol of fa/fb face database, which contains 1196 gallery images and 1195 probe images. One advantage of MSOF-based NN classifier is that it could be directly used without training. The cumulative match score curve is shown in Fig. 7. The rank-1 recognition rate is 80%, a promising result.

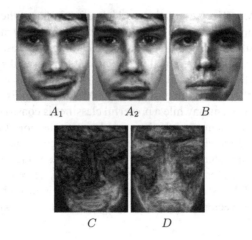

Fig. 5. Examples of dissimilarity measures based on MSOF. The first row: original face images, where A_1 and A_2 are the same person, and B is another person. The second row: difference images calculated via Equ. (1), where C is generated using A_1 and A_2, and D is generated using A_2 and B. The total dissimilarity of (A_1, A_2) pair computed with Equ. (2) is 0.1603, while that of (A_2, B) pair is 0.2974.

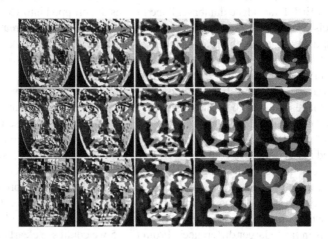

Fig. 6. Examples of MSOF filtered images with 5 scales. Each column is corresponding to one scale, which becomes larger from left to right. For each scale, 8-bits binary string of each SOF encoding is converted to a decimal number ranging from 0 to 255, which is displayed as a pixel label here. Each row is generated with one face image. The three rows are corresponding to image A_1, A_2, and B in Fig. 5 respectively.

Finally, we train two AdaBoost classifiers based on MSOF dissimilarity measure, using the FERET training set of 1002 images. The first AdaBoost classifier is constructed using block-based MSOF Hamming dissimilarity measure (Equ. (3)), and the second one is using histogram-based MSOF dissimilarity measure (Equ. (5)). The results are

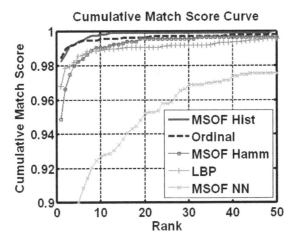

Fig. 7. Cumulative match score curves. "MSOF Hist" is for histogram-based MSOF dissimilarity measure (Equ. (5)); "MSOF Hamm" is for block-based MSOF Hamming dissimilarity measure (Equ. (3)); "MSOF NN" is for Nearest Neighbor classifier using dissimilarity measure of Equ. (2); "Ordinal Feature" is the result of [6], and "LBP" is that of [1].

compared with the approach based on LBP [1] and Ordinal Feature [6] shown in Fig. 7. From the cumulative match score curve, we could see that classifier using histogram-based MSOF dissimilarity measure outperforms all other algorithms, though Ordinal Feature of [6] is slightly better before rank3. The rank-1 recognition rate of histogram-based MSOF is 98.24%, which is an excellent result on FERET database. The performance of block-based MSOF Hamming dissimilarity measure classifier is not the best, but it is also outperforms LBP after rank-8, and it achieves high recognition rates near that of Ordinal Feature after rank-20.

5 Summary and Conclusions

This paper proposes a novel appearance-based representation, called Structured Ordinal Feature (SOF). We show that SOF is invariant to linear transformations on images and can be efficiently computed. It can be further extended to Multi-scale Structured Ordinal Feature (MSOF) to encode both microstructure and macrostructure of image patterns. We also provide several dissimilarity measures based on MSOF for object recognition. Finally we apply MSOF for face recognition. The experiments on FERET database illustrate that our proposed method achieves an excellent performance. We believe that the success of SOF is not limited to faces. Since SOF is general for appearance-based object representation, our future work will be applying SOF on other object classification or recognition problems to investigate its power.

Acknowledgements. This work was supported by the following funding resources: National Natural Science Foundation Project #60518002, National Science and Technology Supporting Platform Project #2006BAK08B06, National 863 Program Projects #2006AA01Z192 and #2006AA01Z193, Chinese Academy of Sciences 100-people project, and the AuthenMetric Research Foundation.

References

1. Ahonen, T., Hadid, A., Pietikainen, M.: Face recognition with local binary patterns. In: Pajdla, T., Matas, J(G.) (eds.) ECCV 2004. LNCS, vol. 3024, pp. 469–481. Springer, Heidelberg (2004)
2. Belhumeur, P.N., Hespanha, J.P., Kriegman, D.J.: Eigenfaces vs. Fisherfaces: Recognition using class specific linear projection. IEEE Transactions on Pattern Analysis and Machine Intelligence 19(7), 711–720 (1997)
3. Crow, F.: Summed-area tables for texture mapping. In: SIGGRAPH, vol. 18(3), pp. 207–212 (1984)
4. Friedman, J., Hastie, T., Tibshirani, R.: Additive logistic regression: a statistical view of boosting. Technical report, Department of Statistics, Sequoia Hall, Stanford Univerity (July 1998)
5. Lades, M., Vorbruggen, J., Buhmann, J., Lange, J., von der Malsburg, C., Wurtz, R.P., Konen, W.: Distortion invariant object recognition in the dynamic link architecture. IEEE Transactions on Computers 42, 300–311 (1993)
6. Liao, S., Lei, Z., Zhu, X., Sun, Z., Li, S., Tan, T.: Face recognition using ordinal features. In: Zhang, D., Jain, A.K. (eds.) Advances in Biometrics. LNCS, vol. 3832, pp. 40–46. Springer, Heidelberg (2005)
7. Liu, C., Wechsler, H.: Gabor feature based classification using the enhanced fisher linear discriminant model for face recognition. IEEE Transactions on Image Processing 11(4), 467–476 (2002)
8. Moghaddam, B., Nastar, C., Pentland, A.: A Bayesain Similarity measure for direct image matching. Media Lab Tech. Report No.393, MIT (August 1996)
9. Ojala, T., Pietikainen, M., Harwood, D.: A comparative study of texture measures with classification based on feature distributions. Pattern Recognition 29(1), 51–59 (1996)
10. Penev, P., Atick, J.: Local feature analysis: A general statistical theory for object representation. Neural Systems 7(3), 477–500 (1996)
11. Sadr, J., Mukherjee, S., Thoresz, K., Sinha, P.: Toward the fidelity of local ordinal encoding. In: Proceedings of the Fifteenth Annual Conference on Neural Information Processing Systems, Vancouver, British Columbia, Canada (December 3-8, 2001)
12. Schapire, R.E., Singer, Y.: Improved boosting algorithms using confidence-rated predictions. In: Proceedings of the Eleventh Annual Conference on Computational Learning Theory, pp. 80–91 (1998)
13. Schneiderman, H.: Toward feature-centric evaluation for efficient cascaded object detection. In: Proceedings of IEEE Computer Society Conference on Computer Vision and Pattern Recognition, Washington, DC, USA, pp. 1007–1013 (June 27 - July 2, 2004)
14. Simard, P.Y., Bottou, L., Haffner, P., Cun, Y.L.: Boxlets: a fast convolution algorithm for signal processing and neural networks. In: Kearns, M., Solla, S., Cohn, D. (eds.) Advances in Neural Information Processing Systems, vol. 11, pp. 571–577. MIT Press, Cambridge (1998)
15. Sinha, P.: Toward qualitative representations for recognition. In: Bülthoff, H.H., Lee, S.-W., Poggio, T.A., Wallraven, C. (eds.) BMCV 2002. LNCS, vol. 2525, pp. 249–262. Springer, Heidelberg (2002)
16. Thoresz, K.J.: On qualitative representations for recognition. Master's thesis, MIT (July 2002)
17. Turk, M.A., Pentland, A.P.: Eigenfaces for recognition. Journal of Cognitive Neuroscience 3(1), 71–86 (1991)
18. Viola, P., Jones, M.: Robust real time object detection. In: IEEE ICCV Workshop on Statistical and Computational Theories of Vision, Vancouver, Canada (July 13, 2001)
19. Wiskott, L., Fellous, J., Kruger, N., Malsburg, C.v.d.: Face recognition by elastic bunch graph matching. IEEE Transactions on Pattern Analysis and Machine Intelligence 19(7), 775–779 (1997)

SODA-Boosting and Its Application to Gender Recognition

Xun Xu and Thomas S. Huang

Beckman Institute, University of Illinois at Urbana-Champaign,
Urbana, IL 61801, USA

Abstract. In this paper we propose a novel boosting based classification algorithm, SODA-Boosting (where SODA stands for Second Order Discriminant Analysis). Unlike the conventional AdaBoost based algorithms widely applied in computer vision, SODA-Boosting does not involve time consuming procedures to search a huge feature pool in every iteration during the training stage. Instead, in each iteration SODA-Boosting efficiently computes discriminative weak classifiers in closed-form, based on reasonable hypotheses on the distribution of the weighted training samples. As an application, SODA-Boosting is employed for image based gender recognition. Experimental results on publicly available FERET database are reported. The proposed algorithm achieved accuracy comparable to state-of-the-art approaches, and demonstrated superior performance to relevant boosting based algorithms.

1 Introduction

Automatic recognition of demographic properties, e.g. gender, age and ethnicity, from face images has many applications in intelligent surveillance, demographic statistics and human-computer interaction. Since early 1990s, gender recognition has attracted considerable attention of the computer vision and patter recognition community for a long time. Early works on this topic were mostly based on neural network [1,2,3,4], where promising performance (more than 90% in accuracy) were reported, although most experiments were conducted on rather small databases (consisting of dozens of images, except [4] where the FERET database was used). From the aspect of patter recognition, gender recognition is a typical two-class problem. In recent years, two most successful "off-the-shelf" classifiers, i.e. SVM [5,6] and AdaBoost [7,8,9], seem to have dominated in this area, because of their higher accuracy and robustness compared to earlier techniques. Both classifiers achieve comparably good recognition accuracy [9]. However, AdaBoost based gender recognizers are generally faster than SVM, which may be a desirable advantage for real-time applications.

In this paper, we present a novel classification algorithm for two-class problem, namely SODA-Boosting, and apply it to gender recognition. This algorithm is along the AdaBoost line. The main contribution lies in the methodology to discover the most discriminative features in an effective and efficient way. AdaBoost [10] is among the most influential recent advances in machine learning, and has

S.K. Zhou et al. (Eds.): AMFG 2007, LNCS 4778, pp. 193–204, 2007.

been widely adopted in computer vision problems. AdaBoost provides an elegant framework to aggregate weak classifiers into a strong one with theoretically provable generalization performance. In computer vision community, the most common practice of applying AdaBoost is defining a huge pool of candidate weak classifiers, and in each iteration seeking the best one through exhaustively traversing the whole feature pool. In order to evade the drawbacks of that approach such as computational load, the proposed algorithm takes a different approach, attempting to directly compute the discriminative features. The proposed algorithm is related to recent algorithms [11,12] which are based on similar motivation. However, SODA-Boosting makes more comprehensive hypotheses on the distribution of the two classes, resulting a stronger learning procedure. The effectiveness of the proposed algorithm is demonstrated by gender recognition experiments reported in this paper, where it achieved accuracy comparable to state-of-the-art gender recognizers, surpassing related boosting algorithms in performance.

Rest of this paper is organized as follows: In Section 2 the SODA-Boosting algorithm is introduced and discussed in detail. Section 3 presents experimental results of gender recognition on the FERET database [13], where SODA-Boosting is compared to many other algorithms. Finally we conclude the paper in Section 4 and briefly discuss future work.

2   SODA-Boosting

Boosting, especially AdaBoost (*Ada*ptive *Boost*ing) [10], is one of the most important and influential recent advances in machine learning, regarded by some researchers as the "best off-the-shelf classifier". During the recent years, it has been widely adopted in computer vision, resulting in many successful applications. As a meta-algorithm that constructs a strong classifier by "boosting" weak classifiers, the key of employing AdaBoost is to design appropriate "weak classifiers" (or "weak hypotheses"). In the computer vision community, the most common practice is defining a huge pool of candidate weak classifiers (depending on the domain knowledge for the problem of interest), and in each iteration seeking the best one (leading to the lowest classification error rate on the weighted training sample set) through traversing the whole feature pool. Such a practice actually treats AdaBoost as a feature selector. This approach has been popularized since successful deployment of Viola-Jones face detector [14]. However, it has several drawbacks:

- The pre-defined feature pool restricts the optimality of the features that can ever be discovered, as the features that will be incorporated into the final classifier are strictly limited to this pool. For example, if linear weak classifiers are the candidates (which is the case for most applications of AdaBoost in computer vision), the feature pool is indeed only a very sparse sampling of the image space (due of the high dimensionality of the space). Even when the feature pool is "over-complete" (implying that its size is

larger than the dimensionality of the data space), there are still too few features to cover the whole space.
- It is computationally expensive. Usually the feature pool is huge, in order to avoid over-sparse sampling of the feature space. Exhaustive traversing such a huge pool in every iteration is clearly rather time consuming.
- The design of candidate weak features largely relies on certain domain knowledge of the problem at hand. Therefore the resulted classifier is not generic, i.e. could not be applied to other problems of different nature. For instance Viola-Jones classifier [14], where rectangular filters are used as weak classifiers, cannot be used in an audio related classification problem where the samples to be classified are MFCC coefficients.

Unlike the conventional practice discussed so far, SODA-Boosting takes another path to discover the weak classifiers. Instead of pre-defining a feature pool and *searching* for "good" features, it attempts to directly *compute* the weak classifiers that are ideal for classification purpose, in a computationally efficient way. In the SODA-Boosting algorithm, we limit the weak classifiers to be "linear-based", i.e. each weak hypothesis is reached by linearly projecting the sample onto a certain vector and thresholding the projection. The key of SODA-Boosting is how to learn such linear projection vectors and their corresponding thresholds, which is detailed in the following subsection.

2.1   SODA: Second Order Discriminant Analysis

In the training procedure of AdaBoost, in each boosting iteration one needs to learn a weak classifier to classify the weighted training samples. In our case, the goal is to seek a linear projection, and construct an effective weak classifier on that projection. Clearly, the weak classifier should have sufficient discriminative power. In SODA-Boosting, we seek such discriminative linear projections via two different techniques, FLD and MRC. With both techniques, the optimal linear projections can be computed in closed-form without exhaustive search or ad-hoc numerical optimization. As we shall see, since both FLD and MRC seek discriminative linear projections by utilizing statistical moments of (up to) second order, we categorize them under a common name SODA (Second Order Discriminant Analysis).

Fisher Linear Discriminant (FLD). FLD is the most well-known technique to find a discriminative linear projection [15]. Suppose we need to classify two classes, $\mathbf{X}^+, \mathbf{X}^- \subset \mathcal{R}^n$. In the training stage we have a labeled sample set $\{(\mathbf{x}_1, y_1), (\mathbf{x}_2, y_2), \ldots, (\mathbf{x}_N, y_N)\}$ where $y_i \in \{+1, -1\}$ indicating $\mathbf{x}_i \in \mathbf{X}^+, \mathbf{X}^-$ respectively. In the boosting framework, each training sample is associated with a weight, say $\{w_1, w_2, \ldots, w_N\}$. In each iteration, the weights are normalized so that $\sum_{i=1}^{N} w_i = 1$. The weighted means of the two classes are given by:

$$\mathbf{m}_+ = \frac{1}{\sum_{y_i=+1} w_i} \sum_{y_i=+1} w_i \mathbf{x}_i, \tag{1}$$

and

$$\mathbf{m}_- = \frac{1}{\sum_{y_i=-1} w_i} \sum_{y_i=-1} w_i \mathbf{x}_i \tag{2}$$

respectively. The weighted scatter matrices are:

$$\mathbf{S}_+ = \sum_{y_i=+1} w_i \left(\mathbf{x}_i - \mathbf{m}_+\right)\left(\mathbf{x}_i - \mathbf{m}_+\right)^T, \tag{3}$$

and

$$\mathbf{S}_- = \sum_{y_i=-1} w_i \left(\mathbf{x}_i - \mathbf{m}_-\right)\left(\mathbf{x}_i - \mathbf{m}_-\right)^T. \tag{4}$$

Defining within class scatter matrix

$$\mathbf{S}_W = \mathbf{S}_+ + \mathbf{S}_-, \tag{5}$$

and between class scatter

$$\mathbf{S}_B = \left(\mathbf{m}_+ - \mathbf{m}_-\right)\left(\mathbf{m}_+ - \mathbf{m}_-\right)^T. \tag{6}$$

FLD is the vector $\mathbf{w}_{FLD}$ that minimizes criterion

$$J_{FLD}\left(\mathbf{w}\right) = \frac{\mathbf{w}^T \mathbf{S}_W \mathbf{w}}{\mathbf{w}^T \mathbf{S}_B \mathbf{w}}. \tag{7}$$

And it turns out that

$$\mathbf{w}_{FLD} = \mathbf{S}_W^{-1}\left(\mathbf{m}_+ - \mathbf{m}_-\right). \tag{8}$$

The weak classifier associated with the FLD feature is given as

$$f_{FLD}\left(\mathbf{x}; \mathbf{w}_{FLD}, T\right) = \begin{cases} +1, \mathbf{w}_{FLD}^T \mathbf{x} > T \\ -1, else \end{cases}, \tag{9}$$

where optimal threshold T is chosen to minimize classification error

$$\varepsilon = \sum_{f_{FLD}(\mathbf{x}_i) \neq y_i} w_i \tag{10}$$

Maximal Rejection Classifier (MRC). FLD works well when the two classes are linearly separable (or at least approximately so) and when their covariance matrices are close to each other. In many practical problems, these conditions are not met. One especially interesting case is the "target detection" configuration [16], where one class (the *target*) is surrounded by the other (the *clutter*), as illustrated in Figure 1. This configuration is common in many computer vision problems, among which object detection is a natural example. As the two classes are by no means linearly separable, the best a linear projection can do to discriminate the two classes is to minimize the overlap between the projected samples from the two classes. An intuitive way to achieve this is seeking a projection vector on which the target class is "squeezed" whereas the clutter class is "pushed aside" as much as possible. Based on this idea, Elad et al [16] proposed a technique called Maximal Rejection Classifier (MRC) to find the discriminative projections, and applied it to face detection. In [12] Xu and Huang showed that face recognition can also be modeled as a two-class problem of this type, and proposed the MRC-Boosting algorithm where the MRC classifiers are aggregated via boosting.

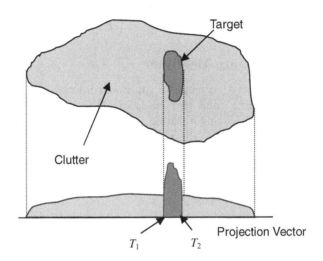

Fig. 1. Target detection configuration and MRC projection

If we treat class $\mathbf{X}^+$ as the target and $\mathbf{X}^-$ as the clutter, the MRC feature is the projection vector $\mathbf{w}_{MRC+}$ which minimizes criterion functional

$$J_{MRC+}\left(\mathbf{w}\right) = \frac{\mathbf{w}^T \mathbf{S}_+ \mathbf{w}}{\mathbf{w}^T \left(\mathbf{S}_W + \mathbf{S}_B\right) \mathbf{w}}. \qquad (11)$$

This criterion seems much similar to that of FLD (7), as it is also in the form of a generalized Rayleigh quotient. However, they chase completely different goals, leading to rather different projection vectors. The MRC feature $\mathbf{w}_{MRC+}$ is found through solving a generalized eigenvalue problem and picking the generalized eigenvector associated with the smallest eigenvalue. The weak classifier associated with MRC feature $\mathbf{w}_{MRC+}$ is

$$f_{MRC+}\left(\mathbf{x}; \mathbf{w}_{MRC+}, T_1^+, T_2^+\right) = \begin{cases} +1, T_1^+ \leq \mathbf{w}_{MRC+}^T \mathbf{x} \leq T_2^+ \\ -1, else \end{cases}, \qquad (12)$$

where the thresholds T_1^+ and T_2^+ are chosen to minimize classification error, similar to (10). Note that unlike the FLD classifier, this weak classifier contains two thresholds, therefore it is not a linear classifier, but "linear-based" [16].

Similarly, if we instead treat class $\mathbf{X}^-$ as the target and $\mathbf{X}^+$ as the clutter, we obtain the other MRC feature $\mathbf{w}_{MRC-}$ which minimizes

$$J_{MRC-}(\mathbf{w}) = \frac{\mathbf{w}^T \mathbf{S}_- \mathbf{w}}{\mathbf{w}^T (\mathbf{S}_W + \mathbf{S}_B) \mathbf{w}}, \tag{13}$$

and the associated weak classifier

$$f_{MRC-}\left(\mathbf{x}; \mathbf{w}_{MRC-}, T_1^-, T_2^-\right) = \begin{cases} -1\,, T_1^- \leq \mathbf{w}_{MRC-}^T \mathbf{x} \leq T_2^- \\ +1\,, else \end{cases} \tag{14}$$

2.2   The SODA-Boosting Algorithm

The SODA-Boosting algorithm employs AdaBoost framework to aggregate the SODA classifiers (i.e., FLD and two kinds of MRC classifiers), leading to a strong classifier. In each boosting iteration, because we don't know which SODA feature is appropriate for current distribution of the two classes (represented by the weighted samples), three hypotheses are made, as illustrated in Figure 2. The first two hypotheses, MRC+ and MRC−, reflect the cases where $\mathbf{X}^+$ is surrounded by $\mathbf{X}^-$ and vice versa, respectively. The last hypothesis reflects the configuration where the two classes are well separated, and can be reasonably discriminated by FLD. For these hypotheses, we employ techniques discussed in the previous subsection to obtain corresponding weak classifiers respectively. Naturally, the one resulting in lowest classification error rate best models current distribution of the two classes, hence will be selected and included into the final strong classifier. The algorithm is listed in Algorithm 1.

2.3   Discussion

SODA-Boosting is closely related to two other boosting based classification algorithms, MRC-Boosting [12] and FisherBoost [11]. MRC-Boosting employs AdaBoost framework to aggregate MRC classifiers. As shown in [12], it works well for face recognition. However, just as the original MRC approach [16], MRC-Boosting was designed specifically for "target detection" type problems, as illustrated in Figure 1. However, for a general two-class discrimination problem, we don't really know whether the distribution of the two classes obey such configuration. Although many problems in computer vision, such as object detection and face recognition, can be modeled as "target detection", this assumption is

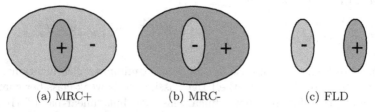

(a) MRC+   (b) MRC-   (c) FLD

Fig. 2. Hypotheses made by SODA-Boosting on the distribution of the two classes

---

Algorithm 1. SODA-Boosting algorithm

Input: $\{(\mathbf{x}_i, y_i), i = 1, 2, \cdots, N : \mathbf{x}_i \in \mathcal{R}^n, y_i \in \{+1, -1\}\}$. The maximal number of weak classifiers K.

Initialize: $w_i = \begin{cases} \frac{1}{2N^+} , y_i = +1 \\ \frac{1}{2N^-} , y_i = -1 \end{cases}$, where N^+ and N^- are the numbers of positive and negative samples respectively.

for $k = 1, 2, \cdots, K$ **do**

    Compute weighted means $\mathbf{m}_+$, $\mathbf{m}_-$ and scatter matrices $\mathbf{S}_+$, $\mathbf{S}_-$, using (1)~(4) respectively.

    Compute FLD feature using (8), obtain the associated weak classifier $f_{FLD}(\mathbf{x})$ according to (9), and calculate its classification error ε_{FLD}.

    Compute MRC+ feature by minimizing (11), obtain the associated weak classifier $f_{MRC+}(\mathbf{x})$ according to (12), and calculate its classification error ε_{MRC+}.

    Compute MRC− feature by minimizing (13), obtain the associated weak classifier $f_{MRC-}(\mathbf{x})$ according to (14), and calculate its classification error ε_{MRC-}.

    Select weak classifier $f_k(\mathbf{x}) \in \{f_{FLD}, f_{MRC+}, f_{MRC-}\}$ with minimal classification error ε_k.

    Update weights: $w_i \leftarrow \frac{1}{Z_k} w_i \exp[-\alpha_k y_i f_k(\mathbf{x}_i)]$, where $\alpha_k = \frac{1}{2} \ln \frac{1-\varepsilon_k}{\varepsilon_k}$ and Z_k is a normalization factor to ensure $\sum_{i=1}^{N} w_i = 1$.

end

Output: Strong classifier $F(\mathbf{x}) = sgn[G(\mathbf{x})]$ where the classification function is $G(\mathbf{x}) = \sum_{k=1}^{K} \alpha_k f_k(\mathbf{x})$.

---

not likely to be true for a general two-class problem. When we don't have a compelling reason that the two classes form a "target detection" configuration, the features (and the associated weak classifiers) sought by MRC wouldn't be effective for classification. On the other hand, FisherBoost does not consider the "target detection" configuration at all, in each iteration it seeks a FLD classifier to discriminate the two classes. As we know, FLD is only effective when the two classes are linearly separable (or at least approximately so). For a complicated two-class problem, especially after the samples are re-weighted as the boosting procedure goes on, the distribution of the two classes may not be such case. At that point, FLD will fail to discover meaningful discriminants.

SODA-Boosting overcomes the limitation of MRC-Boosting and FisherBoost by including both MRC and FLD classifiers into consideration. FLD and MRC are complement to each other, working for rather distinct configurations of the two classes. Considering all these configurations has much stronger discriminative power than just considering one of them. As we shall see in Section 3, putting together FLD and MRC classifiers is actually *not* a trivial combination, it indeed leads to a much stronger learning procedure.

Besides MRC-Boosting and FisherBoost, another relevant approach which also attempts to directly *compute* weak classifiers is KL-Boosting [17]. KL-Boosting discovers discriminative features by seeking linear projection vectors on which the Kullback-Leibler divergence between the two classes are maximized. Unfortunately, such definition of discriminative power can not lead to a closed-form solution, hence an ad-hoc numerical optimization procedure was employed, which is computationally expensive and relatively difficult for implementation. Unlike KL-Boosting, SODA-Boosting (also MRC-Boosting and FisherBoost) is able to find the discriminative features in closed-form, using standard techniques in linear algebra, hence is more efficient.

3   Experiments

We applied the proposed SODA-Boosting algorithm to gender recognition, and report in this section experimental results on the FERET database [13].

In our experiments, 4109 frontal face images from the FERET database were aligned according to eye-corner coordinates supplied with the data, and finally normalized to 40×40. In order to normalize the illumination effect, all images were pre-processed to be of zero-mean and unit variance in pixel value. This data set consists of 703 male individuals and 498 female, the gender ground truth were manually labeled by viewing full face images (i.e. before the faces were aligned and cropped out).

In each run of experiments, we randomly partition the data into training and test set. Each time 80% of the individuals in the database were selected for training, all their images constitute the training set, and the remaining images were used for test. Note that we took a protocol similar to that in [9], where training and test data are separated based on individuals, instead of images themselves, hence any individual in the training set wouldn't have any images in the test set. This is in contrast to some earlier work e.g. [5] where images of one individual might appear in both training and test set (called "mixed data sets" in [9]), resulting in a more optimistic estimate of recognition accuracy. The protocol employed in our experiments and [9], on the other hand, is more close to the practical scenario where the trained gender recognizer will be tested on images of people it never saw before, leading to more accurate evaluation of the generalized performance.

We conducted gender recognition experiments with 10 independent random data partitions, and recorded the average accuracy of different approaches, as shown in Table 1. For comparison purpose, besides the proposed SODA-Boosting algorithm we also reported performance of other classifiers, including SVM, AdaBoost with rectangular filters (used in Viola-Jones face detector [14]) [7], and two algorithms related to the proposed one: FisherBoost [11] and MRC-Boosting [12].

For SVM (SVM-Light implementation [18]), RBF kernel was used (we also tried polynomial kernels, but the performance was inferior to RBF kernel). As reported by [9], the accuracy is sensitive to parameters C and γ. In our experiments, we took $C = 1/N$ (where $N = 1600$ is the dimensionality of the images)

Table 1. Gender recognition accuracy

Algorithm	Accuracy
SODA-Boosting	92.82%
SVM ($\gamma = 1$)	92.38%
SVM ($\gamma = 10^5$)	93.34%
AdaBoost (Viola-Jones)	92.67%
MRC-Boosting (+)	88.69%
MRC-Boosting (−)	89.76%
FisherBoost	89.54%

which is a good choice according to results reported in [9] and two different γ values, $\gamma = 1$ which is the default value of SVM-Light and $\gamma = 10^5$ which was shown by [9] to be optimal (through exhaustive parameter tuning). The number of support vectors varies across runs, on average 860 for $\gamma = 10^5$ and 1450 for $\gamma = 1$ respectively. For all the boosting based algorithms, $K = 500$ weak classifiers were used. The performance of SODA-Boosting (with 500 features) is better than SVM with default γ, and is slightly inferior, although still comparable, to SVM with optimal parameter setting (RBF kernel with $\gamma = 10^5$ and $C = 1/1600$). However, note that SVM employs more features (i.e. support vectors) than SODA-Boosting.

When compared to other boosting based algorithms, SODA-Boosting consistently worked better. For MRC-Boosting, we conducted experiments with two versions (marked with $+/-$) considering male and female as "target" respectively, and both of them achieved inferior performance to SODA-Boosting. In Figure 3 we compare the accuracy of different boosting algorithms as the number of weak classifiers increases. It can be seen that SODA-Boosting cleanly exceeded FisherBoost and two versions of MRC-Boosting everywhere. The asymptotic accuracy of SODA-Boosting was very similar to conventional AdaBoost based algorithm [7]. However, thanks to the effort of directly seeking most discriminative features, SODA-Boosting reached the same accuracy with fewer features than [7]. Although we did not compare SODA-Boosting to recent approach [9] directly, we conjecture that the comparison would reach similar conclusion, as [9] shares the same nature (i.e. boosting very weak features) as [7] and they achieved similar performance. It should be noted that although SODA-Boosting requires fewer features for the same accuracy, it is usually slower than boosting approaches like [7,9] *in classification stage*, because those approaches require much less computation per feature. However, those approaches are specifically designed to classify images, relying on weak features that are all pre-designed based on certain domain knowledge, hence bounded to certain classification problems. On the contrary, SODA-Boosting is a generic algorithm, which is, in theory, applicable to any two-class problem, just like SVM.

The point especially worth noticing is that SODA-Boosting cleanly exceeded both MRC-Boosting and FisherBoost in performance, although the latter two also aggregate FLD and MRC classifiers respectively. This convincingly demonstrates that putting together FLD and MRC weak classifiers is *not* a trivial combination, it indeed leads to a stronger learning procedure, as we mentioned in Section 2.

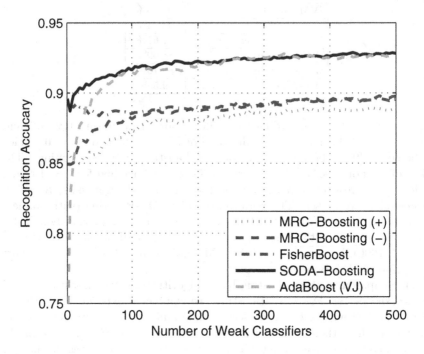

Fig. 3. Accuracy of different boosting algorithms as the number of classifiers increases

4   Conclusion and Future Work

In this paper, we proposed a novel boosting based classification algorithm called SODA-Boosting. Unlike conventional AdaBoost based algorithms widely used in computer vision e.g. [14], SODA-Boosting does not involve any exhaustive search across a huge feature pool, instead it attempts to directly compute discriminative features in a computationally efficient way. Compared to recent approaches [11,12] with similar motivation, the proposed algorithm takes into consideration several distinct hypotheses on the distribution of the two classes, resulting a stronger learning procedure. Application to gender recognition shows that SODA-Boosting achieves considerably better performance than those approaches, reaching accuracy comparable to that of state-of-the-art gender recognizers. In this work, we conducted experiments on the FERET database which only consists of frontal face images obtained under controlled condition (e.g. regular illumination). However, in practical applications, image quality seldom reaches such an ideal level. The images captured from real-world videos usually, if not always, are of rather poor quality, which means low resolution, arbitrary illumination, imaging noises, and most importantly, the faces are often captured in non-frontal views. As future work, we are interested in applying the proposed algorithm to these challenging settings.

References

1. Golomb, B.A., Lawrence, D.T., Sejnowski, T.J.: Sexnet: A neural network identifies sex from human faces. In: NIPS-3: Proceedings of the 1990 conference on Advances in neural information processing systems 3, pp. 572–577. Morgan Kaufmann Publishers Inc., San Francisco, CA, USA (1990)
2. Cottrell, G.W., Metcalfe, J.: Empath: face, emotion, and gender recognition using holons. In: NIPS-3: Proceedings of the 1990 conference on Advances in neural information processing systems 3, pp. 564–571. Morgan Kaufmann Publishers Inc., San Francisco, CA, USA (1990)
3. Tamura, S., Kawai, H., Mitsumoto, H.: Male/female identification from 86 very low resolution face images by neural network. Pattern Recognition 29(2), 331–335 (1996)
4. Gutta, S., Huang, J.R.J., Phillips, P.J., Wechsler, H.: Mixture of experts for classification of gender, ethnic origin, and pose of human faces. IEEE Trans. Neural Networks 11, 948–960 (2000)
5. Moghaddam, B., Yang, M.: Learning gender with support faces. IEEE Transactions on Pattern Analysis and Machine Intelligence 24(5), 707–711 (2002)
6. Graf, A.B.A., Wichmann, F.A.: Gender classification of human faces. In: Bülthoff, H.H., Lee, S.-W., Poggio, T.A., Wallraven, C. (eds.) BMCV 2002. LNCS, vol. 2525, pp. 491–500. Springer, Heidelberg (2002)
7. Shakhnarovich, G., Viola, P.A., Moghaddam, B.: A unified learning framework for real time face detection and classification. In: FGR 2002. Proceedings of the Fifth IEEE International Conference on Automatic Face and Gesture Recognition, p. 16. IEEE Computer Society, Washington, DC, USA (2002)
8. Wu, B., Ai, H., Huang, C.: Lut-based adaboost for gender classification. In: Kittler, J., Nixon, M.S. (eds.) AVBPA 2003. LNCS, vol. 2688, pp. 104–110. Springer, Heidelberg (2003)
9. Baluja, S., Rowley, H.: Boosting sex identification performance. In: AAAI-IAAI 2005 (2005)
10. Schapire, R.E., Freund, Y., Bartlett, P., Lee, W.S.: Boosting the margin: a new explanation for the effectiveness of voting methods. In: Proc. 14th International Conference on Machine Learning, pp. 322–330. Morgan Kaufmann, San Francisco (1997)
11. Tu, J., Zhang, Z., Zeng, Z., Huang, T.: Face localization via hierarchical condensation with fisher boosting feature selection. In: CVPR 2004. IEEE Computer Society Conference on Computer Vision and Pattern Recognition, vol. 02, pp. 719–724 (2004)
12. Xu, X., Huang, T.S.: Face recognition with MRC-Boosting. In: ICCV 2005. 10th IEEE International Conference on Computer Vision, vol. 2, pp. 1770–1777 (2005)
13. Phillips, P.J., Moon, H., Rizvi, S.A., Rauss, P.J.: The feret evaluation methodology for face-recognition algorithms. IEEE Trans. Pattern Anal. Mach. Intell. 22(10), 1090–1104 (2000)
14. Viola, P., Jones, M.J.: Robust real-time object detection. In: IEEE Workshop on Statistical and Theories of Computer Vision, IEEE Computer Society Press, Los Alamitos (2001)

15. Duda, R.O., Hart, P.E., Stork, D.G.: Pattern Classification, 2nd edn. Wiley-Interscience, Chichester (2000)
16. Elad, M., Hel-Or, Y., Keshet, R.: Pattern detection using a maximal rejection classifier. Pattern Recognition Letters 23(12), 1459–1471 (2002)
17. Liu, C., Shum, H.Y.: Kullback-leibler boosting. In: CVPR 2003. IEEE Computer Society Conference on Computer Vision and Pattern Recognition, vol. 01, p. 587. IEEE Computer Society Press, Los Alamitos (2003)
18. Joachims, T.: Making large-Scale SVM Learning Practical. In: Advances in Kernel Methods - Support Vector Learning, MIT Press, Cambridge (1999)

Single Image Subspace for Face Recognition

Jun Liu[1], Songcan Chen[1], Zhi-Hua Zhou[2], and Xiaoyang Tan[1]

[1] Department of Computer Science and Engineering,
Nanjing University of Aeronautics and Astronautics, China
{j.liu,s.chen,x.tan}@nuaa.edu.cn
[2] National Key Laboratory for Novel Software Technology,
Nanjing University, China
zhouzh@nju.edu.cn

Abstract. Small sample size and severe facial variation are two challenging problems for face recognition. In this paper, we propose the SIS (Single Image Subspace) approach to address these two problems. To deal with the former one, we represent each single image as a subspace spanned by its synthesized (shifted) samples, and employ a newly designed subspace distance metric to measure the distance of subspaces. To deal with the latter one, we divide a face image into several regions, compute the contribution scores of the training samples based on the extracted subspaces in each region, and aggregate the scores of all the regions to yield the ultimate recognition result. Experiments on well-known face databases such as AR, Extended YALE and FERET show that the proposed approach outperforms some renowned methods not only in the scenario of *one training sample per person*, but also in the scenario of *multiple training samples per person* with significant facial variations.

1 Introduction

One of the most challenging problems for face recognition is the so-called Small Sample Size (SSS) problem [18,25], i.e., the number of training samples is far smaller than the dimensionality of the samples. Meanwhile, the face recognition task becomes more difficult when the testing samples are subject to severe facial variations such as expression, illumination, occlusion, etc.

To deal with the SSS problem, we propose to represent each single (training, testing) image as a subspace spanned by its synthesized images. The employed synthesized images are the shifted images of the original single face image and thus can be efficiently obtained without additional computation and storage costs. To measure the distance between subspaces, we design a subspace distance metric that is applicable to subspaces with unequal dimensions. Moreover, to improve the robustness to the aforementioned facial variations, we divide a face image into regions, compute the contribution scores of the training samples based on the extracted subspaces in each region, and finally aggregate the scores of all the regions to yield the ultimate classification result. Since the proposed approach generates a subspace for each image (or a partitioned region of an image), it is named as SIS (Single Image Subspace).

Experiments on several well-known databases show that the proposed SIS approach achieves better classification performance than some renowned methods in the scenarios of both *one training sample per person* and *multiple training samples per person*

S.K. Zhou et al. (Eds.): AMFG 2007, LNCS 4778, pp. 205–219, 2007.

with significant facial variations. In what follows, we will briefly review the related work in Section 2, propose the SIS approach in Section 3, report on experimental results in Section 4, and conclude this paper with some discussion in Section 5.

2   Related Work

In dealing with the SSS problem, the following two paradigms are often employed: 1) performing dimensionality reduction to lower the sample dimensionality, and 2) synthesizing virtual samples to enlarge the training set.

Among the many existing dimensionality reduction methods, PCA (Principal Component Analysis, Eigenfaces) [20] and LDA (Linear Discriminant Analysis, Fisherfaces) [1] are well-known and have become the *de-facto* baselines. Later advances on PCA and LDA include Bayesian Intra/Extrapersonal Classifier (BIC) [13], Discriminant Common Vectors (DCV) [4,9], etc.

Our proposed SIS approach works along the second paradigm, i.e., synthesizing virtual samples, whose effectiveness has been verified in quite a few studies [3,11,16,19,23]. In [3], Beymer and Poggio synthesized virtual samples by incorporating prior knowledge, and yielded a classification accuracy of 82% with one real and 14 virtual images compared to 67% with only real samples on a database of 62 persons. Niyogi et al. [14] showed that incorporating prior knowledge is mathematically equivalent to introducing a regularizer in function learning, thus implicitly improving the generalization of the recognition system. In [23], Wu and Zhou enriched the information of a face image by combining the face image with its projection map, and then applied PCA to the enriched images for face recognition. They reported 3-5% higher accuracy than PCA through using 10-15% fewer eigenfaces. Martinez [11] proposed the Local Probabilistic Subspace (LPS) method. Specifically, Martinez synthesized virtual samples by perturbation and divided a face image into several regions where the eigenspace technique was applied to the generated virtual samples for classification. Good performance of LPS was reported on the AR [12] face database. In [16], Shan et al. proposed the Face-Specific Subspace (FSS) method. They synthesized virtual samples by geometric and gray-level transformation, built a subspace for every subject, and classified the testing sample by minimizing the distance from the face-specific subspace. The effectiveness of FSS was verified on face databases such as YALE B [6]. Torre et al. [19] generated virtual samples by using 150 linear and non-linear filters, and built an Oriented Component Analysis (OCA) classifier on each representation. By combining the results of the 150 OCA classifiers, they achieved good performance on the FRGC v1.0 dataset.

The synthesized samples are usually exploited for generating a subspace. There are roughly three styles for generating the subspace: 1) generating a subspace from the whole enlarged training set, e.g., [3,11,23], 2) generating a subspace from all the synthesized images of the same subject, and 3) generating a subspace from all the images passing through the same filter, e.g., [19]. In contrast to these past studies, we generate a subspace from each single (training, testing) image by exploiting its synthesized (shifted) images. To the best of our knowledge, such a style has not been reported in literature.

In addition to the SSS problem, severe facial variations such as expression, illumination and occlusion can often make the face recognition task especially hard [18,25].

To deal with illumination variation, Georghiades et al. [6] proposed an illumination cone method. They exploited the fact that the set of images of a subject in fixed pose but under all possible illumination conditions is a convex cone in the space of images, and assigned to a testing image the identity of the closest approximated illumination cone. This method achieved perfect performance on the Yale Face Database B. Lee et al. [10] dwelled on how to arrange physical lighting so that the acquired images of each subject can be directly used as the basis vectors of a low-dimensional linear space. They proposed the Nine Points of Light (9PL) method with two versions: 9PL with simulated images ($9PL_{sim}$) and 9PL with real images ($9PL_{real}$), and verified their effectiveness on face databases such as Extended YALE. Like the illumination cone and 9PL methods, our SIS approach also employs linear subspace representation. Yet in contrast to illumination cone and 9PL which generate a subspace from all the training images of a subject, our SIS approach builds a subspace for each single (training, testing) image.

To deal with variations of expression and occlusion, Martinetz [11] proposed to divide a face image into several regions, and the LPS method yielded good performance on the AR face database. Tan et al. [17] partitioned a face image into several regions, and trained a Self-Organizing Map (SOM) on each region for feature extraction. The SOM-face method has been proven effective on databases such as AR. Moreover, in [18], it has been indicated that face recognition is less sensitive to facial variations such as expression and occlusion when a face image is divided into several regions that are analyzed separately. Inspired by these works, we also divide a face image into several regions in the proposed SIS approach to improve the robustness to the severe facial variations.

3   The SIS Approach

3.1   Generating Synthesized Samples

Given a face image matrix A of size $M \times N$, we generate the following $m \times n$ number of synthesized (shifted) images with size of $l \times r$:

$$A_{ij} = A(i : (l + i - 1), j : (r + j - 1)),$$
$$1 \leq i \leq m, 1 \leq j \leq n, \tag{1}$$

where m and n are parameters, $l = M - m + 1$ and $r = N - n + 1$.

It is obvious that the shifted images can be obtained without additional computation and storage costs, since they are the shifted parts of the original single image. When $m = n = 1$, there is only one shifted image, i.e., the original face image; when m and n are relatively small, say $m = n = 3$, there are nine shifted images (illustrated in Fig. 1) that resemble the original face image visually; and when m and n are very large, say $m = M$ and $n = N$, there are $M \times N$ number of synthesized images that contain little visual information, since they reduce to points. Therefore, the values of m and n trade off the number of the synthesized images and the information delivered. We have

Fig. 1. Illustration of a face image A and its nine synthesized (shifted) images A_{ij}'s with $m = n = 3$

observed in experiments (in Section 4.5) that $3 \leq m, n \leq 6$ are good choices for the proposed SIS approach.

In fact, the shifted images act as the basis images in the linear spatial filtering [8] of A in the way that:

$$\tilde{A} = \sum_{i=1}^{m} \sum_{j=1}^{n} w_{ij} A_{ij}, \tag{2}$$

where w_{ij}'s are the coefficients of a filter mask with size $m \times n$, and $\tilde{A}$ is the corresponding filtered image.

3.2 Building the Subspace

By using the synthesized images of the single image A, we build a subspace:

$$S_A = span(A_{11}, A_{12}, \ldots, A_{mn}), \tag{3}$$

or equivalently

$$S_a = span(a_{11}, a_{12}, \ldots, a_{mn}), \tag{4}$$

where $a_{ij} = vec(A_{ij})$ is obtained by sequentially concatenating the column vectors of matrix A_{ij}, and $a = vec(A)$. Then, a set of orthonormal basis vectors can be computed for S_a by techniques such as Gram-Schmidt orthogonalization [7] and Singular Value Decomposition [7].

From the viewpoint of linear spatial filtering [8], the subspace S_A in fact contains infinite number of linearly filtered images of A under all possible combinations of mask coefficients w_{ij}'s. Some images contained in S_A are illustrated in Fig. 2, from which we can observe that: 1) some images are able to reveal fine facial details such as eyes, e.g., those in the third and fourth columns; and 2) some images are less sensitive to illumination variation, e.g., those in second and third rows. Therefore, it is expected that the subspace S_A (or equivalently S_a) can be more helpful than the original single image A for face recognition.

3.3 Measuring Subspace Distance

To measure the distance between subspaces, we propose the following subspace distance metric based on orthogonal projection [7]:

$$
\begin{aligned}
dist(S_1, S_2) &= ||PP^T - QQ^T||_F \\
&= \sqrt{k_1 + k_2 - 2||P^T Q||_F^2} \\
&= \sqrt{k_1 + k_2 - 2\sum_{i=1}^{k} cos(\theta_i)^2}
\end{aligned}
\tag{5}
$$

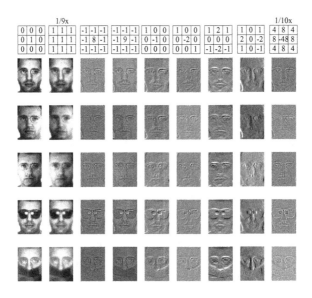

Fig. 2. Illustration of some images contained in the subspace S_A. The employed spatial filters (of size 3×3) are depicted in the first row, with the images filtered by them being shown below.

where $||.||_F$ denotes the *Frobenius* norm, T is the matrix transpose operator, S_1 and S_2 are respectively k_1- and k_2- dimensional subspaces of $\mathbb{R}^{d \times 1}$, $P \in \mathbb{R}^{d \times k_1}$ ($Q \in \mathbb{R}^{d \times k_2}$) contains a set of orthonormal basis vectors for S_1 (S_2), $k = \min(k_1, k_2)$, and θ_i's ($i = 1, 2, \ldots, k$) are the principal angles [7] between S_1 and S_2 in a non-decreasing order.

It is easy to prove that the subspace distance (5) is a metric by checking the three well-known metric properties.

Previously there are some studies on measuring the dissimilarity (or similarity) of subspaces. Golub and Van Loan [7] proposed a distance metric $dist_G(S_1, S_2) = ||PP^T - QQ^T||_2 = cos(\theta_k)$ for subspaces with equal dimensions (i.e., $k = k_1 = k_2$). Moreover, they only employed the biggest principal angle in measuring the distance. In contrast to $dist_G(S_1, S_2)$, our subspace distance metric employs the information of all the principal angles. Yamaguchi et al. [24] proposed to measure the similarity between video sequences by the smallest principal angle between subspaces. In contrast to their work which only employs the smallest principal angle, our distance metric utilizes the information of all the principal angles. Wolf and Shashua [22] proposed to measure the similarity between subspaces with equal dimensions by $\prod_{i=1}^{k} \cos(\theta_i)^2$, and they proved that this similarity makes a positive definite kernel when it is generalized to nonlinear subspaces by the kernel trick. In contrast to their similarity defined on subspaces with equal dimensions, our distance metric can deal with subspaces with unequal dimensions. Moreover, in Wolf and Shashua's method, due to the employed multiplication operator, $\prod_{i=1}^{k} \cos(\theta_i)^2$ will be dominated by some small $cos(\theta_i)$'s, i.e., even if two subspaces share $k - 1$ orthonormal bases, $\prod_{i=1}^{k} \cos(\theta_i)^2$ will still be zero so long as the other basis vectors are orthogonal. It is obvious that our distance metric does not suffer from this problem. Needless to say, (5) can generate a positive definite kernel in the form of $k(S_1, S_2) = exp(-\rho dist(S_1, S_2))$ ($\rho > 0$), since Chapelle et al. [5] pointed out that $k(x, y) = exp(-\rho d(x, y))$ ($\rho > 0$) is a positive definite kernel so long as $d(x, y)$ is a metric.

3.4 Accomplishing Face Recognition

By incorporating 1) the subspace representation of a single image, 2) the subspace distance metric, and 3) the technique of dividing a face image into several regions to deal with facial variations [11,17,18], the SIS approach works as follows:

1) Divide a face image into c overlapping regions of size $R \times C$, with the constraints that *a*) R and C are set about 1/3 of M and N, and *b*) the adjacent regions share half of the image pixels so that some discriminative organs such as eyes are more likely to reside in certain partitioned regions;

2) Build a subspace for the i-th ($i = 1, 2 \ldots, c$) partitioned region by employing (1) and (4). Moreover, based on the subspace representation, (5) will then be used to calculate $dist_j^i$, the distance between a testing sample and the j-th training sample, and a contribution score is obtained as:

$$score_j^i = \frac{\min_{j=1}^s dist_j^i}{dist_j^i}, \tag{6}$$

where s is the number of training samples;

3) Assign to a testing sample the identity of the j^*-th training sample that has the maximal aggregated score as:

$$j^* = \arg\max_j \sum_{i=1}^c score_j^i, j = 1, 2, \ldots, s. \tag{7}$$

The time complexity of the SIS approach in classifying an unknown sample is $O(csRCm^2n^2)$.

4   Experiments

To evaluate the proposed SIS approach, we conduct extensive experiments on three well-known face databases: AR [12], Extended YALE (EYALE) [6,10] and FERET [15].

4.1   Database Description

AR is a very challenging database that consists of over 3,200 frontal images of 126 subjects (70 men, 56 women). Each subject has 26 different images grabbed in two different sessions separated by two weeks, and in each session 13 images under severe variations in expression, illumination and occlusion were recorded. The 26 images of one subject are illustrated in Fig. 3, with the corresponding variations described in Table 1. In this paper, we use a subset provided and preprocessed by Martinez [12]. This subset contains 2,600 face images corresponding to 100 subjects (50 men, 50 women) where each subject has 26 different images under the aforesaid variations. The original resolution of these image faces is 165×120 and we resize them to 66×48.

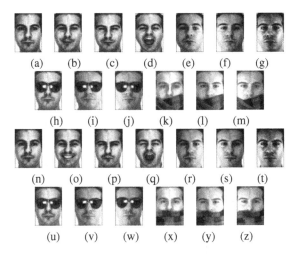

Fig. 3. Illustration of 26 images of one subject from AR

Table 1. Variations of one subject's 26 images on AR

Session 1		Session 2	
Index	Variation(s)	Index	Variation(s)
(a)	neutral	(n)	time
(b-d)	expression	(o-q)	expression & time
(e-g)	light	(r-t)	light & time
(h)	glasses	(u)	glasses & time
(i-j)	glasses & light	(v-w)	glasses & light & time
(k)	scarves	(x)	scarves & time
(l-m)	scarves & light	(y-z)	scarves & light & time

The Extended YALE (EYALE) face database contains 2,432 frontal face images of 38 subjects under 64 different illumination conditions. The images of each subject are partitioned to five subsets according to the illumination conditions illustrated in Fig. 4. Lee et al. [10] manually cropped the images to 192×168, and we resize them to 60×50.

The FERET database consists of a total of 14,051 gray-scale images representing 1,199 subjects, with images containing variations in illumination, expression, pose and so on. In this paper, only frontal faces are considered. These facial images can be divide into five sets: *fa* (1,196 images), *fb* (1,195 images), *fc* (194 images), *dup I* (722 images) and *dup II* (234 images). With the eye locations provided by the FERET program, we crop the image size to 60×60.

4.2 Experimental Settings

The four parameters of SIS are set as follows: m and n are both set to 5, and R and C are set as in Table 2. Moreover, we will evaluate the influence of the four parameters in Section 4.5.

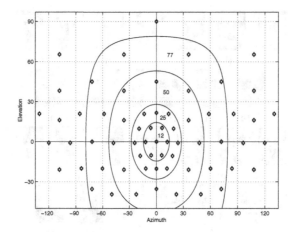

Fig. 4. The azimuth and elevation of the 64 strobes. Each annulus contains the positions of the strobes corresponding to the images of each illumination subset-Subset 1 (12°), Subset 2 (25°), Subset 3 (50°), Subset 4 (77°) Subset 5 (outer annulus) [6].

Table 2. Image size $M \times N$ and region size $R \times C$ on each database

	AR	EYALE	FERET
$M \times N$	66×48	60×50	60×60
$R \times C$	16×18	20×20	20×20

A degenerated variant of the proposed SIS approach is to directly represent each single (training, testing) face image as a subspace spanned by its shifted images, and to conduct the recognition by selecting the subspace which corresponds to a training sample and is with the minimal distance to the subspace corresponding to the testing sample. In this variant, a face image is not divided into several regions (or in other words, c, the number of partitioned regions, equals 1), and thus it is termed as SIS_{nondiv}. In order to study that whether the process of dividing the face image into several regions helps to improve the robustness of SIS, and whether SIS could work well without this process, we have also evaluated this variant in the experiments.

Moreover, we compare the proposed SIS approach with the following eleven face recognition methods: PCA [20], LDA [1], DCV [4,9], BIC [13], Elastic Bunch Graph Matching (EBGM) [21], LPS [11], SOM-face [17], illumination cone [6], 9PL [10] and FSS [16]. The settings of these methods are as follows.

1) For PCA, it is a common practice to lower the dimensionality of the samples and then to employ a nearest neighbor classifier with *Euclidean* distance for classification. Since it is an open problem to select the the optimal number of employed eigenfaces, we exhaustively try all numbers of eigenfaces to report the their best performance.

2) For LDA and DCV, the samples are firstly projected to a subspace whose dimension is the number of classes minus 1, and then a nearest neighbor classifier using *Euclidean* distance is employed for classification.

Table 3. Recognition accuracies (%) on AR in the scenario of one training sample per person (*the best performance in each case has been bolded*)

Index	Image(s)	SIS	SIS$_{nondiv}$	PCA	LPS [11]	SOM-face [17]
(b-d)		**99**	85	88	83	95
(h)		**99**	87	58	80	97
(k)		**98**	89	13	82	95
(o-q)		**86**	69	64	76	81
(u)		**96**	61	29	54	60
(x)		**90**	78	9	48	53
(e-g)		**100**	99	64	N/A	N/A
(i-j)		**96**	60	23	N/A	N/A
(l-m)		**97**	77	9	N/A	N/A
(n)		**100**	95	83	N/A	N/A
(r-t)		**99**	89	34	N/A	N/A
(v-w)		**82**	36	14	N/A	N/A
(y-z)		**84**	63	4	N/A	N/A

3) For BIC, EBGM, LPS, SOM-face, illumination cone, 9PL and FSS, the results are directly cited from the literatures [2,6,10,11,16,17].

4.3   One Training Sample Per Person

In this subsection, we consider face recognition in the scenario of one training sample per person, and conduct the following experiments.

Experiment 1: We employ the first image of each subject from the AR database (i.e., Fig. 3 (a)) for training and the remaining images for testing. Moreover, to evaluate the performance under different facial variations, we categorize the 25 testing samples of each subject into 11 subsets according to the facial variations summarized in Table 1, and report the classification performance in Table 3. From this table, we can observe that: 1) SIS$_{nondiv}$ generally obtains higher classification performance than the holistic methods such as PCA (note that, the comparison with PCA is not fair for SIS$_{nondiv}$, since the recognition accuracies of PCA reported here are the optimal ones by trying all the numbers of projection vectors, and Martinetz [11] reported a recognition rate of less than 70% for (b-d) by using 20 eigenfaces); 2) since holistic methods are sensitive to severe facial variations such as expression, illumination and occlusion [18], it is reasonable that SIS$_{nondiv}$ achieves inferior classification performance to SIS; 3) SIS obviously outperforms PCA; and 4) compared to the recent methods such as LPS and SOM-face that are primarily designed for face recognition with one training sample per person under severe variations, SIS yields better classification performance especially for the testing samples with indexes (u) and (x) that are of severe variations in occlusion and time duration.

Experiment 2: We conduct experiments on FERET by using the *fa* set for training and the remaining sets for testing. Results are presented in Table 4, from which we can

Table 4. Recognition accuracies (%) on FERET (*the best performance in each case has been bolded*)

Method	fb	fc	dup I	dup II
SIS	**91**	**90**	**68**	**68**
PCA, MahCosine [2]	85	65	44	22
Bayesian, MAP [2]	82	37	52	32
EBGM_Standard [2]	88	40	44	22
PCA_Euclidean [2]	74	5	34	14
LDA_Euclidean [2]	61	19	38	14

find that SIS obviously outperforms the state-of-the-art methods evaluated in the CSU Face Identification Evaluation System [2] especially for the sets such as *fc*, *du I* and *du II* that contain significant facial variations.

Experiment 3: We further compare the performance under serious illumination variation on the EYALE face database. The first image of each subject (i.e., the image in the center of Fig. 4 with azimuth and elevation degrees of zero) is employed for training while the remaining images are used for testing. The classification rates are reported in Table 5, from which we can observe that SIS achieves higher recognition rates than PCA especially on Subsets 3, 4 and 5.

The above experiments verify that the proposed SIS approach is a good choice in the scenario of one training sample per person.

4.4   Multiple Training Samples Per Person

In this subsection, we consider face recognition in the scenario of multiple training samples per person and conduct the following experiments.

Experiment 4: We employ the seven non-occluded face images of each subject from the first session of the AR database (i.e., Fig. 3 (a-g)) for training and the remaining images for testing, and present the experimental results in Table 6. From this table, we can find that the proposed SIS approach achieves much higher classification accuracies than the other methods, especially when the testing images are with severe occlusions such as glasses and scarves (Table 6 (h-m, u-z)). Furthermore, comparing the results reported in Tables 3 and 6, we can find that SIS with only one training sample per person can even outperform methods such as LDA, DCV and PCA with seven training samples per person.

Experiment 5: We employ Subset 1 of the EYALE database for training and the remaining subsets for testing, and report the results in Table 7. From this table, we can find that: 1) SIS can obtain competitive performance to the state-of-the-art methods such as illumination cone(including Cones-attached [6], Cones-cast [6]) and 9PL (including $9PL_{real}$ [10] and $9PL_{sim}$ [10]) that are primarily designed for dealing with severe illumination variation; and 2) SIS outperforms methods such as PCA, LDA, DCV and FSS especially on Subsets 4 and 5 that have severe illumination variation. Furthermore, comparing the results of Tables 5 and 7, we can find that SIS using only one training sample per person can even outperform methods such as LDA, DCV, PCA and FSS employing seven training samples per person.

Table 5. Recognition accuracies (%) on EYALE in the scenario of one training sample per person (*the best performance in each case has been bolded*)

Method	Subset				
	1	2	3	4	5
SIS	**100**	**100**	**99**	**95**	**96**
PCA	95	91	21	4	3

Table 6. Recognition accuracies (%) on AR in the scenario of multiple training samples per person (*the best performance in each case has been bolded*)

Index	Images	SIS	LDA	DCV	PCA
(h)		**99**	65	73	58
(i-j)		**100**	51	60	56
(k)		**100**	57	47	14
(l-m)		**99**	50	47	10
(n)		**100**	91	88	84
(o-q)		**99**	82	82	78
(r-t)		**99**	86	84	77
(u)		**97**	37	45	27
(v-w)		**97**	22	33	27
(x)		**92**	25	24	6
(y-z)		**95**	24	18	5

Table 7. Recognition accuracies (%) on EYALE in the scenario of multiple training samples per person (*results in the rows marked by * are obtained by evaluating only the first 10 subjects, while results in the other rows are obtained by evaluating all the 38 subjects*)

Method	Subset			
	2	3	4	5
SIS	100	100	97	99
SIS*	100	100	99	100
Cones-cast [6]*	100	100	100	N/A
9PL$_{real}$ [10]*	100	100	100	N/A
9PL$_{sim}$ [10]*	100	100	97	N/A
Cones-attached [6]*	100	100	91	N/A
FSS [16]*	100	100	87	35
LDA	100	98	37	5
DCV	100	96	32	6
PCA	90	41	6	3

The above experiments verify that the proposed SIS approach is effective in the scenario of multiple training samples per person.

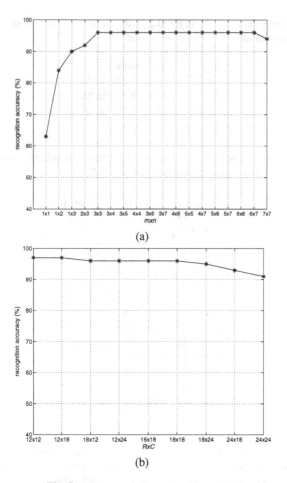

(a)

(b)

Fig. 5. Influence of the parameters of SIS

4.5   Influence of the Parameters

To study the influence of the four parameters m, n, R and C on the performance of SIS, we conduct experiments on the AR database by employing the images with index (a) for training and the images with index (u) for testing.

Experiment 6: We fix $R = 16$ and $C = 18$ and report recognition accuracies by varying values of $m \times n$ in Fig. 5 (a). First, when $m = n = 1$, for a given sub-image, we can only generate one synthesized sub-image that is just the original sub-image. In this case, SIS reduces to applying the correlation method to sub-images for classification, and only achieves a classification accuracy of 63%, which is far less than 96% by using 25 shifted sub-images. Second, when $m, n > 6$, there is a tendency towards performance drop, which may owe to the fact that little information is delivered by the synthesized sub-images with relatively big m and n, as mentioned in Section 3.1. Third, the performance curve is quite stable when the value of $m \times n$ is between 3×3

and 6×6. Note that, the recognition task here is very hard due to severe occlusion by wearing glasses, and thus it is nice to see that SIS is relatively invariant to $m \times n$ in a relatively wide range.

Experiment 7: We fix $m = 5$ and $n = 5$ and report recognition rates by varying values of $R \times C$ in Fig. 5 (b), from which we can observe that the performance curve is relatively stable when R and C are around 1/3 of M and N.

5   Conclusion and Discussion

In this paper, we propose the SIS (Single Image Subspace) approach for face recognition. First, we propose to represent each single image as a subspace spanned by its the synthesized images. Second, we design a new subspace distance metric for measuring the distance between subspaces. Third, to improve the robustness to great facial variations such as expression, illumination and occlusion, we divide a face image into several regions, compute the contribution scores of the training samples based on the extracted subspaces in each region, and aggregate the scores of all the regions to yield the ultimate recognition result.

Experiments on AR, FERET and EYALE show that SIS outperforms some renowned methods such as PCA, LDA, DCV, LPS, SOM-face, BIC, EBGM and FSS in the scenarios of both *one training sample per person* and *multiple training samples per person* with significant facial variations. Moreover, like the well-known methods such as illumination cone and 9PL, SIS yields classification accuracies close to 100% on EYALE.

In our future work we will study the theoretical justification for the proposed SIS approach. We will try to make use of kernel trick to embed the idea of SIS into traditional methods such as LDA. Moreover, we will try to exploit other synthesizing techniques in building the subspace.

Acknowledgments

The authors would like to thank the anonymous reviewers for their constructive comments that improved this paper. This work was supported in part by the National Natural Science Foundation of China under Grant Nos. 60473035 and 60635030, the National 863 project under Grant No. 2007AA01Z169, the Natural Science Foundation of Jiangsu Province under Grant Nos. BK2005122 and BK2006187, and the Innovation Foundation of NUAA under Grand No. Y0603-042.

References

1. Belhumeur, P.N., Hespanha, J.P., Kriegman, D.J.: Eigenfaces vs. Fisherfaces: Recognition using class specific linear projection. IEEE Transactions on Pattern Analysis and Machine Intelligence 19(7), 711–720 (1997)
2. Beveridge, J.R., Bolme, D., Draper, B.A., Teixeira, M.: The CSU face identification evaluation system: its purpose, features, and structure. Machine Vision Application 16(2), 128–138 (2005)
3. Beymer, D., Poggio, T.: Face recognition from one example view. In: Proceedings of the 5th IEEE International Conference on Computer Vision, pp. 500–507. IEEE Computer Society Press, Washington, DC (1995)

4. Cevikalp, H., Neamtu, M., Wilkes, M., Barkana, A.: Discriminative common vectors for face recognition. IEEE Transactions on Pattern Analysis and Machine Intelligence 27(1), 4–13 (2005)
5. Chapelle, O., Haffner, P., Vapnik, V.N.: Support Vector Machines for Histogram-based Image Classification. IEEE Transactions on Neural Networks 10(5), 1055–1064 (1999)
6. Georghiades, A.S., Belhumeur, P.N., Kriegman, D.J.: From few to many: Illumination cone models for face recognition under variable lighting and pose. IEEE Transactions on Pattern Analysis and Machine Intelligence 23(6), 643–660 (2001)
7. Golub, G., Van Loan, C.: Matrix Computations, 3rd edn. The Johns Hopkins University Press (1996)
8. Gonzalez, R.C., Woods, R.E.: Digital Image Processing, 2nd edn. Prentice-Hall, Englewood Cliffs (2004)
9. Liu, J., Chen, S.C.: Discriminant common vecotors versus neighbourhood components analysis and laplacianfaces: A comparative study in small sample size problem. Image and Vision Computing 24(3), 249–262 (2006)
10. Lee, K., Ho, J., Kriegman, D.J.: Acquiring linear subspaces for face recognition under variable lighting. IEEE Transactions on Pattern Analysis and Machine Intelligence 27(5), 1–15 (2005)
11. Martinez, A.M.: Recognizing imprecisely localized, partially occluded and expression variant faces from a single sample per class. IEEE Transactions on Pattern Analysis and Machine Intelligence 25(6), 748–763 (2002)
12. Martinez, A.M., Benavente, R.: The AR face database. Technical Report, CVC (1998)
13. Moghaddam, B., Nastar, C., Pentland, A.: A bayesian similarity measure for direct image matching. In: Proceedings of the 13th International Conference on Pattern Recognition, Vienna, Austria, pp. 350–358 (1996)
14. Niyogi, P., Girosi, F., Poggio, T.: Incorporating prior information in machine learning by creating virtual examples. Proceedings of the IEEE 86(11), 2196–2209 (1998)
15. Phillips, P.J., Wechsler, H., Huang, J., Rauss, P.: The FERET database and evaluation procedure for face recognition algorithms. Image and Vision Computing 16(5), 295–306 (1998)
16. Shan, S., Gao, W., Zhao, D.: Face identification based on face-specific subspace. International Journal of Image and System Technology 13(1), 23–32 (2003)
17. Tan, X., Chen, S.C., Zhou, Z.-H., Zhang, F.: Recognizing partially occluded, expression variant faces from single training image per person with SOM and soft kNN ensemble. IEEE Transactions on Neural Networks 16(4), 875–886 (2005)
18. Tan, X., Chen, S.C., Zhou, Z.-H., Zhang, F.: Face recognition from a single image per person: A survey. Pattern Recognition 39(9), 1725–1745 (2006)
19. Torre, F., Gross, R., Baker, S., Kumar, V.: Representational oriented component analysis (ROCA) for face recognition with one sample image per training class. In: Proceedings of the 23rd IEEE Computer Society Conference on Computer Vision and Pattern Recognition, pp. 266–273. IEEE Computer Society Press, San Diego, CA (2005)
20. Turk, M., Pentland, A.: Eigenfaces for recognition. Journal of Cognitive Neuroscience 3(1), 71–96 (1991)
21. Wiskott, L., Fellous, J., Kruger, N., von der Malsburg, C.: Face recognition by elastic bunch graph matching. IEEE Transactions on Pattern Analysis and Machine Intelligence 19(7), 775–779 (1997)
22. Wolf, L., Shashua, A.: Learning over sets using kernel principal angles. Journal of Machine Learning Research 4(6), 913–931 (2004)
23. Wu, J., Zhou, Z.-H.: Face recognition with one training image per person. Pattern Recognition Letters 23(14), 1711–1719 (2002)

24. Yamaguchi, Q., Fukui, K., Maeda, K.: Face recognition using temporal image sequence. In: Proceedings of the 3rd International Conference on Face & Gesture Recognition, Washington, DC, pp. 318–323 (1998)
25. Zhao, W., Chellappa, R., Phillips, P.J., Rosenfeld, A.: Face recognition: A literature survey. ACM Computing Survey 35(4), 399–458 (2003)

Human Face Processing with 1.5D Models

Ginés García-Mateos[1], Alberto Ruiz-Garcia[1], and Pedro E. López-de-Teruel[2]

[1] Dept. de Informática y Sistemas
[2] Dept. Ing. y Tecn. de Computadores
Universidad de Murcia, 30.100 Espinardo, Murcia, Spain
{ginesgm,aruiz}@um.es, pedroe@ditec.um.es

Abstract. Integral projections reduce the size of input data by transforming 2D images into significantly simpler 1D signals, while retaining useful information to solve important computer vision problems like object detection, location, and tracking. However, previous attempts typically rely on simple heuristic analysis such as searching for minima or maxima in the resulting projections. We introduce a more rigorous and formal modeling framework based on a small set of integral projections –thus, we will call them *1.5D models*– and show that this model-based analysis overcomes many of the difficulties and limitations of alternative projection methods. The proposed approach proves to be particularly adequate for the specific domain of human face processing. The problems of face detection, facial feature location, and tracking in video sequences are studied under the unifying proposed framework.

Keywords: 1.5D object models, integral projections, face detection, facial feature location, face tracking.

1 Introduction

Dimensionality reduction is a required stage in many computer vision applications. This task is usually carried out with techniques like principal components analysis (PCA) [1], linear discriminant analysis (LDA), independent component analysis (ICA), or other feature extraction methods, such as edge or segment detection. Integral projections are among the most frequently used methods to reduce the huge volume of data contained in images, specially in the human face domain [2]. However, projections are often used just in heuristic and *ad hoc* algorithms [2,3,4,5]. A much more theoretically sound basis can be developed to take full advantage of the intrinsic power of the technique. Two aspects will be crucial to define this framework: first, a simple but powerful *modeling* framework for projections, which is generic and trainable; and second, an efficient and robust technique for the *alignment* of resulting 1D signals.

The rest of the paper is structured as follows. Section 2 describes the concept and properties of integral projections, and tackles the problems of modeling and alignment. A feasible face model using projections is presented in section 3. Then, the problems of human face detection, facial feature location, and face tracking in video are studied in sections 4, 5 and 6, always working with projections.

S.K. Zhou et al. (Eds.): AMFG 2007, LNCS 4778, pp. 220–234, 2007.

Experiments and references to related work are included in each section. Finally, the main contributions of the paper are summarized in section 7.

2   Integral Projections and 1.5D Models

Radon transform [6], Hough transform [7], and integral projections are closely related concepts. Let $f(x, y)$ be a continuous 2D function; its Radon transform is another 2D function, $\mathcal{R}[f](\theta, s)$, defined as:

$$\mathcal{R}[f](\theta, s) = \int_{-\infty}^{\infty} \int_{-\infty}^{\infty} f(x, y)\delta(x\cos\theta + y\sin\theta - s)\ dx\ dy \tag{1}$$

where δ is a Dirac's delta. Curiously enough, 58 years after being firstly formulated by Johann Radon in 1914, equation 1 was renamed as "Hough transform to detect lines" [7], in this case applied on discrete images.

Moreover, integral projections are a specific case of equation 1, where θ is a fixed projection angle. For example, let $i(x, y)$ be an image; $\mathcal{R}[i](0, y), \forall y$ is called the **vertical integral projection** of i, and $\mathcal{R}[i](\pi/2, x), \forall x$ the **horizontal projection**[1]. For simplicity, we will denote them with $PV_i(y)$ and $PH_i(x)$.

In a pioneering work by Kanade in the human face domain [2], integral projections were applied on edge images. More recently, some alternative methods have been proposed, such as the **variance projection functions** [5], where the variance of each row or column of pixels –instead of just the sum– is computed. Though these also have some interesting advantages, by definition they are not linear transforms; thus, many of the following properties do not hold.

2.1   Properties and Advantages

Compared to most other dimensionality reduction techniques –specially linear subspace methods, like PCA, LDA and ICA–, integral projections are simpler both in definition and computation. Nevertheless, they offer a very interesting set of properties, which make them preferable in many image analysis applications:

- **Invariance and noise filtering.** Projections are invariant to a number of image transformations such as mirroring, scale, shear and translation along the projection angle. It is also well-known that integral projections are highly robust to white noise [8]. Figure 1 shows a sample facial image under several instances of these transformations, and the corresponding vertical projections; it can be easily seen that, while the former are severely distorted, the latter remain greatly unaffected.
- **Locality.** Integral projections preserve the principle of locality of pixels: two neighbor points in a projection correspond to two neighbor regions in the image. This makes it possible to apply alignment processes *after* projection, whereas in PCA, LDA and ICA, images have to be aligned *before* projection.

---

[1] Some authors call "vertical projection" what we define as "horizontal projection" and *vice versa*, while many others adopt our same definition.

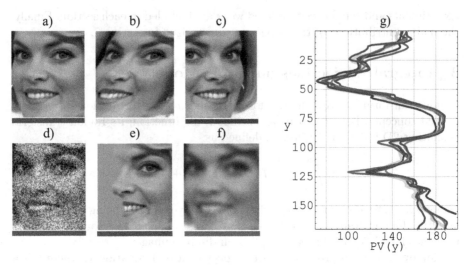

Fig. 1. Invariance of integral projections to various image transforms. a) Original image. b-f) The same image after: b) shear; c) mirroring and translation; d) random noise; e) partial occlusion; f) smoothing. g) The corresponding vertical projections.

In other words, integral projections are less sensitive to miss-alignment in the projected regions.

– **Invertibility.** No information is lost in the process of projection. Using an adequate number of projections at different angles, it is possible to reconstruct original images up to a desired precision level. This result derives from the *central slice theorem* [6], which is the base of computed tomography.

– **Characterization.** According to the previous property, integral projections are preferred when the number of projections needed to represent an object is small. Due to symmetry, this is precisely the case for human faces. Furthermore, projections from very different people share a common underlying structure, as can be seen in figure 2, where images of more than 1000 distinct individuals are projected.

– **Efficiency.** Finally, working with projections is obviously much faster than with full images. Moreover, *integral images* [10] can be used to reduce even more the cost of computing projections, as described below.

2.2 Gaussian Projection Models

Many computer vision systems have benefited from the good properties of integral projections [2,3,4,7]. But, in general, most of them merely analyze the projections heuristically, by searching for local maxima, minima, areas of high variation (maxima of the derivative), or any other similar *ad hoc* techniques. For example, a face is said to be present if the vertical projection presents a minimum in the eyes, a maximum in the nose, and another minimum in the mouth [4]. Considering the highly regular structure of human faces –see figure 2c)– it is clear that a lot of information is being thrown away by these simple heuristic methods.

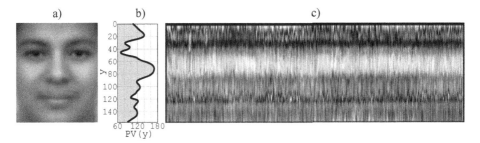

Fig. 2. Characterization of objects with projections. a) Mean male face. b) Vertical integral projection of the mean face (observe the –non-casual– similitude to a profile face). c) 3818 vertical projections of 1196 individuals from the FERET database [9] (each projection is represented as a single column).

To avoid this undesirable loss of information, we propose a mechanism which takes advantage of the whole structure of the projection signal. In particular, let $\mathcal{P} = \{P_1, P_2, \ldots, P_n\}$ be a set of training projections from a certain class of objects. We define a *projection model* as a pair of 1D signals (M, V), where:

- $M(i)$ is the mean of the set $\{P_1(i), P_2(i), \ldots, P_n(i)\}$.
- $V(i)$ is the variance of the set $\{P_1(i), P_2(i), \ldots, P_n(i)\}$.

This way, a set $\mathcal{P}$ of integral projections is modeled as m independent 1D gaussians, being m the domain of $\mathcal{P}$ –that is, the size of each input projection vector–. Figure 4a) shows an example of one of these models, corresponding to the vertical projections of a set of images of human faces.

2.3   Projection Alignment

Alignment (both in domain and codomain) between two different 1D signals is a key problem when working with integral projections. Let us define a family of alignment transformations on 1D signals, t_{abcde}. For any projection P, each transformed value is given by:

$$t_{abcde}(P)(i) := a + b \cdot i + c \cdot P(d + e \cdot i)$$
$$\forall i \in \{(P_{min} - d)/e, \ldots, (P_{max} - d)/e\} \tag{2}$$

This is an *affine transformation* of 1D signals in the XY plane. A visual interpretation of the free parameters (a, b, c, d, e) is shown in figure 3.

Alignment of an input projection P to a given projection model (M, V) can be formulated as the optimization of the following expression:

$$\{a^*, b^*, c^*, d^*, e^*\} = \arg \min_{a,b,c,d,e} \frac{1}{||r||} \sum_{i \in r} \frac{(M(i) - t_{abcde}(P)(i))^2}{V(i)} \tag{3}$$

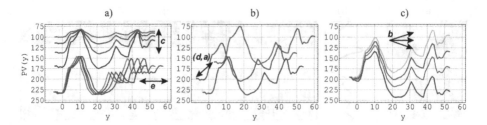

Fig. 3. Interpretation of parameters (a, b, c, d, e) in the alignment function defined in equation 2. a) Scale in signal's value (c) and domain (e). b) Translation in value (a) and domain (d). c) Shear (b), that accounts for non-uniform illumination.

where r is the intersection of domains of M and $t_{abcde}(P)$. For fixed $\{d, e\}$, the minimum squared error solution for the parameters $\{a, b, c\}$ can be obtained in closed form. Then, we can define the following function $mindist$:

$$mindist(d, e) := \min_{a,b,c} dist((M, V), t_{abcde}(P)) \tag{4}$$

where $dist$ is the summation term in equation 3. Unfortunately, $\{d, e\}$ cannot be solved analytically. But, by definition, the range of possible values for both parameters is bounded by a maximum and minimum translation, d, and scale, e. Thus, we propose a simplified version of the Nelder-Mead simplex optimization algorithm [11] based on successive sampling and reduction of the search space in the plane $mindist(d, e)$. The algorithm is described in figure 4.

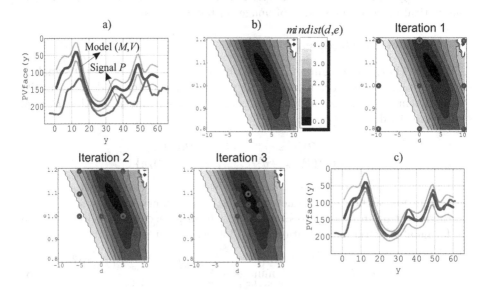

Fig. 4. Illustration of the alignment algorithm. a) Model and signal before alignment. b) Alignment distance, $mindist$, as a function of e and d; and the search space in the first iterations of the algorithm. c) Resulting signal and model after alignment.

3   A 1.5D Face Model

In the rest of this paper we will describe the application of gaussian projection models and the proposed alignment algorithm in the specific domain of face processing. As mentioned before, integral projections are specially adequate for representing human faces, because a very small number of projections is able to retain most information of typical faces. For example, in terms of variance of the gray value of a mean face –see figure 2a)–, the vertical projection alone describes more than 75% of the variance of the original image.

In the following, we will assume that input faces are normalized according to these three rules:

1. Faces are extracted with a predefined resolution of $W \times H$ pixels –typically 24×30– using a *similarity* transform, i.e. a scale/translation/rotation.
2. Faces are horizontally centered, with both eyes at the same height.
3. We set the height of the eyes $h_{eyes} = 0.2H$, and the height of the mouth $h_{mouth} = 0.8H$.

Our face model consists of two integral projection models –thus, we call it *1.5D model*–, which are computed on normalized faces. These models are:

– (MV_{face}, VV_{face}): model of the vertical integral projections of the extracted facial images, PV_{face}.
– (MH_{eyes}, VH_{eyes}): model of the horizontal projections of the eyes' region, PH_{eyes}, approximately between height $0.1H$ and $0.3H$ in extracted images.

Figure 5 shows a sample model computed on 374 faces. Observe the typical patterns of both models, corresponding to dark and light areas of human faces.

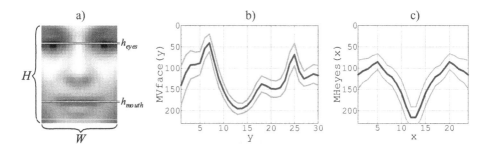

Fig. 5. Face model trained with a set of 374 faces not included in the tests. a) Mean face and parameters of the normalized model: H= height of the extracted faces; W= width; h_{eyes}= height of the eyes; and h_{mouth}= height of the mouth. b) Gaussian projection model of the vertical integral projection of the face, MV_{face}. c) Gaussian projection model of the horizontal projection of the eyes, MH_{eyes}.

4   Human Face Detection

Most face detectors –such as the popular method by Viola and Jones [10]– are based on multi-scale exhaustive search. Sung and Poggio were the first to develop this idea [12]. In essence, a binary (face/non-face) classifier is applied over all possible locations (or *windows*), and at all possible resolutions. These methods are known as *appearance-based* detectors.

4.1   Face Detection Using 1.5D Models

Our face detection technique follows the appearance-based approach, where the binary classifier is designed to work with integral projections and 1.5D models. The structure of the proposed detector is depicted in figure 6.

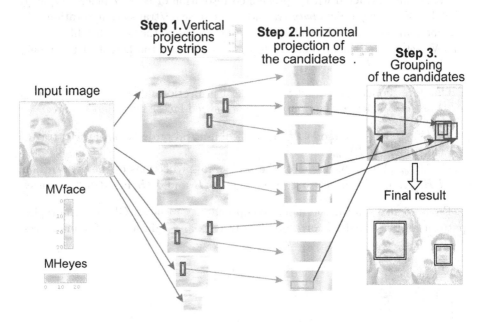

Fig. 6. Global structure of the face detection algorithm. In step 1, a pyramid of scaled vertical integral projections of the input image is computed, and the model MV_{face} is searched for at every position and scale. The resulting candidates are verified, in step 2, using horizontal projections and the corresponding model MH_{eyes}. Finally, tentative candidates are grouped in step 3 to eliminate multiple responses at the same location of the image.

The procedure can be summarized in the following 3 steps:

Step 1. First, the algorithm constructs a *pyramid* of vertical projections from the input image, using a typical scale factor reduction of 1.2. In accordance with the model, the width of the strips is W pixels, and these are computed in steps of $W/4$ pixels (thus, adjacent strips represent in fact partially over-lapped regions). Then, the model of PV_{face} is searched for along the pyramid of projections.

This first step accounts for the uncertainty in the size of the faces, and represents the most expensive part of the process. However, using *integral images* [10], computing the whole pyramid of projections requires just $O(n)$ operations, where n is the number of pixels in the input image.

Step 2. The most relevant candidates obtained in step 1 are verified using PH_{eyes}. For each candidate, if the horizontal projection of the subregion approximately corresponding to the eyes –with slight variations in scale and horizontal position– does not fit with the model MH_{eyes}, the candidate is rejected; otherwise, it is accepted.

Step 3. Finally, the remaining candidates are analyzed in order to avoid multiple responses. Nearby and overlapping candidates are grouped together, and only the best candidate of each group is classified as a detected face.

4.2 Face Detection Results

Integral projections have already been applied to human face detection [3,4], mostly in *localization* scenarios –i.e., supposing that just one face is present in each image–. Figure 7 shows some sample results of the proposed detector on the public CMU/MIT face database [13], demonstrating that our method is able to detect an arbitrary number of faces in complex backgrounds.

Fig. 7. Sample results of the face detector based on integral projections. The images were taken from the CMU/MIT face database [13]. More results available at [14].

We have also evaluated the performance of our detector –both in quantitative and qualitative terms– on a face database developed by the authors' research group, which includes samples taken from TV, TDT, DVD, digital photographs, video-conference cameras, and additional samples taken from the CMU/MIT set –as shown in figure 7–. This database contains a total of 737 images with 853 faces. Our integral projection method (**IntProj**) was compared with two alternative –and publicly available– appearance-based techniques: Viola and Jones'

Table 1. Face detection results on a database with 737 images containing 853 faces. The percentage of correctly detected faces (*detection rate*) is shown for different false positive (FP) settings. FP ratio is relative to the number of images. The computer used was a Pentium IV at 2.6GHz, and the average image size is of 534 × 393 pixels.

Detection method	Detection rate				Time
	FP=5%	FP=10%	FP=20%	FP=50%	(ms)
IntProj	35.6	50.8	67.2	84.2	**85.2**
AdaBoost&Haar [10]	86.1	88.9	90.8	91.8	292.5
Neural Networks [13]	55.0	75.4	85.5	88.6	2337.7
AdaB&Haar + IntProj	**92.7**	**94.0**	**95.0**	**96.1**	295.6

detector [10], based on the AdaBoost algorithm and Haar-like filters, and Rowley's [13], based on neural networks. Additionally, a combination of our method and [10] was also studied. We present a summary of the results of this experiment in table 1, which shows the detection rates corresponding to several arbitrarily chosen false positive rates of the resulting ROC curves for each method.

Though more complex techniques certainly produce better detection rates, the proposed method exhibits a remarkable cost/benefit ratio. Moreover, **IntProj** and **NeuralNet** achieve similar maximum detection rates, while the former is 27 times faster. Considering only the images taken from webcams, **IntProj** reaches a 90% detection rate at 10% false positives per image.

But, clearly, the best performance is given by the combined method, which improves around a 5% the average detection rate of **AdaBoost&Haar**, at a negligible increment in the execution time.

5   Facial Feature Location

As shown in figure 7, our face detector simply outputs a rough location of the existing faces. This is a common characteristic of many methods available in the literature [15], where the faces are described with bounding rectangles. The purpose of facial feature location is to refine that description, providing –in our case– a precise location of the left and right eyes, and the mouth.

5.1   Face Feature Locator Using 1.5D Models

Basically, our facial feature locator performs a refined search of the 1.5D face model (i.e., MV_{face} and MH_{eyes}) on the previously detected faces. The input to this refinement process is the face rectangle generated by the detector. The proposed method consists of three steps (figure 8), all of them relying on the alignment algorithm described in section 2.3.

In the first step, we estimate face orientation, i.e. in-plane rotation[2]. This step makes use of face symmetry in a robust way. The vertical integral projection of

---

[2] The detector introduced in section 4 assumes that faces are approximately upright. In our experiments, an inclination of up to ±10° is allowed, with insignificant degradation in the detection rate.

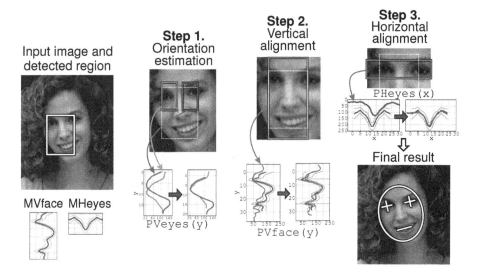

Fig. 8. Global structure of the facial feature location algorithm. In step 1, the orientation of the face is estimated using the vertical projections of both eyes. Then, in step 2, the vertical projection of the whole region is used to find the vertical position of the face. Similarly, the horizontal projection of eyes is computed and aligned in step 3.

the expected left and right eye regions are obtained. Then, both projections are aligned to each other, and the resulting displacement is easily transformed into an estimated inclination angle. This simple method can be very accurate up to angles of 20°.

The angle obtained in step 1 is used to rectify the input face. Then the accurate vertical and horizontal scale and location of the extracted face are determined in steps 2 and 3. The vertical integral projection of the face –along with an extra margin– is computed in PV_{face}, and this signal is aligned with respect to MV_{face}. Parameters $\{d, e\}$, resulting from the alignment algorithm (see equation 3) indicate the vertical translation and scale of the face, respectively.

In a similar way, in step 3 we compute the horizontal integral projection of the eyes' region PH_{eyes}, which is aligned with respect to MH_{eyes} to accurately locate the face horizontally. In this case, parameters $\{d, e\}$ indicate horizontal position and scale. Finally, the coordinates of the eyes and the mouth in the rectified image are mapped back into the original image.

5.2   Facial Feature Location Results

We present some sample results of the proposed method in figure 9. In all cases, the output of the combined face detector described in section 4 is used to feed the locator procedure based on integral projections, described in this section.

Though the proposed facial feature locator is based on face symmetry, it is notably robust even in situations where this symmetry is not so evident, as can

Fig. 9. Some sample results of the face locator based on integral projections. The four images on the left were taken from the CMU/MIT face database [13], and the rest from TV. More results available at [14].

be seen in figure 9. This is mainly due to two reasons: (1) changes in illumination are practically removed by the alignment process; and (2) integral projections remain invariant under small imprecisions in the projected regions –for example, if a part of the background is projected–. Furthermore, our method is able to work both with high and low resolution faces.

We have carried out extensive location experiments with more than 3700 manually labeled faces from the FERET database [9]. None of those faces were used to train the 1.5D face model[3]. The proposed method was compared with some alternative facial feature locators: a neural network-based eye locator by Rowley [13]; a simple template matching method (using correlation and mean eye and mouth patterns); and a modular eigenspace (eigen-eyes, eigen-mouth) technique [1]. The main results are summarized in table 2.

Again, the proposed method achieves a very good cost/benefit ratio. It is able to locate 99% of the faces with an error in the eyes position below 20% of the distance between eyes, taking just 3 ms of computing time per face. Moreover, in 96% of these cases the error is under 10%. Its accuracy is very similar or better than the neural networks locator, but it is about 100 times faster.

6   Face Tracking

Many different approaches have been proposed to deal with human face tracking, based on color, appearance, optical flow, predefined models, eigen-decompositions, and many other heterogeneous techniques. Not surprisingly, Ahlberg and

---

[3] In particular, the face model presented in figure 5 was used both in the detection and location experiments.

Table 2. Facial feature location results on 3743 faces from the FERET database [9]. For each method: **Location rate**: percentage of faces with both eyes with an error below 20%; **Angle diff.**: mean error in inclination angle (in degrees); **Dist. eyes, mouth**: mean distance error of eyes and mouth, respectively (error is always an Euclidean distance, expressed as % of the eye-to-eye distance); **Time**: average location time per face on a Pentium IV at 2.6GHz.

Location method	Location rate (miss-locations)	Angle diff.	Dist. eyes	Dist. mouth	Time (ms)
IntProj	**98.9% (41)**	**0.9°**	4.6%	**9.8%**	**3.1**
Neural Networks [13]	90.8% (343)	1.4°	**4.5%**	10.8%	346.0
Temp. Matching	91.1% (332)	2.0°	7.4%	10.5%	18.9
Eigen Features [1]	93.9% (272)	2.3°	6.2%	11.6%	45.1

Dornaika [16] use the expression "plethora of trackers" when talking about this topic. Here we prove that integral projections can also be applied successfully to this problem, producing a fast, stable and robust tracking method.

6.1   Face Tracking with 1.5D Models

Tracking methods are commonly based on two main components: a *prediction* mechanism, responsible for estimating tracking status in each new frame of a video sequence; and a *relocator*, which actually processes the current frame and computes the resulting position. If the observed motion is expected to be small, the first component can just be obviated; otherwise a more sophisticated predictor is required. In the human face domain, color based methods –such as the popular CamShift [17]– can be used to perform a suitable prediction. They are able to efficiently produce a robust but imprecise estimation of fast movements, that will be refined then by the relocator.

In this context, the problems of face relocation and facial feature location are closely related. Thus, our tracking algorithm shares a common structure with the technique described in section 5. However, there are two important differences:

1. The 1.5D face model –i.e., the projection models for PV_{face} and PH_{eyes}– is computed from the sequence itself. Recall that, in the case of facial feature location, a generic model was used.
2. The orientation estimation step is performed *after* vertical and horizontal alignments, instead of *before*. While in facial feature location the observed inclination can be relatively high, in tracking only a presumably slight variation of inclination needs to be considered.

Besides, an excessive alignment distance is used to detect the end of tracking. A more detailed description of the proposed face tracker can be found in [18].

6.2   Face Tracking Results

The method presented above was designed to perform robust and precise 2D face tracking under complex situations of facial expression, fast motion, low

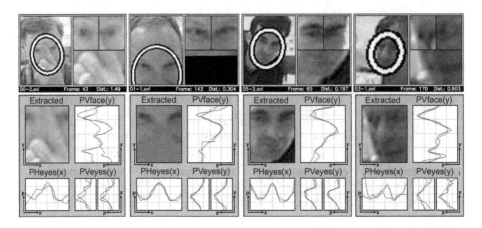

Fig. 10. Some sample results of the face tracker based on integral projections on videos from the NRC-IIT facial video database [19]. For each frame, we show the location of eyes and mouth (upper right), the bounding ellipse (upper left), and the computed projections (below).

Table 3. Face tracking results on 12 videos from the NRC-IIT facial video database [19] (00-1.avi, 00-2.avi, 01-1.avi, ..., 05-02.avi). The total number of faces (frame-by-frame) is 3635. **Tracked faces** and **false positives** are also counted frame-by-frame. Tracking is said to be correct if the obtained location is *close enough* to real eye positions (see caption of table 2); recall that all methods, except CamShift, involve a relocation of the eyes. The computer used was a Pentium IV at 2.6GHz.

Face Tracker	Tracked faces	False positives	Time (ms)
Detector [10]	2032 (55.8%)	368 (9.8%)	42.9
IntProj Null	2893 (79.6%)	493 (12.5%)	8.9
IntProj Color	**3050 (83.9%)**	**300 (7.3%)**	10.8
LK Tracker [20]	2828 (78.2%)	706 (17.1%)	**5.1**
Temp. Match	2387 (66.3%)	947 (23.9%)	11.3
CamShift [17]	1905 (51.5%)	1763 (47.0%)	5.8

resolution, partial occlusion, and poor illumination. The NRC-IIT facial video database [19], publicly available, is a good resource for experimentation under these circumstances. Figure 10 shows some difficult cases from this database.

Using 12 videos from the NRC-IIT set, we have compared the described tracker with three alternative approaches: a pyramidal implementation of Lucas and Kanade's method [20]; a template matching-based tracker; and the CamShift algorithm [17]. In addition, the result of applying Viola and Jones' face detector [10] to all frames is also reported. Table 3 summarizes the performance of these methods. The proposed technique (**IntProj**) was applied both without prediction (**Null**), and with a color based predictor (**Color**).

The low *detection rate* of **Detector** (below 56%) is a good indicator of the intrinsic complexity of the test. **IntProj Color** finds 50% more faces, while being

4 times faster. The high rate of false positives in **LK Tracker** is due to the well known *drift* problem of motion based trackers [16]. Our method attenuates its effects by using a robust model for the face. In **CamShift**, false positives are due to very imprecise locations of the face. In contrast, our tracker is able to provide an accurate location of eyes and mouth even in cases of low resolution.

We have carried out additional experiments using sample videos captured from TV, TDT, video-conference cameras and some DVD scenes. Several samples present great changes in out-of-plane rotation. In general, the range of allowed rotation is approximately ±40° in yaw, and ±20° in pitch. Many of these videos, and the obtained results, can be found at [14]. Basically, all the conclusions mentioned above still hold.

7   Discussion and Conclusions

In this paper we have tackled some of the main problems in face processing under a common framework based on integral projection models and alignment. Whilst projections are a classical and well-known technique in image analysis, little effort has been done to formalize their use. We have discussed the necessity to undertake this effort, by introducing the concept of a *probabilistic projection model* and a robust and general *alignment process*. Both aspects have been thoroughly studied, leading to a gaussian technique to model projections, and a fast iterative model-instance alignment algorithm. Using them in conjunction, we have proposed closely related solutions for several face processing problems, such as face detection on still images, facial feature location, and face tracking.

Our experiments prove that integral projections have a number of advantages with respect to other techniques: improved generalization, immunity to noise, and robustness against facial expressions and individual factors. The accuracy of the proposed algorithm is similar to that of the more complex state-of-the-art methods, with a considerable reduction of the computational cost.

Further applications of the proposed approach include the problems of person recognition, 3D pose estimation, and facial expression recognition [14]. Our future plans include using integral projections within the AdaBoost algorithm [10]. Instead of using Haar-like features, AdaBoost would take projections as the weak classifiers, giving rise to *not-so-weak* elementary classifiers.

Acknowledgements

This work has been supported by the Spanish MEC grant CSD2006-00046.

References

1. Pentland, A., Moghaddam, B., Starner, T.: View-based and modular eigenspaces for face recognition. In: IEEE Computer Society Conf. on CVPR, pp. 84–91 (1994)
2. Kanade, T.: Picture Processing by Computer Complex and Recognition of Human Faces. PhD thesis, Kyoto University (1973)

3. Kotropoulos, C., Pitas, I.: Rule-based face detection in frontal views. In: Proc. I.C. Acoustics, Speech and Signal Processing, vol. 4, pp. 2537–2540 (1997)

4. Sobottka, K., Pitas, I.: Looking for faces and facial features in color images. PRIA: Advances in Mathematical Theory and Applications 7(1) (1997)

5. Feng, G.C., Yuen, P.C.: Variance projection function and its application to eye detection for human face recognition. Pattern Rec. Letters 19, 899–906 (1998)

6. Dean, S.R.: The Radon Transform and Some of Its Applications. John Wiley & Sons, New York (1983)

7. Duda, R.O., Hart, P.E.: Use of the Hough transformation to detect lines and curves in pictures. Comm. ACM 15, 11–15 (1972)

8. Robinson, D., Milanfar, P.: Fast local and global projection-based methods for affine motion estimation. J. of Math. Imaging and Vision 18, 35–54 (2003)

9. Phillips, P.J., Moon, H., Rizvi, S.A., Rauss, P.J.: The FERET evaluation methodology for face-recognition algorithms. IEEE Trans. on Pattern Analysis and Machine Intelligence 22(10), 1090–1104 (2000)

10. Viola, P., Jones, M.J.: Rapid object detection using a boosted cascade of simple features. In: IEEE Intl. Conf. on Comp. Vision and Pattern Recogn., pp. 12–14 (2001)

11. Nelder, J.A., Mead, R.: A simplex method for function minimization. The Computer Journal 7, 308–313 (1964)

12. Sung, K.-K., Poggio, T.: Example-based learning for view-based human face detection. IEEE Trans. on PAMI 20(1), 39–51 (1998)

13. Rowley, H.A., Baluja, S., Kanade, T.: Neural network-based face detection. IEEE Transactions on Pattern Analysis and Machine Intelligence 20(1), 23–28 (1998)

14. García-Mateos, G.: Face processing with IP: http://dis.um.es/~ginesgm/fip/

15. Yang, M.-H., Kriegman, D.J., Ahuja, N.: Detecting faces in images: A survey. IEEE Trans. on Pattern Analysis and Machine Intelligence 24(1), 34–58 (2002)

16. Li, S.Z., Jain, A.K.: Handbook of Face Recognition. Springer, New York (2005)

17. Bradsky, G.D.: Computer vision face tracking as a component of a perceptual user interface. In: Workshop on Appl. of Comp. Vision, pp. 214–219. Princeton University Press, Princeton, NJ (1998)

18. García-Mateos, G.: Refining face tracking with integral projections. In: Kittler, J., Nixon, M.S. (eds.) AVBPA 2003. LNCS, vol. 2688, pp. 360–368. Springer, Heidelberg (2003)

19. Gorodnichy, D.O.: Video-based framework for face recognition in video. In: Second Workshop on FPiV 2005, Victoria, BC, Canada, pp. 330–338 (2005)

20. Bouguet, J.-Y.: Pyramidal implementation of the Lucas Kanade feature tracker. Technical report, Intel Corporation, Microprocessor Research Labs (2000)

21. Stegmann, M.B., Ersboll, B.K., Larsen, R.: FAME–a flexible appearance modeling environment. IEEE Transactions on Medical Imaging 22(10), 1319–1331 (2003)

22. Ma, Y., Ding, X.: Robust precise eye localization under probabilistic framework. In: Proc. of IEEE Conf. on Automatic Face and Gesture Recogn., pp. 339–344. IEEE Computer Society Press, Los Alamitos (2004)

Fusing Gabor and LBP Feature Sets
for Kernel-Based Face Recognition

Xiaoyang Tan and Bill Triggs

INRIA and Laboratoire Jean Kuntzmann, 655 avenue de l'Europe, Montbonnot 38330, France
{xiaoyang.tan,bill.triggs}@imag.fr

Abstract. Extending recognition to uncontrolled situations is a key challenge for practical face recognition systems. Finding efficient and discriminative facial appearance descriptors is crucial for this. Most existing approaches use features of just one type. Here we argue that robust recognition requires several different kinds of appearance information to be taken into account, suggesting the use of heterogeneous feature sets. We show that combining two of the most successful local face representations, Gabor wavelets and Local Binary Patterns (LBP), gives considerably better performance than either alone: they are complimentary in the sense that LBP captures small appearance details while Gabor features encode facial shape over a broader range of scales. Both feature sets are high dimensional so it is beneficial to use PCA to reduce the dimensionality prior to normalization and integration. The Kernel Discriminative Common Vector method is then applied to the combined feature vector to extract discriminant nonlinear features for recognition. The method is evaluated on several challenging face datasets including FRGC 1.0.4, FRGC 2.0.4 and FERET, with promising results.

1 Introduction

One of the key challenges for face recognition is finding efficient and discriminative facial appearance descriptors that are resistant to large variations in illumination, pose, facial expression, ageing, partial occlusions and other changes [32]. Most current recognition systems use just one type of features. However for complex tasks such as face recognition, it is often the case that no single feature modality is rich enough to capture all of the classification information available in the image. Finding and combining complementary feature sets has thus become an active research topic in pattern recognition, with successful applications in many challenging tasks including handwritten character recognition [9] and face recognition[16].

In this paper, we show that face recognition performance can be significantly improved by combining two of the most successful local appearance descriptors, Gabor wavelets [12, 28, 15] and Local Binary Patterns (LBP) [18, 19, 2]. LBP is basically a finescale descriptor that captures small texture details. Local spatial invariance is achieved by locally pooling (histogramming) the resulting texture codes. Given that it is also very resistant to lighting changes, LBP is a good choice for coding fine details of facial appearance and texture. In contrast, Gabor features [12, 28, 15] encode facial shape and appearance information over a range of coarser scales (although they have also been used as a preprocessing stage for LBP feature extraction [30]). Both representations are

S.K. Zhou et al. (Eds.): AMFG 2007, LNCS 4778, pp. 235–249, 2007.
© Springer-Verlag Berlin Heidelberg 2007

rich in information and computationally efficient. Their complementary nature makes them good candidates for fusion.

Here we evaluate and normalize the two modalities independently before combining them (although some works argue that it can be more effective to fuse modalities at an earlier stage of processing [10]). Both feature sets are high-dimensional (typically at least 10^4-D) and simply concatenating them would tend to exacerbate any 'curse of dimensionality' problems. To counteract this we run dimensionality reduction on each modality before fusion. Many dimensionality reduction techniques could be considered – Principal Component Analysis (PCA) [8], Independent Component Analysis (ICA) [20], Non-negative Matrix Factorization (NMF) [14], and Canonical Correlation Analysis (CCA) [13] to mention only some of the linear ones – but here we find that simple PCA suffices. The reduced feature vectors are separately normalized before being concatenated into a single combined feature vector. Finally the Kernel Discriminative Common Vector (KDCV) [4] method is applied to the combined feature vector to provide effective multi-class recognition from relatively few training examples. To illustrate the effectiveness of our approach we present experimental results on three state-of-the-art face recognition datasets containing large lighting variations similar to those encountered in natural images taken under uncontrolled conditions: the Face Recognition Grand Challenge 1.0.4 and 2.0.4 datasets [21] and FERET [22].

2   Related Work

Information fusion for visual recognition can occur at feature-level or at decision-level [10]. Feature-level methods combine several incoming feature sets into a single fused one that is then used in a conventional classifier, whereas decision-level ones combine several classifiers (e.g. based on distinct features) to make a stronger final classifier [11] (this is also called post-classification fusion or mixture of experts).

Face recognition is an area that is well-suited to the use (and hence fusion) of multiple classes of descriptors owing to its inherent complexity and need for fine distinctions. Much of the past work in this area adopts classifier-level fusion, *e.g.* [6,17]. For example, in [17] PCA, ICA and LDA provide the component subspaces for classifier combination. Each test sample is separately projected into these three subspaces and the resulting distance matrices are then fused to make the final decision using either the sum rule [11] or an RBF network. However motivated by the belief that the original features are a richer representation than distance matrices or individual classifier decisions, several works have studied feature-level fusion. J. Yang *et al.* [29] concatenate different features into a single vector and use Generalized PCA for feature exaction. C. Liu *et al.* [16] concatenate shape and texture information in a reduced subspace then use an enhanced Fisher classifier for recognition: their framework has similarities to ours but the underlying features and recognition methods are different.

Selecting appropriate and complementary component features is crucial for good performance. There is some work on fusing different biometric modalities (*e.g.* face and speech [3], face and fingerprint [23]), but most studies concentrate on fusing different representations of a single underlying modality (e.g. 2D and 3D facial shape in [6]). Our work belongs to this category, studying the effectiveness of fusing local 2D texture descriptors at both the feature and the decision stages but focusing mainly on the feature based fusion. Our initial experiments selected two of the most successful local appearance descriptors, Gabor wavelets and LBP, as promising candidates for fusion. As both features are strongly normalized and quite local in nature, we also test whether the inclusion of a less-normalized feature set (raw gray levels) further improves the quality of the combined representation.

Finally, we use a kernel discriminant to extract as much information as possible from the resulting combined features. Methods such as Kernel Principal Component Analysis (KPCA) [25] have proven to be effective nonlinear feature extractors and here we use a related discriminative method, Kernel Discriminative Common Vectors (KDCV). Like other kernel methods, KDCV uses a nonlinear (kernel) mapping to implicitly transform the input data into a high dimensional feature space. It then selects and projects out an optimal set of discriminant vectors in this space, using the kernel trick to express the resulting computation in terms of kernel values in the input space. A simple Nearest Neighbour (NN) classifier is applied to the resulting KDCV feature vector. H. Cevikalp *et al.* [4] have shown that the combination of KDCV and NN significantly outperforms several other kernel methods including KPCA+LDA and SVM in related problems.

3   Fusing Gabor and LBP Feature Sets for Kernel-Based Face Recognition

This section describes the components of our face recognition system in detail: Gabor and LBP features, PCA dimensionality reduction and feature fusion, Kernel DCV feature extraction and Nearest neighbour recognition. The stages of processing are illustrated in Fig. 1.

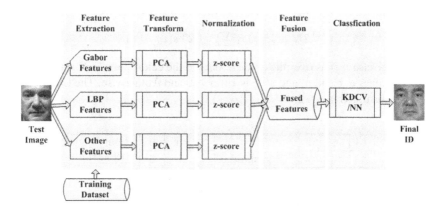

Fig. 1. The overall architecture of our face recognition system

3.1   Gabor Features Representation

Gabor wavelets were originally developed to model the receptive fields of simple cells in the visual cortex and in practice they capture a number of salient visual properties including spatial localization, orientation selectivity and spatial frequency selectivity quite well. They have been widely used in face recognition since the pioneering work of Lades *et al.* [12]. Computationally, they are the result of convolving the image with a bank of Gabor filters of different scales and orientations and taking the 'energy image' (pixelwise complex modulus) of each resulting output image. The filters most commonly used in face recognition have the form

$$\psi_{\mu,\nu}(\mathbf{z}) = \frac{\|\mathbf{k}_{\mu,\nu}\|^2}{\sigma^2} e^{-\frac{\|\mathbf{k}_{\mu,\nu}\|^2 \|\mathbf{z}\|^2}{2\sigma^2}} [e^{i\mathbf{k}_{\mu,\nu}\mathbf{z}} - e^{-\frac{\sigma^2}{2}}] \tag{1}$$

where μ and ν define the orientation and scale of the Gabor kernels, $\mathbf{z} = (x, y)$, $\| \cdot \|$ denotes the norm operator, and the wave vector is $\mathbf{k}_{\mu,\nu} = k_\nu(\cos\phi_\mu, \sin\phi_\mu)$ where $k_\nu = k_{max}/f^\nu$ and $\phi_\mu = \pi\mu/8$ with k_{max} being the maximum frequency and f being the spacing factor between kernels in the frequency domain. Many face recognition studies use 40 Gabor wavelets of five different scales, $\nu \in \{0, 1, 2, 3, 4\}$, and eight orientations, $\mu \in \{0, \ldots, 7\}$, with $\sigma = 2\pi$, $k_{max} = \frac{\pi}{2}$, and $f = \sqrt{2}$. The Gabor wavelet representation is essentially the concatenated pixels of the 40 modulus-of-convolution images obtained by convolving the input image with these 40 Gabor kernels. In practice, before concatenation, each output image is downsampled according to the spatial frequency of its Gabor kernel and normalized to zero mean and unit variance.

3.2 Local Binary Patterns

Ojala *et al.* [18] introduced the Local Binary Pattern operator in 1996 as a means of summarizing local gray-level structure. The operator takes a local neighbourhood around each pixel, thresholds the pixels of the neighbourhood at the value of the central pixel and uses the resulting binary-valued image patch as a local image descriptor. It was originally defined for 3×3 neighbourhoods, giving 8 bit codes based on the 8 pixels around the central one. Formally, the LBP operator takes the form

$$LBP(x_c, y_c) = \sum_{n=0}^{7} 2^n s(i_n - i_c) \tag{2}$$

where in this case n runs over the 8 neighbours of the central pixel c, i_c and i_n are the gray-level values at c and n, and $s(u)$ is 1 if $u \geq 0$ and 0 otherwise. The LBP encoding process is illustrated in fig. 2.

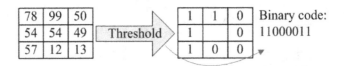

Fig. 2. Illustration of the basic LBP operator

Two extensions to the original operator were made in [19]. The first defined LBP's for neighbourhoods of different sizes, thus making it feasible to deal with textures at different scales. The second defined the so-called *uniform patterns*: an LBP is 'uniform' if it contains at most one 0-1 and one 1-0 transition when viewed as a circular bit string. For example, the LBP code in fig. 2 is uniform. Uniformity is an important concept in the LBP methodology, representing primitive structural information such as edges and corners. Ojala *et al.* observed that although only 58 of the 256 8-bit patterns are uniform, nearly 90 percent of all observed image neighbourhoods are uniform. In methods that histogram LBP's, the number of bins can be thus significantly reduced by assigning all non-uniform patterns to a single bin, often without losing too much information.

LBP's are resistant to lighting effects in the sense that they are invariant to monotonic gray-level transformations, and they have been shown to have high discriminative power for texture classification [18]. T. Ahonen *et al.* introduced an LBP based method for face recognition [1] that divides the face into a regular grid of cells and histograms the uniform LBP's within each cell. Finally, the cell-level histograms are concatenated to produce a global descriptor vector. Like the Gabor descriptor, the LBP descriptor is usually high dimensional. For example, a 128×128 face image with 8×8 pixel cells produces a 15104-D LBP descriptor vector (256 patches with 59 entries/patch).

3.3   Feature-Level Fusion with PCA

Before combining the Gabor and LBP features, we reduce their dimensionality to remove some of the redundancy and noise inherent in them. Given that we will later be feeding the results to a sophisticated nonlinear discriminant feature extractor (KDCV), we do not attempt to select discriminative directions at this stage. Instead we use simple PCA-based dimensionality reduction [8], retaining enough components to give KDCV scope to find good discriminant directions while still significantly reducing the size and redundancy of the data. Other methods could be used (ICA, CCA, NMF, etc), but PCA has the advantage of minimizing reconstruction error without making strong assumptions about the nature or use of the resulting data – we prefer to postpone such assumptions to the classifier stage.

Formally, let faces be represented by n-D vectors $\mathbf{x}$. PCA seeks a set of m orthogonal directions that capture as much as possible of the variability of the face set $\{\mathbf{x}\}$, or equivalently an m-D projection $\mathbf{y}$ of $\mathbf{x}$ from which $\mathbf{x}$ can be reconstructed with as little error as possible. Encoding these directions as an $n \times m$ matrix $\mathbf{U}$ with orthonormal columns, we seek to maximize $\mathrm{tr}(\mathbf{U}^T \mathbf{C} \mathbf{U})$ where $\mathbf{C}$ is the covariance matrix of the face set $\{\mathbf{x}\}$. This leads to an eigenvalue problem $\mathbf{C}\mathbf{U} = \mathbf{U}\Lambda$ where $\Lambda = \mathrm{diag}(\lambda_1, \ldots, \lambda_m)$ is the matrix of eigenvalues of $\mathbf{C}$. For the best reconstruction we need to take the m largest eigenvalues. Then given $\mathbf{x}$, its projection is $\mathbf{y} = \mathbf{U}^T(\mathbf{x} - \boldsymbol{\mu})$ and its reconstruction is $\mathbf{x} \approx \mathbf{U}\mathbf{y} + \boldsymbol{\mu}$ where $\boldsymbol{\mu}$ is the mean of the training set $\{\mathbf{x}\}$. m necessarily satisfies $m \leq \min(n, N-1)$ where N is the number of training samples. In the experiments below $N \ll n$ and we preserve as much discriminant information as we can by taking m to be large enough to include all 'significantly non-zero' eigenvalues, so in practice $m \approx N - 1$.

Letting $\mathbf{x}_1 \in R^{n_1}$ and $\mathbf{x}_2 \in R^{n_2}$ be respectively the Gabor and LBP features of a face image, and $\mathbf{y}_1 = \mathbf{U}_1^T(\mathbf{x}_1 - \boldsymbol{\mu}_1)$, $\mathbf{y}_2 = \mathbf{U}_2^T(\mathbf{x}_2 - \boldsymbol{\mu}_2)$ be the corresponding centred and PCA-reduced vectors, the combined feature vector $\mathbf{z} \in R^{m_1+m_2}$ is then the '*z-score*' normalized combination

$$\mathbf{z} = (\mathbf{y}_1/\sigma_1, \mathbf{y}_2/\sigma_2)^T \tag{3}$$

where σ_1, σ_2 are the (scalar) standard deviations of $\mathbf{y}_1, \mathbf{y}_2$.

3.4 Seeking Optimal Discriminant Subspace with Kernel Trick

The next stage of the process extracts optimally discriminative nonlinear features from the combined feature vector $\mathbf{z}$. This is the only point at which class label information is used during training. It is based on a kernelized variant of Linear Discriminant Analysis (LDA) [24] called KDCV [4]. Classical LDA seeks a low-dimensional projection matrix $\mathbf{P}$ that maximizes the objective function

$$J(\mathbf{P}) = \frac{\mathbf{P}^T \mathbf{S}_B \mathbf{P}}{\mathbf{P}^T \mathbf{S}_W \mathbf{P}} \tag{4}$$

where $\mathbf{S}_B$ denotes the between-class and $\mathbf{S}_W$ the within-class scatter matrix of the training data. Formally the solution is given by the largest-eigenvalue eigenvectors of $\mathbf{S}_W^{-1}\mathbf{S}_B$. However this is not always stably computable. In particular, if there are more feature dimensions than training examples or if the examples lie in a lower dimensional affine subspace – both of which are true in our case – $\mathbf{S}_W$ is rank deficient and its inverse does not exist. The singularity is intrinsic in the sense that directions in the null space of $\mathbf{S}_W$ have no observed covariance so LDA predicts that they should be infinitely discriminant. In particular, if $\mathbf{S}_B$ has a nontrivial projection along these directions, LDA considers the corresponding classes to be perfectly separable. Techniques proposed to solve this classical problem include the perturbation method [31], two stage PCA+LDA [26], and the *null space* methods pioneered by Chen *et al.* [7]. The latter have dominated research in recent years. They focus *only* on the null space of $\mathbf{S}_W$, so they are really complements to traditional LDA not stabilized variants of it. They optimize the *null space based* LDA criterion

$$J(\mathbf{P}) = \max_{|\mathbf{P}^T \mathbf{S}_W \mathbf{P}| = 0} |\mathbf{P}^T \mathbf{S}_T \mathbf{P}| \tag{5}$$

where $\mathbf{S}_T = \mathbf{S}_B + \mathbf{S}_W$ is the total scatter matrix of the training set. Cevikalp *et al.* [4] proved that the optimal discriminant subspace in the sense of (5) is the intersection of the null space $N(\mathbf{S}_W)$ of $\mathbf{S}_W$ and the range space $R(\mathbf{S}_T)$ of $\mathbf{S}_T$, and to find it one can first project the training set sample onto $N(\mathbf{S}_W)$ and then apply PCA. This method is called Discriminative Common Vectors (DCV) [5] because all of the training samples in a class are projected to a unique vector in $N(\mathbf{S}_W)$ called the class' *common vector*. It can be shown that if the affine spans of the training sets are linearly separable, the corresponding common vectors are distinct resulting in a perfect recognition rate [5].

In many face recognition problems the class distributions are not separable using linear DCV but introducing a nonlinear embedding $\phi : R^d \mapsto F$ into a kernel-induced feature space F allows them to be separated. Kernel DCV [4] finds projection vectors that optimize the null space LDA criterion (5) in the induced feature space F by applying KPCA to project the training set onto the range space $R(\mathbf{S}_T^\phi)$ of $\mathbf{S}_T^\phi$, the total scatter matrix induced in F, then finding an orthonormal basis for the null space $N(\mathbf{S}_W^\phi)$ of the within-class scatter matrix $\mathbf{S}_W^\phi$ within this range space. The computation is kernal-izable (expressible using inner products) precisely because it suffices to work within the span of $\mathbf{S}_T^\phi$: although $N(\mathbf{S}_W^\phi)$ typically contains many directions orthogonal to this, they are irrelevant as far as inter-class discrimination is concerned because test sample components in these directions are identical for all classes and hence not useful for discrimination based on this training set.

We will only summarize KDCV briefly here. See [4] for details. Let $\widetilde{\mathbf{K}}$ be the empir-ical kernel matrix of the training set, with eigendecomposition $\widetilde{\mathbf{K}} = \mathbf{U}\Lambda\mathbf{U}^T$ where Λ is the diagonal matrix of nonzero eigenvalues. $\mathbf{U}$, the associated matrix of normalized eigenvectors, doubles as a basis for the span of $\mathbf{S}_T^\phi$. Let $\overline{\boldsymbol{\Phi}}$ be the matrix of the centered training set with respect to the empirical feature space. The matrix that projects the training set onto $R(\mathbf{S}_T^\phi)$ is then $\overline{\boldsymbol{\Phi}}\mathbf{U}\Lambda^{-1/2}$. This is used to obtain the projected within-class scatter matrix $\widetilde{\mathbf{S}}_W^\Phi$, from which a basis $\mathbf{V}$ for the null space of $\widetilde{\mathbf{S}}_W^\Phi$ is obtained:

$$\mathbf{V}^T \widetilde{\mathbf{S}}_W^\Phi \mathbf{V} = 0 \tag{6}$$

The optimal projection matrix $\mathbf{P}$ is then:

$$\mathbf{P} = \overline{\boldsymbol{\Phi}}\mathbf{U}\Lambda^{-1/2}\mathbf{V} \tag{7}$$

3.5   Face Recognition in the Optimal Discriminant Subspace

When a face image is presented to the system, its Gabor and LBP representations are extracted, projected into their PCA subspaces, normalized separately (3) and integrated into a combined feature vector $\mathbf{z}_{\text{test}}$, which is then projected into the optimal discrimi-nant space by

$$\boldsymbol{\Omega}_{\text{test}} = \mathbf{P}^T \phi(\mathbf{z}_{\text{test}}) = (\mathbf{U}\Lambda^{-1/2}\mathbf{V})^T \mathbf{k}_{\text{test}} \tag{8}$$

where $\mathbf{P}$ is the optimal projection matrix given by (7) and $\mathbf{k}_{\text{test}} \in R^M$ is a vector with entries $K(\mathbf{z}_m^i, \mathbf{z}_{\text{test}}) = \langle \phi(\mathbf{z}_m^i), \phi(\mathbf{z}_{\text{test}}) \rangle$, where $\phi(\mathbf{z}_m^i)$ are the mapped training samples. The projected test feature vector $\boldsymbol{\Omega}_{\text{test}}$ is then classified using the nearest neighbour rule and the cosine 'distance'

$$d_{\cos}(\boldsymbol{\Omega}_{\text{test}}, \boldsymbol{\Omega}_{\text{template}}) = -\frac{\boldsymbol{\Omega}_{\text{test}}^T \boldsymbol{\Omega}_{\text{template}}}{\|\boldsymbol{\Omega}_{\text{test}}\|\|\boldsymbol{\Omega}_{\text{template}}\|} \tag{9}$$

where $\boldsymbol{\Omega}_{\text{template}}$ is a face template in the gallery set. Other similarity metrics such as L_1, L_2 or Mahalanobis distances could be used, but [15] found that the cosine distance performed best among the metrics it tested on this database, and our initial experiments confirmed this.

4   Experiments

We now present experiments designed to illustrate the effectiveness of the proposed method. Three publicly available databases containing large illumination variations were used: Face Recognition Grand Challenge version 1 experiment 1.0.4 ('FRGC-104') and version 2 experiment 2.0.4 ('FRGC-204') [21], and the FERET dataset [22].

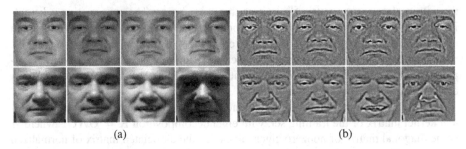

(a)   (b)

Fig. 3. Examples of images from FRGC-104: (a) target images (upper row) and query images (lower row) without illumination preprocessing; (b) the corresponding illumination normalized images from the proposed preprocessing chain.

We first conducted a series of pilot experiments on the FRGC-104 dataset, then we verified the results on FERET and the challenging FRGC-204 dataset.

4.1 Experimental Settings

Prior to analysis, all images undergo geometric and photometric normalization to counter the effects of pose and illumination variations, local shadowing and highlights. First they are converted to 8 bit gray-scale, rigidly scaled and rotated to place the centers of the two eyes at fixed image positions using the eye coordinates supplied with the original datasets, and cropped to 128×128 pixels. Then they are photometrically normalized using the following sequence of steps: strong gamma compression; Difference of Gaussian (DoG) filtering; robust normalization of the range of output variations; and sigmoid-function based compression of any remaining signal highlights. A detailed description of this simple but very effective normalization procedure can be found in [27]. Some examples of preprocessed images are shown in Fig. 3.

The downsampling factor for the Gabor features is set to 64, resulting a dimensionality of 10 240 ($128 \cdot 128 \cdot 40/64$), while the cell size of the LBP features is set to 8×8 pixels, giving a dimensionality of 15 104. For the kernel method we tried polynomial kernels $k(\mathbf{x}, \mathbf{y}) = (\langle \mathbf{x}, \mathbf{y} \rangle)^n$ with degrees $n = 2, 3$ and Gaussian kernels $k(\mathbf{x}, \mathbf{y}) = e^{-\|\mathbf{x}-\mathbf{y}\|^2/(2\sigma^2)}$ with scale parameter chosen on a validation set and reported the best result.

4.2 Results on FRGC-104

The FRGC-104 dataset [21] is challenging because although the gallery images were obtained under carefully controlled conditions, the probe images were captured in uncontrolled indoor and outdoor settings with large changes in illumination, appearance and expression. Fig. 3 shows some examples. For the experiments reported here the gallery contains 152 people with one image per person, while the probe set contains 608 images of the 152 subjects. For training we chose the 886 images of 198 subjects with at least two images per subject from the FRGC-104 training set. There is no overlap between the training, gallery and probe sets. Besides the well-normalized LBP and

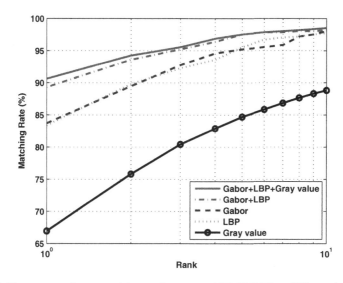

Fig. 4. The comparative recognition performance of KDCV/NN on different feature sets

Table 1. FRGC-104 recognition rate (%) for different feature sets and different recognition methods. The asterisks indicate performance differences that are statistically significant at the 5% level between the given method and the corresponding result in bold.

Input Features	LDA	DCV	KPCA	KDCV
Gabor	52.3*	82.2*	45.1*	83.7*
LBP	50.8*	78.6*	52.7	83.4*
Gray value	36.2*	63.2*	35.2*	66.9*
Gabor+LBP	56.1	89.1	50.0	89.3
Gabor+LBP+Gray value	**59.7**	**89.8**	**53.5**	**90.6**

Gabor local texture features, we also test whether the inclusion of raw gray-level image pixels can improve the results.

Fig. 4 shows the FRGC-104 performance of our Kernel DCV/NN method for several different types of input features. As expected the raw pixel features perform poorly owing to their sensitivity to various common appearance variations, while both Gabor wavelets and LBP features give much better, and here very similar, performance. However, fusing the Gabor and LBP features still provides a significant performance gain – about 6.0% relative to either feature set individually – which suggests that these two feature sets do indeed capture different and complementary information. Incorporating the somewhat unreliable information provided by raw gray-levels provides a modest further improvement, reaching a rank 1 recognition rate of over 90%. This suggests that there is scope for further improvement by including additional higher-quality feature sets.

We also checked the effects of using our combined features in several other popular face recognition frameworks including LDA, DCV and KPCA. The results are shown in Table 1. The recognition performance of every method was improved by using the

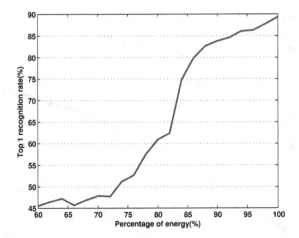

Fig. 5. The influence of PCA dimension (percentage of total energy preserved during the PCA) on FRGC-104 recognition rate

combined features as input. Among the methods compared, KDCV consistently performs best, particularly on the combined features 'Gabor+LBP+Gray value'.

The influence of different PCA projection dimensions (as represented by the percentage of the total energy retained by the projection) is illustrated in fig. 5. The figure reveals a positive, albeit somewhat irregular, correlation between PCA energy (projection dimensionality) and recognition rate, underlining the importance of preserving as much as possible of the original information during the projection. In particular, increasing the energy retained from 70% to 85% gives a 30% improvement in recognition rate. However, note that the maximum possible PCA dimension is limited by the number of training samples and that for larger samples than those used here some overfitting may occur if all of the dimensions are used.

To compare the relative effectiveness of feature-level and decision-level fusion we conducted some experiments based on a simple decision-level fusion method. We project each test image onto three KDCV discriminant subspaces trained respectively with Gabor wavelets, LBP features and gray-value features, and for each feature class we compute the cosine distances between the test image and the gallery templates. The *z-score* normalization procedure (3) is applied to the three distance matrices, and they are then combined by simple addition. As before, test samples are assigned to the class containing the closest template under the combined distance metric and we considered several different feature combinations.

The results for 'Gabor + LBP' and 'Gabor + LBP + Gray value' are shown in fig. 6. The decision-level 'Gabor + LBP' method predominates. As a general rule, both decision-level and feature-level fusion benefited from using a mixture of different feature types. The main exception was that for decision-level fusion, the 'Gabor+LBP' scheme worked significantly better than the 'Gabor+LBP+Gray value' one. Decision-level fusion by simple averaging tends to be sensitive to the performance of the worst of its component classifiers, and to perform best when they are both *diverse* and *uniformly accurate*, whereas here the raw pixel based classifier is significantly weaker than

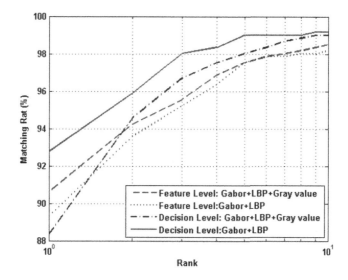

Fig. 6. The comparative face recognition performance of feature level fusion and decision-level averaging on FRGC-104

Table 2. CPU times (s) for FRGC-104 recognition runs on a 2.8 GHZ single processor PC

Features	Gabor	LBP	Gray value	Gabor+LBP	Gabor+LBP+Gray value
CPU Time	73.9	74.2	72.8	60.5	61.96

the other two, thus decreasing the overall system performance. In contrast, feature-level fusion provided a performance increment for each new feature set included in its pool.

Regarding computational cost, average CPU times for complete recognition runs on FRGC-104 on our 2.8 GHz single processor PC are shown in Table 2. Note that the combined feature sets actually have *lower* cost than the individual features: after reduction, the combined features have lower dimensionality than the individual ones and most of the run time is spent doing KDCV and NN search in this reduced space.

4.3   Results on FERET

A second series of experiments was conducted on the FERET dataset. This contains five standard partitions: 'fa' is the gallery containing 1196 grayscale images and 'fb', 'fc',

Fig. 7. Some sample images from the FERET dataset

Table 3. Comparative recognition rates of various methods on the FERET partitions

Method	fb	fc	dup1	dup2
Fisherfaces[30]	0.94	0.73	0.55	0.31
Best Results of [22]	0.96	0.82	0.59	0.52
Best Results of [1]	0.97	0.79	0.66	0.64
Best Results of [30]	0.98	0.97	0.74	0.71
Our 'Gabor+LBP' method	0.98	0.98	0.90	0.85

'dup1' and 'dup2' are four sets of probe images. The diversity of the probe images is across gender, ethnicity and illumination ('fc'), expression ('fb') and age/time ('dup1' and 'dup2'). Some examples of FERET images are shown in fig. 7. All of the images were preprocessed as described in section 4.1. The gallery set is always available to a face recognition system so in addition to the distributed training set we used the images in 'fa' to train the Kernel DCV classifier. As there is only one image per person in 'fa', these images do not contribute to the null space of the within-class scatter matrix, but they do help to shape the between-class distribution and to increase the dimensionality of final discriminative subspace.

We compared the proposed 'Gabor+LBP' method to several previously published results on FERET including Fisherfaces, the best result in FERET'97 [22], and the recent results of [1] and [30]. The rank-1 recognition rates of the different methods on the FERET probe sets are shown in table 3. The performance of the proposed method is comparable to or better than existing state-of-the-art results on this dataset, especially on the challenging probe sets 'dup1' and 'dup2'. Besides better performance, our method also requires much less memory than weighted LGBPHS [30], which allows it to scale efficiently to large datasets such as FRGC version 2.

4.4   Results on FRGC-204

FRGC-204 is the most challenging FRGC experiment [21]. It extends the FRGC-104 dataset, defining a standard tripartite partition into a training set of 12,776 images (including both images with controlled lighting and uncontrolled ones), a target set of 16,028 controlled images, and a query set of 8,014 uncontrolled images. Again the preprocessing method described in section 4.1 was used. To allow a better comparison with the state of the art on this dataset we used the training set of [15], which includes 6,388 images selected from the full FRGC-204 training set.

The results of FRGC version 2 experiments are usually reported using the Receiver Operating Characteristic (ROC) curves for Face Verification Rate (FVR) as a function of False Accept Rate (FAR). For a given distance matrix three types of ROC curves can be generated by the Biometric Experimentation Environment (BEE): ROC-I, ROC-II,and ROC-III, corresponding respectively to images collected within a semester, within a year, and between semesters. Owing to space limitations we report results only for ROC-III (the most commonly reported benchmark) – see fig. 8. The figure shows that the proposed 'Gabor+LBP' method increases the FVR over separate Gabor or LBP

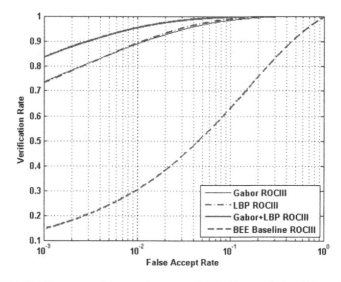

Fig. 8. FRGC-204 face recognition performance (ROC-III curves) for Gabor, LBP and Gabor+LBP methods. The FRGC baseline performance is also included for comparison.

from 73.5% to 83.6% at 0.1% FAR. The best previous performance that we are aware of on this dataset at 0.1% FAR is 76.0% FVR [15].

5 Conclusions

This paper investigated the benefits of combining two of the most successful feature sets for robust face recognition under uncontrolled lighting: Gabor wavelets and LBP features. We found that these features are more complementary than might have been expected, with the combination having only around 2/3 of the errors of either feature set alone. The method was tested in a novel face recognition pipeline that includes: robust photometric image normalization; separate feature extraction, PCA-based dimensionality reduction and scalar variance normalization of each modality; feature concatenation; Kernel DCA based extraction of discriminant nonlinear features; and finally cosine-distance based nearest neighbour classification in the KDCA reduced subspace. The proposed face recognition method is scalable to large numbers of individuals and easy to extend to additional feature sets. We illustrated its performance with a series of comparative experiments on the challenging FRGC version 1 experiment 4, FRGC version 2 experiment 4, and FERET datasets.

Acknowledgements

The authors would like to thank the anonymous reviewers for their constructive suggestions and H. Cevikalp for helpful discussions. The research used the FERET and FRGC face datasets collected respectively under the FERET and FRGC programs.

References

[1] Ahonen, T., Hadid, A., Pietikainen, M.: Face recognition with local binary patterns. In: Pajdla, T., Matas, J(G.) (eds.) ECCV 2004. LNCS, vol. 3021, pp. 469–481. Springer, Heidelberg (2004)

[2] Ahonen, T., Hadid, A., Pietikainen, M.: Face description with local binary patterns: Application to face recognition. IEEE TPAMI 28(12) (2006)

[3] Ben-Yacoub, S., Abdeljaoued, Y., Mayoraz, E.: Fusion of face and speech data for person identity verification. IDIAP-RR 03, IDIAP (1999)

[4] Cevikalp, H., Neamtu, M., Wilkes, M.: Discriminative common vector method with kernels. IEEE TNN 17(6), 1550–1565 (2006)

[5] Cevikalp, H., Neamtu, M., Wilkes, M., Barkana, A.: Discriminative common vectors for face recognition. IEEE TPAMI 27(1), 4–13 (2005)

[6] Chang, K., Bowyer, K., Flynn, P., Chen, X.: Multi-biometrics using facial appearance, shape and temperature. In: Proc. AFGR 2004, pp. 43–48 (2004)

[7] Chen, L.-F., Liao, H.-Y.M., Ko, M.-T., Lin, J.-C., Yu, G.-J.: A new lda-based face recognition system which can solve the small sample size problem. Pattern Recognition 33(10), 1713–1726 (2000)

[8] Hotelling, H.: Analysis of a complex of statistical variables into principal components. J. Educational Psychology 24, 417–441 (1933)

[9] Huang, Y.S., Suen, C.Y.: A method of combining multiple experts for the recognition of unconstrained handwritten numerals. IEEE TPAMI 17(1), 90–94 (1995)

[10] Jain, A., Nandakumar, K., Ross, A.: Score normalization in multimodal biometric systems. Pattern Recognition 38(12), 2270–2285 (2005)

[11] Kittler, J., Hatef, M., Duin, R.P., Matas, J.: On combining classifiers. IEEE TPAMI 20(3), 226–239 (1998)

[12] Lades, M., Vorbruggen, J.C., Buhmann, J., Lange, J., von der Malsburg, C., Wurtz, R.P., Konen, W.: Distortion invariant object recognition in the dynamic link architecture. IEEE Trans. Comput. 42(3), 300–311 (1993)

[13] Lai, P.L., Fyfe, C.: Kernel and nonlinear canonical correlation analysis. IJCNN 04, 4614 (2000)

[14] Lee, D.D., Seung, H.S.: Algorithms for non-negative matrix factorization. In: NIPS, pp. 556–566 obtainable2 (2000)

[15] Liu, C.: Capitalize on dimensionality increasing techniques for improving face recognition grand challenge performance. IEEE TPAMI 28(5), 725–737 (2006)

[16] Liu, C., Wechsler, H.: A shape- and texture-based enhanced fisher classifier for face recognition. IEEE TIP 10(4), 598–608 (2001)

[17] Lu, X., Wang, Y., Jain, A.: Combining classifiers for face recognition. In: ICME 2003. Multimedia and Expo. 2003 (2003)

[18] Ojala, T., Pietikainen, M., Harwood, D.: A comparative study of texture measures with classification based on feature distributions. Pattern Recognition 29 (1996)

[19] Ojala, T., Pietikainen, M., Maenpaa, T.: Multiresolution gray-scale and rotation invarianat texture classification with local binary patterns. IEEE TPAMI 24(7), 971–987 (2002)

[20] Comon, P.: Independent component analysis-a new concept? Signal Processing 43, 287–314 (1994)

[21] Phillips, P.J., Flynn, P.J., Scruggs, W.T., Bowyer, K.W., Chang, J., Hoffman, K., Marques, J., Min, J., Worek, W.J.: Overview of the face recognition grand challenge. In: Proc. CVPR 2005, San Diego, CA, pp. 947–954 (2005)

[22] Phillips, P.J., Moon, H., Rizvi, S.A., Rauss, P.J.: The FERET evaluation methodology for face-recognition algorithms. IEEE TPAM 22(10), 1090–1104 (2000)

[23] Ross, A., Jain, A.: Information fusion in biometrics. Pattern Recogn. Lett. 24(13), 2115–2125 (2003)

[24] Fisher, R.R.: The use of multiple measurements in taxonomic problems. Ann. Eugen 7, 179–188 (1936)

[25] Scholkopf, B., Smola, A.J.: Learning with Kernels: Support Vector Machines, Regularization, Optimization, and Beyond. MIT Press, Cambridge (2001)

[26] Swets, D.L., Weng, J.: Using discriminant eigenfeatures for image retrieval. IEEE TPAMI 18(8), 831–836 (1996)

[27] Tan, X., Triggs, B.: Enhanced local texture feature sets for face recognition under difficult lighting conditions. In: Zhou, S.K., et al. (eds.) AMFG 2007. LNCS, vol. 4778, pp. 168–182. Springer, Heidelberg (2007)

[28] Wiskott, L., Fellous, J.-M., Kruger, N., von der Malsburg, C.: Face recognition by elastic bunch graph matching. IEEE TPAMI 19(7), 775–779 (1997)

[29] Yang, J., Yang, J.-Y.: Generalized k-l transform based combined feature extraction. Pattern Recognition 35(1), 295–297 (2002)

[30] Zhang, W., Shan, S., Gao, W., Zhang, H.: Local Gabor Binary Pattern Histogram Sequence (LGBPHS): A novel non-statistical model for face representation and recognition. In: Proc. ICCV 2005, Beijing, China, pp. 786–791 (2005)

[31] Zhao, W., Chellappa, R., Krishnaswamy, A.: Discriminant analysis of principal components for face recognition. In: FG 1998, Washington, DC, USA, p. 336 (1998)

[32] Zhao, W., Chellappa, R., Phillips, P.J., Rosenfeld, A.: Face recognition: A literature survey. ACM Computing Survey 34(4), 399–485 (2003)

A Unified Framework of Subspace and Distance Metric Learning for Face Recognition

Qingshan Liu[1,2] and Dimitris N. Metaxas[1]

[1] The department of computer Sciences, Rutgers University
[2] National Laboratory of Pattern Recognition, CAS, China

Abstract. In this paper, we propose a unified scheme of subspace and distance metric learning under the Bayesian framework for face recognition. According to the local distribution of data, we divide the k-nearest neighbors of each sample into the intra-person set and the inter-person set, and we aim to learn a distance metric in the embedding subspace, which can make the distances between the sample and its intra-person set smaller than the distances between it and its inter-person set. To reach this goal, we define two variables, that is, the intra-person distance and the inter-person distance, which are from two different probabilistic distributions, and we model the goal with minimizing the overlap between two distributions. Inspired by the Bayesian classification error estimation, we formulate it by minimizing the Bhattachyrra coefficient between two distributions. The power of the proposed approach are demonstrated by a series of experiments on the CMU-PIE face database and the extended YALE face database.

1 Introduction

Face recognition is a hot topic in the communities of computer vision and pattern recognition due to its potential applications in biometrics, surveillance, human-computer interface, and multimedia. A lot of methods have been proposed in the past decades [31].

Since Principal Component Analysis(PCA) achieved much success in EigenFace [25], subspace learning methods have been widely used for facial feature representation. The general goal of subspace learning is to find some transformation to project high-dimensional data into a low-dimensional subspace. Defining different objective functions will produce different subspaces. We will review some popular subspace methods in Section 2. However, same as most pattern recognition problems, similarity measurement or classification scheme is needed to further analyze the relationship of the data or to predict their labels based on the extracted features for face recognition. The simple Euclidean distance is often used to measure the similarities between two face images in the subspace, but it is not a better metric in most cases. Distance metric learning is a technique to learn a distance based similarity measurement and classification scheme, and has attracted much attention in machine learning and computer vision in recent years. Its original goal is to directly learn the distance metric from the available training data, in order to improve the performance of distance-based classifiers. Due to the encouraging effectiveness of the simple nearest neighbor rule, most studies focused on learning the similarity matrix of the Mahalanobis distance to improve the performance

S.K. Zhou et al. (Eds.): AMFG 2007, LNCS 4778, pp. 250–260, 2007.

of the nearest neighbor classification. A common strategy is to minimize various separation criteria between the classes assuming equivalent relations over all the data or the k-nearest neighbors. A brief review will be given in Section 2. However, for high dimensional data, such as face image data (the dimension of an image with the size of 100×100 is up to 10^4), learning the metric matrix directly in such a high dimensional space, not only results in high computational cost, but also is sensitive to noise.

In this paper, we propose a unified scheme of subspace and distance metric learning for face recognition under the Bayesian framework. In order to learn a local distance metric with subspace dimensionality reduction, we divide the k-nearest neighbors of each sample into the intra-person set and the inter-person set according to the local distribution of the data, and we aim to make the distances between the sample and its intra-person set smaller than the distances between it and its inter-person set in the embedding subspace, so as to handle the high-dimensional data well. We define two variables in the subspace, i.e., the intra-person distance and the inter-person distance, and model them with two different probability distributions. Thus, the problem can be converted to minimize the overlap between two distributions. Inspired by the Bayesian classification error estimation, we formulate it by minimizing the Bhattachyrra coefficient measurement between two distributions, and the solution can be obtained by the gradient descent optimization. The proposed work has some special characteristics: 1) It is based on the local neighbors, so it does not make assumption on the global distribution of the data like Linear Discriminant Analysis (LDA). 2) It can be directly used for multi-class problems without any modification or extension. 3) It links to Bayesian classification error and has an intuitionistic geometric property due to adoption of the Bhattachyrra coefficient measurement. We conduct the experiments on two benchmarks, the CMU-PIE face database [21] and the extended YALE face database [15], and the experimental results show the promising performance of the proposed work compared to the state-of-the-arts.

2   Related Work

Subspace learning is a popular approach of face recognition. It maps the high dimensional face image data into a low dimensional subspace based on some criteria. Eigenface [25]and Fisherface [5] [30]are two classic methods, which are based PCA and LDA respectively. PCA seeks to maximize the covariance over the whole data, so it is optimal for data reconstruction, but it is not optimal for classification. The idea of LDA is to find a linear subspace projection that maximizes the between-class scatter and minimizes the within-class scatter. However, LDA assumes that each class has a similar within-class distribution of samples. Kernel PCA (KPCA) and Kernel LDA (KDA) combine the nonlinear kernel trick with PCA and LDA to get nonlinear principal component and discriminant subspaces [19] [16]. However, for the kernel methods, the kernel function design is still an open problem, and different kernels will give different performances. Manifold based subspace methods, such as LLE [17] and ISOMAP [23], aim to preserve the local geometric relations of the data in both the original high dimensional space and the transformed low dimensional space, while they often have a problem of "out of sample". Local Preserving Projection (LPP) gives a linear approximation of manifold structure to deal with this problem [13]. In [8], the idea of LDA is integrated into LPP to enhance the discriminating performance of LPP. In [22], M. Sugiyama proposed to compute the within-class scatter and between-class scatter in LDA with a weighting scheme inspired by LPP. A generalized interpretation for these methods based on graph analysis is discussed in [28]. From the view of subspace dimensionality reduction, our work is similar to LDA, which aims to find a transformation of separating one class from the others, and it can be also extended with the kernel trick. However, our work is different from LDA in that: no constraints are made on the global distribution of the data, because it is based on the local neighbors' distribution, and it preserves the neighborhood relationship of the data during the dimension reduction as in manifold learning.

Subspace learning can be thought as a method of feature representation, while distance metric learning is related to constructing a data classification scheme. It is well known that the nearest neighbor rule is simple and surprisingly effective. However, its performance crucially depends on the distance metric. For different distance metrics, it will produce different nearest neighbor relationships. Most previous studies aim to improve the performance of the nearest neighbor classification by learning a distance metric based on the Mahalanobis distance from the labeled samples. E. Xing et al [27] tried to find an optimal Mahalanobis metric from contextual constrains in combination with a constrained K-means algorithm. B. Hilled et al [4] [20] proposed a much simpler approach called Relevance Component Analysis (RCA), which identities and downscales global unwanted variability within data. However, it does not consider the between class pair-wise information, which will influence its performance on classification [14]. K. Q. Weinberger et al [26] proposed to learn the distance metric by penalizing large distances between each input and its neighbors and by penalizing small distances between each input and all other inputs that do not share the same label. Its solution is based on complex quadratic programming. Torresani and Lee [24] extended this method with dimensional reduction, but its objective function is non-convex. Neighborhood Component Analysis (NCA) aimed at directly maximizing a stochastic variant of the leave one out *K-NN* score on the training set [12]. Later, A. Globerson et al [11] converted the formula of NCA to a convex optimization problem with a strong assumption that all the samples in the same class were mapped to a single point and infinitely far from points in different classes. Actually, this assumption is unreasonable for practical data. In [29], the bound optimization algorithm [18] was adopted to search a local distance metric for the non-convex function. Most of the above methods do not consider the dimensionality reduction for high dimensional data except for RCA [4] [20], NCA [12], and [24]. However, the proposed method is different from them in that it links to Bayesian classification error and has an intuitionistic geometric property due to adoption of the Bhattachyrra coefficient measurement.

3 Our Work

In this section, we propose a new unified framework of subspace and distance metric learning, which is inspired by the Bayesian classification error estimation. We first present our purpose and then give a Bhattacharyya coefficient based solution.

3.1   The Purpose

Let $X = \{x_1, x_2, \cdots, x_n\} \in R^D$ denote the training set of n labeled samples in C classes. Let $l(x_i)$ be the label of sample x_i, i.e., $l(x_i) \in \{1, 2, \ldots, C\}$. Most distance metric learning methods seek to directly find a similarity matrix Q based on the Mahalanobis distance to maximize the performance of the nearest neighbor classification. The Mahalanobis distance between samples x_i and x_j is defined as follows:

$$P_{i,j} = (x_i - x_j)^T Q(x_i - x_j). \tag{1}$$

However, learning Q directly in a high dimensional space, such as the image space, will be sensitive to noise to some extent, besides being computationally expensive.

Since Q is a $D \times D$ semi-definite matrix, it can be rewritten as: $Q = AA^T$. If the dimension of A is $D \times d$, $d < D$, (1) is equivalent to calculating the Euclidean distance in the transformed subspace with A.

$$P_{i,j} = \|A^T x_i - A^T x_j\|^2 = (x_i - x_j)^T AA^T (x_i - x_j). \tag{2}$$

Thus, the distance metric Q for high dimensional data can be computed by an explicit embedding transformation A. In this paper, we will focus on how to first learn this transformation A, and then compute Q. Actually the transformation A is corresponding to subspace dimension reduction, so this idea is equivalent to integrating the subspace and distance metric learning together.

Before presenting the details of our approach, we first give some definitions. The set $N_r(x_i)$ is the k-nearest neighbors of sample . Same as in [26] [24], the neighbors are computed by the Euclidean distance in the original data space. We divide $N_r(x_i)$ into two sets using the labels of the samples, $N_r(x_i) = S_i \bigcup D_i$, where the labels of the set S_i are same as the label of x_i, $x_s \in S_i$, $l(x_s) = l(x_i)$, and the samples in D_i have different labels from the sample x_i, $x_d \in D_i$, $l(x_d) \neq l(x_i)$,. We call them the intra-person set and inter-person set respectively in this paper.

Intuitively, a good distance metric should make each sample close to the samples in the same class and far from the samples in the different classes. Based on the nearest neighbor classification scheme, we can compare each sample against its k-nearest neighbors. We aim to find a distance metric that makes each sample far from the samples in its inter-person set and close to the samples in its intra-person set. Thus, our goal can be described as follows:

Given any samples x_i and its two kinds of neighbors $x_s \in S_i$ and $x_d \in D_i$, the intra-person distance $P_{is}(A)$ between x_i and x_s should be smaller than the inter-person distance $P_{id}(A)$ between x_i and x_d:

$$P_{is}(A) = \|A^T (x_i - x_s)\|^2, x_s \in S_i, \tag{3}$$

$$P_{id}(A) = \|A^T (x_i - x_d)\|^2, x_d \in D_i, \tag{4}$$

$$P_{is}(A) < P_{id}(A), for \forall i, s, d. \tag{5}$$

3.2 Bhattacharyya Coefficient Based Solution

For convenience, we define the variable $P_s(A)$ to represent all the intra-person distances, $P_s(A) = \{P_{is}(A)\}$ for all the i and s, and the variable $P_d(A)$ to represent all the inter-person distances, $P_d(A) = \{P_{id}(A)\}$ for all the i and d. Assuming that $P_s(A)$ and $P_d(A)$ are from two distributions respectively, $P_s(A) \sim \rho_s(P(A))$ and $P_d(A) \sim \rho_d(P(A))$, we can achieve our goal to find a transformation A that minimizes the overlap between these two distributions. Figure 1 gives an illustration, where x represents the distance $P(A)$. It can be found that minimizing the overlap means to separate the intra-person distances $P_s(A)$ from the inter-person distances $P_d(A)$ as much as possible, and it is also equivalent to minimizing the up-boundary of the classification error as much as possible under the Bayesian framework.

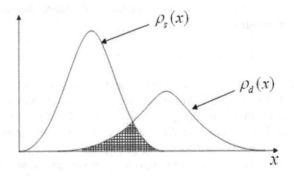

Fig. 1. An illustration of minimizing the overlap

The Bhattacharyya coefficient is a divergence-type measure which has an has an intuitionistic geometric interpretation [9]. Moreover, it is a popular technique to estimate the boundary of the classification error, i.e., the overlap between two distributions [10]. Given two distributions, $\rho_1(x)$ and $\rho_2(x)$, their Bhattacharyya coefficient is $\int \sqrt{\rho_1(x)\rho_2(x)}dx$. A small Bhattacharyya coefficient means a small overlap between two distributions which may lead to a small classification error. Thus, we define the objective function with Bhattacharyya coefficient between $\rho_s(P(A))$ and $\rho_d(P(A))$ as follows:

$$J_B(A) = \max_A(-\ln \int \sqrt{\rho_s(P(A))\rho_d(P(A))}dP(A)). \qquad (6)$$

In this paper, we regard the variables of the intra-person distance and inter-person distance as two different Gaussian distributions. We define the mean and variance of all the $P_s(A)$ distances as $\mu_s(A)$ and $\Sigma_s(A)$, and the mean and covariance of all the $P_d(A)$ vectors as $\mu_d(A)$ and $\Sigma_d(A)$ i.e.,

$$\rho_s(P(A)) = N(\mu_s(A), \Sigma_s(A)), \qquad (7)$$

$$\rho_d(P(A)) = N(\mu_d(A), \Sigma_d(A)), \qquad (8)$$

where $N(\mu, \Sigma)$ represents a Gaussian distribution with mean μ and covariance Σ. Now the objection function (6) can be written as [10]:

$$J_B(A) = \max_A \left\{ \frac{1}{4} \frac{(\mu_s(A) - \mu_d(A))^2}{\Sigma_s(A) + \Sigma_d(A)} + \frac{1}{2} \ln \frac{\Sigma_s(A) + \Sigma_d(A)}{2\sqrt{\Sigma_s(A)\Sigma_d(A)}} \right\} \tag{9}$$

Denote $E(\cdot)$ represents the expectation operation, and $Tr(X)$ is the trace of the matrix X. Since any $\|A^T x_{ij}\|^2 = Tr(A^T x_{ij} x_{ij}^T A)$, where $x_{ij} = x_i - x_j$, we have

$$\mu_s(A) = E(P_s(A)) = E(Tr(A^T x_{is} x_{is}^T A)) = Tr(A^T E(x_{is} x_{is}^T) A) = Tr(A^T M_s A) \tag{10}$$

$$\mu_d(A) = E(P_d(A)) = E(Tr(A^T x_{id} x_{id}^T A)) = Tr(A^T E(x_{id} x_{id}^T) A) = Tr(A^T M_d A) \tag{11}$$

$$\Sigma_s(A) = E(P_s(A) - \mu_s(A))^2 = E(P_s(A))^2 - \mu_s^2(A) \tag{12}$$

$$\Sigma_d(A) = E(P_d(A) - \mu_d(A))^2 = E(P_d(A))^2 - \mu_d^2(A) \tag{13}$$

The solution of (9) can be obtained by the gradient descent algorithm, such as the conjugate gradient method. For simplicity, we ignore (A) in all the $J_B(A)$, $\mu_s(A)$, $\Sigma_s(A)$, $\mu_d(A)$, and $\Sigma_d(A)$. The differentiation of J_B with respect to A is as follows:

$$\frac{\partial J_B}{\partial A} = \frac{(\mu_s - \mu_d)(\frac{\partial \mu_s}{\partial A} - \frac{\partial \mu_d}{\partial A}) + (\frac{\partial \Sigma_s}{\partial A} + \frac{\partial \Sigma_d}{\partial A})}{2(\Sigma_s + \Sigma_d)} - \frac{(\mu_s - \mu_d)^2(\frac{\partial \Sigma_s}{\partial A} + \frac{\partial \Sigma_d}{\partial A})}{4(\Sigma_s + \Sigma_d)^2} - \frac{\frac{\partial \Sigma_s}{\partial A}}{2\Sigma_s} - \frac{\frac{\partial \Sigma_d}{\partial A}}{2\Sigma_d} \tag{14}$$

where

$$\frac{\partial \mu_s}{\partial A} = 2M_s A \tag{15}$$

$$\frac{\partial \mu_d}{\partial A} = 2M_d A \tag{16}$$

$$\frac{\partial \Sigma_s}{\partial A} = 4E(Tr(A^T x_{is} x_{is}^T A) x_{is} x_{is}^T A) - 4Tr(A^T M_s A) M_s A \tag{17}$$

$$\frac{\partial \Sigma_d}{\partial A} = 4E(Tr(A^T x_{id} x_{id}^T A) x_{id} x_{id}^T A) - 4Tr(A^T M_d A) M_d A \tag{18}$$

From the above description, we can see that the proposed method tries to find the embedding subspace during learning the distance metric inspired by the Bayesian classification error estimation. The transformation A does not change the k-nearest neighborhood relationship of the data, which is similar to the local preserving property of manifold learning, but it is different from popular manifold learning methods in that it aims to make each sample far from its inter-person set and close to its intra-person set. Although we use the Gaussian distribution to model the the variables of the intra-person distances and inter-person distances in the subspace, they are based on the local neighbors, so we do not make assumption on the global distribution of the data compared to LDA. Compared with most distance metric learning methods, the proposed method uses the Bhattacharyya coefficient measurement, which has intuitionistic geometric interpretation and links to Bayesian classification error under the Bayesian framework. The proposed method can handle high dimensional data well.

4   Experiments

We test the proposed method on the two benchmarks, i.e., the CMU-PIE face database [21] and the extended YALE face database [15]. The data of the two face databases are available in [1]. In our experiments, we take the PCA as the baseline, where we keep 98% energy of eigenvalues. We compare the proposed method with related works, i.e., LDA, RCA, and NCA. The codes of RCA and NCA are downloaded from [2] and [3] respectively. For RCA, we use the prior label information to form the chunklets. In addition, we also compare the proposed method with the Bayesian face subspace (BFS) [6]. In the Bayesian face subspace, the face images are modeled by the intra-face and the inter-face subspaces, which are represented by PCA directly in the input data space. For the Bayesian face subspace, we construct the principal subspace with the 90% energy of the eigenvalues, and the complemental subspace with the rest of 10% energy. In the experiments, we set the number of neighbors k as the training numbers of each class minus 1.

4.1   CMU-PIE Face Database

The CMU PIE face database contains 68 subjects and 41368 images [25]. Each subject has 13 different poses, 43 different illuminations, and 4 different expressions. In this paper, our dataset is composed of all the images from five near frontal poses $(C05, C07, C09, C27, C29)$ including all the illumination and expression variations as in [7] [1]. There are 170 face images for each subject in our dataset. The images are cropped by fixing two eyes, and the cropped image size is 32×32. No image preprocessing is performed except normalizing the image into unit vector as in [7] [1]. Figure 2 shows some samples of one subject.

We randomly select 30 images from each subject for training, and the other 140 images of each subject for testing. The experiments are randomly run 50 times, and all the results reported in Figure 3 are the average of 50 times experiments. Because there are 68 classes, the maximum feature dimension of LDA is 68-1 = 67. From Figure 3, we can see that MBC is better than PCA, LDA, RCA, NCA, and BFC. The minimum classification error of MBC is 5.46%, while those of PCA, LDA, RCA, NCA, and BSF are 29.4%, 7.84%, 14.62%, 6.76%, and 6.76% respectively. The performance of MBC is still better than the modified LPP [7]. In [7] [1] , the modified LPP obtained the minimum average classification error of 7.5% over 50 times experiments under the same testing protocol, i.e., 30 images are randomly selected from each subject, and the rest images of each subject are used for testing.

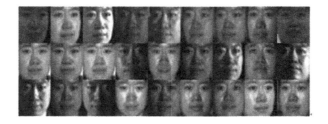

Fig. 2. Samples of the CMU-PIE database

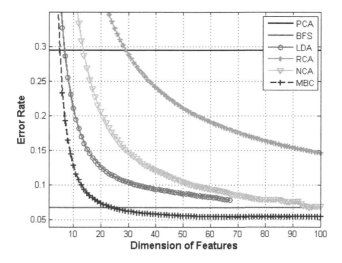

Fig. 3. Testing error rate on the CMU-PIE database

4.2   Extended YALE Face Database

The extended YALE face database has 38 subjects, each subjects has 64 near frontal view images under different illuminations [1] [15]. The images are cropped to 32×32, and images are normalized into unit vectors as in [7] [1]. Figure 4 shows some image samples. Same as the experiments on the CMU-PIE database, we randomly select 30 images from each individual for training, and the rest 34 images per subject are used for testing. The experiments are run 50 times, and Figure 5 reports their average results. Because the training data has 38 classes, the maximum feature dimensions of LDA is 38-1 = 37. The minimum classification error of MBC is 2.5%, while those of PCA, LDA, RCA, NCA, and BSF are 25.59%, 13.34%, 10.88%, 4.93%, and 3.93% respectively. The performance of MBC is still better than the modified LPP [7], for the minimum classification error of the latter reported is 7.5% under a similar testing in [7] [1].

Fig. 4. Samples of the extended YALE database

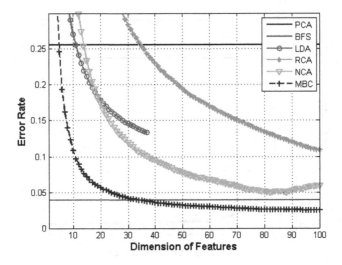

Fig. 5. Results on the extended YALE database

5   Conclusions

In this paper, we presented a unified scheme of subspace and distance metric learning under the Bayesian framework for face recognition. We divided the k-nearest neighbors of each sample into the intra-person set and the inter-person set according to the local distribution of the data, and we attempted to learn a distance metric in the embedding subspace, which made the distances between the sample and its intra-person set smaller than the distances between it and its inter-person set in the embedding subspace. To reach this goal, we defined two variables in the subspace, i.e., the intra-person distance and the inter-person distance, and modeled them with two different probabilistic distributions. Then we converted our problem to that of minimizing the overlap between these two distributions. Inspired by Bayesian classification error estimation, Our goal was equivalent to minimizing their Bhattachyrra coefficient measurement. The proposed framework made no assumption on the global distribution of the data. Moreover, it links to Bayesian error. We proved the power of the proposed approach on the CMU-PIE face database and the extended YALE face database.

Acknowledgements

We would like to thanks the reviewers' comments. The first author would also like to thank for the support of the NSFC (No. 60405005 and 60675003). This work is done at Rutgers University.

References

1. http://ews.uiuc.edu/dengcai2/data/data.html
2. http://www.cs.huji.ac.il/aharonbh/
3. http://www.eng.biu.ac.il/goldbej/papers.html
4. Bar-Hillel, A., Hertz, T., Shental, N., Weinshall, D.: Learning a mahalanobis metric from equivalence constrains. Journal of Machine Learning Research (2005)
5. Belhumeur, P.N., Hespanha, J.P., Kriegman, D.J.: Eigenfaces vs. fisherfaces: Recognition using class specific linear projection. IEEE Trans. Pattern Analysis and Machine Intelligence 19(7), 711–720 (1997)
6. Moghaddam, B., Jebara, T., Pentland, A.: Bayesian face recognition. Pattern Recognition 33(11), 1771–1782 (2000)
7. Cai, D., He, X., Han, J.: Using graph model for face analysis. Tech. Report UIUCDCS-R-2636, University of UIUC (2005)
8. Chen, H.T., Chang, H.W., Liu, T.L.: Local discriminant embedding and its variants. In: Proc. of Int. Conf. Computer Vision and Pattern Recognition (CVPR) (2005)
9. Comaniciu, D., Ramesh, V., Meer, P.: Kernel-based object tracking. IEEE Trans. on Pattern Analysis and Machine Intelligence 25(5), 564–577 (2003)
10. Fukunaga, K.: Introduction to statistical pattern recognition. Academic Press, New York (1990)
11. Globerson, A., Roweis, S.: Metric learning by collapsing classes. In: Advances in Neural Information Processing Systems (NIPS) (2005)
12. Goldberger, J., Roweis, S., Hinton, G., Salakhutdinov, R.: Neighborhood component analysis. In: Advances in Neural Information Processing Systems (NIPS) (2004)
13. He, X.F., Niyogi, P.: Locality preserving projections. In: Advances in Neural Information Processing Systems (NIPS) (2003)
14. Hoi, S.C., Liu, W., Lyu, M.R., Ma, W.Y.: Learning distance metrics with contextual constraints for image retrieval. In: Proc. of Int. Conf. Computer Vision and Pattern Recognition (CVPR) (2006)
15. Lee, K.-C., Ho, J., Kriegman, D.: Acquiring linear subspaces for face recognition under variable lighting. IEEE Trans. Pattern Analysis and Machine Intelligence 27(5), 1–15 (2005)
16. Mika, S., Ratsch, G., Weston, J.: Fisher discriminant analysis with kernels. In: Proc. of Neural Networks for Signal Processing Workshop (1999)
17. Roweis, S.T., Saul, L.K.: Nonlinear dimensionality reduction by locally linear embedding. Sciences 290(5500), 2323–2326 (2000)
18. Salakhutdinov, R., Roweis, S.T.: Adaptive over- relaxed bound optimization methods. In: Proc. of Int. Conf. Machine Learning (ICML) (2003)
19. Scholkopf, B., Smola, A., Muller, K.R.: Nonlinear component analysis as a kernel eigenvalue problem. Neural Computation 10(5), 1299–1319 (1998)
20. Shental, N., Hertz, T., Weinshall, D., Pavel, M.: Adjustment learning and relevant component analysis. In: Europen Conf. on Computer Vision (ECCV) (2003)
21. Sim, T., Baker, S., Bsat, M.: The cmu pose, illumination, and expression database. IEEE Trans. on PAMI 25(12), 1615–1618 (2003)

22. Sugiyama, M.: Local fisher discriminant analysis for supervised dimensionality reduction. In: Proc. of Int. Conf. Machine Learning (ICML) (2006)
23. Tenenbaum, J.B., de Silva, V., Langford, J.C.: A global geometric framework for nonlinear dimensionality reduction. Sciences 290(5500), 2319–2323 (2000)
24. Torresani, L., Lee, K.C.: Large margin component analysis. In: Advances in Neural Information Processing Systems (NIPS) (2006)
25. Turk, M., Pentland, A.: Eigenfaces for recognition. Journal of Cognitive Neuroscience 3(1), 72–86 (1991)
26. Weinberger, K.Q., Blitzer, J., Saul, L.K.: Metric learning for large margin nearest neighbor classification. In: Advances in Neural Information Processing Systems (NIPS) (2005)
27. Xing, E., Ng, A., Jordan, M., Russell, S.: Distance metric learning, with application to clustering with side-information. In: Advances in Neural Information Processing Systems (NIPS) (2004)
28. Yan, S.C., Xu, D., Zhang, B.Y., Zhang, H.J.: Graph embedding: A general framework for dimensionality reduction. In: Proc. of Int. Conf. Computer Vision and Pattern Recognition (CVPR) (2005)
29. Yang, L., Jin, R., Sukthankar, R., Liu, Y.: An efficient algorithm for local distance metric learning. In: AAAI (2006)
30. Zhao, W., Chellappa, R., Phillips, P.J.: Subspace linear discriminant analysis for face recognition. Tech. Report CAR-TR-914, University of Maryland (1999)
31. Zhao, W., Chellappa, R., Rosenfeld, A., Phillips, P.J.: Face recognition: A literature survey. CS-Tech. Report-4167, University of Maryland (2000)

Face Recognition Based on Pose-Variant Image Synthesis and Multi-level Multi-feature Fusion

Congcong Li, Guangda Su, Yan Shang, Yingchun Li, and Yan Xiang

Electronic Engineering Department, Tsinghua University, Beijing, 100084, China
li.congcong@gmail.com

Abstract. Pose variance remains a challenging problem for face recognition. In this paper, a scheme including image synthesis and recognition is proposed to improve the performance of automatic face recognition system. In the image synthesis part, a series of pose-variant images are produced based on three images respectively with front, left-profile, right-profile poses, and are added into the gallery in order to overcome the pose inconsistence between probes and images in the database. In the recognition part, a multi-level fusion method based on Gabor-combined features and gray-intensity features (GCGIF) is presented. Both amplitude features and phase features extracted through Gabor filters are utilized. Fusion is introduced in both the face representation level and the confidence level. Experiment results show that the integrated scheme achieve superior recognition performance.

Keywords: Face recognition, face synthesis, pose variance, Gabor, fusion method.

1 Introduction

In the past few years, techniques on face recognition have been developed a lot. Many algorithms have achieved good recognition performance in controlled conditions that faces are in frontal poses, in harmonious illumination and in neutral expression. However, there are still many open problems when face recognition technology is put into application. The face recognition vender test (FRVT) 2002 reports [1] that recognition under illumination, expression and pose variations still remains challenging. Results show that recognition rate decreases sharply when one side for matching is a face rotated to a large angle and the other is a frontal face.

Aiming to improve face recognition performance under pose variance, one way easily being thought of is to change the matching condition by adjusting face pose in one image the same with that of the other image for matching. Based on this idea, synthesizing face images in novel views is considered to be an important way and has been discussed by many researchers for a period.

In the past few years, many methods of synthesizing face image in novel views have been proposed. One common way to synthesize novel views of a face is to recover its 3D structure. Some current algorithms utilize a morphable 3D model to generate face images novel views from a single image. W. Zhao et al. [2] proposed a

S.K. Zhou et al. (Eds.): AMFG 2007, LNCS 4778, pp. 261–275, 2007.
© Springer-Verlag Berlin Heidelberg 2007

SFS (Shape from Shading)-based view synthesis technique to generate a frontal image from a profile image. It is also a single image based methods where no example based learning is carried out. These methods face to a problem in common: when only one face image is available, the texture within occluded region becomes undefined.

Vetter et al. [3, 4] use the linear object class approach to deal with the problem. It is a hybrid method that needs multiple images per person for training and only one image in database per person is available in recognition. It is assumed that a new face's texture can be represented as a linear combination of the texture from a group of example faces in the same view, and the combination coefficients can be used to synthesize the face image in another view. However, another difficulty appears. Since the generated texture is a linear combination of the textures in training database, some individual characteristic information would be lost, such as little scar, beauty spot, and so on.

Besides the two categories of methods, another category of methods are multiple image based methods where multiple images of variant poses per person are available. To collect multiple images per person in the database directly by capturing is hardly carried out; however, with synthesis technique, we can generate multiple images through only one or a limited quantity of images. It is the method category that this paper adopted.

The proposed work in this paper mainly aims to be applied to criminal identification. In the original criminal database, there are commonly three face images of every person who has a criminal history, respectively in the frontal pose, left profile pose and right profile pose. In our work, we utilize these three images to synthesize more images of the same person with different rotation angles. The synthesized images are then put into the database to increase the pose variety. In the recognition stage, when a probe comes, it is first estimated about its pose, and then compared with a sub-database selected according to the principle that images in the sub-database has the most similar pose with that of the probe.

The synthesis work is carried on based on Stereopsis and projective geometry. Before synthesis, ASM algorithm is improved to ensure the accuracy of face alignment. 3D shape reconstruction and triangle-based cubic spline interpolation are introduced for generating the shape in new pose. Multi-resolution spline technique is adopted in texture synthesis. Proper integration of all these techniques results in satisfying synthesis performance which retains major characteristics of a face.

Besides the synthesis work, this paper also studies the area of face recognition algorithm. Although the synthesis work has helped to adjust the pose of images in the database similar to that of the probe, another problem is left. That is, how to make the recognition algorithm robust for two profile image matching. Therefore, in this work, we tried to introduce Gabor wavelet feature since Gabor features have the properties of orientation selectivity, spatial frequency selectivity, and insensitivity in positioning error. At the same time, gray-intensity feature was discarded; instead, it was combined with Gabor features at different stage by trials. Finally, we present a two-level fusion algorithm for recognition based on Gabor-amplitude features, Gabor-phase features and Gray-Intensity features. This method combines the Gabor amplitude features and phase features in the PCA level to form Gabor-combined features, which are then joined with gray intensity features in the confidence level to form the final classifier.

Combining the synthesis work and the recognition work, this paper makes contributions in mainly three aspects:

1. It generates multiple images in variant poses from three images per person and makes the images on sides for recognition have similar pose so that the recognition performance is improved.
2. Since the synthesis is based on more than one image, the texture contained in the three original images can cover all area of the face so that individual details are retain;
3. Since the synthesis is carried on aforehand before recognition, it brings no time problem for recognition, and thus the proposed scheme is suitable for real-time face identification applications.

The rest of the paper is organized as follows: Section 2 provides an overview of the whole proposed scheme; Section 3 introduces major techniques in the proposed image synthesis course including face alignment, shape reconstruction, texture synthesis and pose estimation. Section 4 demonstrates the framework and the detail of the proposed two-level fusion recognition method based on multiple image features. Experiment results are given in Section 6, and this paper is concluded in section 7.

2   Overview of the Proposed Scheme

Aiming to solve the problem of recognizing an image with face pose in a large rotation angle, an integrated scheme is designed, which consists of two parts: database image synthesis part and face image recognition part. As shown in Fig.1, before recognition, synthesis work would be done based on three categories of databases, respectively with frontal poses, left-profile poses and right-profile poses. Through synthesis, the database will be enlarged by adding images with other poses. In therecognition stage, when a probe comes, the proposed system will first estimate its face pose and then pick out a sub-database whose images have the most similar pose with that of the probe. So the recognition work will carried on between the probe and

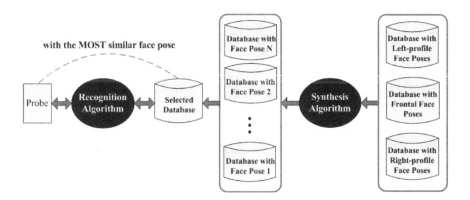

Fig. 1. Overview of the whole scheme

the selected sub-database. Therefore, the most important work in this scheme is the synthesis stage and the recognition stage, both of which have crucial affect on the final recognition performance.

3 Pose-Variant Face Image Synthesis

This section gives an overview of the synthesis proposed in our scheme and introduces briefly the key techniques utilized for synthesis.

3.1 Synthesis Framework

Frontal, left-side and right-side face images are utilized together to produce images with any possible pose. These synthesized images then compose sub-datasets of the gallery, each of which represents a pose type. Fig.2 illustrates the whole synthesis process. Face alignment, new shape generation and new texture synthesis are crucial parts in the synthesis stage.

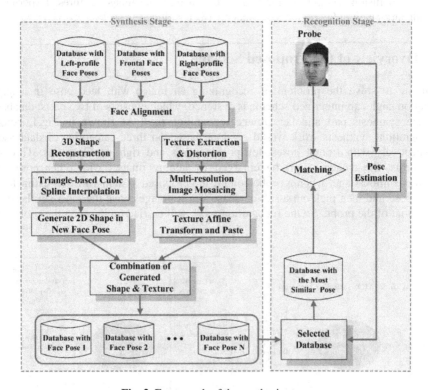

Fig. 2. Framework of the synthesis stage

3.2 Face Alignment

An improved ASM (Active Shape Models) method is chosen to extract the face feature points in this paper. It is hard for the conventional ASM to get accurate result on each feature point; what's more, the performance depends heavily on the initial positions of the landmarks. According to the structure of face, the edge information and part information of face are introduced to the matching process of ASM, which improved the performance of ASM [5].

The face images are firstly normalized. Then the improved ASM algorithm help to extract 105 feature points to represent the front face shape and 57 feature points to represent the profile face shape respectively, as shown in Fig.3.

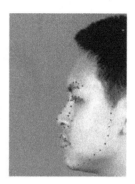

Fig. 3. Feature points extracted by the improved ASM algorithm

To ensure the corresponding relation between feature points in different images, feature points of some face parts like contour are connected and fitted by polynomial curve. As shown in Fig. 4, half of the contour is fitted at two stages. At the first stage shown in the left, feature points are roughly fitted and the point parallel to the corner of mouth is considered to be a subsection point. Then the contour is fitted separated by two curves as shown in the right. Then the contour feature points are adjusted on the curves in well-proportioned distribution. Besides fitting the contour, similar operations are also carried onto the other facial parts. The alignment of the face feature points provides an important basis for shape reconstruction of frontal face, which would be mentioned in the next section.

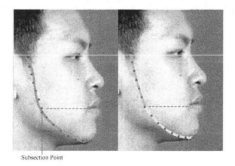

Subsection Point

Fig. 4. A two-stage fitting to the contour with polynomial curves

3.3 Shape Reconstruction

One face image includes shape information and pure texture image. So a face image can be separated into shape information and texture information. If we have these two kinds of information, we can form a new face image.

The 3D shape of a given face is reconstructed based on the aligned feature points extracted from the three source images. For each 3D point, its x and y coordinate values can be obtained from the frontal image and its z coordinate value can be obtained from either profile image, as shown in the Fig.5 below.

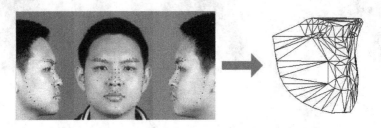

Fig. 5. Demonstration of 3D shape reconstruction based on stereoscopy

The 3D shape formed directly from the source images contains only 105 points, which are not enough for representing the face shape. So based on these sparse feature points, we introduce the triangle-based cubic spline interpolation technique [6][7][8] to generate dense regularly spaced grid, as shown in Fig.6.

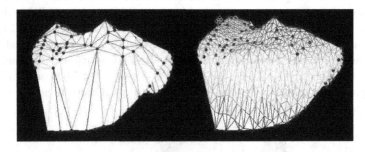

Fig. 6. Dense regularly spaced grid generation for representing face shape

With the dense grid, we can generate the 2D face shape in new pose based on stereoscopy. Since some parts of the face would be occluded in the new pose, we need to compute the new edges of all face parts, especially the nose part and the contour part.

3.4 Texture Synthesis

As mentioned in Section. 1, one advantages of the proposed method in this paper is that there is enough information for texture synthesis. To make full use of the textures

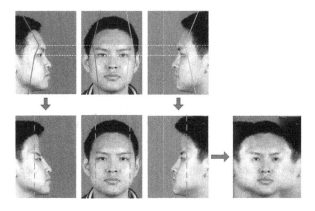

Fig. 7. Image transform and multi-resolution mosaic

of three source images, transform is carried on according to a set of principles as shown in Fig.7. Based on the curves marked in Fig.7, images in the first row is transformed to those in the second row, which are then cut and combined with the help of multi-resolution spline technique [9] to generate the mosaic image in right-down corner.

In order to generate the image in new pose, the new 2D shape points and their corresponding positions in the mosaic image are needed. Since in 3.4 we have already gained the new 2D shape points, we can also compute out their corresponding positions in the mosaic images by utilizing the relationship between 3D coordinates and 2D coordinates and all the parameters in the image transform and mosaic course.

After the corresponding points are confirm, Delaunay triangularization following the same principle is introduced to form multiple triangles to connect the points. Then the triangle based affine transform is used to span the selected part of the mosaic face image to fit for the destination shape. Equation (1) describes this affine transform process.

$$\begin{bmatrix} x' \\ y' \end{bmatrix} = \begin{bmatrix} a & b \\ c & d \end{bmatrix} \begin{bmatrix} x \\ y \end{bmatrix} + \begin{bmatrix} O_x \\ O_y \end{bmatrix} \tag{1}$$

Fig.8 is an example of the affine transform for texture synthesis.

Fig. 8. Process of affine transform for texture synthesis

3.5 Pose Estimation

As shown in Fig.2, in order to select the sub-database whose images have the similar pose as the probe, the probe's probe should be estimated. In this work, we require the input probe with a rotation angle no larger than $45°$. The probe is first preprocessed such as feature-positioned and normalized. It is rectified and normalized geometrically according to the auto located key-point positions. In the geometric normalization step, not only the eyes but also the chin middle point would be automatically located. Then each face image would be scaled and rotated so that the eyes are positioned in line and the distance between the chin point and the center of the eyes equals a predefined length. After that, the face image is cropped to a given size. The examples of training images in TH database (built by ourselves) are shown in Fig.9.

Fig. 9. The training face images in TH database

It is essential to extract features from images utilizing the composite PCA (principle component analysis) and projecting face images to the eigenspace. Given a set of samples $X_i \in \mathbb{R}^N$ represented face images by column vectors. The transformation matrix can be formed by using eigenvectors which normalized to unit matrix T .The projection of X_i into the N-dimensional subspace can be expressed as

$$\alpha = \{\alpha_1, \cdots, \alpha_N\} = X_i^T \cdot T \tag{2}$$

The shape feature is shown in Fig.10 in next page. The feature points can give geometric characteristic. AB and $A'B'$ are the distance between two eyes when pose angle is 0 and β degree respectively. Set radius as 1.

$$A'E' = A'B' = \sin(\theta + \beta) + \sin(\theta - \beta) = 2\sin\theta\cos\beta \tag{3}$$

Since distance $AB = 2\sin\theta$, then pose angle

$$\beta = \arccos(\frac{A'E'}{AB}) \tag{4}$$

Set weights of two weight parameters α and β after two groups of features are gained. The new eigenvector ξ is

$$\xi = p \cdot \alpha + q \cdot \beta , \text{ where } p + q = 1 \tag{5}$$

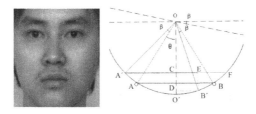

Fig. 10. Shape feature points and the configuration of pose variance

SVM (support vector machine) is to find the optimal linear hyperplane which the expected classification error for unseen test samples is minimized [10]. According to the structural risk minimization principle, a function that classifies the training data accurately will generalize best regardless of the dimensionality of the input space.

Each training sample x_i is associated with coefficient a_i. Those samples whose coefficient a_i is nonzero are Support Vectors (SV) of the optimal hyperplane. $f(x)$ is an optimal SVM classified function. $y_i \in (+1, -1)$.

$$f(x) = \sum_{vector} y_i a_i K(x_i, x) + b \tag{6}$$

where K is a kernel function. Here we use linear kernel, $\phi(x_i) = x_i$, then $K(x_i, x_j) = x_i \cdot x_j = x_i^T x_j$.

The PCA projection values of samples to eigenspace were as SVM input parameters and the optimal hyperplane that correctly separates data points were found. Combining the PCA and SVM classifier, we can draw better classification results. Then the pose angle will be acquired.

4 Multi-level Multi-feature Fusion Method

This section introduces the recognition algorithm proposed in our work, which is a two-level fusion method based on three types of image features.

4.1 Fusion Framework

Three types of face representations are introduced in this method, including gray-level intensity features, Gabor amplitude features and Gabor phase features. Fig.11 illustrates the process of feature extraction and the design of two-level fusion. In the PCA level, shown in the left gray frame, we make a fusion between Gabor amplitude features and phase features. These two features are then treated as a whole in the later steps. Another fusion is introduced in the confidence level between the matching result based on Gabor-combined features and that based on gray intensity features, as shown in the right gray frame. This two-level fusion method based on Gabor-combined features and gray-intensity features is called GCGIF method in the subsequent part of this paper.

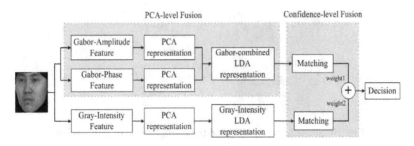

Fig. 11. Design of the proposed method GCGIF

4.2 Feature Extraction

Extracting Gray-level Intensity Feature: Face images are rectified and normalized geometrically according to the auto located key-point positions, as mentioned in Section 3.5. After these processes, the face image is cropped to a given size (90*120). To reduce the affection of different hairstyles and backgrounds, a mask is put on the face image. Moreover, histogram equalization is introduced to decrease the influence from light and complexion variation. The preprocessing procedure is shown in Fig.12 (a).

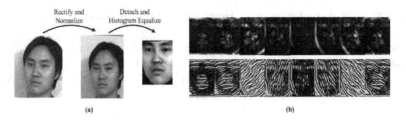

Fig. 12. (a) formation of gray intensity feature; (b) examples of Gabor amplitude features and phase features

Extracting Gabor Features: Gabor wavelet has been introduced to image analysis due to its biological relevance and its ability in representing spatial locality and orientation. In our experiments, we consider both Gabor amplitude and phase for face image representation.

The 2D Gabor wavelet components can be defined as equations (7) and (8):

$$G_{\bar{k},+}(\bar{r}) = k^2 \exp\left(-k^2 \left\|\bar{r} - \bar{r}_0\right\| / 2\delta^2\right)\left\{\cos\left[\bar{k}(\bar{r} - \bar{r}_0)\right] - \exp\left(-\delta^2 / 2\right)\right\} / \delta^2 \qquad (7)$$

$$G_{\bar{k},-}(\bar{r}) = k^2 \exp\left(-k^2 \left\|\bar{r} - \bar{r}_0\right\|^2 / 2\delta^2\right)\sin\left[\bar{k}(\bar{r} - \bar{r}_0)\right] / \delta^2 \qquad (8)$$

where $\bar{k} = k \exp(j\theta_v)$, $k = k_{max} / \lambda^u$, $\theta_v = \pi v / n$.

Here $\bar{k}$ is the filter wave-vector, determines the spatial frequency and orientation tuning of the filter. If $n = 8$, $u \in \{0,1,2,3,4\}$, $v \in \{0,1,\cdots,7\}$, $\delta = \pi$, $k_{max} = \pi / 2$, and $\lambda = 2$, a family of Gabor filters with 5 scales and 8 orientations are generated.

When a gray-intensity image is convolved with these Gabor filters, responses of the filters would be combined into a vector, with components given below:

$$R_{\vec{k},\pm}(\vec{r}_0) = \int G_{\vec{k},\pm}(\vec{r}_0,\vec{r})I(\vec{r})d\vec{r} \tag{9}$$

where I represents the input gray intensity image.

Then Gabor amplitude features and phase features of the corresponding face image could be computed as follows:

$$R_{\vec{k}} = \sqrt{R_{\vec{k},+}^2 + R_{\vec{k},-}^2} \;,\;\; \psi_{\vec{k}} = \arctan(R_{\vec{k},-} / R_{\vec{k},+}) \tag{10}$$

Fig.12(b) gives examples of outputs from Gabor filters, with amplitude features in the first row and the corresponding phase features in the second row, both are at the condition of $u = 2$.

The Gabor wavelet transform of an image is the collection of the coefficients of all the pixels (90*120). To reduce the dimensionality, the pixels are sampled to 24*32. To further reduce the redundancy of features, PCA (Principle Component Analysis)[11] and LDA (Linear Discriminant Analysis)[12] are employed.

4.3 Selection of Fusion Mechanism

We study fusion mechanism at both the representation level and the confidence level, as shown in Fig.13 and Fig.14.

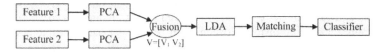

Fig. 13. Feature fusion at the PCA level

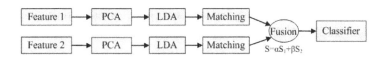

Fig. 14. Feature fusion in the confidence level

At the representation level, vectors extracted by PCA from different kinds of features are combined firstly. Then the combined vector enters LDA. At last, the feature vector obtained by LDA is the final representation for the face image and would be used for matching before the final decision.

The mechanism of confidence-level fusion works as shown in Fig.14. Different features are first processed by PCA and LDA and the LDA results are used for matching respectively. Then different feature-matching results are calculated into final similar-scores based on the weighted sum rule.

Both the above fusion mechanisms may help improve the recognition task. Which mechanism should be utilized is decided through experiment trials here.

Table 1. Recognition performance without fusion

Without Fusion	Gabor-Amplitude PCA-LDA	Gabor-Phase PCA-LDA	Gray-Intensity PCA-LDA
Recognition Rate	70.0%	63.8%	67.8%

Table 2. Recognition performance with different fusion manners

Features for Fusion		Fusion Level	Recognition Rate
Feature1	Feature2		
Gabor-Amplitude	Gabor-Phase	PCA	**74.5%**
Gabor- Amplitude	Gabor-Phase	Confidence ($\alpha : \beta = 5{:}2$)	72.3%
Gabor-Combined	Gray-Intensity	PCA	78.4%
Gabor-Combined	Gray-Intensity	Confidence ($\alpha : \beta = 3{:}2$)	**81.9%**

Face recognition performance is evaluated based on part of the TH-database [13]. The gallery consists of images of 160 people with one frontal image per person. The probe dataset consists of 320 images whose left-right rotation angle is either -15 or +15 degree. The recognition rate means the fraction of probes that have rank top fifth in the identification task. Table.1 shows the recognition performance based on each type of features without fusion.

Table.2 compares the performance of different fusion mechanisms. Comparing with Table.1, it is obvious that fusions of features do help to improve the recognition performance. Due to greater correlation between Gabor amplitude and phase features, we first consider making fusion between them. The upper part of Table.2 shows that combing Gabor amplitude and phase features in PCA level outgoes that in confidence level, so the former is adopted to form the Gabor-combined features. Then the nether part of Table.2 shows that further fusion between Gabor-combined feature and gray-intensity feature in the confidence level is better and should be adopted. The reason behind the results may be that features with more inherent relativity, just like amplitude feature and phase feature both extracted by Gabor filters, adapts to fusion at an earlier stage.

According to results in Table.2, the fusion mechanism for GCGIF algorithm was formed as Fig.11 illuminated. Several classic algorithms are also evaluated in our experiments, including the PCA algorithm, the combined PCA and LDA algorithm (PCA+LDA) --both based on gray intensity features-- and the PCA+LDA algorithm based on Gabor amplitude features (G PCA+LDA). A previously released fusion algorithm MMP-PCA (Multi-Modal Part face recognition method based on Principal Component Analysis) [14], is also tested for reference. Table.3 shows that GCGIF delivers the best result in the above mentioned experiment condition.

Table 3. Recognition performance of different methods

Methods	PCA–LDA	G PCA-LDA	MMP-PCA	GCGIF
Recognition Rate	67.8%	70.0%	76.3%	**81.9%**

5 Experiment Results

In this section we describe our experiments on the TH face database. The TH face database contains face images of 160 persons with left-right rotation angles from -90 degree to +90 degree in the interval of 15 degree. We select the frontal, left-profile, right-profile images as original gallery and select images from -45 degree to 45 degree in the interval of 15 degree to form probe sets. Images in every probe set have the same face pose.

In our experiment, the frontal, left-profile, right-profile images are first utilized to synthesize multiple face images with left-right rotation angles from -45 degree to +45 degree in interval of 5 degree, through the proposed synthesis framework introduced in Section.3. The synthesized images then constitute multiple sub-databases, each of which represents an individual pose.

Fig.15 gives two examples of face synthesis based on three images. For each person, the first row are original images with frontal, left-profile and right-profile poses; the following two rows are the synthetic face images with poses from -45 degree to 45 degree at an interval of 5degree.

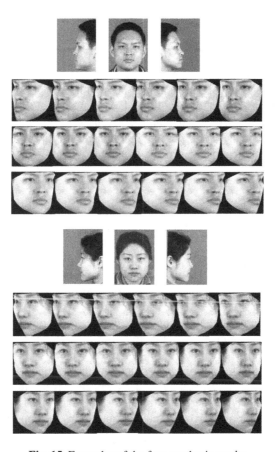

Fig. 15. Examples of the face synthesis results

The recognition experiments are based on an identification task. Recognition rate is tested on each probe set. The recognition rate means the fraction of probes that have rank top fifth in the identification task. The recognition algorithm adopted the GCGIF algorithm presented in Section 5. To better evaluate the proposed scheme in this paper, we compare the recognition performances in database with synthesized images and in database without synthesized image. In both the situations, the gallery consists of images of 160 people and each probe set contains 160 face images. The experiment results are shown in Table. 4.

Table 4. Recognition performance in the original gallery and that in the synthetic gallery

Probe (Pose)	Recognition rate in the database containing only frontal, left-profile, right-profile images	Recognition rate in the database containing frontal, left-profile, right-profile images and also synthesized images
L 15	81.3%	**85.0%**
L 30	58.1%	**75.6 %**
L 45	29.4%	**54.4%**
R 15	81.9%	**86.3%**
R 30	56.9%	**75.0%**
R 45	25.6%	**55.6%**

Table. 4 shows the recognition performance of different probe sets. In Table.4, "L xx" means the images in the set has a face pose with xx degree's rotation to its left. Similarly, "R" means "Right". From Table.4, we can see that the recognition rates in the third column are much higher than the second column in the same row, which indicates that the synthesis of pose-variant images for the database did help to improve the recognition performance significantly.

6   Conclusions

In this paper, we design an integrated scheme for pose-variant face recognition. There are mainly two contributions.

First, Synthesis is introduced to produce a series of pose-variant face images based on three images with frontal, left-profile and right-profile poses respectively in order to overcome the difficulty of image matching between faces with inconsistent poses. The generated images are then added to the gallery to increase the pose variety of each individual before the recognition work. In the recognition stage, when a probe comes, it will first be estimated about its pose and then be compared with images in a sub-dataset with the most similar pose. Since the synthesis is processed before the recognition work, the recognition speed has not been affected. Although a small quantity of unavoidable estimation and alignment errors may affect the final reconstruction accuracy, experiment results show that most of the information important for recognition has been retained and helps to improve the recognition performance.

Secondly, a two-level fusion algorithm for face recognition based on Gabor-Combined features and Gray-Intensity features, GCGIF, is presented in order to improve the recognition performance. This method combines the Gabor amplitude features and phase features in the PCA level to form Gabor-combined features, which are then joined with gray intensity features in the confidence level. This two-level fusion mechanism is selected through experimental trials and rational conjecture on correlation between features. Experimental results show that GCGIF achieves superior performance.

Due to these two contributions, experiments show that the proposed scheme achieves great improvement for pose-variant face recognition. Without expensive time cost, this method is suitable for real-time identification applications.

References

1. Phillips, P.J., Grother, P., Ross, J., Blackburn, D., Tabassi, E., Bone, M.: Face Recognition Vendor Test 2002: Evaluation Report (March 2003)
2. Zhao, W., Chellappa, R.: SFS based view synthesis for robust face recognition. Int. C. Automatic Face and Gesture Recognition, 285–292 (2000)
3. Vetter, T.: Synthesis of novel views from a single face image. International Journal of Computer Vision 28(2), 103–116 (1998)
4. Vetter, T., Poggio, T.: Linear object classes and image synthesis from a single example image. IEEE Transactions on Pattern Analysis and Machine Intelligence 19(7), 733–742 (1997)
5. Du, C., Su, G.D., Lin, X.G., Gu, H.: An Improved Multi-resolution Active Shape Model for Face Alignment. Jounal of Optoelectronics Laser 15(12), 706–710 (in Chinese, 2004)
6. Barber, C.B., Dobkin, D.P., Huhdanpaa, H.T.: The Quickhull Algorithm for Convex Hulls. ACM Transactions on Mathematical Software 22(4), 469–483 (1996)
7. National Science and Technology Research Center for Computation and Visualization of Geometric Structures (The Geometry Center), University of Minnesota (1993)
8. Watson, D.E.: Contouring: A Guide to the Analysis and Display of Spatial Data. Pergamon,Tarrytown, NY (Elsevier Science, Inc.) (1992)
9. Burt, P.J., Andelson, E.H.: A Multiresolution Spline With Application to Image Mosaics. ACM Transactions on Graphics 2(4), 217–236 (1983)
10. Vapnik, V.: Statistical Learning Theory. John Wiley & Sons, New York (1998)
11. Turk, M., Pentland, A.: Eigenfaces for Recognition. Journal of Cognitive Neuroscience 3, 72–86 (1991)
12. Martinez, A.M., Kak, A.C.: PCA versus LDA. IEEE Trans. on PAMI 23(2), 228–233 (2001)
13. Li, C.C., Su, G.D., Meng, K., Zhou, J.: Technology Evaluations on TH-FACE Recognition System. In: Zhang, D., Jain, A.K. (eds.) Advances in Biometrics. LNCS, vol. 3832, pp. 589–597. Springer, Heidelberg (2005)
14. Su, G.D., Zhang, C.P., Ding, R., Du, C.: MMP-PCA face recognition method. Electronics Letters 38(25) (2002)

Towards Pose-Invariant 2D Face Classification for Surveillance

Conrad Sanderson[1], Ting Shang[1,2], and Brian C. Lovell[1,2]

[1] NICTA, 300 Adelaide St, Brisbane, QLD 4000, Australia
[2] ITEE, University of Queensland, Brisbane, QLD 4072, Australia

Abstract. A key problem for "face in the crowd" recognition from existing surveillance cameras in public spaces (such as mass transit centres) is the issue of pose mismatches between probe and gallery faces. In addition to accuracy, scalability is also important, necessarily limiting the complexity of face classification algorithms. In this paper we evaluate recent approaches to the recognition of faces at relatively large pose angles from a gallery of frontal images and propose novel adaptations as well as modifications. Specifically, we compare and contrast the accuracy, robustness and speed of an Active Appearance Model (AAM) based method (where realistic frontal faces are synthesized from non-frontal probe faces) against bag-of-features methods (which are local feature approaches based on block Discrete Cosine Transforms and Gaussian Mixture Models). We show a novel approach where the AAM based technique is sped up by directly obtaining pose-robust features, allowing the omission of the computationally expensive and artefact producing image synthesis step. Additionally, we adapt a *histogram-based bag-of-features* technique to face classification and contrast its properties to a previously proposed *direct bag-of-features* method. We also show that the two bag-of-features approaches can be considerably sped up, without a loss in classification accuracy, via an approximation of the exponential function. Experiments on the FERET and PIE databases suggest that the bag-of-features techniques generally attain better performance, with significantly lower computational loads. The *histogram-based bag-of-features* technique is capable of achieving an average recognition accuracy of 89% for pose angles of around 25 degrees.

1 Introduction

In the 21st century, international usage and interest in Closed-Circuit Television (CCTV) for surveillance of public spaces is growing at an unprecedented pace in response to global terrorism. A similar escalation of the installed CCTV base occurred in London late last century in response to the continual bombings linked to the conflict in Northern Ireland. Based on the number of CCTV cameras on Putney High Street, it is "guesstimated" [1] that there are around 500,000 CCTV cameras in the London area and 4,000,000 cameras in the UK. This suggests that in the UK there is approximately one camera for every 14 people. However, whilst it is relatively easy, albeit expensive, to install increasing numbers of cameras, it

S.K. Zhou et al. (Eds.): AMFG 2007, LNCS 4778, pp. 276–289, 2007.

is quite another issue to adequately monitor the video feeds with security guards. Hence, the trend has been to record the CCTV feeds without monitoring and to use the video merely for a forensic, or reactive, response to crime and terrorism, often detected by other means.

In minor crimes such as assault and robbery, surveillance video is very effective in helping to find and successfully prosecute perpetrators. Thus one would expect that surveillance video would act as a deterrent to crime. Recently the immense cost of successful terrorist attacks on soft targets such as mass transport systems has indicated that forensic analysis of video after the event is simply not adequate. Indeed, in the case of suicide bombings there is simply no possibility of prosecution after the event and thus no deterrent effect. A pressing need is emerging to monitor all surveillance cameras in an attempt to detect events and persons-of-interest.

The problem is that human monitoring requires a large number of personnel, resulting in high ongoing costs and questionable reliability due to the attention span of humans decreasing rapidly when performing such tedious tasks. A solution may be found in advanced surveillance systems employing computer monitoring of all video feeds, delivering the alerts to human responders for triage. Indeed such systems may assist in maintaining the high level of vigilance required over many years to detect the rare events associated with terrorism — a well-designed computer system is never caught "off guard". A key technology for prevention of crime and terrorism is the reliable detection of persons-of-interest through face recognition.

While automatic face recognition of cooperative subjects has achieved good results in controlled applications such as passport control, CCTV conditions are considerably more challenging. Nuisance factors such as varying illumination, expression, and pose can greatly affect recognition performance. According to Phillips et al. head pose is believed to be the hardest factor to model [2]. In mass transport systems, surveillance cameras are often mounted in the ceiling in places such as railway platforms and passenger trains. Since the subjects are generally not posing for the camera, it is rare to obtain a true frontal face image. As it is infeasible to consider remounting all the cameras (in our case more than 6000) to improve face recognition performance, any practical system must have effective pose compensation or be specifically designed to handle pose variations. Examples of real life CCTV conditions are shown in Figure 1.

A further complication is that we generally only have one frontal gallery image of each person of interest (e.g. a passport photograph or a mugshot). In addition to robustness and accuracy, scalability and fast performance are also of prime importance for surveillance. A face recognition system should be able to handle large volumes of people (e.g. peak hour at a railway station), possibly processing hundreds of video streams. While it is possible to setup elaborate parallel computation machines, there are always cost considerations limiting the number of CPUs available for processing. In this context, a face recognition algorithm should be able to run in real-time or better, which necessarily limits complexity.

Previous approaches to addressing pose variation include the synthesis of new images at previously unseen views [3,4], direct synthesis of face model parameters [5] and local feature based representations [6,7,8]. We note in passing that while true 3D based approaches in theory allow face matching at various poses, current 3D sensing hardware has too many limitations [9], including cost and range. Moreover unlike 2D recognition, 3D technology cannot be retrofitted to existing surveillance systems.

In [4], Active Appearance Models (AAMs) were used to model each face, detecting the pose through a correlation model. A frontal image could then be synthesized directly from a single non-frontal image without the need to explicitly generate a 3D head model. While the AAM-based face synthesis allowed considerable improvements in recognition accuracy, the synthesized faces have residual artefacts which may affect recognition performance.

In [5], a "bag of features" approach was shown to perform well in the presence of pose variations. It is based on dividing the face into overlapping uniform-sized blocks, analysing each block with the Discrete Cosine Transform (DCT) and modelling the resultant set of features via a Gaussian Mixture Model (GMM). The robustness to pose change was attributed to an effective insensitivity to the topology of the face. We shall refer to this method as the *direct bag-of-features*.

Inspired by text classification techniques from the fields of natural language processing and information retrieval, alternative forms of the "bag of features" approach are used for image categorisation in [10,11,12]. Rather than directly calculating the likelihood as in [5], histograms of occurrences of "visual words" (also known as "keypoints") are first built, followed by histogram comparison. We shall refer to this approach as the *histogram-based bag-of-features*.

This paper has four main aims: (i) To evaluate the effectiveness of a novel modification of the AAM-based method, where we explicitly remove the effect of pose from the face model, creating pose-robust features. The modification allows the use of the model's parameters directly for classification, thereby skipping the computationally intensive and artefact producing image synthesis step. (ii) To adapt the histogram-based bag-of-features approach to face classification and contrast its properties to the direct bag-of-features method. (iii) To

Fig. 1. Examples of typical non-frontality of faces in surveillance conditions

evaluate the extent of speedup possible in both bag-of-features approaches via an approximation of the exp() function, and whether such approximation affects recognition accuracy. **(iv)** To compare the performance, robustness and speed of AAM based and bag-of-features based methods in the context of face classification under pose variations.

As we are currently in the process of creating a suitable dataset for face classification in CCTV conditions (part of a separately funded project), the experiments reported in this paper instead use the FERET and PIE datasets [13,14].

The paper is structured as follows. In Section 2 we overview the AAM-based synthesis technique and present the modified form. In Section 3 we overview the two bag-of-features methods. Section 4 is devoted to an evaluation of the techniques on the FERET and PIE datasets. Concluding remarks and further avenues of research are given in Section 5.

2   ASMs and AAMs

In this section we describe face modelling based on deformable models popularised by Cootes et al., namely Active Shape Models (ASMs) [15] and Active Appearance Models (AAMs) [16]. We first provide a brief description of the two models, followed by pose estimation via a correlation model and finally frontal view synthesis. We also show that the synthesis step can be omitted by directly removing the effect of the pose from the model of the face, resulting in (theoretically) pose independent features.

2.1   Face Modelling

Let us describe a face by a set of N landmark points, where the location of each point is tuple (x, y). A face can hence be represented by a $2N$ dimensional vector:

$$\mathbf{f} = [\, x_1, x_2, \cdots, x_N, \; y_1, y_2, \cdots, y_N \,]^T. \tag{1}$$

In ASM, a face shape is represented by:

$$\mathbf{f} = \bar{\mathbf{f}} + \mathbf{P}_s \mathbf{b}_s \tag{2}$$

where $\bar{\mathbf{f}}$ is the mean face vector, $\mathbf{P}_s$ is a matrix containing the k eigenvectors with largest eigenvalues (of a training dataset), and $\mathbf{b}_s$ is a weight vector. In a similar manner, the texture variations can be represented by:

$$\mathbf{g} = \bar{\mathbf{g}} + \mathbf{P}_g \mathbf{b}_g \tag{3}$$

where $\bar{\mathbf{g}}$ is the mean appearance vector, $\mathbf{P}_g$ is a matrix describing the texture variations learned from training sets, and $\mathbf{b_g}$ is the texture weighting vector.

The shape and appearance parameters $\mathbf{b}_s$ and $\mathbf{b}_g$ can be used to describe the shape and appearance of any face. As there are correlations between the shape and appearance of the same person, let us first represent both aspects as:

$$\mathbf{b} = \begin{bmatrix} \mathbf{W}_s \mathbf{b}_s \\ \mathbf{b}_g \end{bmatrix} = \begin{bmatrix} \mathbf{W}_s \mathbf{P}_s^T (\mathbf{f} - \bar{\mathbf{f}}) \\ \mathbf{P}_g^T (\mathbf{g} - \bar{\mathbf{g}}) \end{bmatrix} \tag{4}$$

where $\mathbf{W}_s$ is a diagonal matrix which represents the change between shape and texture. Through Principal Component Analysis (PCA) [17] we can represent $\mathbf{b}$ as:

$$\mathbf{b} = \mathbf{P}_c \mathbf{c} \tag{5}$$

where $\mathbf{P}_c$ are eigenvectors, $\mathbf{c}$ is a vector of appearance parameters controlling both shape and texture of the model, and $\mathbf{b}$ can be shown to have zero mean. Shape $\mathbf{f}$ and texture $\mathbf{g}$ can then be represented by:

$$\mathbf{f} = \bar{\mathbf{f}} + \mathbf{Q}_s \mathbf{c} \tag{6}$$
$$\mathbf{g} = \bar{\mathbf{g}} + \mathbf{Q}_g \mathbf{c} \tag{7}$$

where

$$\mathbf{Q}_s = \mathbf{P}_s \mathbf{W}_s^{-1} \mathbf{P}_{cs} \tag{8}$$
$$\mathbf{Q}_g = \mathbf{P}_g \mathbf{P}_{cg} \tag{9}$$

In the above, $\mathbf{Q}_s$ and $\mathbf{Q}_g$ are matrices describing the shape and texture variations, while $\mathbf{P}_{cs}$ and $\mathbf{P}_{cg}$ are shape and texture components of $\mathbf{P}_c$ respectively, i.e.:

$$\mathbf{P}_c = \begin{bmatrix} \mathbf{P}_{cs} \\ \mathbf{P}_{cg} \end{bmatrix} \tag{10}$$

The process of "interpretation" of faces is hence comprised of finding a set of model parameters which contain information about the shape, orientation, scale, position, and texture.

2.2   Pose Estimation

Following [18], let us assume that the model parameter $\mathbf{c}$ is approximately related to the viewing angle, θ, by a correlation model:

$$\mathbf{c} \approx \mathbf{c}_0 + \mathbf{c}_c \cos(\theta) + \mathbf{c}_s \sin(\theta) \tag{11}$$

where $\mathbf{c}_0$, $\mathbf{c}_c$ and $\mathbf{c}_s$ are vectors which are learned from the training data. (Here we consider only head turning. Head nodding can be dealt with in a similar way).

For each face from a training set Ω, indicated by superscript $[i]$ with associated pose $\theta^{[i]}$, we perform an AAM search to find the best fitting model parameters $\mathbf{c}^{[i]}$. The parameters $\mathbf{c}_0$, $\mathbf{c}_c$ and $\mathbf{c}_s$ can be learned via regression from $\left(\mathbf{c}^{[i]} \right)_{i \in 1, \cdots, |\Omega|}$ and $\left(\left[1, \cos(\theta^{[i]}), \sin(\theta^{[i]}) \right] \right)_{i \in 1, \cdots, |\Omega|}$, where $|\Omega|$ indicates the cardinality of Ω.

Given a new face image with parameters $\mathbf{c}^{[new]}$, we can estimate its orientation as follows. We first rearrange $\mathbf{c}^{[new]} = \mathbf{c}_0 + \mathbf{c}_c \cos(\theta^{[new]}) + \mathbf{c}_s \sin(\theta^{[new]})$ to:

$$\mathbf{c}^{[new]} - \mathbf{c}_0 = [\ \mathbf{c}_c\ \mathbf{c}_s\ ] \left[\ \cos(\theta^{[new]})\ \ \sin(\theta^{[new]})\ \right]^T. \tag{12}$$

Let $\mathbf{R}_c^{-1}$ be the left pseudo-inverse of the matrix $[\ \mathbf{c}_c\ \mathbf{c}_s\ ]$. Eqn. (12) can then be rewritten as:

$$\mathbf{R}_c^{-1}\left(\mathbf{c}^{[new]} - \mathbf{c}_0\right) = \left[\ \cos(\theta^{[new]})\ \ \sin(\theta^{[new]})\ \right]^T. \tag{13}$$

Let $[\ x_\alpha\ y_\alpha\ ] = \mathbf{R}_c^{-1}\left(\mathbf{c}^{[new]} - \mathbf{c}_0\right)$. Then the best estimate of the orientation is $\theta^{[new]} = \tan^{-1}(y_\alpha/x_\alpha)$. Note that the estimation of $\theta^{[new]}$ may not be accurate due to land mark annotation errors or regression learning errors.

2.3   Frontal View Synthesis

After the estimation of $\theta^{[new]}$, we can use the model to synthesize frontal face views. Let $\mathbf{c}_{res}$ be the residual vector which is not explained by the correlation model:

$$\mathbf{c}_{res} = \mathbf{c}^{[new]} - \left(\mathbf{c}_0 + \mathbf{c}_c \cos(\theta^{[new]}) + \mathbf{c}_s \sin(\theta^{[new]})\right) \tag{14}$$

To reconstruct at an alternate angle, $\theta^{[alt]}$, we can add the residual vector to the mean face for that angle:

$$\mathbf{c}^{[alt]} = \mathbf{c}_{res} + \left(\mathbf{c}_0 + \mathbf{c}_c \cos(\theta^{[alt]}) + \mathbf{c}_s \sin(\theta^{[alt]})\right) \tag{15}$$

To synthesize the frontal view face, $\theta^{[alt]}$ is set to zero. Eqn. (15) hence simplifies to:

$$\mathbf{c}^{[alt]} = \mathbf{c}_{res} + \mathbf{c}_0 + \mathbf{c}_c \tag{16}$$

Based on Eqns. (6) and (7), the shape and texture for the frontal view can then be calculated by:

$$\mathbf{f}^{[alt]} = \bar{\mathbf{f}} + \mathbf{Q}_s \mathbf{c}^{[alt]} \tag{17}$$
$$\mathbf{g}^{[alt]} = \bar{\mathbf{g}} + \mathbf{Q}_g \mathbf{c}^{[alt]} \tag{18}$$

Examples of synthesized faces are shown in Fig. 2. Each synthesized face can then be processed via the standard Principal Component Analysis (PCA) technique to produce features which are used for classification [4].

2.4   Direct Pose-Robust Features

The bracketed term in Eqn. (14) can be interpreted as the mean face for angle $\theta^{[new]}$. The difference between $\mathbf{c}^{[new]}$ (which represents the given face at the estimated angle $\theta^{[new]}$) and the bracketed term can hence be interpreted as removing the effect of the angle, resulting in a (theoretically) pose independent

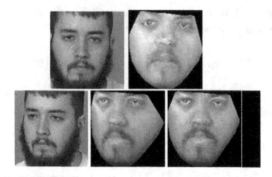

Fig. 2. Top row: frontal view and its AAM-based synthesized representation. Bottom row: non-frontal view as well as its AAM-based synthesized representation at its original angle and $\theta^{[alt]} = 0$ (i.e. synthesized frontal view).

representation. As such, $\mathbf{c}_{res}$ can be used directly for classification, providing considerable computational savings — the process of face synthesis and PCA feature extraction is omitted. Because of this, we're avoiding the introduction of imaging artefacts (due to synthesis) and information loss caused by PCA-based feature extraction. As such, the pose-robust features should represent the faces more accurately, leading to better discrimination performance. We shall refer to this approach as the *pose-robust features* method.

3   Bag-of-Features Approaches

In this section we describe two local feature based approaches, with both approaches sharing a block based feature extraction method summarised in Section 3.1. Both methods use Gaussian Mixture Models (GMMs) to model distributions of features, but they differ in how the GMMs are applied. In the first approach (*direct bag-of-features*, Section 3.2) the likelihood of a given face belonging to a specific person is calculated directly using that person's model. In the second approach (*histogram-based bag-of-features*, Section 3.3), a generic model (not specific to any person), representing "face words", is used to build histograms which are then compared for recognition purposes. In Section 3.4 we describe how both techniques can be sped up.

3.1   Feature Extraction and Illumination Normalisation

The face is described as a set of feature vectors, $X = \{\mathbf{x}_1, \mathbf{x}_2, \cdots, \mathbf{x}_N\}$, which are obtained by dividing the face into small, uniformly sized, overlapping blocks and decomposing each block[1] via the 2D DCT [21]. Typically the first 15 to 21 DCT coefficients are retained (as they contain the vast majority of discriminatory

---

[1] While in this work we used the 2D DCT for describing each block (or patch), it is possible to use other descriptors, for example SIFT [19] or Gabor wavelets [20].

information), except for the 0-th coefficient which is the most affected by illumination changes [6].

To achieve enhanced robustness to illumination variations, we have incorporated additional processing prior to 2D DCT decomposition. Assuming the illumination model for each pixel to be $\hat{p}_{(x,y)} = b + c \cdot p_{(x,y)}$, where $p_{(x,y)}$ is the "uncorrupted" pixel at location (x, y), b is a bias and c a multiplier (indicating the contrast), removing the 0-th DCT coefficient only corrects for the bias. To achieve robustness to contrast variations, the set of pixels within each block is normalised to have zero mean and unit variance.

3.2   Bag-of-Features with Direct Likelihood Evaluation

By assuming the vectors are independent and identically distributed (i.i.d.), the likelihood of X belonging to person i is found with:

$$P(X|\lambda^{[i]}) = \prod_{n=1}^{N} P(\mathbf{x}_n|\lambda^{[i]}) = \prod_{n=1}^{N} \sum_{g=1}^{G} w_g^{[i]} \mathcal{N}\left(\mathbf{x}_n|\mu_g^{[i]}, \mathbf{\Sigma}_g^{[i]}\right) \tag{19}$$

where $\mathcal{N}(\mathbf{x}|\mu, \mathbf{\Sigma}) = (2\pi)^{-\frac{d}{2}}|\mathbf{\Sigma}|^{-\frac{1}{2}} \exp\left\{-\frac{1}{2}(\mathbf{x} - \mu)^T \mathbf{\Sigma}^{-1}(\mathbf{x} - \mu)\right\}$ is a multi-variate Gaussian function [17], while $\lambda^{[i]} = \{w_g^{[i]}, \mu_g^{[i]}, \mathbf{\Sigma}_g^{[i]}\}_{g=1}^{G}$ is the set of parameters for person i. The convex combination of Gaussians, with mixing coefficients w_g, is typically referred to as a Gaussian Mixture Model (GMM). Its parameters are optimised via the Expectation Maximisation algorithm [17].

Due to the vectors being treated as i.i.d., information about the topology of the face is in effect lost. While at first this may seem counter-productive, the loss of topology in conjunction with overlapping blocks provides a useful characteristic: the precise location of face parts is no longer required. Previous research has suggested that the method is effective for face classification while being robust to imperfect face detection as well as a certain amount of in-plane and out-of-plane rotations [6,22,5].

The robustness to pose variations can be attributed to the explicit allowance for movement of face areas, when comparing face images of a particular person at various poses. Furthermore, significant changes of a particular face component (e.g. the nose) due to pose variations affect only the subset of face areas that cover this particular component.

3.3   Bag-of-Features with Histogram Matching

The technique presented in this section is an adaption of the "visual words" method used in image categorisation [10,11,12]. First, a training set of faces is used to build a generic model (not specific to any person). This generic model represents a dictionary of "face words" — the mean of each Gaussian can be thought of as a particular "face word". Once a set of feature vectors for a given face is obtained, a probabilistic histogram of the occurrences of the "face words" is built:

$$h_X = \frac{1}{N} \left[\sum_{i=1}^{N} \frac{w_1 p_1 (x_i)}{\sum_{g=1}^{G} w_g p_g (x_i)}, \sum_{i=1}^{N} \frac{w_2 p_2 (x_i)}{\sum_{g=1}^{G} w_g p_g (x_i)}, \cdots, \sum_{i=1}^{N} \frac{w_G p_G (x_i)}{\sum_{g=1}^{G} w_g p_g (x_i)} \right]$$

where w_g is the weight for Gaussian g and $p_g (x)$ is the probability of vector x according to Gaussian g.

Comparison of two faces is then accomplished by comparing their corresponding histograms. This can be done by the so-called χ^2 distance metric [23], or the simpler approach of summation of absolute differences [24]:

$$d(h_A, h_B) = \sum_{g=1}^{G} \left| h_A^{[g]} - h_B^{[g]} \right| \tag{20}$$

where $h_A^{[g]}$ is the g-th element of h_A. As preliminary experiments suggested that there was little difference in performance between the two metrics, we've elected to use the latter one.

Note that like in the direct method presented in the previous section, information about the topology of the face is lost. However, the direct method requires that the set of features from a given probe face is processed using all models of the persons in the gallery. As such, the amount of processing can quickly become prohibitive as the gallery grows[2]. In contrast, the histogram-based approach requires the set of features to be processed using only one model, potentially providing savings in terms of storage and computational effort.

Another advantage of the histogram-based approach is that the face similarity measurement, via Eqn. (20), is symmetric. This is not the case for the direct approach, as the representation of probe and gallery faces differs — a probe face is represented by a set of features, while a gallery face is represented by a model of features (the model, in this case, can be thought of as a compact approximation of the set of features from the gallery face).

3.4   Speedup Via Approximation

In practice the time taken by the 2D DCT feature extraction stage is negligible and hence the bulk of processing in the above two approaches is heavily concentrated in the evaluation of the exp() function. As such, a considerable speedup can be achieved through the use of a fast approximation of this function [25]. A brief overview follows: rather than using a lookup table, the approximation is accomplished by exploiting the structure and encoding of a standard (IEEE-754) floating-point representation. The given argument is transformed and injected as an integer into the first 32 bits of the 64 bit representation. Reading the resulting floating point number provides the approximation. Experiments in Section 4 indicate that the approximation does not affect recognition accuracy.

---

[2] For example, assuming each model has 32 Gaussians, going through a gallery of 1000 people would require evaluating 32000 Gaussians. Assuming 784 vectors are extracted from each face, the number of exp() evaluations is around 25 million.

4   Experiments

As mentioned in the introduction, we are currently in the process of creating a suitable dataset for face classification in CCTV conditions. As such, in these experiments we instead used subsets of the PIE dataset [14] (using faces at -22.5^o, 0° and $+22.5^o$) as well as the FERET dataset [13] (using faces at -25°, -15°, 0°, $+15^o$ and $+25^o$).

To train the AAM based approach, we first pooled face images from 40 FERET individuals at -15°, 0°, $+15^o$. Each face image was labelled with 58 points around the salient features (the eyes, mouth, nose, eyebrows and chin). The resulting model was used to automatically find the facial features (via an AAM search) for the remainder of the FERET subset. A new dataset was formed, consisting of 305 images from 61 persons with successful AAM search results. This dataset was used to train the correlation model and evaluate the performances of all presented algorithms. In a similar manner, a new dataset was formed from the PIE subset, consisting of images for 53 persons.

For the synthesis based approach, the last stage (PCA based feature extraction from synthesized images) produced 36 dimensional vectors. The PCA subsystem was trained as per [4]. The pose-robust features approach produced 43 dimensional vectors for each face. For both of the AAM-based techniques, Mahalanobis distance was used for classification [17].

For the bag-of-features approaches, in a similar manner to [5], we used face images with a size of 64×64 pixels, blocks with a size of 8×8 pixels and an overlap of 6 pixels. This resulted in 784 feature vectors per face. The number of retained DCT coefficients was set to 15 (resulting in 14 dimensional feature vectors, as the 0-th coefficient was discarded). The faces were normalised in size so that the distance between the eyes was 32 pixels and the eyes were in approximately the same positions in all images.

For the direct bag-of-features approach, the number of Gaussians per model was set to 32. Preliminary experiments indicated that accuracy for faces at around 25° peaked at 32 Gaussians, while using more than 32 Gaussians provided little gain in accuracy at the expense of longer processing times.

For the histogram-based bag-of-features method, the number of Gaussians for the generic model was set to 1024, following the same reasoning as above. The generic model (representing "face words") was trained on FERET *ba* data (frontal faces), excluding the 61 persons described earlier.

Tables 1 and 2 show the recognition rates on the FERET and PIE datasets, respectively. The AAM-derived pose-robust features approach obtains performance which is considerably better than the circuitous approach based on image synthesis. However, the two bag-of-features methods generally obtain better performance on both FERET and PIE, with the histogram-based approach obtaining the best overall performance. Averaging across the high pose angles ($\pm 25^o$ on FERET and $\pm 22.5^o$ on PIE), the histogram-based method achieves an average accuracy of 89%.

Table 3 shows the time taken to classify one probe face by the presented techniques (except for PCA). The experiments were performed on a Pentium-M

Table 1. Recognition performance on the FERET pose subset

Method	Pose			
	$-25°$	$-15°$	$+15°$	$+25°$
PCA	23.0	54.0	49.0	36.0
Synthesis + PCA	50.0	71.0	67.4	42.0
pose-robust features	**85.6**	88.2	88.1	66.8
Direct bag-of-features	83.6	93.4	**100.0**	72.1
Histogram bag-of-features	83.6	**100.0**	96.7	**73.7**

Table 2. Recognition performance on PIE

Method	Pose	
	$-22.5°$	$+22.5°$
PCA	13.0	8.0
Synthesis + PCA	60.0	56.0
pose-robust features	83.3	80.6
Direct bag-of-features	**100.0**	90.6
Histogram bag-of-features	**100.0**	**100.0**

machine running at 1.5 GHz. All methods were implemented in C++. The time taken is divided into two components: (1) one-off cost per probe face, and (2) comparison of one probe face with one gallery face.

The one-off cost is the time required to convert a given face into a format which will be used for matching. For the synthesis approach this involves an AAM search, image synthesis and PCA based feature extraction. For the pose-robust features method, in contrast, this effectively involves only an AAM search. For the bag-of-features approaches, the one-off cost is the 2D DCT feature extraction, with the histogram-based approach additionally requiring the generation of the "face words" histogram.

The second component, for the case of the direct bag-of-features method, involves calculating the likelihood using Eqn. (19), while for the histogram-based approach this involves just the sum of absolute differences between two histograms (Eqn. (20)). For the two AAM-based methods, the second component is the time taken to evaluate the Mahalanobis distance.

As expected, the pose-robust features approach has a speed advantage over the synthesis based approach, being about 50% faster. However, both of the bag-of-features methods are many times faster, in terms of the first component — the histogram-based approach is about 7 times faster than the pose-robust features method. While the one-off cost for the direct bag-of-features approach is much lower than for the histogram-based method, the time required for the second component (comparison of faces after conversion) is considerably higher, and might be a limiting factor when dealing with a large set of gallery faces (i.e. a scalability issue).

Table 3. Average time taken for two stages of processing: (1) conversion of a probe face from image to format used for matching (one-off cost per probe face), (2) comparison of one probe face with one gallery face, after conversion.

Method	Approximate time taken (sec)	
	One-off cost per probe face	Comparison of one probe face with one gallery face
Synthesis + PCA	1.493	< 0.001
pose-robust features	0.978	< 0.001
Direct bag-of-features	0.006	0.006
Histogram bag-of-features	0.141	< 0.001

When using the fast approximation of the exp() function, the time required by the histogram-based method (in the first component) is reduced by approximately 30% to 0.096, with no loss in recognition accuracy. This makes it over 10 times faster than the pose-robust features method and over 15 times faster than the synthesis based technique. In a similar vein, the time taken by the second component of the direct bag-of-features approach is also reduced by approximately 30%, with no loss in recognition accuracy.

5   Conclusions and Further Avenues

In this paper we have made several contributions. We proposed a novel approach to Active Appearance Model based face classification, where pose-robust features are obtained without the computationally expensive image synthesis step. Furthermore, we've adapted a *histogram-based bag-of-features* technique (previously employed in image categorisation) to face classification, and contrasted its properties to a previously proposed *direct bag-of-features* method. We have also shown that the two bag-of-features approaches, both based on Gaussian Mixture Models, can be considerably sped up without a loss in classification accuracy via an approximation of the exponential function.

In the context of pose mismatches between probe and gallery faces, experiments on the FERET and PIE databases suggest that while there is merit in the AAM based methods, the bag-of-features techniques generally attain better performance, with the histogram-based method achieving an average recognition rate of 89% for pose angles of around 25 degrees. Furthermore, the bag-of-features approaches are considerably faster, with the histogram-based method (using the fast exp() function) being over 10 times quicker than the pose-robust features method.

We note that apart from pose variations, imperfect face localisation [22] is also an important issue in a real life surveillance system. Imperfect localisations result in translations as well as scale changes, which adversely affect recognition performance. To that end, we are currently extending the histogram-based bag-of-features approach to also deal with scale variations.

Acknowledgements

This project is supported by a grant from the Australian Government Department of the Prime Minister and Cabinet. NICTA is funded by the Australian Government's *Backing Australia's Ability* initiative, in part through the Australian Research Council. The authors thank Abbas Bigdeli, Shaokang Chen and Erik Berglund for useful suggestions.

References

1. McCahill, M., Norris, C.: Urbaneye: CCTV in London. Centre for Criminology and Criminal Justice, University of Hull, UK (2002)
2. Phillips, P., Grother, P., Micheals, R., Blackburn, D., Tabassi, E., Bone, M.: Face recognition vendor test 2002. In: Proc. Analysis and Modeling of Faces and Gestures, p. 44 (2003)
3. Blanz, V., Grother, P., Phillips, P., Vetter, T.: Face recognition based on frontal views generated from non-frontal images. In: Proc. IEEE Int. Conf. Computer Vision and Pattern Recognition, vol. 2, pp. 454–461. IEEE Computer Society Press, Los Alamitos (2005)
4. Shan, T., Lovell, B., Chen, S.: Face recognition robust to head pose from one sample image. In: Proc. 18th Int. Conf. Pattern Recognition (ICPR), vol. 1, pp. 515–518 (2006)
5. Sanderson, C., Bengio, S., Gao, Y.: On transforming statistical models for non-frontal face verification. Pattern Recognition 39, 288–302 (2006)
6. Cardinaux, F., Sanderson, C., Bengio, S.: User authentication via adapted statistical models of face images. IEEE Trans. Signal Processing 54, 361–373 (2006)
7. Lucey, S., Chen, T.: Learning patch dependencies for improved pose mismatched face verification. In: IEEE Conf. Computer Vision and Pattern Recognition, vol. 1, pp. 909–915. IEEE Computer Society Press, Los Alamitos (2006)
8. Wiskott, L., Fellous, J., Kuiger, N., Malsburg, C.V.: Face recognition by elastic bunch graph matching. IEEE Trans. Pattern Analysis and Machine Intelligence 19, 775–779 (1997)
9. Bowyer, K., Chang, K., Flynn, P.: A survey of approaches and challenges in 3D and multi-modal 3D+2D face recognition. Computer Vision and Image Understanding 101, 1–15 (2006)
10. Csurka, G., Dance, C., Fan, L., Willamowski, J., Bray, C.: Visual cetegorization with bags of keypoints. In: Workshop on Statistical Learning in Computer Vision (co-located with ECCV 2004) (2004)
11. Sivic, J., Zisserman, A.: Video google: A text retrieval approach to object matching in videos. In: Proc. 9th International Conference on Computer Vision (ICCV), vol. 2, pp. 1470–1477 (2003)
12. Nowak, E., Jurie, F., Triggs, B.: Sampling strategies for bag-of-features image classification. In: Leonardis, A., Bischof, H., Pinz, A. (eds.) ECCV 2006. LNCS, vol. 3954, pp. 490–503. Springer, Heidelberg (2006)
13. Phillips, P., Moon, H., Rizvi, S., Rauss, P.: The FERET evaluation methodology for face-recognition algorithms. IEEE Trans. Pattern Analysis and Machine Intelligence 22, 1090–1104 (2000)
14. Sim, T., Baker, S., Bsat, M.: The CMU pose, illumination, and expression database. IEEE. Trans. Pattern Analysis and Machine Intelligence 25, 1615–1618 (2003)

15. Cootes, T., Taylor, C.: Active shape models - 'smart snakes'. In: Proc. British Machine Vision Conference, pp. 267–275 (1992)
16. Cootes, T., Edwards, G., Taylor, C.: Active appearance models. IEEE Trans. Pattern Analysis and Machine Intelligence 23, 681–685 (2001)
17. Duda, R., Hart, P., Stork, D.: Pattern Classification, 2nd edn. Wiley, Chichester (2001)
18. Cootes, T., Walker, K., Taylor, C.: View-based active appearance models. In: Proc. 4th IEEE International Conference on Automatic Face and Gesture Recognition, pp. 227–232. IEEE Computer Society Press, Los Alamitos (2000)
19. Lowe, D.G.: Distinctive image features from scale-invariant keypoints. International Journal of Computer Vision 60, 91–110 (2004)
20. Lee, T.S.: Image representation using 2D Gabor wavelets. IEEE Trans. Pattern Analysis and Machine Intelligence 18, 959–971 (1996)
21. Gonzales, R., Woods, R.: Digital Image Processing. Addison-Wesley, Reading (1992)
22. Rodriguez, Y., Cardinaux, F., Bengio, S., Mariethoz, J.: Measuring the performance of face localization systems. Image and Vision Computing 24, 882–893 (2006)
23. Wallraven, C., Caputo, B., Graf, A.: Recognition with local features: the kernel recipe. In: Proc. 9th International Conference on Computer Vision (ICCV), vol. 1, pp. 257–264 (2003)
24. Kadir, T., Brady, M.: Saliency, scale and image description. International Journal of Computer Vision 45, 83–105 (2001)
25. Schraudolph, N.: A fast, compact approximation of the exponential function. Neural Computation 11, 853–862 (1999)

Robust Face Recognition Strategies Using Feed-Forward Architectures and Parts

Hung Lai, Fayin Li, and Harry Wechsler

Department of Computer Science, George Mason University
Fairfax, VA 22030, USA
hlai@gmu.edu,fayin.li@gmail.com,wechsler@cs.gmu.edu

Abstract. This paper describes new feed-forward architectural and configural/holistic strategies for robust face recognition. This includes adaptive and robust correlation filters that lock on both appearance and location, and recognition-by-parts using boosting over strangeness driven weak learners. The utility of the proposed architectural strategies, shown with respect to different databases, includes occlusion, disguise, and temporal changes. The results obtained confirm and complement key findings on the ways people recognize each other, among them that the facial features are processed holistically and that the eyebrows are among the most important features for recognition.

Keywords: adaptive and robust correlation filters (ARCF), biometrics, boosting, configural, disguise, occlusion, face recognition, feed-forward, holistic, recognition-by-parts, strangeness, transduction, weak learners.

1 Introduction

One of the grand challenges for computational intelligence is to understand how people process and recognize each other's face and to develop reliable face recognition systems. The face recognition challenge underlies *biometrics*, the science of authenticating people by measuring their physical or external appearance (and/or their behavioral or internal traits). There has recently been a flurry of activity whereby insights about how the primates carry out recognition activities are projected on the very design of novel biometric architectures for face recognition with the implicit expectation for robustness to image degradations. Representative examples of such insights include the feed-forward ventral visual architecture to learn a generic dictionary of shape-components for task-specific categorization [23,24], fMRI studies on holistic and configural processing [28,20], and the psychophysical key findings reported by Sinha et al. [25] on the ways people recognize each other and their implications for face recognition. This paper describes new computational blocks that expand the scope for the feed-forward ventral architectures to include configural processing characteristic of decision-making using recognition-by-parts that account for denial and deception. The computation involved is driven by adaptive and robust correlation filters (ARCF) or boosting and strangeness as described later. The results obtained confirm several results reported by Sinha et al. [25], among them that of the different facial

S.K. Zhou et al. (Eds.): AMFG 2007, LNCS 4778, pp. 290–304, 2007.

features, eyebrows are among the most important for recognition. In addition, and most important the new strategies and corresponding computational blocks proposed are shown to display robustness to occlusion and disguise.

2   Feed-Forward Architectures

Serre et al. [24] have recently proposed a quantitative model that "accounts for the circuits and computations of the feed-forward path of the ventral stream of visual cortex". This model is consistent with a general theory of visual processing that extends the hierarchical model of Hubel & Wiesel from primary to extra-striate visual areas. The proposed feed-forward architecture assumes that recurrent paths characteristic of back-projections are inactive, and that learning proceeds in an unsupervised fashion leading to a "generic dictionary of shape-components from V2 to IT, which provides an invariant representation to task-specific categorization circuits in higher brain areas." The hierarchical and invariant aspect draws from the Neocognitron [8], while the generic dictionary, inspired by the universal basis driven by the statistics of natural scenes [21], is the result of adaptation.

The feed-forward aspect is a rather restricted version of the latency and evidence accumulation concepts advanced by Thorpe et al. [26] and reiterated by the result 18 reported by Sinha et al. [25]. Evidence accumulation involves a steady progression in the way the visual information is processed and analyzed. Asynchronous spike propagation and rank order coding were proposed to explain the speed with which "neurons in the monkey temporal lobe can respond selectively to the presence of a face" [22]. The most strongly activated neurons or processing units fire first, greater impact is assigned to the spikes with shortest latency to stimulus onset, and the order and relative strength is the (temporal) code used for recognition. Such processing squares well with sparse coding driven by suspicious coincidences [2] and has been shown to "generalize well to novel views of the same face and to be remarkably resistant to image noise and reduction in contrast" [5].

The feed-forward strategy proposed is limited to the ventral ("what") part and omits the complementary dorsal ("where") cortical path that encodes for spatial information. To make configural/holistic processing suitable for face recognition coarse coding of shape fragments ("parts") with retinotopy ("geometry") is required. The adaptive and robust correlation filters proposed in Sect. 4 handle both the *what* and *where* components. The feed-forward architecture also leaves out the decision-making aspect characteristic of classification and recognition, which is characteristic of higher-brain areas involved in linking perception, memory, and action. Ad-hoc implementations, such as support vector machines (SVM), are used for classification by the feed-forward architectures recently proposed [24]. Our recognition scheme using boosting and strangeness driven weak learners (see Sect. 6) is biologically motivated from a functional viewpoint but no specific biological hardware is proposed here for its realization.

3   Configural and Holistic Processing

Yovel and Kanwisher [28] have shown, using fMRI studies of the Fusiform Face Area(FFA), that face perception is domain rather than process specific. "Canonical or configural configurations of face parts were found to trigger greater response vs. randomly rearranged parts within the face outline in the amygdala, superior temporal sulcus (STS), and FFA" [9]. Face processing, however, is more than just configural. Face perception "engages a domain - specific system for processing both configural and part-based information about faces" [28]. This accommodates viewpoint or pose changes, occlusion and/or disguise, and temporal changes.

What about encoding for face recognition? "For stimuli such as faces, which are likely to be encountered by every member of the species, configural representations or golden ratio templates may be most effective because the basic stimulus configuration is invariant across the environments in which individuals may live. Thus the predictability of species-specific stimuli may allow for the creation through evolution of complex pattern recognition systems. These systems are tuned at birth but remain plastic through development" [11]. Face recognition involves both holistic and configural processing. "Holistic processing is characterized by the integration of facial information into a gestalt, whereas configural processing usually describe sensitivity to the precise spatial layout of the facial features" [6]. Evidence for the holistic face space comes from "the detrimental effects of manipulations that disrupt the holistic structure of the face but leave individual features intact" [16]. Moscovitch et al. [18] have argued that only a vertical half (face) is necessary to activate configural face processing. McKone et al. [16] have shown that holistic processing can operate in isolation from (local) feature-based identification. Heisele et al. [10] have recently proposed a component-based ("recognition-by-parts") framework for face detection and identification. They search for components that are similar across classes of objects, vary less under pose changes than the image pattern of the whole object, and handle partial occlusion. The framework proposed requires that the locations of the components relative to each other are not fixed. The best performance reported was achieved with a system in which the detection of components was confined to small regions around the expected positions of the components. Our realization for recognition-by-parts described in Sect. 6 relaxes the latter requirement using the golden ratio template.

4   Adaptive and Robust Correlation Filters (ARCF)

Configural and holistic face recognition can benefit from the use of the whole face and from an encoding where the face parts record both appearance and location. We describe here a novel face recognition-by-parts approach using Adaptive and Robust Correlation Filters (ARCF) whose filter banks are optimized match (correlation) filters for the above component-based and holistic mix of face components. ARCF expand on Minimum Average Correlation Energy(MACE) filters and adaptive beam-forming from radar/sonar and are similar to Tikhonov regularization. The cluster and strength of the ARCF correlation peaks indicate the confidence of the face authentication made, if any. This ability thus expands the scope of the feed-forward architectures discussed earlier. The correlation scores and their relative alignment are combined using LDA for recognition purposes (but could be as easily be combined using boosting using strangeness as described in Sect. 6). The adaptive aspect of ARCF comes from its derivation using both training and test data, while their robust aspect comes from being optimized to decrease their sensitivity to distortion.

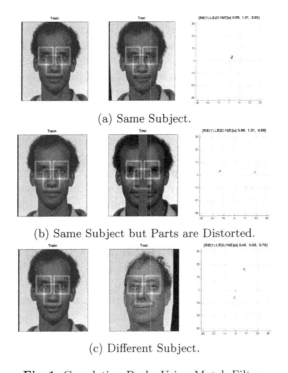

(a) Same Subject.

(b) Same Subject but Parts are Distorted.

(c) Different Subject.

Fig. 1. Correlation Peaks Using Match Filters

Given the output of correlation filters (CF) the strength of the correlation peak indicates how well the training and test images match, while the location of the peaks indicates the relative shift between the training and test images. Recognition-by-parts involves matching the corresponding parts and their relative location. One only needs to maintain the relative locations of the parts during training and testing to check for their alignment. This is accomplished by using masks that expose only the parts and zero out the rest of the face (or alternatively using golden ratio templates as described in Sect. 6). As an example, three masks are used to extract out the face parts corresponding to the right eye(RE), left eye(LE), and nose(N), with the area outside the mask zeroed out. The masks are used to design three match filters (MF) that are then used for recognition-by-parts. In the first example, the test image is from the same subject(see Fig. 1(a)). The matching scores (correlation peaks) for the face components are high and the peak locations align. The next example (see Fig. 1(b)) illustrates the case of parts that match but miss proper alignment for the same subject. The test image has been artificially cut at the middle and the nose is split. MF shows good matching for the eye components, but poor matching for the corresponding nose component. The peak locations do not align, and authentication thus fails. The last example illustrates the case for different subjects(see Fig. 1(c)). The peaks from MF are weak and misaligned, and authentication fails.

Different correlation filters are available [12] and their performance with respect to training and noise vary. MF is optimum against white noise but it can train from only one exemplar s. Synthetic Discriminant Functions(SDF) train from multiple exemplars and are robust only to white noise. Robustness to general non-white noise leads to the Minimum Variance Synthetic Discriminant Filter(MVSDF). Similar to SDF and MF, the MVSDF filters are affected from the presence of side-lobes, which are secondary peaks away from the true correlation peak, even when training and testing with the same image. This problem is addressed using the Minimum Average Correlation Energy(MACE) filter which minimizes the correlation side-lobes. It is, however, extremely sensitive to noise. To improve on the MACE filter robustness to noise and distortion, the Optimal Trade-off Filter (OTF) filter was proposed.

The above correlation filters do not take advantage of the information provided by the test data. Similar to beam-forming [4], the filter should be designed to adapt and automatically tune out the actual noise/distortion observed in test data without making any arbitrary assumptions about the structure of the noise. The result is an adaptive correlation filter whose output correlation surface has an optimally low average side-lobe level. It, however, is still sensitive to noise/distortion. To make the correlation peak robust, we introduce an adjustable loading parameter that can be derived using an approach motivated by beam-forming or Tikhonov regularization. This leads to a robust filter based on the magnitude of the match filter weight. The adaptive (A) and robust (R) components for the new adaptive and robust correlation filter (ARCF) proposed here are explained below.

Adaptiveness. If the noise/distortion in the test data can be measured, it can be minimized directly. This approach has been used by both MVSDF and OTF when Q_n, the noise power spectrum or covariance, is known. When Q_n is unknown, it is assumed to be white. We take a different approach, motivated by adaptive beam-forming, to learn the noise/distortion in the test data, and automatically adjust the correlation filter to minimize it. This is accomplished by minimizing the output correlation energy due to test data while subject to a unit response to training data.

$$\text{Minimize } h^H D_x h \tag{1}$$

$$\text{Subject to } S^H h = d \text{ where } S = [s_1, \cdots, s_M] \text{ and } d = 1_M$$

where D_x is a diagonal matrix containing the power spectrum of test exemplar. The Adaptive Correlation Filter (ACF) solution, $h = D_x^{-1}S(S^H D_x^{-1}S)^{-1}d$, is similar to the MACE filter except that D_s is now replaced by D_x. The use of test data D_x, in addition to training data S, is different from previous approaches, and proves beneficial. The filter tunes itself to noise present in the test data. The output correlation surface has an optimally low side-lobe level, irrespective of the actual structure of the noise. This is different from MACE, which lacks an optimization criterion to reject the noise from test data. It is also different from MVSDF and OTF where the noise information Q_n must be known or has to be assumed to be white.

Robustness. A robust CF should produce a stable correlation peak that changes very little even when there is a large change in the strength of the distortion/noise. To minimize the sensitivity of the correlation peak to noise/distortion, we minimize the rate of change of the squared correlation peak with respect to the strength of the noise/distortion. Let the squared correlation peak be $p = E\|h^H x\|^2$.

$$
\begin{aligned}
p &= E\{h^H xx^H h\} = E\{h^H(s+n)(s+n)^H h\} \\
&= E\{h^H(ss^H + sn^H + ns^H + nn^H)h\} = h^H ss^H h + h^H E\{sn^H + ns^H + nn^H\}h \\
&= h^H ss^H h + h^H Qh = h^H ss^H h + \xi h^H Nh
\end{aligned}
\tag{2}
$$

where the covariance N is normalized so that the average of the diagonal elements is 1, and ξ is the strength parameter. We seek to minimize $dp/d\xi = h^H Nh$. The ARCF formulation becomes

$$
\text{Minimize the output correlation energy} \quad h^H D_x h \tag{3}
$$
$$
\text{Subject to unit response to training signal} \quad S^H h = d
$$
$$
\text{Subject to sensitivity constraint} \quad h^H Ih \leq \alpha
$$

The solution is $h = (D_x + \varepsilon I)^{-1}S[S^H(D_x + \varepsilon I)^{-1}S]^{-1}d$ with ε chosen to satisfy the constraint $h^H Ih \leq \alpha$. The solution for $\varepsilon = 0$ is $h = D_x^{-1}S[S^H D_x^{-1}S]^{-1}d$. It has the same form as the MACE filter, which is sensitive to noise/distortion. The solution $h = S[S^H S]^{-1}d$ is found when $\varepsilon = \infty$. This is the same SDF filter and the correlation peak has maximum robustness to white noise. The magnitude of the SDF weight is the smallest among the adaptive correlation filters with white noise robustness. ε is chosen to satisfy the constraint $h^H h \leq k\|h_{SDF}\|^2$ where $k \geq 1$.

Fig. 2(a) shows how different filters compare in matching the left eye part for both appearance and location. One can see that ARCF outscores MF, MACE, and OTF in terms of discriminating between the true peak corresponding to the left eye and the false peak caused by the right eye. In addition, one notes that ARCF displays the lowest average side-lobe, which indicates its robustness to noise. The advantage of ARCF over the competing CFs becomes even more pronounced when noise is added. The false peak for OTF shows now as the strongest (see Fig. 2(b)). The ARCF architecture for recognition-by-parts is shown in Fig. 3. Face parts for an enrolled subject and their counterparts from

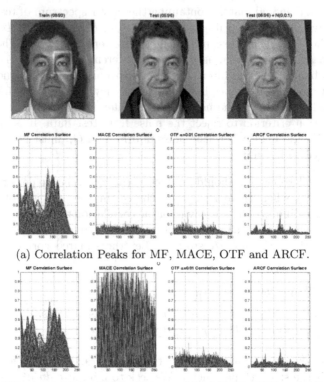

(a) Correlation Peaks for MF, MACE, OTF and ARCF.

(b) Effect of Additive White Noise on MF, MACE, OTF and ARCF.

Fig. 2. Matching the Left Eye using Correlation Filters

test data claiming the same identity are combined on a part-by-part basis to build corresponding ARCF filters. The outputs from ARCF are combined using LDA to learn the optimal separation direction and are then projected on the direction axis to find the overall score. ROC at FAR = 1% using the overall scores from both authentic claims and impostors determines the optimal a-priori decision thresholds for future authentication claims.

5   Transduction

Transductive inference / transduction is different from inductive inference. It is a type of local inference ("estimation") that moves from particular(s) to particular(s). One directly estimates the values of the function (only) at the points of interest from the training data [29]. Transduction incorporates unlabeled data, characteristic of test samples, in the decision-making process responsible for their labeling. The roles of what is "known" and "unknown" are complementary. Transduction seeks to find, from all possible authentications for unknown faces, the one that is most probable to the gallery of known faces. Transduction

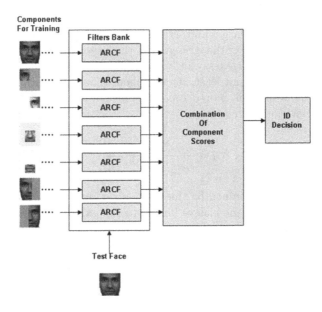

Fig. 3. ARCF Recognition-by-Parts Architecture

"works because the test set provides a nontrivial factorization of the [discrimination] function class" [3]. One key concept behind transduction is the symmetrization lemma [29]. The simplest mathematical realization for transductive inference is the method of k-nearest neighbors. Similar and complementary to transduction is semi-supervised learning (SSL) [3].

Face recognition requires comparing face images according to the way they are different from each other and ranking them accordingly. Scoring and ranking is done using the strangeness and p-values. Let $\sharp(z)$ be the length of the binary string z and $K(z)$ be its Kolmogorov complexity. The randomness deficiency $D(z)$ for string z [13,27] is $D(z) = \sharp(z) - K(z)$. The larger the randomness deficiency is, the more regular and more probable the string z is [27]. Transduction chooses from all the possible labeling for test data the one that yields the largest randomness deficiency. Randomness deficiency is, however, not computable [13]. One has to approximate it instead using a slightly modified Martin-Löf test for randomness. The values taken by such randomness tests are referred to as p-values with respect to some strangeness measure. The strangeness α_i measures the uncertainty for a data point or face (part) with respect to its true or putative (assumed) identity label and the labels for all the other face patterns. It is the ratio of the sum of the k nearest distances d from the same class y divided by the sum of the k nearest distances from all the other classes $(\neg y)$.

$$\alpha_i = \frac{\sum_{j=1}^{k} d_{ij}^y}{\sum_{j=1}^{k} d_{ij}^{\neg y}}. \tag{4}$$

The strangeness of an exemplar increases when the distances from the exemplars of the same class become larger and/or when the distances from the other classes become smaller. The smaller the strangeness, the larger its randomness deficiency is. Alternatively the strangeness can be defined as Eq. 5, in a fashion similar to Cohort models. Last but not least, the strangeness and classification margin are related via a monotonically non-decreasing function where a small strangeness amounts to a large margin.

$$\alpha_i = \frac{\sum_{j=1}^{k} d_{ij}^{y}}{min_{c \neq y} \sum_{j=1}^{k} d_{ij}^{c}} \tag{5}$$

The p-values are determined by the relative rankings of putative authentications against each one of the classes known to the gallery using the strangeness measure. The standard p-value construction shown below, where l is the cardinality of the training set T, constitutes a valid randomness (deficiency) test approximation [17] for some transductive (putative label y) hypothesis.

$$p_y(e) = \frac{\sharp\{i : \alpha_i \geq \alpha_{new}^{y}\}}{l+1} \tag{6}$$

The interpretation for p-values is similar to statistical testing of likelihood ratios used to support or discredit the null hypothesis. When the null hypothesis is rejected for each identity class known, one declares that the test image lacks mates in the gallery and the identity query is answered with "none of the above." Such a rejection is characteristic of open set recognition [14].

6   Boosting Using Strangeness

The face representation used for recognition-by-parts should span a multi - resolution grid that captures partial information at different scales in order to accommodate different surveillance scenarios including human identification from distance (HID). The golden ratio template [1] is used as the geometrical / topological framework where candidates for local face patches are found (see Fig. 4). The template provides a rough spatial map for the facial features ("landmarks").

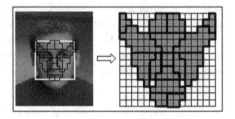

Fig. 4. Golden Ratio Face Template

Given the positions of eyes, the center o_i and minimal width/height r_i of each region in the face image, determined by their corresponding size in the golden ratio template, become the center of the feature ("patch") and its initial scale. In order to encode the local and global information of the face, multiple face components are extracted at different scale at each position. The k-th component of region i has the scale $r_{ik} = s^{k-1}r_i$ with $s = \sqrt{2}$. A Gaussian pyramid [15] is built by blurring the original image and the same number of patches are extracted at each level of the pyramid to encode $1st$ order statistics. Given that the golden ratio template consists of 16 regions, and given the scale level N_s and the blurring level N_b, there are $16N_sN_b$ first order local patches extracted from each face image. Second order local patches are also extracted. The motivation is related to the importance of suspicious coincidence [2], when "two candidate feature A and B should be encoded together if the join appearance probability $P(A, B)$ is much greater than $P(A)P(B)$". The $2nd$ order patches are extracted from two local regions that neighbor each other in the golden ratio template. This accommodates local configural constraints. The size of each patch is represented by an ellipse with center x and parameters a and b. Given two neighborhood regions i and j with scales r_{ik}, r_{jk} and centers x_i and x_j, the $2nd$ order local patch is extracted at center $x = (x_i + x_j)/2$, $a = (\|x_i - x_j\| + (r_{ik} + r_{jk}))/2$ and $b = max(r_{ik}, r_{jk})$. $27N_sN_b$ second order local patches are thus extracted. Fig. 5 shows the first and second order local patches at their initial scale, respectively.

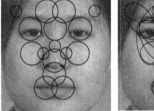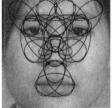

Fig. 5. First and Second Order Patches

Next one computes a descriptor for each local patch that is highly distinctive yet is as invariant as possible to image variability. The SIFT descriptor [15] satisfies such requirements and is used to represent each local region. This yields a 128 dimensional feature vector which is normalized to unit length in order to reduce the sensitivity to image contrast and brightness changes during the testing stage. Each face is represented by $43N_sN_b$ 1st and 2nd order patches with SIFT descriptor. Alternatively one could use Gabor descriptors.

The parts are clusters of local patches and are modeled by an exemplar-based representation. The corresponding model free and non-parametric weak learners ("parts") compete to build up strong classifiers. The relative (confidence) weighting and order (ranking) for the weak learners is determined from their strangeness. Patch selection corresponds to feature selection, which is implemented using iterative backward elimination and cross-validation. Features characterized by high strangeness are iteratively discarded. Variable selection is complementary to feature selection and seeks the most discriminative SIFT components. The patches selected are aggregated into parts using their relative locations across the golden ratio template and K-means clustering. The strangeness based multi-class weak learner selected at each iteration in boosting [7] corresponds to the most discriminative part. The confidence and thresholds required for the strangeness based weak learners are found using cross-validation. The same approach works for weakly supervised learning when the object or face of interest shares the image space with clutter, and segmentation is not required. The explanation comes from the fact that the parts are found as clusters of non-accidental and repeating structures. The parts lock on "semantic" structures rather than clutter.

The strangeness driven weak learners are trained and validated in a fashion similar to open set recognition [14]. Each class is represented by parts in terms of patches and their features. The coefficients and thresholds for the weak learners, including the thresholds needed for rejection, are learned using validation images. The best feature correspondence for each part is sought between a validation and a training face image over the features defining that part. This makes the recognition robust because it allows for different patches or features to score for parts from faces carrying a similar ID in a fashion similar to Hough transforms and accumulator arrays. The strangeness of the best feature found is computed for each validation image under all its putative class labels c $(c = 1, \cdots, C)$. Assuming M validation images from each class, one derives M "positive" strangeness values for each class c, and $M(C-1)$ "negative" strangeness values corresponding to the case when the putative label of the validation and training image are the same or not, respectively. The strangeness values are ranked for all the parts available, and the best weak learner h_i is the one that maximizes the recognition rate over the whole set of validation images V for some part i and threshold θ_i. Upon completion, boosting yields the strong classifier $H(x)$, which is a collection of discriminative parts filling the role of weak learners. For non-frontal faces and/or partly occluded faces, a region of interest (ROI) that looks like a face needs to be located first. Boosting works as before while searching for parts within the ROI. Patches are found and clustered as parts, their correspondence to known parts from enrolled faces is established, and strong classifiers indexed by pose are activated.

7   Experimental Results

We report here on the feasibility of the ARCF architecture for face recognition subject to occlusion, disguise, varying illumination, and temporal changes. The three reported similarity scores are F (Full Face), H (best of Half-Faces), and P (combination of nose, mouth, and best of eyes). The decision thresholds learned a-priori from one data base, e.g., FERET, carry over successfully to another data base, e.g., AR. The face images used for training come from *http://makeoversolutions.com*, while the test images are obtained from the

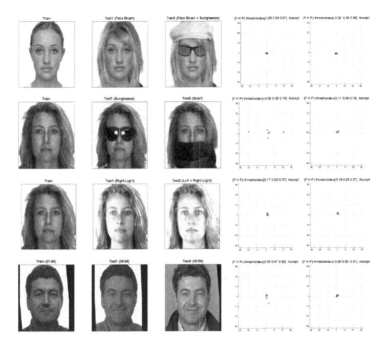

Fig. 6. Experimental Results of ARCF architecture

training ones by applying face blush and sunglasses (see Fig. 6(a)). Authentication succeeds to uncover the identity behind the disguise.

Fig. 6(b) shows the strong correlation peaks for the parts not occluded are aligned. Authentication succeeds to uncover the identity behind the occlusion. The weak correlation peaks for the full face and eyes and mouth cannot prevent ARCF from locking on the correct identification in both cases while holistic components do not help with recognition for occluded faces. The correlation peaks in Fig. 6(c) are strong and all aligned, and authentication suacceeds although illumination varies. Fig. 6(d) shows the correlation peaks of test images acquires two years later compared to training images. The peaks are strong and aligned. Authentication succeeds.

Biometric experiments using the interplay between strangeness and boosting were performed on frontal faces collected at the University of Notre Dame during 2002-2003, and now part of the FRGC face image database [19]. The face images were acquired under different and sometimes uncontrolled lighting conditions and/or with different facial expressions. We sampled 200 subjects from the data base; for each one there are 48 images of which 16 were acquired in an uncontrolled environment. The local patches are extracted and the corresponding SIFT descriptors are computed using $N_s = 5$ and $N_b = 4$. Each face is represented by $P = 43N_s = 215$ parts with $N_b + 1 = 5$ feature instances. For each subject, we randomly select 12 images as training set, another 12 images as the validation set and the remaining 24 images as testing set. Euclidian distance is

Fig. 7. Examples of the Best Feature for Faces after Boosting Learning

used to compute the strangeness. The top-1 rank identification rates using 1st order patches and strangeness based boosting were 97.5% and 97.9% without and with symmetry, respectively. The corresponding rates using both 1st and 2nd order patches were 98.1% and 98.9%, respectively. The results obtained confirm several results reported by Sinha et al. [25], among them Result 5 that of the different facial features, eyebrows were indeed found most important for recognition using boosting and strangeness (see Fig. 7).

8   Conclusions

This paper describes new feed-forward architectural and configural/holistic strategies for robust face recognition. This includes adaptive and robust correlation filters (ARCF) that lock on both appearance and location, and recognition-by-parts using boosting over strangeness driven weak learners. The feasibility and utility of the proposed architectural strategies, shown with respect to different data bases includes occlusion, disguise, varying illumination, and temporal changes. The results obtained also confirm and complement several results on the ways people recognize each other [25]. One near-term venue that holds promise for future research expands feed-forward (and hierarchical) architectures towards higher-brain areas using the ARCF correlation filters as intermediate representational building blocks that address the dorsal ("where") cortical path and boosting mediated by ARCF strangeness. The other long-term venue is to take advantage of the temporal dimension as discussed next.

Objects, in general, and faces, in particular, are known to be processed sequentially over time [5]. The human faces should be processed across discrete and local units of space and time and generate spatiotemporal patches. Rather than crawling around to merely score and rank human faces, the progressive recognition-by-parts scheme, similar to Really Simple Syndication (RSS), could "ping" discrete parts and/or events to competing face recognition "browsers" to share, update, and plan on how to proceed with their biometric mission. The above spatiotemporal and progressive scheme resonates well with recent fMRI results showing that "category-specific activity is cueing the memory system to retrieve studied items" [20]. Recalling a particular event involves reactivating the constellation of representations that was active during that event, a phenomenon that Tulving has referred to as "mental time travel." This suggests that constellations are much more than merely facial parts assembled together, and that recalling an event (or face) "involves a process of contextual reinstatement." In particular when specific details ("parts") are recalled, "these details can be used to further refine the retrieval cue, which leads to recall of additional details, and so on." The temporal dimension glues the parts for solving the whodunit even when the bits ("patches") and pieces ("parts") are not seen in the right order. View generalization can also be mediated by temporal association despite the fact that image-level differences between two views of the same face are much larger than those between two different faces viewed at the same angle.

References

1. Anderson, K., McOwan, P.: Robust real-time face tracker for cluttered environments. Computer Vision and Image Understanding 95, 184–200 (2004)
2. Barlow, H.B.: Unsupervised learning. Neural Computation 1, 295–311 (1989)
3. Chapelle, O., Scholkopf, B., Zien, A.: Semi-Supervised Learning. MIT Press, Cambridge (2006)
4. Cox, H., Zeskind, R.M., Owen, M.M.: Robust Adaptive Beam-forming. IEEE Trans. on ASSP 35(10) (1987)
5. Delorme, A., Thorpe, S.: Face Identification Using One Spike per Neuron: Resistance to Image Degradation. Neural Networks 14, 795–803 (2001)
6. Duchaine, B., Nakayama, K.: Dissociations of Face and Object Recognition in Developmental Prosopagnosia. J. of Cognitive Neurosciences 17(2), 1–13 (2005)
7. Freund, Y., Schapire, R.: A decision-theoretic generalization of on - line learning and an application to boosting. Journal of Computer and System Science 55(1), 119–139 (1997)
8. Fukushima, K.: Neocognitron: A Self-Organizing Neural Network Model for a Mechanism of Pattern Recognition Unaffected by Shift in Position. Biological Cybernetics 36(4), 193–202 (1980)
9. Golarai, G., Eberhardt, D.L., Grill-Spector, K., Gabrieli, G.D.D.: Representation of Parts and Canonical Face Configuration in the Amygdala, Superior Temporal Sulcus (STS) and the Fusiform "Face Area"(FFA). Vision 4(8), 131a (2004)
10. Heisele, B., Serre, T., Poggio, T.: A Component-Based Framework for Face Detection and Identification. Int. J. of Comp. Vision 74(2), 167–181 (2007)
11. Kanwisher, N., Moscovitch, M.: The Cognitive Neuroscience of Face Processing: An Introduction. J. of Cognitive Neuropsychology 17(1-3), 1–11 (2000)
12. Kumar, B.V.K., et al.: Correlation Pattern Recognition for Face Recognition. Proc. IEEE 94(11), 1963–1976 (2006)
13. Li, M., Vitanyi, P.: An Introduction to Kolmogorov Complexity and Its Applications, 2nd edn. Springer, Heidelberg (1997)
14. Li, F., Wechsler, H.: Open Set Face Recognition Using Transduction. IEEE Trans. on PAMI 27(11), 1686–1697 (2005)
15. Lowe, D.G.: Distinctive image features from scale - invariant key points. Int. Journal of Computer Vision 60(2), 91–110 (2004)

16. McKone, E., Martini, P., Nakayama, K.: Categorical Perception of Face Identity in Noise Isolates Configural Processing. Journal of Experimental Psychology: Human Perception and Performance 27(3), 573–599 (2001)
17. Melluish, T., Saunders, C., Gammerman, A., Vovk, V.: The Typicalness Framework: A Comparison with the Bayesian Approach, TR-CS, Royal Holloway College, Univ. of London (2001)
18. Moscovitch, M., Winocur, G., Behrmann, M.: What is Special About Face Recognition? Journal of Cognitive Neuroscience 9, 555–604 (1997)
19. Phillips, P.J., Flynn, P.J., Scruggs, T., Bowyer, K.W., Chang, J., Hoffman, K., Marques, J., Min, J., Worek, W.: Overview of the face recognition grand challenge. In: Computer Vision and Pattern Recognition (CVPR), New York (2005)
20. Polyn, S., et al.: Category-Specific Cortical Activity Precedes Retrieval During Memory Search. Science 310, 1963–1966 (2005)
21. Ruderman, D.L.: The Statistics of Natural Images. Network: Computation in Neural Systems 5, 517–548 (1994)
22. Rullen, R.V., Gautrais, J., Delorme, A., Thorpe, S.: Face Processing Using One Spike per Neuron. BioSystems 48, 229–239 (1998)
23. Serre, T., et al.: Robust Object Recognition with Cortex-Like Mechanisms. IEEE Trans. on Pattern Analysis and Machine Intelligence 29(3), 411–425 (2007)
24. Serre, T., et al.: A Feed-Forward Architecture Accounts for Rapid Categorization. Proc. National Academy of Sciences (PNAS) 104(15), 6424–6429 (2007)
25. Sinha, P., et al.: Face Recognition by Humans: Nineteen Results All Computer Vision Researchers Should Know About. Proceedings of the IEEE 94(11), 1948–1962 (2006)
26. Thorpe, S., Fize, D., Marlot, C.: Speed of Processing in the Human Visual System. Nature 381, 520–522 (1996)
27. Vovk, V., Gammerman, A., Saunders, C.: Machine Learning Application of Algorithmic Randomness. In: 16th Int. Conf. on Machine Learning (ICML), Bled, Slovenia (1999)
28. Yovel, G., Kanwisher, N.: Face Perception: Domain Specific, Not Process Specific. Neuron 44, 889–898 (2004)
29. Vapnik, V.N.: Statistical Learning Theory. Wiley, Chichester (1998)

Author Index

Lecture Notes in Computer Science

Sublibrary 6: Image Processing, Computer Vision, Pattern Recognition, and Graphics

Vol. 4170: J. Ponce, M. Hebert, C. Schmid, A. Zisserman (Eds.), Toward Category-Level Object Recognition. XI, 618 pages. 2006.

Vol. 4153: N. Zheng, X. Jiang, X. Lan (Eds.), Advances in Machine Vision, Image Processing, and Pattern Analysis. XIII, 506 pages. 2006.

Vol. 4142: A. Campilho, M. Kamel (Eds.), Image Analysis and Recognition, Part II. XXVII, 923 pages. 2006.

Vol. 4141: A. Campilho, M. Kamel (Eds.), Image Analysis and Recognition, Part I. XXVIII, 939 pages. 2006.

Vol. 4122: R. Stiefelhagen, J.S. Garofolo (Eds.), Multimodal Technologies for Perception of Humans. XII, 360 pages. 2007.

Vol. 4109: D.-Y. Yeung, J.T. Kwok, A. Fred, F. Roli, D. de Ridder (Eds.), Structural, Syntactic, and Statistical Pattern Recognition. XXI, 939 pages. 2006.

Vol. 4091: G.-Z. Yang, T. Jiang, D. Shen, L. Gu, J. Yang (Eds.), Medical Imaging and Augmented Reality. XIII, 399 pages. 2006.

Vol. 4073: A. Butz, B. Fisher, A. Krüger, P. Olivier (Eds.), Smart Graphics. XI, 263 pages. 2006.

Vol. 4069: F.J. Perales, R.B. Fisher (Eds.), Articulated Motion and Deformable Objects. XV, 526 pages. 2006.

Vol. 4057: J.P.W. Pluim, B. Likar, F.A. Gerritsen (Eds.), Biomedical Image Registration. XII, 324 pages. 2006.

Vol. 4046: S.M. Astley, M. Brady, C. Rose, R. Zwiggelaar (Eds.), Digital Mammography. XVI, 654 pages. 2006.

Vol. 4040: R. Reulke, U. Eckardt, B. Flach, U. Knauer, K. Polthier (Eds.), Combinatorial Image Analysis. XII, 482 pages. 2006.

Vol. 4035: T. Nishita, Q. Peng, H.-P. Seidel (Eds.), Advances in Computer Graphics. XX, 771 pages. 2006.

Vol. 3979: T.S. Huang, N. Sebe, M.S. Lew, V. Pavlović, M. Kölsch, A. Galata, B. Kisačanin (Eds.), Computer Vision in Human-Computer Interaction. XII, 121 pages. 2006.

Vol. 3954: A. Leonardis, H. Bischof, A. Pinz (Eds.), Computer Vision – ECCV 2006, Part IV. XVII, 613 pages. 2006.

Vol. 3953: A. Leonardis, H. Bischof, A. Pinz (Eds.), Computer Vision – ECCV 2006, Part III. XVII, 649 pages. 2006.

Vol. 3952: A. Leonardis, H. Bischof, A. Pinz (Eds.), Computer Vision – ECCV 2006, Part II. XVII, 661 pages. 2006.

Vol. 3951: A. Leonardis, H. Bischof, A. Pinz (Eds.), Computer Vision – ECCV 2006, Part I. XXXV, 639 pages. 2006.

Vol. 3948: H.I. Christensen, H.-H. Nagel (Eds.), Cognitive Vision Systems. VIII, 367 pages. 2006.

Vol. 3926: W. Liu, J. Lladós (Eds.), Graphics Recognition. XII, 428 pages. 2006.

Vol. 3872: H. Bunke, A.L. Spitz (Eds.), Document Analysis Systems VII. XIII, 630 pages. 2006.

Vol. 3852: P.J. Narayanan, S.K. Nayar, H.-Y. Shum (Eds.), Computer Vision – ACCV 2006, Part II. XXXI, 977 pages. 2006.

Vol. 3851: P.J. Narayanan, S.K. Nayar, H.-Y. Shum (Eds.), Computer Vision – ACCV 2006, Part I. XXXI, 973 pages. 2006.

Vol. 3832: D. Zhang, A.K. Jain (Eds.), Advances in Biometrics. XX, 796 pages. 2005.

Vol. 3736: S. Bres, R. Laurini (Eds.), Visual Information and Information Systems. XI, 291 pages. 2006.

Vol. 3667: W.J. MacLean (Ed.), Spatial Coherence for Visual Motion Analysis. IX, 141 pages. 2006.

Vol. 3417: B. Jähne, R. Mester, E. Barth, H. Scharr (Eds.), Complex Motion. X, 235 pages. 2007.

Vol. 2396: T.M. Caelli, A. Amin, R.P.W. Duin, M.S. Kamel, D. de Ridder (Eds.), Structural, Syntactic, and Statistical Pattern Recognition. XVI, 863 pages. 2002.

Vol. 1679: C. Taylor, A. Colchester (Eds.), Medical Image Computing and Computer-Assisted Intervention – MICCAI'99. XXI, 1240 pages. 1999.